Korean For Dummies®

Cheat Sheet

English Question	Korean Translation	Pronunciation
How's it going?	annyeonghaseyo?	an-nyoung-ha-sae-yo?
Do you speak English?	yeongeo haljul aseyo?	young-uh hal-jool a-sae-yo?
Can you help me?	jeo jom dowa jusillaeyo?	juh jom do-wa-joo-shil-lae-yo?
What is your name?	seonghami eotteokke doeseyo?	sung-ha-mee uh-ttuh-kae dwae-sae-yo?
What time is it?	myeotsieyo?	myuht-shi-ae-yo?
How much is this?	ige eolmajyo?	ee-gae ul-ma-jyo?
Where is the bathroom?	hwajangsiri eodiiseoyo?	hwa-jang-shi-ree uh-dee-ee-ssuh-yo?
Can you repeat that?	dasi malsseum haejusillaeyo?	da-shi mal-sseum hae-joo-shil-lae-yo?
Can you slow down a bit?	jom cheoncheoni malsseum haejusileyo?	jom chun-chun-nee mal-sseum hae-joo-shil-lae-yo?
Where is it?	eodi itjiyo?	uh-dee eet-jee-yo?

Everyday Expressions

English Expression	Korean Translation	Pronunciation
Hello.	annyeong.	an-nyoung.
Please.	jebal.	jae-bal.
Thank you.	gomapseumnida.	go-map-sseum-nee-da.
Thank you.	gamsahamnida.	gam-sa-ham-nee-da.
I'm sorry.	joesonghamnida.	jwae-song-ham-nee-da.
I don't know.	moreugetseumnida.	mo-reu-get-sseum-nee-da.
I don't understand.	mot aradeutgetseumnida.	mot a-ra-deut-get-sseum-nee-da.
Excuse me.	sillyehamnida.	shil-lae-ham-nee-da.

Calendar Terms

English	Korean Translation	Pronunciation	English	Korean Translation	Pronunciation
January	irwol	ee-rwol	July	chirwol	chi-rwol
February	iwol	eeh-wol	Augus		pa-rwol
March	samwol	sam-wol	Septe		
April	sawol	sa-wol	Octo		
May	owol	oh-wol	Nove		
June	yuwol	yoo-wol	Dec		

(continued)

For Dummies: Bestselling Book Series for Beginners

Korean For Dummies

Cheat Sheet

Calendar Terms (continued)

English	Korean Translation	Pronunciation
Monday	**woryoil**	*wo-ryo-il*
Tuesday	**hwayoil**	*hwa-yo-il*
Wednesday	**suyoil**	*soo-yo-il*
Thursday	**mogyoil**	*mo-gyo-il*
Friday	**geumyoil**	*geu-myo-il*
Saturday	**toyoil**	*to-yo-il*
Sunday	**iryoil**	*ee-ryo-il*

Question Words

English Question	Korean Translation	Pronunciation
Who?	**nugu?**	*noo-goo?*
What?	**mueot?**	*moo-uht?*
Where?	**eodi?**	*uh-dee?*
How	**eotteoke?**	*uh-ttuh-kae?*
When?	**eonje?**	*uhn-jae?*
Why?	**wae?**	*wae?*

Numbers

Number	Sino-Korean Number (Pronunciation)	Korean Number (Pronunciation)	Number	Sino-Korean Number (Pronunciation)	Korean Number (Pronunciation)
1	**il** (*Il*)	**hana** (*ha-na*)	16	**sip yuk** (*ship-yook*)	**yeol yeoseot** (*yuhl yuh-sut*)
2	**i** (*ee*)	**dul** (*dool*)	17	**sip chil** (*ship-chil*)	**yeol ilgop** (*yuhl il-gop*)
3	**sam** (*sam*)	**set** (*set*)	18	**sip pal** (*ship-pal*)	**yeol yeodeol** (*yuhl yuh-duhl*)
4	**sa** (*sa*)	**net** (*net*)	19	**sip gu** (*ship- goo*)	**yeol ahop** (*yuhl a-hop*)
5	**o** (*o*)	**daseot** (*da-sut*)	20	**i sip** (*ee-ship*)	**seumul** (*seu-mool*)
6	**yuk** (*yook*)	**yeoseot** (*yuh-sut*)	30	**sam sip** (*sam- ship*)	**seoreun** (*suh-reun*)
7	**chil** (*chil*)	**ilgop** (*il-gop*)	40	**sa sip** (*sa-ship*)	**maheun** (*ma-heun*)
8	**pal** (*pal*)	**yeodeol** (*yuh-duhl*)	50	**o sip** (*o-ship*)	**shwin** (*sween*)
9	**gu** (*goo*)	**ahop** (*a-hop*)	60	**yuk sip** (*yook-ship*)	**yesun** (*yae-soon*)
10	**sip** (*ship*)	**yeol** (*yuhl*)	70	**chil sip** (*chil-ship*)	**ilheun** (*il-heun*)
11	**sip il** (*shipil*)	**yeol hana** (*yuhl ha-na*)	80	**pal sip** (*pal-ship*)	**yeodeun** (*yuh-deun*)
12	**sip i** (shipee)	**yeol dul** (*yuhl dool*)	90	**gu sip** (*goo-ship*)	**aheun** (*a-heun*)
13	**sip sam** (*shipsam*)	**yeol set** (*yuhl set*)	100	**baek** (*baek*)	**baek** (*baek*)
14	**sip sa** (*shipsa*)	**yeol net** (*yuhl net*)			
15	**sip o** (*ship o*)	**yeol daseot** (*yuhl da-sut*)			

For Dummies: Bestselling Book Series for Beginners

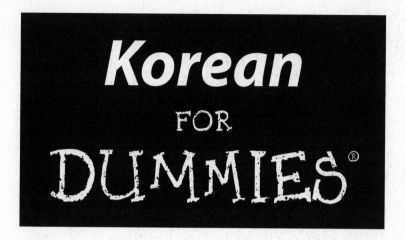

by Jungwook Hong and Wang Lee

Wiley Publishing, Inc.

Korean For Dummies®

Published by
Wiley Publishing, Inc.
111 River St.
Hoboken, NJ 07030-5774
www.wiley.com

Copyright © 2008 by Wiley Publishing, Inc., Indianapolis, Indiana

Published simultaneously in Canada

WILEY

About the Author

Wang Lee was born in Seoul, Korea, and he moved at an early age to the Middle East. He spent two years in Kuwait and another six and a half in Saudi Arabia. At the age of 13, he moved with his family to the United States and has been there ever since. He graduated from Shimer College in 2000, with a B.A. in Humanities. Since then, he's been working as an interpreter and a translator. He has worked for various school districts helping children with disabilities and has worked as a translator in many different fields ranging from the medical profession to the auto industry. He tutors Korean children in English and writes in his spare time.

Dedication

This book is dedicated to my parents, Sang Gil and Tae Kyun Lee, and my sister, Eun Jung. I am forever in their debt for all the love and support they were kind enough to show. None of this would have been possible without their help and guidance.

Author's Acknowledgments

When I was a little kid, I was fortunate enough to travel the world and live in many different places. It had a large part in shaping the person that I became. I was only three or four when my family moved to Kuwait. My sister, being a couple years older than myself, attended school while we were there. She went to a British school and I first learned English looking over her shoulders. I didn't learn to read then; I just memorized what she was reading and correlated that with the pictures that were on the pages. Later, when my family moved to Saudi Arabia, I continued to learn English from a British lady named Mrs. Brodure. For the first few years of my English-speaking career, I said things like "parcels" instead of "packages," "bonnet" instead of "hood," "lift" instead of "elevator," and the like.

When I moved to the States, I quickly learned that my bilingual skills were a valuable asset. It was a very marketable skill, in fact. I quickly realized that something that came quite naturally to me was something that many people struggled with. I knew that I was fortunate to learn English at an early age, which enabled me to communicate with perfect pronunciation and pass myself off as a native speaker. Then, I would raise a few eyebrows by turning around and speaking perfect Korean as well. My parents at home made sure I spoke Korean very well.

So my first set of thanks goes out to my parents, who taught me Korean and made sure I read and spoke it well. To my father, who always brought home a Korean newspaper for me to read, and for my mother, who was always there for me and pushed me to test my limits.

A most sincere thanks to my sister, Eun, and my brother-in-law, Jin Won Jung, who helped me maintain my sanity while I was sick and in the hospital. A special thanks to my sister, without whom this project would not have been possible.

To my nephew Miles, though he's just 14 months old, he taught me to smile and take delight in the little things, like pointing and laughing, and putting things in your mouth.

To Mike Grossinger, for coming through for me time and time again, no matter what I needed. He has been a sympathetic ear as well as a sounding board for my ideas and rough translations, even though he doesn't speak a word of Korean.

To Eric Hoch, for fixing my computer when it was on the fritz and I was freaking out, worried that I'd lost all my work. His calm patience and computer repair skills saved my hide more than once.

To Tom Cyr, who was always there to help me take the edge off, who also seemed to know exactly when I needed to take a break.

A sincere thanks goes out to Barb Doyen, my agent, who found this work for me. Without her, I would have never been involved with the *For Dummies* project and the fine folks at Wiley. I have to thank her also for having faith in me even when I doubted myself. Her steadfastness, like fuel, allowed me to keep going.

To Jennifer Connolly, my project manager, whose seemingly unending patience I tested time and time again, with one delay after another, and who was a tremendous help to me every step of the way.

To Stacy Kennedy, Acquisitions Editor at Wiley, who along with Jennifer, showed an incredible amount of patience with me and stuck with me through all the hassles, problems, and delays. I owe both of you a great deal of gratitude.

Publisher's Acknowledgments

We're proud of this book; please send us your comments through our Dummies online registration form located at www.dummies.com/register/.

Some of the people who helped bring this book to market include the following:

Acquisitions, Editorial, and Media Development

Project Editors: Jennifer Connolly, Natalie Harris

Acquisitions Editor: Stacy Kennedy

Copy Editors: Jennifer Connolly, Sarah Faulkner

Technical Editors: Sung-Eun Won, Teresa Lee

Media Development Coordinator: Jenny Swisher

Assistant Producer: Shawn Patrick

Quality Assurance: Angie Denny

Senior Editorial Manager: Jennifer Ehrlich

Editorial Supervisor: Carmen Krikorian

Media Development Manager: Laura VanWinkle

Editorial Assistants: Erin Calligan Mooney, Joe Niesen, Jennette Einaggar, Leeann Harney, David Lutton

Cartoons: Rich Tennant (www.the5thwave.com)

Composition Services

Project Coordinator: Patrick Redmond

Layout and Graphics: Claudia Bell, Melanee Habig, Stephanie D. Jumper

Proofreaders: Melissa Bronnenberg, Mildred Rosenzweig, Amanda Steiner

Indexer: Joan K. Griffitts

Special Help: Constance Carlisle

Publishing and Editorial for Consumer Dummies

Diane Graves Steele, Vice President and Publisher, Consumer Dummies

Joyce Pepple, Acquisitions Director, Consumer Dummies

Kristin A. Cocks, Product Development Director, Consumer Dummies

Michael Spring, Vice President and Publisher, Travel

Kelly Regan, Editorial Director, Travel

Publishing for Technology Dummies

Andy Cummings, Vice President and Publisher, Dummies Technology/General User

Composition Services

Gerry Fahey, Vice President of Production Services

Debbie Stailey, Director of Composition Services

Contents at a Glance

Introduction 1

Part I: Getting Started 7
Chapter 1: Getting Down the Basics 9
Chapter 2: The Nitty-Gritty: Basic Korean Grammar and Numbers.......................... 25
Chapter 3: Introductions and Greetings 49

Part II: Korean in Action 69
Chapter 4: Getting to Know You: Making Small Talk 71
Chapter 5: Eating and Drinking.. 93
Chapter 6: Shopping Made Easy... 111
Chapter 7: Exploring the Town 125
Chapter 8: Enjoying Yourself: Recreation and Sports 139
Chapter 9: Making Connections: Phone, Mail, Fax, and Internet 151
Chapter 10: At the Office and Around the House... 165

Part III: Korean on the Go 189
Chapter 11: Money, Money, Money.. 191
Chapter 12: Asking Directions 203
Chapter 13: Staying at a Hotel... 215
Chapter 14: Transportation 233
Chapter 15: Planning a Trip... 247
Chapter 16: Handling an Emergency.. 263

Part IV: The Part of Tens 277
Chapter 17: Ten Ways to Get a Quick Handle on Korean 279
Chapter 18: Ten Things to Avoid Doing in Korea 283
Chapter 19: Ten Favorite Korean Expressions.. 289
Chapter 20: Ten Phrases That Make You Sound Korean 293

Part V: Appendixes 301
Appendix A: Korean Verbs 303
Appendix B: Mini-Dictionary.. 307
Appendix C: Answer Key 331
Appendix D: On the CD... 337

Index 341

Table of Contents

Introduction 1

About This Book 1
Conventions Used in This Book 2
Foolish Assumptions 3
How This Book Is Organized 3
   Part I: Getting Started 4
   Part II: Korean in Action 4
   Part III: Korean on the Go 4
   Part IV: The Part of Tens 4
   Part V: Appendixes 4
Icons Used in This Book 5
Where to Go From Here 5

Part 1: Getting Started 7

Chapter 1: Getting Down the Basics 9

Getting the Basic Sounds 10
The Basic Vowel Sounds 10
   Distinguishing among vowel sounds 12
   Pronouncing eu and ui 12
The Basic Consonant Sounds 13
   Pronouncing jj, kk, pp, and tt 14
   Telling the difference between s and ss 15
   Pronouncing the Korean r,l sound 16
   Muting consonants at the end of a syllable 16
Sounding Fluent 17
   Don't stress 17
   Pronounce each syllable 17
   Speak in a steady rhythm 18
   Basic phrases 18
Saying It with Body Language 21
   Beckoning 21
   Bowing 21
   Nodding 22
   Shaking hands 22

Chapter 2: The Nitty-Gritty: Basic Korean Grammar and Numbers . . . 25

Speaking Politely 25
Knowing the Basic Parts of Speech 27
   Nouns 28
   Pronouns 29

Verbs 31
Adjectives 36
Suffixes 37
Adverbs 37
Particles 38
Asking Questions 40
Counting Korean Style 41
Native Korean numbers 42
Sino-Korean numbers 43
Counters 44

Chapter 3: Introductions and Greetings **49**

Making Introductions 49
Greetings and salutations 50
Bowing and shaking hands 51
Getting formal or informal 51
Introducing yourself 55
Introducing a friend or a peer 57
Introducing a senior or your parents 58
Asking for Names 61
Giving Thanks and Saying Sorry 64
Saying Goodbye 65

Part II: Korean in Action *69*

Chapter 4: Getting to Know You: Making Small Talk **71**

Asking Questions with Essential Words and Formal Usages 71
"Where Are You From?" 73
Describing your home community...74
Talking about where someone lives 76
Discussing ethnicity and citizenship 77
The Weather, the Seasons, and Everything In Between 80
Talking About Jobs and Occupations 83
Describing the Members of Your Family 87
Exchanging Contact Information...90

Chapter 5: Eating and Drinking **93**

Dig In! Let's Eat! 93
Understanding meal time 94
Satisfying your hunger..95
Sitting down to eat 95
Practicing good table manners...98

Getting to Know Korean Cuisine 98
    Popular dishes 99
    Setting time for a meal 100
    Liking and disliking with adjectives 100
Dining Out 101
    Understanding what's on the menu 101
    Ordering at a restaurant 102
    Ordering at a roadside shop 103
    Chatting with the waitstaff 106
    Finding restrooms 106
    Paying for your meal 106
    Drinking, Korean style 107

Chapter 6: Shopping Made Easy **111**
Navigating Stores 111
    Visiting department stores, markets, and small shops 112
    Browsing around 114
    Asking for help 115
Comparing Merchandise 116
    Comparing several items 117
    Pointing out the best item 117
Shopping for Clothes 117
    Checking for sizes 118
    Asking about colors 119
    Trying on clothes 120
Shopping for Specific Items 121
    Groceries 122
    Electronics 122
    Antiques and souvenirs 122
All About Buying: Pricing, Bargaining, Purchasing, Refunding 123

Chapter 7: Exploring the Town **125**
Knowing the Time and Day 125
    Days, weeks, months 126
    Telling time 126
    Telling time relative to now 127
Exploring Fun Places 129
    Visiting museums and galleries 130
    Going to concerts, theatres, and performances 130
    Korean films 130
    Korean noraebang 132
    Bar- and club-hopping 134
Giving and Receiving Invitations 135
    Getting something started 135
    Inviting your friends to your house 136

Chapter 8: Enjoying Yourself: Recreation and Sports 139

Naming Your Hobbies...139
Exploring Nature 142
Admiring and discovering the landscape......................................144
Korean seasons 145
Talking about the Arts 147
Playing Sports and Gaming..148
Playing games 148
Gaming at a Korean PC bang...148

Chapter 9: Making Connections: Phone, Mail, Fax, and Internet . . .151

Phoning Made Easy..151
Finding a phone 152
Making the call..152
Asking for someone...155
Leaving a message...157
Buying stamps 160
Asking for special services...160
Sending a Fax 161
Looking for an Internet Connection..161

Chapter 10: At the Office and Around the House 165

Getting Down to Work...166
Finding things at the office...166
Using computers 169
Finding people at the office..170
Asking for directions..171
Attending Meetings 173
Making introductions..173
Speaking up in a meeting..173
Making the Rounds: Business Dinners 174
Drinking politely 175
Declining drinks..176
Making Yourself at Home 176
The place where you live...176
The smallest room...177
Visting Koreans at Home...178
Taking the tour..178
Chilling out 179
Eating and drinking 181
Staying over 184
Cleaning up..186

Part III: Korean on the Go *189*

Chapter 11: Money, Money, Money 191
  Knowing Korean Currency 191
  Changing Currency 192
  Working the ATM 196
  Paying for Your Purchases 197
    Using cash 197
    Using plastic 199
    Using personal checks 201

Chapter 12: Asking Directions 203
  Asking for Directions 203
    Finding your way with "where?" 204
    Specifying which direction 207
    Specifying distance 209
  Giving Directions 210
    Referring to locations on the street 210
    Providing actions with directions 210
    Making directions flow 211

Chapter 13: Staying at a Hotel 215
  Sorting Out the Accommodation Options 215
    Traditional hotels 216
    Motels 216
    Korean motels and B&Bs 217
    Hostels 217
    Saunas and public baths 217
  Finding Accommodations 218
  Making Reservations 220
    Asking for details 223
    Checking out the room 224
  Complaining 101 226
    Broken machinery 226
    Noisy neighbors 227
    Other problems 228
  Checking Out 228

Chapter 14: Transportation 233
  Getting Around at the Airport 233
    Making it past the check-in counter 234
    Getting past Immigration and Customs 238
    Leaving the airport 238

Getting Around Town..239
  Hailing a cab...239
  Taking a bus 240
  Riding the subway 240
  Getting on the train 244

Chapter 15: Planning a Trip **247**
Picking a Good Time for Travel...247
  Checking out the seasons..247
  Naming months and counting days 248
  Korean holidays 252
  Naming off the years 254
  Specifying dates and times..255
Choosing Your Destination 256
Packing for Your Trip..259
Getting the Help of a Travel Agency 259

Chapter 16: Handling an Emergency **263**
Shouting for Help 263
Calling the Police..264
  Reporting an accident to the police................................264
  Finding the lost and found 266
Getting Medical Help 267
  Finding a doctor 267
  Describing what ails you 269
  Discussing your medical history.....................................272
  Making a diagnosis 272
  Following the prescription...273
Getting Legal Help...274

Part IV: The Part of Tens.................................277

Chapter 17: Ten Ways to Get a Quick Handle on Korean **279**
Find Koreans (or Other Korean Speakers) Near You...............279
Use Korean Language Tapes, CDs, and Other Multimedia Resources....280
Visit Korean Restaurants and Bars 280
Sing Korean Songs 280
Watch Korean Movies..280
Watch Korean Drama...281
Surf the Net for Korean Web Sites 281
Look Up Words in a Korean Dictionary 281
Make Korean Word and Phrase Lists.......................................282
Go to Korea!...282

Chapter 18: Ten Things to Avoid Doing in Korea **283**

Bragging or Accepting Compliments 283
Making Someone Lose Face in Public 284
Sitting or Eating Before the Seniors in the Group 284
Calling Your Boss or Teachers by Their First Names 285
Saying "Ssi" After Your Own Name 285
Walking into a House with Your Shoes on 285
Crossing Your Legs When You Sit 286
Kissing in Public 287
Taking the First "No, Thank You" Literally 287
Picking Up Your Rice Bowl and Using Your Spoon to Eat 287

Chapter 19: Ten Favorite Korean Expressions **289**

ppalli 289
gwaenchanayo 289
jeongmal, jinjja, cham 290
a, geuraeyo 290
jamkkanmanyo 291
mwo haeyo 291
mollayo 291
joayo 291
jal doetneyo 292
jeoreon, ireon 292

Chapter 20: Ten Phrases That Make You Sound Korean **293**

akkapda 293
eojjeol su eopgun 294
geureonde itjanayo 294
jom 295
jjajeungnanda 295
jukgetda 296
kkeunnaejunda 297
neukkihada 297
siwonhada 298
sugohaeyo 299

Part V: Appendixes **301**

Appendix A: Korean Verbs **303**

Appendix B: Mini-Dictionary **307**

Appendix C: Answer Key 331

Appendix D: On the CD 337
   Tracks on the CD...337
   System Requirements..340
   Customer Care...340

Index...*341*

Introduction

You probably know more about Korean than you think you do. Maybe you own a Korean-made cellphone or car. You may have had some Korean food or watched a Korean film, and maybe you've even heard something interesting about Korea in the news. But if you want to learn how to speak Korean, you're probably interested in speaking and interacting with Korean people. Perhaps you're doing business with a company in Korea, or perhaps you're planning to travel to Korea. Whatever the case, *Korean For Dummies* will go a long way toward helping you get a handle on the Korean language.

Some people say that speakers of different languages perceive things differently. If that's truly the case, perhaps learning a bit of Korean will help you see things the way a Korean does. Regardless of whether the language changes your perception, however, Koreans will perceive *you* differently when you try speaking some Korean. Speaking their language will certainly give them a good first impression! If you want to befriend people at school, on the job, or while traveling, show them that you're not only interested in them, but also that you're trying to understand and live by their culture.

Korean For Dummies helps you take those first steps toward understanding some Korean and tells you about some Korean mannerisms. As with anything, the first few steps can be the hardest to take, but they're worthwhile. After you make some friends using the Korean that you pick up from this book, you'll know that learning Korean is rewarding and fun!

About This Book

If you don't like memorizing tables upon tables of grammatical rules and declensions, or if you love it but don't have much time, this book is for you. Each chapter is organized so that you can look up and say a little something in the many situations that you may encounter while shopping, traveling, eating, and so on.

Learn a few words and sentences as you go along through this book, and surprise Koreans with a few well-placed phrases. Pick up this book when you need it, and flip through the sections that you find useful. Each section has a few phrases and cultural pointers that are meant to give Koreans a "Where did you learn that from?" sort of reaction. And if you're interested, you can learn a few sentence structures that you can add to as you become more comfortable with the language. The chapters are structured so that you can take away the bits that you need when you need them, so get ready to learn by speaking a little bit at a time as opposed to memorizing a whole lot at once.

Conventions Used in This Book

I use a few conventions in this book to help your reading go smoothly:

- ✔ Web addresses appear in `monofont`.
- ✔ Korean terms are in **boldface** to make them stand out.
- ✔ Korean words are spelled out phonetically, so that you see how to pronounce them.
- ✔ Definitions, which are shown in parentheses, follow the phonetically spelled Korean words the first time they appear in a section.
- ✔ Throughout the book, I give a nonliteral translation of the dialogues and phrases and, when necessary, I add a literal translation to help you better understand not only the phrase that you're saying, but also how and when to use it.
- ✔ Degrees of politeness are very important in Korean phrases. For important sentences, the formal polite, informal polite, intimate, and plain degrees of politeness are pointed out as necessary.
- ✔ Verb and adjective conjugations are given in the following order: dictionary stem and informal polite stem.

Anytime you're learning a language, you want to reinforce the material that you're learning by putting your lessons in the correct context. I use the following elements to help you do just that:

- ✔ **Talkin' the Talk:** These dialogues include bits and pieces of material from each lesson. They put the material in a daily context and show you the situations in which they may happen. Each dialogue has a brief introduction to the scenario in which the conversation takes place and often includes cultural tidbits. Each dialogue has the Korean words spelled out phonetically so that you can see their English pronunciations, so reading through them should be a breeze. If they're not so easy to read at first, look for dialogues that have a CD icon next to them — you can listen to those dialogues on the CD that comes with the book. In no time, you'll get the hang of speaking Korean!

✔ **Words to Know:** On the blackboards in this section, important words are highlighted for you to have at your disposal. I include the informal polite form of the verbs. (Chapter 2 has more information on verb forms and their various endings.)

✔ **Fun & Games:** These sections include a few exercises to help jog your memory and reinforce what you learn in the chapter. The exercises help you gauge your performance, so make sure you give them a try.

Foolish Assumptions

Here are a few foolish assumptions that I made about you while writing this book:

✔ You don't know much Korean aside from a phrase or two that you picked up from films or from your friends.

✔ You're not planning to take a proficiency test any time soon, nor are you trying to start translating literature or begin interpreting. All you want to do is learn a few bits of Korean here and there in order to communicate with some Koreans around you.

✔ You don't want to wake up in a cold sweat after memorizing tables upon tables of grammatical rules and conjugations.

✔ You want to have fun while learning Korean.

How This Book Is Organized

This book is organized thematically into four parts and a set of appendixes. Each part focuses on a particular theme, such as shopping, introductions, or eating out at a restaurant.

Part I: Getting Started

This portion of the book introduces you to Korean pronunciation and gives you an overview of basic Korean grammar. If you can, make sure that you go through Part I carefully, because it will significantly help your understanding of what's happening throughout the rest of the book.

Part II: Korean in Action

Here, you begin learning Korean — and Korean culture — for everyday life. Meeting someone? Eating? Shopping? Look through this section if you want to look for information and expressions that you can use with your friends.

Part III: Korean on the Go

This part of the book gives you more task-specific expressions to use when you want to travel. If you need to exchange currency, book a hotel room, or ask for directions, go through this chapter.

Part IV: The Part of Tens

Even if you're really strapped for time, you should go through Part IV. Here I include ten ways to learn Korean quickly, ten phrases to make you sound more Korean, ten expressions that Koreans like to use, and ten things you shouldn't do in front of Koreans. These sections are short and easy to remember, so go through them when you can.

Part V: Appendixes

This part contains various references that you may want to turn to while flipping through the rest of the chapters. You can find verb tables that show the conjugations of regular and irregular verbs, and a mini-dictionary for Korean-to-English and English-to-Korean words. In addition, check the answers to the Fun & Games sections at the end of each chapter, and look for the list of tracks that appear on the audio CD.

Icons Used in This Book

Throughout the book, I use icons in the margins and sidebars to help you find information quickly. Here are the icons to look for:

This icon highlights tips that make learning Korean easier.

This icon is used to point out information that bears repeating and remembering.

Avoid saying or doing things that have this warning sign icon. It marks the faux pas that you may make while speaking or interacting with Koreans.

Throughout the text, these icons mark bits about Korean culture and travel.

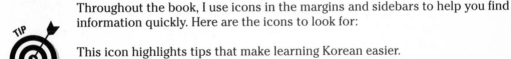

The audio CD that accompanies this book gives you a chance to listen to native speakers of Korean. You may have a few Korean friends at your disposal to pronounce various phrases, but when they're not there, use the CD to learn Korean faster. This icon lets you know what's on the CD.

Where to Go from Here

To get a sense of what's going on behind the scenes in terms of grammar, read Chapter 2. Korean grammar is very different from English grammar. I don't present all there is to know about Korean grammar, because that's beyond the scope of this book. You can, however, find enough grammar info to figure out what's going on and possibly figure out which words are playing what role when you listen to your Korean friends.

Chapter 2 aside, listening and speaking are the focus of this book. And although I try to provide you with as much information on specific topics as I can, the best way to learn is by trial and error. Learning a language involves learning how to interact with people, and no book or language course — however well designed — can trump actual conversation with someone. Go on and read a topic that strikes your fancy, listen to the audio CD, try using a Korean phrase here and there, but most importantly try speaking with a Korean speaker whenever you can. You'll undoubtedly form friendships and fond memories along the way.

Part I
Getting Started

The 5th Wave   By Rich Tennant

In this part . . .

If you've never been introduced to the Korean language before now, this part is for you. You can become familiar with Korean pronunciation and get an overview of basic Korean grammar. Try to go through Part I carefully because it lays the foundation for understanding the rest of the book.

Chapter 1

Getting Down the Basics

· ·

In This Chapter

▶ Sounding off with Korean phonetics

▶ Pronouncing the basic vowels and consonants

▶ Working on sounding fluent

▶ Practicing some Korean phrases

▶ Using Korean gestures

· ·

Surprising a **woneomin** (*won-uh-min;* native speaker) of Korea by perfectly pronouncing a **mungu** (*moon-goo;* phrase or a **munjang** (*moon-jang;* sentence) of their language can be **jaemi** (*jae-mee;* fun). And the purpose of this chapter is to help you do exactly that. Here you will learn how to pronounce Korean and get a hang of a few common **haengdong** (*hang-dong;* gestures). It shouldn't take long for you to begin fooling your Korean **chingudeul** (*chin-goo-deul;* friends) into thinking that you've secretly been spending time mastering the language.

Like **unjeon** (*oon-jun;* driving), riding a **jajeongeo** (*ja-juhn-guh;* bike) or tightrope **geotgi** (*gut-gee;* walking), the only way to get better at pronouncing Korean is by practicing. And the only way to fix your mistakes is by making them. So in this chapter, I introduce words like **chimdae** (*chim-dae;* bed), **angyeoung** (*an-gyoung;* eye glasses), **chitsol** (*chi-sol;* toothbrush), and **keopi** (*kuh-pee;* coffee) so you can practice saying words throughout your daily routine, and also teach you some basic sentences and phrases so you can start communicating in Korean. The more Korean you incorporate into your daily routine and **daehwa** (*dae-hwa;* conversations) you have, the better your understanding of Korean will become. Try to get a Korean friend to work with you. Practicing accurate pronunciation will not only help you **deutgi** (*deut-gee;* listen) and **malhagi** (*mal-ha-gee;* speak), but it will also win you brownie points, as Koreans will think highly of you for taking the time to master the finer points of their native language.

In the following sections, I present the sounds in their Romanized alphabetical order. Although it might take a while to get used to Korean sounds, there are no new concepts to learn such as tone or pitch.

Getting the Basic Sounds

Korean, like English, is a phonetic **eoneo** (*un-uh;* language). Each character of the Korean **sseugi** (*sseu-gee;* writing) system represents a sound, be it a vowel or a consonant. Although Korean has its own writing system, Hangeul, learning Korean using Korean script will require that you learn various sound change rules. So instead throughout this book, I will Romanize (write the sounds of Korean out in English) Korean phonetics, or sounds, using the English alphabet.

The Romanization method that I have chosen is the revised Romanization of Korean approved by the Korean government in year 2000. Using Romanization, I will write out how the characters sound so you can jump into conversation immediately without learning these rules. In addition, I have also included the pronunciation of the Korean words in brackets with English translation.

If you have the time, I highly recommend that you learn the Korean script, Hangeul. Hangeul was developed in the mid 1400s by the King Sejong's mandate to create a writing system that could easily be learned by commoners. Today, almost all of Korea relies on Hangeul for written communication, and Romanization is used exclusively for foreigners. Learning Hangeul will give you access to a wealth of online resources, so if you want to learn Korean more effectively, make sure you eventually take the time to learn Korean script.

Pronounce Korean words as though you are British, Scottish, or Australian rather than an American. For example, pronounce *an-gyeong* as *ahn-gyoung* not *an-gyoung*. Pronounce the *an* as *ahn* rather than *an*.

The Basic Vowel Sounds

Every Korean consonant must be accompanied by a vowel. Sometimes a group of vowels can form a word, as in the case of **uyu** (*oo-yoo*) which means *milk,* and **yeoyu** (*yuh-yoo*) which means *leisure/ease.* You should have little difficulty pronouncing most of the vowels, but some will sound almost indistinguishable from one another, and some will simply be tricky to pronounce.

First, try going over the sounds listed in Table 1-1. Don't worry if you have trouble figuring out how to pronounce some of the sounds. I go over how to distinguish and pronounce some of the trickier ones later in this chapter.

Phonetically, *ae* and *e* are two different sounds. Hence, they should be distinguished as such, although their difference may be blurred by most native speakers in causal speech.

Table 1-1		Vowel Sounds
Vowel	*English Word with the Sound*	*Korean Word with the Sound*
a ㅏ	ah-ha	**jadongcha** (*ja-dong-cha;* car)
ae	hand	**chaek** (*chaek;* book)
e ㅔ	get	**gagye** (*ga-ge;* store)
eo	uh	**geoul** (*guh-ool;* mirror)
eu	gull	**oneul** (*o-neul;* today)
i ㅣ	eat	**i** (*ee;* teeth)
o ㅗ	so	**chitsol** (*chi-ssol;* toothbrush)
oe	wet	**hoesa** (*hwae-sa;* company, corporation)
u	boo	**mul** (*mool ;* water)
ui ㅢ	boy	**uija** (*ui-ja;* chair)
wa	water	**hwajangsil** (*hwa-jang-shil;* bathroom)
wae	wet	**wae** (*whae;* why)
we	wet	**wigyeyang** (*we-gae-yang;* stomach ulcer)
wi	we	**wiheom** (*wee-hum;* danger)
wo	won	**mwo** (*mwo;* what)
ya	yam	**chiyak** (*chi-yak;* toothpaste)
yae	yesterday	**yae** (*yae;* that person; informal)
ye	yeti	**jipye** (*jee-pae;* dollar bills)
yeo	yuck	**angyeong** (*an-gyoung;* eye glasses)
yo	yo	**yokjo** (*yog-jo;* bathtub)
yu	you	**hyusik** (*hyoo-sheeg;* rest)

In Korean, pronounce *a* as *ah* (like *spa*) as in British English instead of *ae* (like *day*) in U.S. English.

Distinguishing among vowel sounds

Can Koreans tell the difference among the following three groups of sounds?

> *ae* (sounds like the *a* in hand), *e* (sounds like the *e* in get), and
> *oe* (sounds like the *o* in hope)

The answer is **ye** (*yae;* yes) and **aniyo** (*a-ni-yo;* no). If native Korean speakers were to **anjas** (*an-ja;* sit down) and split hairs over the **bareum** (*ba-reum;* pronunciation) of the three groups of sounds, they most likely could. But for the most part, especially in **maeil** (*mae-ill;* daily) conversation, they don't. So do not worry if you cannot distinguish between the sounds *ae, e,* and *oe,* because most Koreans do not worry either. The only way to distinguish between them is when you see them written down. Therefore, just by hearing them, most Koreans cannot tell the difference between above sounds.

Try these examples:

> *wae* (sound like the *we* in *wet*) **waegeurae** (*wae-geu-rae;* what is it)
>
> *oe* (also sound like *we* in wet) **oetori** (*wae-to-ree;* alone)
>
> *yae* (sound like *ye* in yeah) **yaeya** (*yae-ya;* hey, kid)
>
> *ye* (sound like the *ye* in *yesterday*) **ye** (*yae;* yes)

As you can see with the pronunciations written in brackets, above words are very difficult to distinguish just by hearing the words itself. It is more important to listen to the words used in sentences.

Pronouncing eu and ui

The *eu* sound does not exist in English. Fortunately, it isn't that **eoryoepda** (*uh-ryup-da;* hard) to **baeuda** (*bae-oo-da;* learn). Imagine that a friend or a sibling has hit you hard in the **bae** (*bae;* stomach) and you've just had the wind knocked out of you. Most likely you'll be clenching your **i** (*ee;* teeth) and groaning. Keep imagining the pain that you are in, but now focus on your groaning. Your teeth should be clenched tightly and your **mom** (*mohm;* body) should be tense. Now, try groaning a few times, and focus on the sound that you make. Keep your **ip** (*eep;* mouth) in the same position. Now try making a clear sound while keeping your mouth in that same shape.

The *ui* sound is a combination of the *eu* sound and the *i* sound. You start off with an *eu* sound, then quickly shift into an *i* sound. It might have been easier to remember if *ui* were written as *eui,* but I'd like you to learn standard Romanization so just keep this in mind.

By this point, you should have the *eu* and *ui* sounds down. I hope that wasn't too painful.

The Basic Consonant Sounds

Try saying the words *ski, gas,* and *kid.* You should notice that you let more air out when you pronounce *gas* than when you do *ski,* and again that you let even more air out when you say *kid* than you do when you say *gas.* Korean pronunciation relies heavily on how much air you let out when you pronounce consonants.

As you listen to the CD, try to focus on how much air is being let out for each letter.

Table 1-2 lists some basic consonant sounds. Please note that when a same consonant has two different sounds, I have **bolded** the consonant in question to differentiate between examples being used. *Note:* The revised form of Romanization no longer uses apostrophes.

Table 1-2	Consonant Sounds	
Consonant	*English Word with the Sound*	*Korean Word with the Sound*
ch	chat	**chimdae** (*chim-dae;* bed)
h	hat	**haneul** (*ha-neul;* sky)
j	chose	**jigeum** (*jee-geum;* now)
jj	match	**jeo jjok** (*juh-jjok;* that way)
k	cap	**kal** (*kal;* knife)
k,g	kooky	**gukgi** (*gook-gee;* national flag)
k,**g**	good	**gilga** (*geel-ga;* roadside)
kk	ski	**kkeut** (*kkeut;* end)
m	mom	**meori** (*muh-ree;* head)
n	no	**namu** (*na-moo;* tree)
ng	sung	**sang** (*sang;* table)
p	pass	**pal** (*pal;* arm)
b, **p**	paper	**japida** (*ja-pee-da;* get caught
b, p	baby	**babo** (*ba-bo;* dummy)
pp	happy	**ppang** (*ppang;* bread)
r, l	roll	**ramyum** (*ra-myun;* instant noodle)

(continued)

Table 1-2 *(continued)*

Consonant	English Word with the Sound	Korean Word with the Sound
s	so	**sul** (*sool;* alcohol)
ss	boss	**ssal** (*ssal;* rice)
t	tada	**tada** (*ta-da;* to burn or to ride [depends on the context])
t, d	tone	**datda** (*dat-da;* to close)
t, **d**	ed	**badak** (*ba-dag;* floor)
tt	star	**ttokttok** (*ttog-ttog;* knock knock)

k, g and *d, t* are read as *g* and *d* before a vowel, as in **gilga** (*geel-ga;* street), **gagu** (*ga-goo;* furniture), **doldam** (dol-*dam;* stone wall) and **don** (*don;* money), and as *k* and *t* when followed by another consonant or form the final sound of a word, as in **dokdo** (*dok-do;* dokdo island), **yokjo** (*yog-jo;* bathtub), **chaek** (*chaeg;* books), **geotda** (*guht-da;* to walk) and **datda** (*dat-da;* to close).

The *r,l* sound differs in that it is pronounced as *r* before a vowel, as in **baram** (*ba-ram;* wind), **ramyun** (*ra-myun;* instant noodles) and as *l* everywhere else as in **balral** (*bal-ral;* energetic).

Pronouncing jj, kk, pp, and tt

Most people have little trouble pronouncing *j* and *ch*, but the *jj* sound is often a source of frustration. To understand first how the *jj* sound is pronounced (and later, the *kk, pp,* and *tt* sounds), try saying *jazz, match,* and *champ.* You should notice that the *ch* sound has the most air coming out of your mouth and *j* the next. It should seem as though you are trying to prevent any air from coming out. For this reason, the *j, ch,* and also *jj* sounds are called *affricates.* They are phonetically a combination of a stop and a fricative, hence the term *affricate,* which involves a friction of airflow as well as the obstruction of airflow at different stages of its production.

In fact, the *jj, kk, pp,* and *tt* sounds are actually stops of the *ch, k, p,* and *t* sounds. So when you pronounce *jj, kk, pp,* and *tt,* try letting less air rush out of your mouth than you would when you are saying *ch, k, pp,* and *t.* Try these examples:

chong (*chong;* gun)

jeojjok (*juh-jjok;* over there)

jjok-jii (*jjok-jee;* memo)

kkeut (*kkeud;* end)

kkot (*kkot;* flower)

kong (*kong;* bean)

pal (*pal;* arm)

ppalli (*ppal-li;* fast)

ppang (*ppang;* bread)

tang (*tang;* bang)

ttang (*ttang;* ground)

tteok (*tteog;* rice cake)

Telling the difference between s and ss

Again, the name of the game in pronouncing the *s* and *ss* sounds is airflow. However, the defining characteristic of these two sounds is that they involve hissing sounds when they are produced, hence their name 'sibilant.' The *ss* sound involves more friction of airflow compared to the *s* sound. The *s* sound in the words *sound* and *cinema* is like the Korean *ss* sound. Try saying the words **ssal** (*ss*al; rice) and **ssada** (*ss*a-da: cheap).

On the other hand, the Korean *s* sound is closer to an English *z* sound compared to the *ss* sound. But, *s* is quite different from *z* in English in that the former is voiceless and the latter voiced. Try saying *zada* first, but then say the *z* sound imagining that you've lost your voice. You should have an *s* sound that is significantly softer, and also longer, than what you are used to. If you have trouble differentiating the two, try pronouncing the *s* sound twice as long as you would the *ss* sound. Try these examples:

ssal (*ss-al;* rice), **sal** (*sal;* skin)

ssada (*ssa-da;* cheap), **sada** (*sa-da;* buy)

One more thing to know about the *s* and the *ss* sound is that when they are combined with an *i* sound, as *si* and *ssi,* they are read *shi* and *sshi,* as in these examples:

ssi (*sshi;* Mr., Mrs., Miss), **si** (*shi;* poem)

Pronouncing the Korean r,l sound

If you **gullida** (*gool-lee-da;* roll) your **hyeo** (*hyuh;* tongue) across the **cheon-jang** (*chun-jang;* roof) of your mouth, you should notice a flat hard part near the teeth and a ridge where you should notice an incline. When you say *d* as in *day* and *dog*, or *l* as in *lamb* and *log*, your tongue stays on the hard part near your **i** (*ee;* teeth). In the case of *l* in English, the tip of your tongue touches the alveolar ridge, but when you pronounce an *r* sound as in *run* and *rock*, the tip of your tongue stays behind the ridge on the roof of your mouth, somewhere on the incline.

The key to pronouncing the Korean *r,l* sound is to keep only the tip of your tongue on the ridge between the *r* and *l* sounds. If you have trouble pronouncing the *r,l* sound, just think of it as the *l* sound pronounced by putting the tip of your tongue on the ridge that I was talking about earlier. Try these examples.

> **chitsol** (*chi-ssol;* toothbrush)
>
> **hangari** (*hang-a-ree;* jar, pot)
>
> **nara** (*na-ra;* country)
>
> **pal** (*pal;* arm)
>
> **ramyun** (*ra-myun;* instant noodles)
>
> **uri** (*oo-ree;* us, we)

Muting consonants at the end of a syllable

When Korean syllables or **daneo** (*da-nuh;* words) end in a *g* or a *d* sound, Koreans will mute the *g* or *d* sound. More specifically speaking, syllable-final *g* and *d* are unreleased sounds. When pronouncing these sounds, the airflow is closed very rapidly. Koreans do this by not letting as much air rush out of their mouths as they would when they would pronounce a *g* or a *d* sound at the beginning of a syllable. As **isanghan** (*ee-sang-han;* strange) as this may sound, even English speakers do this when they say the *d* in *good morning*.

For pronice, try these examples (*kkeut* should sound a lot like *good*):

> **kkeut** (*kkeud;* end)
>
> **chitsol** (*chi-ssol;* toothbrush)
>
> **chaek** (*chaeg;* book)
>
> **yok-jo** (*yog-jo;* bathtub)

hyu-sik (*hyu-sheeg;* rest)

jeojjok (*juh-jjog;* over there)

ttok-ttok (*ttog-ttog;* knock knock)

badak (*ba-dag;* floor)

Sounding Fluent

Once you have a grasp of the basic Korean **sori** (*so-ree;* sounds), mimicking the intonation, and cadence of a Korean speaker should take just a **jogeum** (*jo-geum;* little) more work. But this does not mean that path to excellent Korean pronunciation is one without **yuhok** (*yoo-hok;* temptations). In this section, I provide three tips for mastering Korean pronunciation and making your Korean sound even more natural.

Koreans use many English words on a daily basis. A few of them sound similar to the original English words but for others you might have to use your imagination. Most of these words should be easy to memorize and help you better understand Korean pronunciation.

Don't stress

English words and sentences are full of stressed and unstressed syllables. For example, the sentence "Ko-*rean* pro-nun-ci-*a*-tion is *sim*-ple" is stressed at three points. The same sentence in Korean, "**Hangugeo bareumeun swiwoyo** (*han-goo-guh ba-reum-eun shee-wo-yo;* Korean pronunciation is easy)," is said with no stress at all. It is possible to emphasize a particular word in a sentence by saying each syllable in that word **cheoncheonhi** (*chun-chun-hee;* slowly) and **keuge** (keu-gae; loudly), but if you ever feel tempted to put stress on a syllable within a word in Korean, resist.

Pronounce each syllable

In this book, I provide the Romanization for the Korean word and sentences, then I write out how each word is pronounced breaking words up into syllables. Although it may be tempting read each syllable quickly, if you enunciate each syllable clearly it will be easier for you to pronounce words accurately, and easier for Koreans to understand you. Remember to speak like an Australian or British person, such as pronouncing *a* as *ah*.

CULTURAL WISDOM

Puzzling English words in Korean

Some English words have had their meanings changed over the course of their assimilation into the Korean language. Don't be surprised when you hear familiar English words used with different meanings.

✔ *Panties:* **Paen-tee** does not only refer to women's underwear; it also refers to men's underwear. Do not get the wrong idea if

your male co-worker says he prefers boxer-style **sa-gag-paen-tee** to briefs.

✔ *Training:* **Choo-ree-ning** does not mean *training.* Instead, it refers to the gym pants that you wear when you train.

✔ *Villa:* **Beel-la** is not a house in the countryside, but a condominium or apartment complex.

Speak in a steady rhythm

At times, English sentences can sound like a waltz, a minuet, a serenade or sometimes even like a jazz piece. This is all because speakers of English can vary the rhythm of the words within a sentence. Although Koreans may raise or lower the tone of their **moksori** (*mok-so-ree;* voices), the best rhythm of Korean speech is a steady one, almost like a march. It might even help if you clap your hands at a steady beat and pronounce each syllable as you clap. Remember, if you feel the **piryo** (*pee-ryo;* need) to vary the rhythm of a Korean sentence, resist.

Basic phrases

Table 1-3 provides some basic phrases that you can begin practicing now so that even if you don't sound fluent, you can show that you're trying.

Table 1-3	Basic Korean Phrases	
Korean	*Pronunciation*	*Translation*
cheoncheonhi malhaejusaeyo	*chun-chun-hee mal-hae-joo-sae-yo*	Speak slowly please.
[some word] eui tteutsi hangugeoro/yeongeoro mwoyaeyo?	*[some word] eui tteut-shee han-goo-guh-ro/ young-uh-ro mwo-yae-yo?*	What does [some word] mean in Korean/English?
[some word] eul bareumhae jusaeyo	*[some word] rul ba-reum-hae-joo-sae-yo*	Please pronounce [some word].

Korean	Pronunciation	Translation
gomawoyo	*go-ma-wuh-yo*	Thank you.
anieyo	*a-ni-yae-yo*	No, or No thank you.
gwaenchanayo	*gwen-chan-a-yo*	It's all right.
joayo	*jo-a-yo*	Good, I agree.
byeolmalsseumeseyo	*byeol-mal-sseum-e-se-yo*	Don't mention it.
silyaehaeyo	*shil-lae-hae-yo*	Excuse me.
mianhaeyo	*mee-an-hae-yo*	Sorry.

Talkin' the Talk

Jessica and Jewu are friends. Jessica has learned some Korean and surprises Jewu.

Jessica: **jaeussi annyeonghaseyo**
jae-woo-sshi an-nyoung-ha-sae-yo?
Jae-Woo, are you doing well? [literal translation: Are you in peace?]

Jewu: **ye. geureondae jaessikassi hangugeo gongbuhaeyo?**
ye. geu-ruhn-dae jae-ssi-ka sshi han-goo-guh gong-boo-hae-yo?
Yes. By the way, Jessica, are you studying Korean?

Jessica: **ye. jinanjuae babodeuleulwihan hangukeochaekeul saseo bwaseoyo.**
ye. jee-nan-joo-ae ba-bo-deul-eul-wee-han han-goo-guh chaeg-eul sa-suh bwa-ssuh-yo.
Yes. Last week, I bought *Korean For Dummies,* then started reading it.

Jewu: **jeongmaryo? bareumi cham jeonghwakhaneyo.**
jung-mal-yo? ba-reum-ee cham-jung-hwak-ha-nae-yo.
Really? Your pronunciation is very accurate.

Jessica:	**anieyo. ajik mani bujokhaeyo. jaeussi, "eoryeowoyo" reul hangugmallo eotteoke bareumhaeyo?**
	a-nee-ae-yo. a-jeek man-ee boo-jok-hae-yo. jaeu sshi, "uh-ryuh-wo-yo"-reul han-gug-mal-lo uh-ttuh-kae ba-reum-hae-yo?
	Not really. I'm still far from fluent. Jae-Woo, how do you pronounce *difficult* in Korean?
Jewu:	**Eoryeowoyo. "Eoryeowoyo"ga eoryeowoyo?** (*Uh-ryuh-wo-yo. "Uh-ryuh-wo-yo"-ga Uh-ryuh-wo-yo?*)
	Difficult. Is "difficult" difficult to pronounce?
Jessica:	**ye, jaeussi gomawoyo.**
	ye, jae-woo sshi go-ma-wo-yo.
	Yes. Thank you, Jae-Woo.

Words to Know

beoseu	(buh-sseu)	Bus
haembeogeo	(ham-buh-guh)	Hamburger
hompeiji	(hom-pae-ee-jee)	Home page
imeil	(ee-mae-il)	E-mail
inteonet	(in-tuh-net)	Internet
kamera	(ka-me-ra)	Camera
keopi	(kuh-pee)	Coffee
keumpeuteo ma-u-seu	(kum-peu-tuh ma-oo-sseu)	Computer mouse
neetai	(nek-ta-ee)	Necktie
radio	(ra-dee-o)	Radio
syeocheu	(syuh-cheu)	Shirt
tel-le-bi-jyeon	(te-rae-bee-juhn)	Television

Saying It with Body Language

If actions speak louder than words, when in the company of Koreans, *respect* is the word that all your body should be saying. Although the repertoire of Korean has expanded to handshakes and sometimes even hugs, aside from bows, it is up to the person of seniority who initiates all of these activities. Juniors are to keep their hands at their sides and listen attentively, unless their seniors initiate a hug or a handshake.

Amongst peers, Koreans will use a wide range of body language. Most body language will translate without any problems, but you should be careful about a few gestures. Before you try these gestures yourself, first try to observe the native Koreans around you and maybe even ask them to explain why they are doing what they are doing. Once you get a sense of what's going on try them yourself. Doing so will pleasantly surprise the people around you.

Beckoning

When Koreans beckon their peers or friends they will use an arm and make a scooping motion in the direction that they want the listener to go. When Koreans signal or beckon their superiors they will use both arms and at times it will seems as though they're trying to signal a fighter jet on a runway.

One thing you will most likely never see, and should avoid is beckoning anyone using a single finger. It is insulting and rude. Apologize immediately if you catch yourself doing so.

Bowing

There are two kinds of bows done in Korean culture:

- An informal bow, in which you tilt your head slightly
- A more formal bow, in which you bow with the upper half of your body

The informal bow is used when greeting a co-worker or an acquaintance. To your boss or anyone else you meet in a formal setting (or when addressing someone older than you, whom you respect), make sure you use the formal bow. And for your close friends, you can wave your hands, do an informal bow, or whatever else strikes your fancy like a high five, or even air guitar but expect to get some strange glances.

If you've taken tae-kwon-do, you were taught to look at the other person's feet, but there's no need to do this in social settings. In fact, it might be preferable to look a foot or two in front of your feet.

Nodding

When listening to a senior you will see Koreans put their hands to their side, tilt their body a bit forward and listen attentively while nodding slightly and saying **ye** (*ye;* yes) at appropriate intervals. The more frozen the listener seems, the more important the speaker is to the listener.

But even amongst friends you will see Koreans sometimes nod and say **geuraeyo** (*geu-rae-yo;* Is that so?) or **jeongmal** (*jung-mal;* really?) to show that they are paying attention to the speaker.

Shaking hands

As I had told you in the introduction, it is up to the senior to initiate a handshake. The grip of the handshake should be like any handshake anybody from America should be used to, only if you are shaking hands with a senior or in a formal setting, put your left hand below your right elbow as if you were supporting your right arm. However, there is a gender difference when it comes to shaking hands. Generally speaking, Korean women do not shake hands that much, unless at a business setting. Even at that time, Korean women do not use two hands the way it's described here. However, there are always exceptions.

Fun & Games

Fill in the blanks with equivalent Korean words:

1. Bicycle

_____

2. Bed

Chimdae _____

3. Greetings

_____

4. Shaking hands

_____

5. Body

_____

6. Danger

_____

7. Friend

_____

8. Over there

_____

9. Toothbrush

_____

10. Bread

_____

Chapter 2

The Nitty-Gritty: Basic Korean Grammar and Numbers

In This Chapter

▶ Understanding the parts of speech

▶ Knowing how to ask questions

▶ Figuring out numbers

For most of us mere mortals, grammar is intimidating. And when faced with learning a new language, grammar can be a major turn-off. But the truth is, if you can read this textbook, you already know a lot of grammar even though you might not know exactly what rules you are using. You simply know what "feels" right.

In this chapter, I go over some simple tips and tricks on combining the ingredients of a sentence using the same parts that make up an English sentence, such as nouns, verbs, adjectives, and adverbs. Then I take concrete examples from everyday speech and eventually ease you into composing similar Korean sentences.

So be patient. Read over the text, go over the dialogues, and listen to the accompanying CD. By the end of the chapter, you should be able to string together and read a number of sentences. In no time, you'll be able understand others and express yourself with style.

Speaking Politely

Formal English is coming to a slow demise. The few times that we ever hear or use it is in situations that we'd rather avoid, such as during job interviews, public speeches, and in conversations with police officers and judges. On the other hand, formal Korean is very much alive and well. In fact, there are four degrees of conversational politeness in Korean, formal polite, informal polite, intimate, and plain.

Perhaps the number of polite forms that Korean has shows just how much emphasis Koreans place on showing the proper levels of respect to the listener or someone being talked about. But, showing too much respect is just as awkward as showing too little respect. And if one hopes to say they have mastered Korean, it is necessary to master the polite forms of the Korean language.

The good news is that you don't need to have a full understanding of all the different polite forms of Korean to carry on daily conversations. Informal polite form of speech is all that you need for daily conversations when you are just starting to learn Korean. As you become more fluent in the Korean language, you can worry about the other forms of politeness. However, for those of you who are more interested in grammar, in Korean, you set the degree of politeness that you use by changing the ending of the verb or adjective that comes at the end of the sentence. For those of you who are curious about when to use different degrees of politeness in Korean, Table 2-1 will provide general guidelines.

Table 2-1	Speech Styles
Form	*Used With*
Formal Polite	Someone much older than you, your teacher, your boss, customers of your business, your in-laws, a judge, and sometimes your parents. Basically people who have seniority over you, and to whom you want to show respect.
Informal Polite	Your colleague, an acquaintance, church minister, shop keeper, people you do not know (e.g., people you meet on the street, bus, train, and park). Basically everyone who does not have seniority over you, but you want to show some respect to.
Intimate	Your close friends, your sibling, your children, your student. Basically anyone really close to you.
Plain	In newspaper or magazine articles. Usually to an unknown audience.

In this book, I will stick with informal polite form of the Korean language. It is formal enough so that you never sound rude, and it is informal enough so that it can be used in a variety of situations. However, in incidences where formal polite form is necessary, I will tell you both formal polite and informal polite forms of Korean. When you say **jeoneun hangungmareul baewoyo** (*juh-neun han-goong-ma-reul bae-wo-yo;* I am learning Korean) you are using the informal polite form. This form is more than enough for everyday conversations.

I recommend starting off with the informal polite form, then eventually moving on to other degrees of politeness of speech as you become more fluent in Korean language.

Knowing the Basic Parts of Speech

English sentences are mostly made of nouns, verbs, adjectives, and adverbs. Korean sentences are also mostly made up of these same parts. There are no outlandish grammatical terms that you have to learn or master in order to learn Korean. However, the order of the sentence in Korean is different from English sentences. The basic word order in English is subject-verb-object, whereas the basic word order for Korean is subject-object-verb. Please see examples of different grammatical orders in two languages below:

English: I love you.

Korean: **naneun dangsineul saranghaeyo** (*na-neun dang-shin-enl sa-rang-hae-yo;* I love you). Literal translation: I you love.

English: I eat Kimchee.

Korean: **jeoneun gimchireul meogeoyo** (*juh-neun gim-chee-reul muh-guh-yo;* I eat Kimchee). Literal translation: I Kimchee eat.

English: I study Korean.

Korean: **jeoneun hangugeoreul gongbuhaeyo** (*juh-neun han-goo-guh-reul gong-boo-hae-yo;* I study Korean). Literal translation: I Korean study.

Here are a few other cool things to know about the Korean language:

✔ There is no need to distinguish between singular and plural nouns. For example, in Korean, a person and people are both called **saram** (*sa-ram;* person, people).

✔ There is no such a thing as subject-verb agreement (e.g., I am, It is, They are).

✔ You don't have to change word order to ask a question. In Korean you would ask, "This is a cat?" instead of "Is this a cat?" Asking a question is indicated by raising the intonation at the end of the sentence.

✔ Changing the tense of a verb follows a highly consistent pattern.

✔ You don't have to worry about memorizing the genders of the nouns. There are no masculine or feminine way of speech in Korean as in other languages such as Spanish, German, or French.

These points should help you on your path to learning Korean. Soon, you'll amaze your Korean friends with your new Korean language skills.

Easy grammar, hard language?

You may now ask, "If Korean grammar is so easy, why is it considered such a difficult language?" Well, that's a good question. The reason is most likely due to the many polite forms of the Korean language and because of particle words like *at, to,* and *from* that are written as separate words in English are attached behind nouns in Korean. In addition, depending on the degree of respect you want to show to the subject of the conversation, these particles can change. These particles, however, are not as bad as you may think; I provide concrete examples in the "Particles" section, later in this chapter.

Nouns

Korean, like English, has several types of nouns:

- Proper nouns for specific people, places, and things. For example, **hanguk** (*han-goog;* Korea), **hangugeo** (*han-goo-guh;* Korean language), **Socrates** (*so-keu-ra-te-seu;* Socrates), and **Seoul** (*Suh-ool;* Seoul).

- Common nouns for common things. For example, **jadongcha** (*ja-dong-cha;* car), **jip** (*jeeb;* house), **saram** (*sa-ram;* person, people), gil (*geel;* road).

- Abstract nouns for things like **ideology** (*Ee-de-ol-lo-jee;* ideology), and **jeongui** (*jung-ee;* justice).

- Mass nouns for non-discrete thing such as **mul** (*mool;* water), **sul** (*sool;* alcoholic beverages) and **bul** (*bool;* fire).

Some of your Korean friends might tell you that there are politer ways to refer to common nouns. See examples below:

Food: **jinji** (*jin-ji*) instead of **bap** (*bap*)

Name: **seongham** (*sung-ham*) or **jonham** (*jon-ham*) instead of **ireum** (*ee-reum*)

Home: **daek** (*daek*) instead of **jip** (*jeeb*)

You can use the politer form of common nouns to people that you want to show respect. However, most of the time, you can get by without them. If there is a situation in which you should use the honorific form of the noun, I will make sure to bring it to your attention.

Pronouns

Pronouns take the place of nouns to reduce repetition in a sentence and are indispensable when asking questions. Here are a few examples of interrogative pronouns, demonstrative pronouns, and personal pronouns along with a few pointers.

Interrogative pronouns

Question words such as **nugu** (*noo-goo;* who), **mwo** (*muh;* what), **eoneu** (*uh-neu;* which), **eotteon** (*uh-ttun;* what kind of), **eonje** (*un-jae;* when), and **eodi** (*uh-dee;* where)

Demonstrative pronouns

In English, the difference between this and that, and here and there has to do with the relative location of a thing to the speaker. *This* is closer to the speaker than *that*, and *here* is closer than *there*. In Korean, the word for *here* is **yeogi** (*yuh-gee*), but for the word *there*, there are two options depending on whether or not the place is closer to the listener. If the place is closer to the listener, but far away from the speaker, then it is **geogi** (*guh-gee;* there), if it is far from both the speaker and the listener then it is **jeogi** (*juh-gee;* there).

Personal pronouns

Korean also has several personal pronouns, but they are used less extensively. This is especially true with the case of the pronoun *You*. It sounds more natural and more polite if you call someone by their name as opposed to addressing them using a personal pronoun. If you don't know the person's name, try using **jeogiyo** (*juh-gee-yo;* hey there).

> I: **jeo** (*juh;* humble form of I, used with people you want to show respect to), **na** (*nah;* form of I used when talking with close friends and younger family members).

> You: **seonsaeng** (*sun-saeng;* sir), **eoreusin** (*uh-reu-shin;* when referring to elderly), **jane**(*ja-nae;* to address younger people), **geudae** (*geu-dae;* to address your girlfriend/boyfriend/spouse), **yeoreobun** (*yuh-ruh-boon;* to address groups of people), **neo** (*nuh;* used in informal settings amongst peers).

i (*ee;* this), **geu** (*geu;* that near the listener), and **jeo** (*juh;* that over there) are added before various nouns such as person and things to make them pronouns.

> He: **i namja** (*ee-nam-ja;* this man), **geu namja** (*geu-nam-ja;* that man near the listenr), **ju namja** (*juh-nam-ja;* that man over there)

> She: **i yeoja** (*ee-yeo-ja;* this women), **geu yeoja** (*geu-yeo-ja;* that women near the listener), **jeo yeoja** (*juh-yeo-ja;* that women over there)

However, using the **namja** (*nam-ja;* man/men) and **yeoja** (*yeo-ja;* woman/women) to refer to someone, isn't that polite. Instead use **bun** (*boon;* no English translation. It is used when referring to a person you want to show respect to. Used for both genders.) to get **i bun** (*ee-boon;* this person), **geu bun** (*geu-boon;* that person near the listener) and **jeo bun** (*juh-boon;* that person over there) when you're referring to: a stranger, a person with seniority over you or when you are in a formal setting. Use **i saram** (*ee-sa-ram; this person*), **geu saram** (*geu-sa-ram;* that person near the listener) and **jeo saram** (*juh-sa-ram;* that person over there) when you are using informal polite Korean.

> It: Use **geot** (*guht;* thing) or its contraction **geo** (*guh;* things). These are interchangeable. You can just pick one way and stick to it. Add **i** (*ee;* this), **geu** (*geu;* that), and **geo** (*guh;* that) to get **i geot** (*ee-guht;* this thing), **geu geot** (*geu-guht;* that thing neat the listener), jeo **geot** (*juh-guht;* that thing over there), or **i geo** (*ee-guh;* this thing), **geu geo** (*geu-guh;* that thing near the listener), **jeo geo** (*juh-guh;* that thing over there).

> We: **uri** (*oo-ree;* we/us) used in casual conversation, **jeohui** (*juh-hee;* we/us) used when speaking in front of an authority figure or a crowd.

> Them: **i deul** (*ee-deul;* these people), **geu deul** (*geu-deul;* those people near the listener), **jeo deul** (*juh-deul;* those people over there) when speaking of other people casually, **i bundeul** (*ee-boon-deul;* these people), **geu bundeul** (*geu-boon-deul;* those people) and **jeobundeul** (*juh-boon-deul;* those people) when speaking of people that you are trying to show respect for.

Depending on context, the sentence **geogi saram isseoyo** (*guh-gee sa-ram-ee-ssuh-yo*) can mean "there are people there." or "there is a person there." And, in most cases, you don't have to explicitly indicate that there is more than one. But if you want to, just add **deul** (*deul;* it's like adding's" at the end of a word to make things plural in English) behind a pronoun or even a noun to show there are more than one. For example, the word for this respected person is **i bun** (*ee-boon*), and these respected people is **i bundeul** (*ee-boon-deul*). Isn't this easy?

Yours, mine, and (not necessarily) ours

In Korean, you might notice that people tend to use the word **uri** (*woo-ri;* we/us) and **jeohui** (*juh-hee;* we/us when speaking to person with seniority over you), a lot more when talking about things they own, especially if they are talking about a thing that they use communally with other people, such as family members or co-workers. Hence they refer to company property and homes as **uri jib** (*oo-ree-jeeb;* our house), **juhui mitingnum** (*juh-hee-mee-ting-room;* our meeting room), and **uri dongne** (*oo-ree-dong-nae;* our neighborhood), as opposed to **ne**

jib (*nae-jeeb;* my house), or **ne dongne** (*nae-dong-nae;* my neighborhood).

This is also true when speaking of shared relationships. If you are a part of company, it is **uri hoesa** (*oo-ree-hwae-sa;* our company). Koreans will further say that their child is "**uri ai** (*oo-ree-a-ee;* our child)," and yes, they even use the term, **uri nampyun** (*oo-ree-nam-pyun;* our husband), and **uri jibsaram** (*oo-ree-jeeb-sa-ram;* our wife) when referring to their own spouses. Just because a Korean uses the word **uri** (*uri;* our), don't get any wrong ideas.

Possessive pronouns

Whose is whose is about as important as what is what, and if you want to make the fact that this book, chair, or table belongs to you, add a **ui** (*~ui;* ~'s) after any pronoun or noun. For example; **i geoseun jeoui chaegieyo** (*ee-geo-seun juh-ae chaeg-ee-ae-yo;* this is my book). Just like in English, the person that owns is placed to the left of the thing that is owned. The formula would be as follows: possessor + possessed.

However, Koreans will rather often omit the **ui** (*~ui;* ~'s) in everyday conversation. For example, Koreans will often use **uri hoesa** (*oo-ree-hwae-sa;* our company), **uri giji** (*oo-ree gee-jee;* our base camp) and **jon eomma** (*jon-um-ma;* John's mom) and omit the **ui**. Although **ui** maybe omitted in everyday conversations, it is important to know that **ui** reflects possession.

Verbs

In English, verbs conjugate according to person and number. In Korean, this doesn't happen. Verbs such as "to be" and "to have" are the same for him [e.g., Tom] or her [e.g., Jane] and you and me.

This doesn't mean that verbs in Korean are a one size fits all kind of deal. Not only do verbs indicate whether or not you are speaking about the past, present, and show intent of future action, but they also show the level of respect that you hold for the subject in your sentence. Hence, if you want to effectively insult your enemy, or impress your in-laws, you must understand how to use verbs.

Knowing the basic verb forms

The verbs of a sentence are conjugated using the stems of the dictionary and informal polite form.

- ✔ **Dictionary form:** The dictionary form of the verb is what you use to look up a verb in the dictionary. Alone, they behave like English infinitives such as to see, to go. All the dictionary forms of verbs end in **da** (*da;* no English translation). Few examples are **boda** (*bo-da;* to see), **mannada** (*man-na-da;* to meet), and **itda**.(*it-da;* to have).

- ✔ **Verb stem:** The verb stem is simply the dictionary form minus the **da** at the end. The verb stem is never used by itself. The stems of the words used in the example above are: **bo** (*bo;* to see), **man** (*man;* to meet), and **it** (*it;* to have).

- ✔ **Informal polite form:** The important thing to remember with informal polite form of the Korean language is that the sentence ends with **yo** (*yo;* no English translation). I.e., the Informal polite form of the verb always ends in a **yo**. For example, **bwayo** (*bwa-yo;* see), **mannayo** (*man-na-yo;* meet) and **iseoyo** (*ee-ssuh-yo;* have). **Yo** at the end of the sentence shows that you respect the person you are speaking to.

  For example: **jeoneun chingureul mannayo** (*juh-neun chin-goo-reul man-na-yo;* I am meeting a friend).

When I introduce a new verb, I will present it in both the dictionary form and informal polite form. Just remember that the dictionary form ends with "**da**" while the informal polite form ends with "**yo**".

Conjugating verbs

The key to conjugating verbs lies in the final syllable of the stem. And in almost all regular conjugations, conjugating the verb depends on one of two things.

Whether or not the stem ends in a vowel or a consonant

Whether or not the last syllable contains one of the following two vowels, *a* and *o,* which are called *bright vowels* by many linguists

For example, the stems **meok** (*muk;* eat), **nol** (*nol;* play) and **it** (*it;* have), end in **eo, o,** and **i** vowels.

Some of you might find it odd that I am going to show you how to conjugate the dictionary form of the word to the informal polite form, especially when I am going to present the two forms anyway. But I am going to do this because learning how to conjugate the informal polite form from the dictionary form will makes it easier to understand and memorize many of the irregular verbs.

1. First, take the dictionary form Stem and check whether or not the last vowel is an **a, or o**.

2. Next, if it is one of these two vowels, add a **ayo** (*a-yo;* no English translation) to the verb stem. If it isn't, add **eoyo** (*uh-yo;* no English translation).

For example, from the dictionary forms **alda** (*al-da;* to know)**, batda**(*bat-da;* to receive), **eopda** (*uhp-da;* to not have) and **itda** (*it-da;* to have) their stems are **al, bat, eop and it**. The last vowel of the stems are **a, a, eo** and **i** respectively. Hence, the informal polite forms are **alayo** (*al-a-yo;* to know), **batayo** (*bat-a-yo;* to receive), **eopseoyo** (*eop-ssuh-yo;* to not have) and **itseoyo** (*ee-ssuh-yo;* to have). Table 2-2 gives you some examples.

Table 2-2	Conjugating Dictionary Forms of Verbs	
Korean	*Pronunciation*	*English*
boda (dictionary)	*bo-da*	to see
bo (verb stem)	*bo*	to see
bwayo (informal polite)	*bwa-yo*	to see
doeda (dictionary)	*dwae-da*	to become
doe (verb stem)	*dwae*	to become
doeyo (informal polite)	*dwae-yo*	to become
hada (dictionary form)	*ha-da*	to do
ha (verb stem)	*ha*	to do
haeyo (informal polite)	*hae-yo*	to do
itda (dictionary)	*it-da*	have or to
it (verb stem)	*it*	be at some
iseoyo (Informal polite)	*ee-ssuh-yo*	location
juda (dictionary)	*joo-da*	to give
ju (verb stem)	*joo*	to give
jwoyo (informal polite)	*jwo-yo*	to give

Getting tense (past, present, and future)

Using verbs to modify nouns in English is a complicated ordeal. You need to pay attention to tense and agreement. In Korean, the only thing that you have to worry about is tense.

In Korean, when it comes to tenses, all you really need is to know how to say things in the past and the present tense. Hence, you can say **oneul seoure dochakhaeyo** (*o-neul suh-oo-rae do-chak-hae-yo;* I'm arriving at Seoul today), and **naeil seoure dochakhaeyo** (*nae-il suh-oo-rae do-chak-hae-yo;* I'll be arriving at Seoul tomorrow) without having to worry about conjugating the verb. Future tense is usually used when you are unsure of what will happen, or want to explicitly show intention.

> **Future: jeoneun naeil mannal salami iseoyo** (*juh-neun nae-il man-nal ra-ram-ee ee-ssuh-yo;* There is someone I will meet tomorrow).

> **Present: jeoneun jigeum mannaneun salami iseoyo** (*juh-neun jee-geum man-na-neun sa-ram-ee ee-ssuh-yo;* There is someone I am meeting now).

> **Past: jeoneun eoje mannan salami iseoyo** (*juh-neun uh-jae man-nan sa-ram-ee ee-ssuh-yo;* There is someone I met yesterday).

Changing a verb to a noun modifier is easy. You take the stem of the dictionary form, check for whether the final syllable ends in a consonant or a vowel, then add the following markers or particles. Even when the verb modifying the noun is a part of a more complicated phrase, place it immediately to the left of the noun it modifies. For verbs whose action will and is going to happen: add a **l** for dictionary stems that end in vowels and **eul** for dictionary stems that end in consonants.

chareul tal saram iseoyo? (*cha-reul tal-sa-ram ee-ssuh-yo?;* Is someone going to ride the car?) For example: **gachi georeul saram iseoyo?** (*ga-chee guh-reul sa-ram ee-ssuh-yo;* Is anyone going to walk with you?)

For verbs whose actions are happening and are ongoing: Add **neun** to the dictionary stem regardless of what it ends in.

For example: **ganeun saram iseoyo?** (*ga-neun sa-ram ee-ssuh-yo?;* Is anybody leaving?) For example: **gachi geonneun saram iseoyo?** (*ga-chee geun-neun sa-ra ee-ssuh-yo;* Is someone walking with you?)

For verbs whose actions have happened or took place : add a **n** to a verb stem whose final syllable ends in a vowel and **eon** for dictionary stems with consonant endings.

For example: **i yeonghwa bon saram iseoyo?** (*ee young-hwa bon sa-ram ee-ssuh-yo?;* Has anyone seen this film?) For example: **noriteoeseo noldeon saramiseoyo?** (*noree-tuh-ae-suh nol-deun-sa-ram ee-ssuh-yo?;* Was anyone playing at the playground?)

Making Korean verbs with English verbs and adjectives

Many Koreans will add **haeyo** (*~hae-yo;* it is~) onto an English verb or adjective and use it as if it were a Korean word. Look at the following sentences.

Oh~ dress-**ga** elegant-**haeyo**. (Oh the dress is elegant)

[Some situation in a Korean soap opera]-**ga** dramatic-**haeyo**. [Oh, (the situation in the drama) is dramatic]

Plato-**ga** Memorial gym-**esu** work-out-**haeyo**. (Plato works out at Memorial Gym)

Jeo-**neun** swimming pool-**esu**, warm-up-**haeyo** (I warm up in the swimming pool.)

In fact you can use English verbs and adjectives to make Korean ones. If you put **haeyo** after an English verb or adjective and incorporate it into a Korean sentence, you can speak a grammatically correct sentence that one of your Korean friends will most likely understand. So if you say something like, John-i television-**eul** living-room-**esu** watch-**haeyo**, or This meatloaf-**ga** rock-hard-**haeyo**, your Korean friends will be able to respond accordingly. Try practicing using particles, adjective, and verbs in this manner, and you'll be speaking Korean in no time.

Talkin' the Talk

 Jason and Alice are friends. Jason is asking Alice if she'll go to the movies with him.

Jason:	**aelliseussi, gachi yeonghwa bol saram iseoyo?**
	al-li-sseu-sshi, ga-chi young-hwa bol sa-ram ee-ssuh-yo?
	Alice, do you have someone to watch movies with?
Alice:	**aniyo jeiseunssi gachi bolsarami eopseoyo**
	a-ni-yo, jei-son-sshi. ga-chi bol sa-ram-ee uhp-ssuh-yo
	No, Jason. I don't have someone to watch movies with.
Jason:	**geureom jeorang gachi bosillaeyo**
	geu-rum, juh-rang ga-chi bo-shil-lae-yo?
	Then, would you like to watch a movie with me?
Alice:	**jeongmaryo? geureom jochyo**
	jung-mal-yo? geu-rum jo-cho
	Really? I'd like that.
Jason:	**geureom naeil 12sie yeonghwagwan apeseo mannayo**
	geu-rum, nae-il 12shi-ae young-hwa-gwan a-pae-suh man-na-yo
	Then, let's meet in front of the movie theater at 12 noon.

Alice:	**gomawoyo jeiseunssi, naeil bwayo**
	go-ma-wo-yo, jei-son-sshi. nae-il-bwa-yo.
	Thank you, Jason. See you tomorrow.

Words to Know

ap	ap	Front
eoje	uh-jae	Yesterday
gachi	ga-chi	Together
jigeum	jee-geum	Now
maeil	mae-il	Everyday
naeil	nae-il	Tomorrow
pyo	pyo	Ticket
saram	sa-ram	Person/people
yeonghwa	young-hwa	Movies
yeonghwagwan	young-hwa-gwan	Movie theater

Adjectives

In English, adjectives can come before a noun and function as the "good" in "good wine," or they can function as the "is good" in "the wine is good." Here in this section, let's go over how to use adjectives as descriptive verbs and as noun modifiers.

Using adjectives like verbs

Korean adjectives have a dictionary form and conjugate just like verbs. Using adjectives in Korean may be strange at first because Korean adjectives mimic much of the behavior of verbs.

> **aiga eoryeoyo** (*a-ee-ga uh-ryuh-yo;* child is young)
>
> **jeoneun bappayo** (*juh-neun ba-ppa-yo;* I'm busy)
>
> **doni manayo** (*do-nee ma-na-yo;* there is lots of money)
>
> **hwajangpumi bissayo** (*hwa-jang-poom-ee bee-ssa-yo;* make up is expensive)

Notice that there are only two Korean words in each sentence: the subject and the adjective.

There is no linking verb such as *is* or *was*. To use an adjective all you need is the subject, and the conjugated form of the adjective placed at the end of the sentence. If you want to say "the apple is red," in Korean, all you have to say is **sagwaga ppalgaeyo** (*sa-gwa-ga ppal-gae-yo*) "apple red."

Suffixes

Enhancing verbs and adjectives with suffixes is a lot like changing tenses because all you are doing is adding an additional suffix to an informal polite or dictionary stem. And, if you learn how to enhance verbs by using suffixes, you can use the same suffixes to a wide range of adjectives and verbs. Hence, your range of expression increases extremely quickly.

In Table 2-2, I use English nouns (refer to "Making Korean verbs with English verbs and adjectives," earlier in this chapter) so you focus more on how the suffixes are used. Also, I write the endings of the suffixes in dictionary form so you can conjugate to whichever tense or form of politeness you need. And for suffixes that require minor changes according to whether the stem ends in a consonant or in a vowel, I first write the form of the suffix that comes after a consonant and then the one that comes after a vowel.

One final thing to remember is that you can "stack" suffixes. For example, you can add the suffix **eul geosida** (*eul-guh-shi-da*)/**reul geosida** (*reul-guh-shi-da*) "to probably be" and **eul suitda** (*eul-soo-it-da*)/**reul suitda** (*reul-soo-it-da*) "can" on the verb "eat" to get **meogeulsu isseul geosida** (*muh-geul-boo-ee-sseul-guh-shi-da*) "can probably eat." So if you think that someone is using more than one suffix, you are most likely right.

Adverbs

You don't need to worry about conjugating adverbs or worry about tinkering around with stems. Adverbs don't conjugate.

There are largely two types of adverbs in Korean. The first is the type of adverbs that are meant to modify the sentence as a whole such as accordingly, also, besides, however, and hence. These adverbs are placed at the beginning of a sentence of phrase. The other type of adverbs are those that that modify the adjectives, verbs, and other adverbs of a sentence or phrase. A few examples are very, less, more, sometimes, and often. Although some of these adverbs can be placed almost anywhere within a sentence or a phrase, the safest way to use adverbs is to place them immediately to the left of the word they modify.

Two adverbs that are important are **mot** (*mot;* can't) and **an** (*an;* won't). **mot** and **an** implies that the subject of the sentence, usually the speaker, cannot do or be something. Both **mot** and **an** are placed to the immediate left of the verb or adjective they modify, and neither of them can be used to modify other adverbs.

> **mot,** can only be used with verbs and implies that the speaker cannot do something.
>
> For example: **jeoneun gimchireul <u>mot</u> meogeoyo** (*juh-neun gim-chi-reul mot muh-guh-yo;* I can't eat Kimchee). **gimchi alleojiga iseoyo** (*gim-chi al-luh-ji-ga it-ssuh-yo;* I have Kimchee allergies).
>
> **an,** when used with a verb, means that you choose not to do something. For example: **adamssineun gogireul <u>an</u> meogeoyo** (*a-dam-sshi-neun go-gee-reul an-muh-guh-yo;* Adam won't eat meat), **chaesikjuuijaeyo** (*chae-shik joo-ui-ja-ae-yo;* He's a vegetarian).
>
> **an,** can also be used with adjectives to mean that the thing spoken about does not have the quality of the adjective.
>
> For example: **gimchiga an maewoyo** (*gim-chi-ga an mae-wo-yo;* The Kimchee isn't spicy).

Particles

In Korean, the basic word order is subject-object-verb (refer to "Knowing the Basic Parts of Speech," earlier in this chapter), but in most cases, even object-subject-verb is fine so long as the verb stays at the end of the sentence. If we were to say, Eric drinks juice, in Korean we could say Eric juice drinks, or juice Eric drinks. But you can immediately see a problem: How do you know what is being drunk and whot is doing the drinking?

Dropping understood words

In spoken English, people drop words from their sentences all the time. They will shorten "Will you come over to my house today." to "Come over." "Are you leaving the office?" to "Leaving?", "Were you also a part of this, Brutus?" to "Brutus?" We can see that we can drop huge parts of a sentence without a breakdown of communication. Of course, this is only when the speakers can tell what is being said from the context of the conversation.

Koreans do the same thing. Only dropping words is a little more frequent in daily conversation. Koreans are particularly fond of dropping personal pronouns and other words that they anticipate their listeners will understand, as in these examples:

✔ **manna seo bangawoyo** (*man-na-suh ban-ga-wo-yo*). (I) am glad to meet (you)

✔ **Led Zeppelinuen?** (*Led Zeppeli-neun?*) (What about) Led Zeppelin?

✔ **Charlesreul?** (*Charles-reul?*) (Who did what to/ What happened to) Charles?

✔ **Saranghaeyo** (*sa-rang-hae-yo*). (I/you/he/she/it/they) love/ loves (something or someone).

These examples might make you wonder if Koreans spend most of their days scratching their heads trying to figure out what the other person just said. Although it is fun to imagine, the truth is this happens less often than you would expect, but if it ever does, Koreans are quick to ask what they just missed, so don't be ashamed to ask questions.

Korean gets around this problem by adding particles at the end of each noun that marks or indicates what role a word plays within the sentence. Here, the particle for the performer of the action is **-ga**, the subject marker, and the particle for the action receiver is **-reul**, the object marker. Hence, we can see that both of the following sentences mean Eric drinks juice:

> Eric-**ga** juice-**reul** drink-**haeyo**
>
> juice-**reul** Eric-**ga** drink-**haeyo**

Sentence particles

Sentence particles are difficult to translate consistently into English because they mark what role a word plays within a sentence as opposed to having an explicit meaning. And hence, a single particle can be translated in more than one way given a different context. For example, the particle **-eseo** specifies when or where a verb takes place, hence, "Eric drinks juice at the market," "Oh, the dress is elegant," and "I warm up in the swimming pool" are translated as "Eric-**ga** juice-**reul** market-**eseo** drink-**haeyo**," "Oh~ dress-**ga** elegant-**haeyo**," and "**juneun** swimming pool-**eseo**, warm-up-**haeyo**."

Common particles

Common particles include **i/ga** (subject market), **eun/neun** (subject marker), **eul/reul** (subject marker), **e/esu** (from), **kkaji** (to/until), **euro** (to), **buteo** (from) and **ui** (indicates possession). This list of common particles is by no means comprehensive, but much daily conversation can be made by using these particles alone. The role of particles is largely determined by what kind of sentence the particle is used in.

Asking Questions

To make an informal polite sentence into a question all you have to do is raise the tone of your voice in a rising intonation at the end of the sentence. Think for a second of how you could turn "Asking a question in Korean is easy," into a question in English. One way would be by moving the "is" to the beginning of the sentence, which would give you "Is asking a question in Korean easy?" The other would be by raising the tone of your voice at the end of a sentence, like asking "Asking a question in Korean is easy?"

If you were given the statement in informal polite Korean, such as **hanguge-oro jilmuneul mandeuneun geosi swiwoyo** (*han-goo-guh-ro jil-moon-eul man-deu-neun guh-shee shee-wo-yo;* Asking a question in Korean is easy) all you have to do is use the same tone of voice as when you would when you say "Asking a question in Korean is easy?"

Talkin' the Talk

Chris and Jung are waiting for food at a restaurant.

Jung: chrisssineun eoneu nara saram eeaeyo?
chris-sshi-neun uh-neu-na-ra sa-ram-ee-ae-yo?
Where are you from, Chris?

Chris: ah, jeoneun meeguk saramieaeyo. jangnyeonae virginiaeseo waseoyo.
oh, juh-neun mee-gook sa-ram-ee-ae-yo. jak-nyun-ae virginia-ae-suh wa-ssuh-yo.
Oh, I'm an American person. I came from Virginia last year.

Jung: hangukeumsigi anmaewoyo?
han-goog-eum-shi-gee an-mae-wo-yo?
Isn't Korean food too spicy?

Chris: jogeum maewoyo. hajiman jeoneun hanguk eum-sigeul jungmal joahhaeyo.
jo-geum mae-wo-yo. ha-jee-man juh-neun han-goog eum-shi-geul jung-mal jo-a-hae-yo.
It is a little spicy. But I really like Korean food.

Jung: murihaji maseyo. pirohamyeon mul jom asyeoyo.
moo-ree-ha-jee-ma-sae-yo. pee-ryo-ha-myun mool-jom-ma-syuh-yo.
Take it easy now. Drink some water if you need to.

Words to Know

chaesik juuija	chae-shik-joo-ui-ja	Vegetarian
gogi	goo-gee	Meat
eumsik	eum-shik	Food
jogeum	jo-geum	Little
nara	na-ra	Country
saranghaeyo	sa-rang-hae-yo	I love you

Counting Korean Style

To say you know how to count in Korean, you have to know two distinct counting systems. One is of Korean origin, native Korean numbers, and the other is of Chinese origin, Sino-Korean numbers. These two systems are used to count different things, and unfortunately what number system you use depends on what you want to count. Let's start off by learning Korean numbers then learn Chinese numbers.

Native Korean numbers

You can use Korean numbers to count from 1 to 99, and if you ever need to go beyond 99 you can start using Sino-Korean numbers. Although it isn't the best thing to do, some Koreans will even use Sino-Korean numbers for numbers bigger than 20.

Table 2-3 lists Korean numbers.

Table 2-3	Korean Numbers
Number	*Korean Name (Pronunciation)*
1	**hana** (*ha-na*) *han
2	**dul** (*dool*) *du
3	**set** (*set*) *se
4	**net** (*net*) *ne
5	**daseot** (*da-sut*)
6	**yeoseot** (*yuh-sut*)
7	**ilgop** (*il-gop*)
8	**yeodeol** (*yeo-deol*)
9	**ahop** (*a-hop*)
10	**yeol** (*yuhl*)
20	**seumul** (*seu-mool*) *seumu
30	**seoreun** (*suh-reun*)
40	**maheun** (*ma-heun*)
50	**swin** (*sween*)
60	**yesun** (*ye-soon*)
70	**ilheun** (*il-heun*)
80	**yeodeun** (*yuh-deun*)
90	**aheun** (*a-heun*)

Now, say you want to count a number larger than 10 using Korean numbers, let's say you feel like saying the number 22. In Korean you would say **seumul-dul** (*seu-mool-dool;* 22). Essentially, what you are saying is 20, 2, just like you would in English, **seumul** (*seu-mool;* 20) **dul** (*dool;* 2).

Although whether you use Korean numbers, or Sino-Korean numbers depends largely on what things you are counting, as a general rule of thumb, Korean numbers are used for counting distinct things one by one. For example, the replicates of pushups and kicks you do in a **taekwondo dojangs** (*tae-kwon-do-do-jang;* Place where you learn Taekwondo), the number of people you meet, and the bottles of beer that you drink are counted using Korean numbers.

You might have noticed that five numbers (See Table 2-3 with *) **hana, dul, set, net** and **seumul** have a second form that I have marled with an asterisk (*). You use this secondary form when you combine these numbers with counters with which to count things. For example, bottles as **byeong** (*byoung;* used to count bottles), sheets as **jang** (*jang;* used to count paper), people as **myeong** (*myoung;* used to count people) and animals as **mari** (*ma-ree;* used to count animals). Aside from the five numbers that I have written, you can just use the numbers themselves in Table 2-4. Hence, you would say **seumu myeong** (*seu-moo-myoung*) for 20 people and **seumulne byeong** (*seu-mool-nae-byoung*) for 24 bottles.

Sino-Korean numbers

Sino-Korean numbers are used just as often as Korean numbers so you need to know both number systems to say that you can count. Table 2-4 lists the Sino-Korean numbers.

Table 2-4	Sino-Korean Numbers
Number	*Korean Name (Pronunciation)*
0	**yeong** (young)
1	**il** (ill)
2	**I** (ee)
3	**sam** (sam)

(continued)

Table 2-4 *(continued)*

Number	Korean Name (Pronunciation)
4	**sa** (sa)
5	**o** (oo)
6	**yuk** (yook)
7	**chil** (chil)
8	**pal** (pal)
9	**gu** (goo)
10	**sip** (ship)
100	**baek** (baeg)
1000	**cheon** (chun)
10,000	**man** (man)
100,000	**shimman** (ship-man)
1,000,000	**baengman** (baeg-man)
10,000,000	**cheonman** (chun-man)
100,000,000	**eok** (uck)

Although you read Sino-Korean a lot like you would numbers in English, there are two big differences. First, you don't add "one" in front of numbers like one hundred, or one thousand, just say hundred, **baek,** or thousand, **chun,** The next thing is that you have to say explicitly ten, **sip,** after reading the number in the tenth place. Hence, you would say 17 in Sino-Korean numbers as **sipchil** (*ship-chil*) and 29 as **isipgu** (*ee-ship-goo*).

Counters

If you want to say the time, you need to use both the Sino-Korean and the Korean counting systems. The hour, **si** (*shi*), is told by using Korean counters. And minutes, **bun** (*boon*), are read using Sino-Korean numbers. In Korean 6:45 is read **yeoseotsi sasibobun** (*yuh-suht-shi sa-ship-o-boon*). The counters are added after the numbers themselves.

When numbers are used in sentences, you have to add counters immediately after them. Suppose you wanted to say, "I'm meeting two colleagues." In Korean, you would say, "I colleagues two people meet," **jeoneun dongnyo dumyeongeul mannayo** (*juh-neun dong-nyo doo-myoung-eul man-na-yo;* I'm meeting two colleagues). You have to place who or what you are counting, the number of the things you are counting and finally the counter.

Now, what determines the number system you use? Well . . . the counter, be it plates of food, flocks of geese, and members of a team. Unfortunately Korean has no clear rules for defining which counter is tied with which number system.

Table 2-5 lists some common Korean counters and Table 2-6 gives you some common Sino-Korean counters.

Table 2-5	**Counters That Use Korean Numbers**		
English	*Korean*	*English*	*Korean*
Things	**gae** (*gae*)	Bowls	**geureut** (*geu-reut*)
People (informal)	**saram** (*sa-ram*)	Animals	**mari** (*ma-ree*)
People (formal)	**myeong** (*myoung*)	Books	**gwun** (*gwon*)
People (honorific)	**bun** (*boon*)	Sheets	**jang** (*jang*)
Parts	**bubun** (*boo-boon*)	Months	**dal** (*dal*)
Bottles	**byeong** (*byoung*)	The hour	**si** (*shi*)
Cup	**jan** (*jan*)	Hours	**sigan** (*si-gan*)
Plates	**jeobsi** (*juhp-shi*)	Years old	**sal** (*sal*)

Table 2-6	**Counters That Use Sino-Korean Numbers**
English	*Korean (Pronunciation)*
Korean currency	**won** (*won*)
Dollars	**dalleo** (*dal-luh*)
Miles	**mail** (*ma-il*)
Kilometers	**killometeo** (*kil-lo-me-ter*)

(continued)

Table 2-6 *(continued)*

English	*Korean (Pronunciation)*
Minutes	**bun** (*boon*)
Days	**Il** (*il*)
Months	**wol** (*wol*)
Years	**nyeon** (*nyeon*)
Kilograms	**killo** (*kee-ro*)
Pounds	**paundeu** (*pa-oon-deu*)
Floors	**cheung** (*cheung*)

Fun & Games

Fill in the blanks with equivalent English and Korean words:

1. Which form of politeness should you use in everyday conversation?

_____

2. Is respect a big thing in Korea?

_____

3. How many different ways are there to count in Korean?

_____

4. What is the Korean word used to count bottles?

_____

5. What is the Korean word used to count animals?

_____

Chapter 3

Introductions and Greetings

- -

In This Chapter

▶ Introducing yourself and your friends

▶ Addressing people formally or informally

▶ Being polite

▶ Saying goodbye

- -

A warm **insa** (*in-sa;* greeting) and a solid **sogae** (*so-gae;* introduction) can leave a good first impression. Done correctly, introductions help you express your sincere **hogam** (*ho-gam;* interest) in not only the **saram** (*sa-ram;* person) that you're talking to, but also **hangungmal** (*han-goog-mal;* Korean language) and culture. Although most people understand you even when you botch your introduction, in some cases, you can annoy or offend the person you want to get to know. In this section I show you how to begin and end the first few minutes of **daehwa** (*dae-hwa;* conversation) on a solid note.

Making Introductions

If you're going to be meeting people, chances are you have to make introductions at one point or another. In Korean, your introduction depends on the person you're introducing and the person to whom you're making the introduction.

In English, you state someone's **ireum** (*ee-rum;* name) and any specific information, such as a job, in a basic introduction. You may say something like, "This is my friend Huckleberry. He's a team leader at Mischief and Misconduct Co." In Korean, the introduction is similar, but you say the specific information about the person, such as a **jikjang** (*jik-jang;* job) title or who he is (a friend or relative, for example), before his name. The following sections give you the Korean words you need to know.

Greetings and salutations

An introduction begins with a **insa** (*in-sa;* greeting), usually a simple hello. Korean offers a few kinds of greetings, such as the following:

- ✔ **Annyeonghaseyo** (*an-young-ha-sae-yo;* Hello/hi, informal polite): This word is the most-often taught and used greeting of the Korean language. It didn't originally mean *hello;* rather, it was a question regarding well-being that meant, "Are you doing well?" But the greeting has lost most of its original meaning and now you can use it the same way as any greeting. This has formal polite counterpart, however, it is more than enough to use this informal polite form. See the section "Getting formal or informal," later in this chapter, for more information.

- ✔ **Cheoeumboepgetseumnida** (*Chuh-eum bwep-get-sseum-ni-da;* It's nice to meet you for the first time, formal polite): Use this greeting when you're meeting someone for the first time. For example, when you are meeting your Korean friend's parents for the first time or when you are at a job interview. Do not use this greeting if you have already met the person you are greeting before.

- ✔ **Mannaseobangapseumnida** (*man-na-suh ban-sseum-ni-da;* It's a pleasure to meet you, formal polite): Usually this greeting follows.

If you happen to know the people you're speaking to, perhaps through work or acquaintances, Korean offers a few more greetings that you may want to try:

- ✔ **Jal jinaeseoyo** (*jal-ji-nat-ssuh-yo;* Are you doing well?): This phrase is another way of asking how someone is doing and can be used like 'How are you?'

- ✔ **Oraeganmanineyo** (*O-rae-gan-man-ee-nae-yo;* Long time no see.) This greeting can be used when you haven't seen someone for a while. Can be used at everyday setting.

- ✔ **Siksa hasyeoseoyo?** (*Shik-sa-ha-syut-ssuh-yo;* Have you eaten?): This greeting is used when you are greeting someone after or around meal times. If someone asks you this question, it doesn't mean that they want to eat with you — part of Korean custom involves checking to see whether those around you have had a good meal.

- ✔ **Geudongan byulil eobseusyutseubnikka?** (*Geu-dong-an byul-il uhp-sseu-syuh-sseum-ni-kka;* Is everything all right? formal)

- ✔ **Geudongan byeoril reopseoseoyo?** (*Geu-dong-an byul il-uhp-ssut-suh-yo;* Is everything all right?): Literal translation of this greeting is "Nothing bad has happened, right?" This greeting can be used to check if everything is going well with the person you are greeting.

When someone is asking you above questions, you may want to answer these questions with **ye** (*ye;* yes) or **aniyo** (*a-ni-yo;* no).

Bowing and shaking hands

Koreans usually shake hands during introductions and greetings when they haven't seen each other in a while. When you shake hands, you bend your waist slightly and put your right hand forward. Your left hand should look as if it's supporting the right arm by holding the wrist or elbow. Sometimes Koreans hold their chests or stomachs instead of holding the wrist or an elbow.

The senior person in a group initiates handshakes, but whichever person first sees the other can initiate bows. Make sure to accompany the bow with a nice greeting (see the previous section for some ideas on appropriate greetings).

Bowing is an **jungyohan** (*joong-yo-han;* important) part of Korean **munhwa** (*moon-hwa;* culture) and communication. You use bows to accompany greetings, apologies, and expressions of gratitude. You also use bows to show regard and respect. Bow from the **heori** (*huh-ri;* waist), but only a little, and make sure to tilt your head. People who haven't bowed before often make the **silsu** (*shil-soo;* mistake) of bowing too much, and sometimes they look straight at the other person or at the other person's **bal** (*bal;* feet). Doing so makes it seem as though you're trying to challenge the other person to a bout of Tae kwon do. If you can, try watching a few Koreans bow before trying it yourself.

Getting formal or informal

Korean is big on politeness. When you're getting ready to make introductions, you need to **ihae** (*ee-hae;* understand) which form of politeness people are using with you, so that you can pick the right form of politeness when speaking to others.

In introductions, you need two degrees of politeness: formal polite and informal polite Korean. Both are equally appropriate and respectful, and the difference between the two is subtle. Perhaps the easiest way to think of it is to examine the differences between occasions where you wear formal attire versus casual attire. You wear formalwear when you want to give a professional or courteous **insang** (*in-sang;* impression), and you choose casualwear when you want to be more easy-going and relaxed. Likewise, you use formal Korean as you would wear formal dress, and informal Korean as you would casualwear. **Namja** (*nam-ja;* men) tend to use more formal Korean, and **yeoja** (*yuh-ja;* women) use both forms or even mix the two. However, it is perfectly okay to use informal polite Korean in everyday living for both men and women.

The degree of politeness you use is determined by the ending you put on at the end of a sentence. I give you a concrete example using the verb **ida** (*ee-da;* to be). If you want to know more about conjugating verbs, check out Chapter 2.

Although informal polite form is used more often in **maeil** (*mae-il;* everyday) conversations, depending on who you are speaking to (e.g., someone older than you, your teacher, in-laws, or at a job interview) you need to use formal polite form of the conversation. However, if this is getting too detailed, just remember the informal polite form. This should get you by without offending someone.

For formal polite form, use the following endings:

- [some word] **imnida** (*-im-ni-da*): This ending can be used when you are introducing or talking about yourself, family, and friends. You use this ending with the word ending with a vowel [some word] **ida** (*ee-da;* to be) to get [some word] **imnida**. This ending is usually used with words ending with a vowel, with some exceptions. However, the exceptions are beyond the scope of this book, and therefore will not be discussed. An example of this ending is, **jeoneun Inigo Montoyaimnida.** (*juh-neun inigo mon-to-ya-im-ni-da;* My name is Inigo Montoya.)

- [some word] **seumnida** (*-sseum-ni-da*): This ending is usually used with words ending with a consonant. **Jota** (*jo-ta;* good) can become **jossumnida** (*jo-ssum-ni-da;* it is good). For example. **Nalssiga josseumnida** (*nal-sshi-ga jo-sseum-ni-da;* the weather is good).

- [some word] **imnikka**/[some word] **seumnikka**: Use this ending when you want to ask a question politely.

  For example,

    1) **Chinguga robeoteuimnikka** (*chin-goo-ga ro-bo-teu-im-ni-kka;* Is your friend Robert?)

    2) **Nalssiga josseumnikka** (*nal-sshi-ga jo-sseum-ni-kka;* Is the weather good?)

When you want to talk with your boss or your **bumo** (*boo-mo;* parents), or talk about them with your friends, you need different endings. If you want to show that you respect your parents and your **sangsa** (*sang-sa;* boss), you add **-ssi** after their name. For example, **jenipeossiimnida** (*je-ni-puh-sshi-im-ni-da;* This is Jennifer). Adding **-ssi after people's name** gives you the honorific degree of politeness. The formal polite honorary form of introducing someone by using the **[some word] ida** (*ee-da;* to be) is **[some word] ishimnida/[some word] ishimnikka** ([some word] *ee-shim-ni-da/[some word] ee-shim-ni-kka:* to be but in ultra polite form). However, don't use the [some word] ssi after your name, or the honorary form when speaking about yourself unless you want to look like you have serious ego problems.

Examples of the honorary form include the following:

> **Ibuni eomeoniisimnikka** (*ee-boo-ni uh-muh-ni-ees-him-ni-kka;* Is this person your mother?)

> **Ibuneun jeoui abeojiisimnida.**: (*ee-bu-neun juh-ae a-buh-jee-ee-shim-ni-da;* This person is my father.)

For informal polite endings, use the following:

- ✔ **[some word] ieyo** (*[some word] ee-yae-yo;* this is [some word]): Use this ending to make statements and also when asking questions. To make a statement, speak with a normal tone. If you want to ask a question, raise the tone of your voice at the end of the sentence, just like you do in English.

- ✔ **[some word] iseyo** (*[some word] ee-sae-yo;* this is [some word]): You use **-iseyo** just as you do **-ieyo,** only you use it when you talk about or talking to people you want to show respect to.

When talking, Koreans sometimes move back and forth between formal polite endings and informal polite endings. However, during everyday conversations, do not worry too much about the degree of politeness. If you use informal polite form of the conversation, you are well on your way without offending anyone. Just make sure to add **[some word] ssi** at the end of someone's name to show respect.

Koreans impose a strict hierarchy among themselves, even when they're among only people of a similar **nai** (*na-ee;* age) group. You may notice that the **hubae** (*who-bae;* junior) bows to the **sunbae** (*sun-bae;* senior) Korean, and that the junior acts a little more reserved when he's in the presence of someone who's his senior. And if you listen carefully enough, you may hear the "junior" using a more respectful form of Korean when they talk to their "senior." This self-imposed hierarchy is a social custom in Korea that stems from Confucianism and still plays an important role in modern Korean culture. If you ignore this hierarchy, especially the hierarchy of "age" (even if it's only one year older) you will be in deep trouble.

Korean has no set rule for deciding seniority, but it's based on a combination of age and status within an organization. Although the idea may seem a tad overbearing and restrictive, Koreans think that seniority and the hierarchy that it entails bring order and a sense of community. Koreans often use the expression **wi areaga itda** (*wee-aa-rae-ga-it-da;* to have a top and bottom) to refer to communities that observe seniority.

Seniority is more than one-sided respect on the part of juniors for seniors. Seniors are also expected to council and provide for their juniors, and traditionally, seniors oversee gatherings, give advice, and even pay for meals. Koreans believe this tradition of respect and care allows people to form tighter personal bonds.

For this reason, most Koreans appreciate it if you can follow a senior or junior role in your immediate relationship with them. But even if you're the perfect senior or junior with one individual, you leave a black mark if he sees you raising your **moksori** (*mok-so-ri;* voice) to your parents, disrespecting a senior, or neglecting a junior. In this instance, your Korean friends will say that you have **wi areaga eopda** (*wee-aa-rae-ga uhp-da;* to have no top and bottom). If you hear this from someone, this means that he/she thinks you are very rude and you have no respect for your seniors. If you want Koreans to believe that you understand their culture, begin by observing seniority with them and the people around you.

Talkin' the Talk

 Hyeonghuon So and Eric Choi work in the same building. Here is how they may greet each other. Note how they mix formal and informal Korean.

Hyeonghun So:	annyeonghaseyo Eric sshi. (bows slightly)
	an-young-ha-sae-yo Eric-sshi
	Are you doing well, Eric?

Eric Choi:	a ye. oraenmanimnida. geudongan byeoril eopseusyeotjyo? (bows slightly and approaches to shake hand)
	a-ye. o-raen-man-im-ni-da. geu-dong-an byul-il-uhp-sseu-syut-jo?
	Ah, yes. It's been a long time. Has everything been all right for you?

Hyeonghun So:	byeoril eopseotseumnida. najunge hanbeon siksana gachi hapsida.
	byul-il-uhp-ssut-ssum-ni-da. na-joong-ae han-buhn sik-sa-na gat-ee hap-si-da.
	There's nothing much. Let's grab some food later.

Eric Choi: ye, ye joayo. (the two shake hands, bowing
                    slightly for the second time)
                    ye, ye jo-a-yo.
                    Sure, sure, that sounds good.

Words to Know

daehwa	dae-hwa	Conversation
insa	in-sa	Greetings
najunge	na-joong-ae	Later
nalssi	nal-sshi	Weather
saram	sa-ram	Person
siksa	shik-sa	Food/meal

Introducing yourself

You can't always rely on **dareunsaram** (*da-reum-sa-ram;* someone else) to make introductions. Introducing yourself isn't hard — all you do is give your name and affiliation. Start with one of these informal polite phrases:

- ✔ **jeoneun . . . ieyo** (*juh-neun [your name] ee-ae-yo;* I am [your name])

- ✔ **je ireumeun . . . ieyo** (*jae-ee-rum-eun [your name] ee-ae-yo;* My name is [your name].)

- ✔ **jeoneun . . . iragohaeyo** (*juh-neun [your name] ee-ra-go hae-yo;* They call me [your name].)

Koreans, especially in formal settings, give their affiliation before they give their name. They use the word **[some word] eseo geunmuhaneun** *[your company name] ae-suh geun-moo-ha-neun;* I work at [your company name].). Conversely, some people say just the name of their workplace or affiliation, rest for a second, and then say their name. Check out the following examples:

Juneun eunhaengaeseo ilhaneun Seuteisieyo. (*Juh-neun eun-hang-ae-suh il-ha-neun Seu-te-shi-ae-yo;* I'm affiliated with bank: my name is Stacy.)

Juneun baekhwajeomaeseo geunmuhaneun Allisseu Haeriseuirago haeyo. (*Juh-neun baek-hwa-jum-ae-suh geun-moo-ha-neun Al-li-sseu Hae-ri-sseu-ra-go-hae-yo:* I work at the department store, and they call me Alice Harris.)

Talkin' the Talk

Jae Woo, and Christina Ridgeway introduce themselves at a party.

Jae Woo:	**yeoreobun annyeonghaseyo. jeoneun AIG hoesawon ijaewooibnida.** (bows) *yuh-ruh-boon, an-young-ha-sae-yo. juh-neun AIG hwae-sa-won ee-jae-woo-im-ni-da* Hello everyone. My name is Jae Woo Lee, and I am an employee at AIG.
Christina:	**yeoreobun annyeonghaseyo. jeoneun hanguk insam-gonsa daeri keuriseutina rijiweiragohaeyo.** (bows) *yuh-ruh-boon, an-young-ha-sae-yo. juh-neun han-goog im-sam-gong-sa dae-ri keu-ri-seu-ti-na ri-ji-wei-ra-go-hae-yo* Hello everyone. My name is Christina Ridgeway, and I am a representative of the Korea Tobacco and Ginseng company.

Words to Know

baekhwajeom	baek-hwa-jum	Department store
eunhaeng	eun-hang	Bank
ireum	ee-rum	Name
hoesawon	hwae-sa-won	Company employee
hubae	who-bae	Junior
jeoneun	huh-neun	I'm/I am
seonbae	seon-bae	Senior
sogae	so-gae	To introduce
yeoreobun	yuh-ruh-boon	Everyone

Introducing a friend or a peer

To start an introduction, begin with **je chingureul sogaehalkkeyo** (*je-chin-goo-reul so-gae-hal-kkae-yo;* Let me introduce you to my friend.) You can replace **chingu** (*chin-goo;* friend) with words such as **dongnyo** (*dong-ryo;* co-worker).

The next thing to do in an introduction is give specific information about the person you're introducing. For example, you may want to give her position in a company and then her name: **i sarameun byeonhosa haena aendeoseunimnida.** (*ee-sa-ram-eun byun-ho-sa hae-na an-der-seun-im-ni-da;* This person is Hannah Anderson, a lawyer.) Here, **i saram** (*ee-sa-ram*) means "this person," but if you're less familiar with the person you're introducing, or if you want to be a little more respectful, use **i buneun** (*ee-boo-neun*), which is a gender neutral term that's close to "this gentleman," or "this lady."

When you talk about someone's affiliation, start from big to small. In English, you usually start from small to big, so this rule may be tough to remember. In English, you begin an introduction by giving the person's name, the person's status within the organization, and then the organization's name. (For example, This is Hannah Anderson, a CEO at Paper Company, Inc.) In Korean, personal introductions begin with the organization the person is affiliated with, and end with the person's name. Check out the following examples:

> **ibuneun uri daehakkyo beopdaee gyesin udeuro wilseunimnida.**
> (*ee-boon-eun uri-dae-hak-gyo byup-dae-ae gae-shin u-de-ro wil-seun-im-ni-da:* This gentlemen belongs to the law school of our university: his name is Woodrow Wilson.)

> **i sarami je dongsaeng Jeieyo:** (*ee-sa-ram-ee jae-dong-saeng jae-ae-yo;* This person is my younger brother, Jae.)

> **i chinguneun samsung junja gwajang ijaeneyo:** (*ee-chin-goo-neun sam-sung-jun-ja gwa-jang ee-jae-oo-ae-yo;* This is my friend, a director in the finance department of Samsung electronics, Lee Jae Woo.)

You use the big-to-small rule when you're giving **juso** (*joo-so;* addresses) in Korean, as well. In English, you start with the house **beonho** (*bun-ho;* number) and end with the state. In Korean, you write an address the other way around, by starting off with the state (or province, as it's known in Korea) and ending with the house number.

You determine the formality of your speech by whatever it is that you want to convey. You use the formal polite, informal polite, or honorific forms based on how much respect you're showing the person you're speaking about.

You can think of the following people as your peers:

- **dongnyo** (*dong-nyo;* colleagues)
- **chingu** (*chin-goo;* friends)
- **jipsaram/anae** (*jeep-sa-ram/aa-nae;* your wife)
- **nampyun** (*nam-pyun;* your husband)
- **ttal** (*ttal;* daughters)
- **adeul** (*a-deul;* sons)
- **namjachingu** (*nam-ja-chin-goo;* boyfriends)
- **yeojachingu** (*yuh-ja-chin-goo;* girlfriends)
- **hubae** (*who-bae;* juniors)
- **dongsaeng** (*dong-saeng;* younger brothers or sisters)

Introducing a senior or your parents

When you're introducing two people in Korean culture, you always begin by introducing the junior to the senior, and then you tell the junior who you're introducing him or her to. If the senior person is your senior as well, make sure you use the appropriate politeness markers. The following examples show you what I mean:

> **i buneun uri eomeoniseyo** (*ee-boon-eun oo-ree uh-muh-ni-sae-yo;* This person our my mother; *Literally:* This is our mother.) For more information on why Koreans use *our* instead of *my,* see Chapter 2.

> **i bunkkeseo siripdaehak gyosunimimisin hong gyosunimisimnida.** (*ee-boon-kkae-suh shi-rip-dae-hak gyo-soo-nim-ee-shin hong gyo-soo-nim-ee-sim-ni-da;* This person is Professor Hong from **Sirip** university.)

In Korean, you call your mother **eomeoni** (*uh-muh-ni;* mother) and your father **abeoji** (*a-buh-ji;* father). You can call your friend's mother and father **ajeossi** (*a-juh-sshi;* Mr.) and **ajumma** (*a-joom-ma;* Ms./Mrs.), but you can also call them **eomeoni** and **abeoji,** just as you do your parents. Calling them your mom and dad doesn't mean that you're abandoning your parents. If you're around a group of parents, you want to be more specific. For example, if you're talking about your friend Lola's mom and dad, say **lola eomeonim** and **lola abeonim.** By adding **[someone's name] nim** (*[someone's name] nim;* more respectfully calling someone) after someone's name or position, you are showing more respect to that person. However, if you want to sound more formal, call them **Lola ssi eomeoni** and **Lola ssi abeonim.**

Usually, when your friends introduce you to their parents, they don't tell you their names. You're just going to have to call them mom and pop. When children introduce their parents or grandparents to other elders, they spell out their names, letter by letter. So, if your father's name is **Choe Nam Hyun,** you say **uri abeoji jonhameun Choe ja, Nam ja, Hyun ja simnida** (*oo-ree a-buh-ji jon-ham-eun Choe-ja Nam-ja Hyun-ja-shim-ni-da*; My father's name is the letter Choe, the letter Nam, and the letter Hyun.)

Talkin' the Talk

Jessica wants to introduce her boyfriend Eric to her mother, Amanda Im.

Jessica:	**eomeoni, je namjachingureul sogaehageseoyo.** *uh-muh-ni, jae-nam-ja-chin-goo-reul so-gae-ha-get-ssuh-yo* Mom, I'll introduce you to my boyfriend.
Amanda:	**o, geurae.** *oo-geu-rae* Oh, sure.
Jessica:	**ireumeun erigieyo.** *ee-rum-eun erig-ee-ae-yo* His name is Eric.
Eric:	**annyeonghaseyo eomeonim. cheoeumboepgetseumnida** *an-young-ha-sae-yo uh-muh-nim. chuh-eum-boep-get-sseum-ni-da* Hello, mom. It's a pleasure to meet you.
Amanda:	**o, geure, erigeun mwohani?** *oo-geu-rae, erig-eun-mo-ha-ni?* Oh, sure, Eric, what do you do?
Eric:	**a, ye, daehagwon gongbuhamnida.** *a-ye, dae-hak-won gong-boo-ham-ni-da* Ah, yes, I'm studying in graduate school.

Words to Know

abeoji	a-buh-ji	Father
ajeossi	a-jo-sshi	Mr
ajumma	a-joom-ma	Ms/Mrs
bumo	boo-mo	Parents
byeonhosa	byun-ho-sa	Lawyer
daehagwon	dae-hak-won	Graduate school
eomeoni	uh-muh-ni	Mother
gongbu	gong-boo	Study
siheom	shi-hum	Test/exam
yeonpil	yuhn-pil	Pencil

You can usually think of the following people as your seniors:

- **sangsa** (*sang-sa;* your superior, your boss)
- **seonsaengnim** (*sun-sang-nim;* teacher; you can also use this term as a sign of respect)
- **gyosunim** (*gyo-soo-nim;* professor)
- **sonnim** (*son-nim;* a client)
- **sajangnim** (*sa-jang-nim;* business owner; use this word to show respect)
- **hyeong** (*hyung;* older brother; use this term if you're male)
- **nuna** (*noo-na;* older sister; use this term if you're male)
- **eoni** (*un-ni;* older sister; use this term if you're female)
- **oppa** (*op-pa;* older brother; use this term if you're female

Asking for Names

Before you ask someone her name, break the ice by saying a quick **joesong-hamnida** (*jwae-song-ham-ni-da;* I'm sorry, formal polite)/**joesonghaeyo** (*jwae-song-hae-yo;* I'm sorry, informal polite), or **sillyehamnida** (*shil-lae-ham-ni-da;* excuse me, formal polite) **sillyehaeyo** (*shil-lae-hae-yo;* excuse me, informal polite). Then politely ask **seonghami eotteoke doesimnikka** (*sung-ham-ee uh-ttuh-kae dwae-shim-ni-kka;* what is your name, formal polite form) **seonghami eotteoke doeseyo** (*sung-ham-ee uh-ttuh-kae dwae-sae-yo;* what is your name, informal polite). Although you can use the informal form of speech when asking for names, most Koreans use the formal polite form of speech. However, for everyday living, it is perfectly okay to use the easier informal polite form. Usually the formal polite form is used with business/work setting and also when talking to a complete strangers.

You may want to combine your icebreaker with the word "but," for a more natural sounding transition. In this case, say **joesonghamnidaman . . .** (*jwae-song-ham-ni-da-man;* I'm sorry, but . . .) or **sillyehamnidaman . . .** (*shil-lae-ham-ni-da-man;* Excuse me, but . . .). These two phrases are formal polite form. Although there is informal polite form of these phrases, in this case, it is better to use the formal polite form.

The key to asking for someone's name is knowing how to say **i** (*ee:* this), **jeo** (*juh;* that), and **geu** (*geu;* that). Use **i** when referring to someone next to you. Use **jeo** for someone who's far away from both the listener and the speaker and you can see them. Use **geu** for someone near the speaker, and also to refer to people who aren't present at the moment. Check out these examples to see how to use **i, ju,** and **keu:**

- ✔ **i yeojabun** (*ee-yuh-ja-boon;* this lady)

- ✔ **i namjabun** (*ee-nam-ja-boon;* this gentleman)

- ✔ **i bun** (*ee-boon;* this person)

- ✔ **jeo bun** (*juh-boon;* that person over there)

- ✔ **jeo yeojabun** (*juh-yuh-ja-boon;* that lady over there)

- ✔ **jeo namjabun** (*juh-nam-ja-boon;* that gentleman over there)

- ✔ **geu bun** (*geu-nam-ja-boom;* that person who is not present)

- ✔ **geu yeojabun** (*geu-yuh-ja-boon;* that lady who is not present)

- ✔ **geu namjabun** (*geu-nam-ja-boon;* that gentleman who is not present)

Describing people

Pointing is rude in Korean culture, so you want to know how to describe a few features about people. The following list will get you started:

- **kiga** jageun (*ki-ga-ja-geun;* short)

- **kiga keun** (*ki-ga-keun;* tall)

- **angyeongeul sseun** (an-*gyung-eul-sseun;* wears glasses)

- **angyeongeul ansseun** (an-*gyung-eul an-sseun;* doesn't wear glasses)

- **meoriga jjalbeun** (*muh-ri-ga jjal-beun;* short-haired)

- **meoriga gin** (*muh-ri-ga gin;* long-haired)

- **. . . oseul ibeun** (*oseul ibeun;* wears . . . clothes) Fill in the blanks with an appropriate color.

- jeo saramieyo? (*juh-sa-ram-ee-yo;* That person, informal polite)

- ye, geu yeopsaram marieyo (*Ye, yep-sa-ram-mal-ee-ae-yo;* Yes, that person next to you, informal polite.)

- aniyo, geu yeopsaram marieyo (*aniyo, yep-sa-ram-mal-ee-ae-yo;* No, that person next to you, informal polite.)

If you want to ask a person's name, simply add **seonghami eotteoke doeseyo** (*sung-ham-ee uh-ttuh-kae-dwae-sae-yo;* what is your name, formal polite). Use this form when you want to show respect to someone. i.e., when asking the name of your friend's parents, someone senior than you. You can also ask **ireumi mwoeyo** (*ee-rum-ee-mo-ae-yo;* what is your name, informal polite). Use this in everyday conversation, to someone younger than you, and also to your friend's friend.

Talkin' the Talk

June and Tim are at a family reunion, but June forgets a relative's name and decides to ask Tim.

June: **tim, jeobun ireumi mwoeyo?**
tim, juh-boon ee-rum-ee mo-ae-yo?
Tim, what's that person's name?

Tim: **jeo namja buniyo?**
juh nam-ja boon-ee-yo?
That guy?

June: **aniyo, geu yeopsaramiyo. meoriga gin yeojabuniyo.**
a-ni-yo. Geu-yuhp-sa-ram-ee-yo. muh-ree-ga geen yuh-ja-boon-ee-yo.
No, the person next to him. The woman with long hair.

Tim: **a, jeo buniyo? jeo bunui seonghami Son jihiseyo.**
a, juh-boon-ee-yo? juh-boon-ae sung-ham-ee Son-jee-hee-sae-yo.
Ah, that person. That person's name is Jihi Son.

June: **tim, gomawoyo.**
tim, go-ma-wo-yo
Thanks Tim.

Talkin' the Talk

 Jane and Alice are planning a picnic. They are talking about the weather.

Jane: **alice, pikkeunik ganeunnal nalssiga eotteoteyo?**
alice, pic-keu-nik ga-neun-nal nal-sshi-ga uh-ttuh-tae-yo?
Alice, how's the weather on the day of the picnic?

Alice: **eung, radioeseo deureonneunde biga ondaeyo**
ung, ra-di-o-ae-suh deu-rut-neun-dae bee-ga-on-dae-yo
Yeah, I heard on the radio that it's going to rain.

Jane: **geureom eotteohajiyo?**
grum, uh-ttuh-ka-ji-yo?
Then what should we do?

Alice: **daeume nalssiga joeulttae gayo.**
da-eum-ae nal-sshi-ga jo-eul-ttae ga-yo
Let's go next time when the weather is good.

Jane: **geuraeyo, geureoja.**
geu-rae-yo, geu-ruh-jyo.
Alright, let's do that.

Words to Know

gajok	ga-jok	Family
gomo	go-mo	Aunt on dad's side
imo	ee-mo	Aunt on mom's side
ki	kee	Height
meori	muh-ree	Head
nun	noon	Eye
samchon	sam-chon	Uncle

Giving Thanks and Saying Sorry

A **miso** (*mi-so;* smile), a word of thanks, and a sincere apology can get you out of tight situations and may take you a long way with people from another culture. Here are some basic phrases that you may want to have at your disposal:

- **gamsahamnida** (*gam-sa-ham-ni-da;* thank you, formal polite): This is the most common "Thank you" phrase Koreans use. If you cannot remember all the "Thank you" phrases, just remember this one and you will be just fine. This phrase is more commonly used when someone has given you something, or has done something for you.

- **gamsahaeyo** (*gam-sa-hae-yo;* thank you, informal polite): This phrase is used mainly between friends or with people you have met before and have some kind of relationships.

- **gomapseumnida** (*go-map-sseum-ni-da;* thank you, formal polite): This is the next common "Thank you" phrase used in Korea. You can use this and *gamsahamnida* interchangeably. It is perfectly okay to just use one of these phrases.

- **gomawoyo** (go-ma-wo-yo; thank you, informal polite): This phrase is usually used if you know the person you are speaking to, just like *gamsahaeyo.*

Although informal polite form is okay to use, when Koreans are thanking someone, they usually use the formal polite form. Use of formal polite form makes the person who you are thanking feel more important and respected. Using informal polite form to thank someone is okay if you have met before and know each other, friends or people who are junior than you.

- ✔ **singyeong sseo jusyeoseo . . .** (*shin-gyoung-ssuh joo-syuh-suh;* for caring, formal polite). This phrase is usually used with **gamsahamnida** or **gomapseumnida'**. It is never used alone. When you have the need to use this phrase, it is usually at a formal setting.

- ✔ **jalhaejusyeoseo . . .** (*jal-hae-joo-syuh-suh;* for being so nice, formal polite). This phrase is usually used with **gamsahamnida** or **gomapseumnida'**. It is never used alone. When you have the need to use this phrase, it is usually at a formal setting.

- ✔ **joesonghamnida** (*jwae-song-ham-ni-da;* I'm sorry, formal polite). This is the usual phrase Korean use when saying sorry to strangers or people you want to show respect to.

- ✔ **joesonghaeyo** (*jwae-song-hae-yo;* I'm sorry, informal polite). This form of sorry can also be used at everyday setting with people you already know.

- ✔ **mianhamnida** (*mi-an-ham-ni-da;* I'm sorry, formal polite). This is the usual phrase Korean use when saying sorry to strangers or people you want to show respect to.

- ✔ **mianhaeyo** (*mi-an-hae-yo;* I'm sorry, informal polite). This form of sorry can also be used at everyday setting with people you already know.

- ✔ **pyekkichyeo deuryoseo mianhamnida** (*pae-kki-chuh deu-ryo-suh mi-an-ham-ni-da;* Sorry for causing such trouble, formal polite). When you are saying this phrase, it is usually in a formal setting. For example, at a business meeting, or when apologizing to people with seniority. Therefore, I have omitted the informal polite form of this phrase.

- ✔ **pyekkichyeo deuryeoseo jowesonghamnida** (*pae-kki-chuh deu-ryo-suh jwae-song-ham-ni-da;* Sorry for causing such trouble). When you need to use this phrase, it will also be at a formal setting. Therefore, the informal polite form of this phrase has been excluded.

Saying Goodbye

Saying goodbye in Korean sometimes depends on whether you're staying or going. If you're seeing your friend off from your house in the evening, you exchange farewells and call it a **bam** (*bam;* night). But in Korean, you tell the person leaving from the place to "go well" and the person staying to "stay well." If you meet your friend at a restaurant, or some other location besides either of your homes or offices, you can also use these farewells.

Check out the different terms and note when to use each:

- ✔ **annyeonghi gyeseyo** (*An-young-hee gye-sae-yo;* goodbye when you are the person leaving, *Literally:* stay well): Use these phrases with seniors and peers when you're leaving and your friend is staying where she is. This is the most common *good bye* used in Korean.

- ✔ **annyeonghi gaseyo** (*An-young-hee ga-sae-yo;* goodbye when you are the person staying, *Literally:* go well): Use these phrases when you are the person staying and your friend is the person leaving the place. This is the most common *goodbye* used in Korean.

- ✔ **jal isseyo** (*jal-ee-ssuh-yo;* goodbye, *Literally:* stay well): Use this phrase with juniors and peers when you're leaving and your friend is staying where he is.

- ✔ **jal gaseyo** (*jal-ga-se-yo;* goodbye, *Literally:* go well): Use this phrase as your friend or people who are junior leaves a place where you're staying.

Korean also has some common goodbyes that you can use whether or not you're staying or going. You can use the following in almost any situation:

- ✔ **daeume tto bwayo** (*da-eum-ae tto bwa-yo;* see you again next time): Use this phrase if you want to meet the person again next time. Can be used to people both senior and junior than you.

- ✔ **annyeonghi jumuseyo** (*an-young-hi joo-mu-sae-yo;* good night, *Literally:* sleep well): This phrase is usually used to people you want to respect is sleeping at the same place as you or if you are talking to them on the phone and it's time to sleep. These phrases cannot be used casually as 'good night' in English, which can be used even if the person is not sleeping at the same house. For example, your parents, in-laws.

- ✔ **jaljayo** (*jal-ja-yo;* good night, *Literally:* sleep well): Use this phrase if people younger than you is sleeping at the same place as you or if you are on the phone with them and it's bed time. For example, your son or daughter in law.

- ✔ **sugohaseyo** (*su-go-ha-sae-yo;* keep up the good work): This phrase can be used to encourage people at any time. Can be used with people senior or junior than you.

Talkin' the Talk

 Danny approaches Megan at a bar and, unfortunately, Megan feels a strong urge to leave.

Danny:	**chum chusillaeyo?**
	choom choo-shil-lae-yo?
	Do you want to dance?

Megan: **joesonghaeyo. jigeum gayahaeyo.**
jwae-song-hae-yo jee-geum ga-ya-hae-yo
I'm sorry. I have to go now.

Danny: **geureom . . . jeonhwabeonhorado?**
geu-rum . . . juhn-hwa-bun-ho-ra-do?
Then . . . your number?

Megan: **mianhaeyo, jeonbeonhoga eopseoyo.**
mi-an-hae-yo, juhn-hwa-bun-ho-ga uhp-ssuh-yo
I'm sorry. I don't have a telephone number.

Danny: **ye?**
ye?
Yes? (actually closer to Huh?)

Megan: **annyeonghi gaeseyo.**
an-young-hee gae-sae-yo
Goodnight.

Words to Know

bam	*bam*	Night
chum	*choom*	Fance
daeume	*da-eum-ae*	Next time
gidaryeoyo	*gi-da-ryo-yo*	To wait
jam	*jam*	Sleep
jeonhwabeonho	*jeon-hwa-bun-ho*	Phone number
jip	*jeeb*	House
nat	*nat*	Day

Fun & Games

Fill in the blanks with equivalent English words:

1. annyeonghaseyo (an-young-ha-sae-yo)

_____

2. gamsahamnida (gam-sa-ham-ni-da)

_____

3. joesonghamnida (jwae-song-ham-ni-da)

_____

4. sillyehamnida (shil-lae-ham-ni-da)

_____

5. ireum (ee-rum)

_____

6. eomeoni (uh-muh-ni)

_____

7. abeoji (a-buh-ji)

_____

8. gajok (ga-jok)

_____

9. seonsaengnim (sun-saeng-nim)

_____

10. byeonhosa (byun-ho-sa)

_____

Part II
Korean in Action

The 5th Wave   By Rich Tennant

"I wasn't sure how to ask in Korean for our shoes back after the meal, so I just ordered them for dessert."

In this part . . .

Sure, you can learn all there is to know about conjugating verbs, distinguishing nouns from adjectives, as well as sentence construction in Korean. But what about everyday life? How can you communicate with your Korean friends or make Korean friends? Look through this part to find information and expressions that you can use with your friends.

Chapter 4

Getting to Know You: Making Small Talk

In This Chapter

▶ Conversing about nationality, languages, and current residence

▶ Talking about the weather, work, and family

▶ Giving out — and getting — contact information

*B*reaking the ice with a little **daehwa** (*dae-hwa;* conversation), in any language, helps you get to know people better and lays down the **cheotgeoreum** (*chut-guh-reum;* first steps) for future friendships. Small talk makes great practice for conversation because the topics for conversation are usually predictable. If you want to know how to use Korean to find out where another person is from and discover a little more about their **gajok** (*ga-jok;* family), read on.

Chapter 3 shows you how to break the **eoreum** (*uh-reum;* ice) and introduce yourself, and in this chapter, I will show you how to carry the conversation further. Remember that I will be using the informal polite form of Korean language in this book. However, I may use formal polite forms from time to time in some situations, where more formality is required. I hope that by going over this chapter, you will be a little more familiar and comfortable with speaking in Korean.

Asking Questions with Essential Words and Formal Usages

Certain words and questions are essential for small talk in Korean, and you need to familiarize yourself with them to converse effectively: **nugu** (*noo-goo;* Who)? **museun** (*moo-seun;* What)? **eonje** (*un-jae;* When)? **eodi** (*uh-dee;* Where)? **eotteoke** (*uh-ttuh-kkae;* How)? Take some time to become familiar with the Korean forms of these words before moving on to make small talk:

mueot (*moo-ut;* What)

mwo (*mwo;* What; shorter version of **mueot**)

mwo is shortened version of **mueot**. These two words are interchangeable, although **mueot** can sound a little more formal than **mwo.**

eolmadongan (*ul-ma-dong-an;* How long: used to define period of time)

eolmana (*ul-ma-da;* How long: shortened version of **eolmadongan**)

eolmana is shortened version of **eolmadongan.** These two words are interchangeable, although **eolmadongan** can sound a little more formal than **eolmana.**

Here are few examples of sentences using basic question words.

nuguseyo? (*noo-goo-sae-yo;* Who are you?)

igeoseun mueosieyo? (*ee-guh-seun moo-us-ee-ae-yo;* What is this?)

igeoseun mwoeyo? (*ee-guh-seun mwo-ae-yo;* What is this?)

myeot sieyo? (*myuht-shi-ae-yo;* What time is it?)

eoneujjogeuro gaya haeyo? (*uh-neu-jjo-geu-ro ga-ya-hae-yo;* Which way do I go?)

eonje mannalkkayo? (*un-jae man-nal-kka-yo;* When should we meet?)

hwajangsiri eodieyo? (*hwa-jang-shil-ee uh-dee-ae-yo;* Where is the bathroom?)

agiga wae ureoyo? (*a-gi-ga whae-oo-ruh-yo;* Why is the baby crying?)

eolmadongan gidaryeoya haeyo? (*ul-ma-dong-an gi-da-ryuh-ya hae-yo;* How long should I wait?)

eolmana gidaryeoya haeyo? (*ul-ma-na gee-da-ryuh-ya hae-yo;* How long should I wait?)

geogireul eotteoke gayo? (*guh-gee-reul uh-ttuh-kkae ga-yo;* How do I get there?)

igeoseul eolmaeyo? (*ee-guh-seun ul-ma-ae-yo;* How much is this?)

When you are speaking in Korean, it is perfectly okay to ask the **hanguk saram** (*han-goog sa-ram;* Korean person) to **doepiri** (*dwae-poo-ree;* repeat) themselves if you did not **ihae** (*ee-hae;* understand) what they were saying. They'll be glad to help. Handy phrases to learn while you're learning Korean for the first time are as follow:

cheoncheonhi malsseumhae juseyo? (*chun-chun-hee mal-sseum-hae joo-sae-yo;* Speak slowly please?)

hanbeonman deo malsseumhae juseyo? (*han-bun-man duh mal-sseum-hae joo-sae-yo;* Please tell me once more?)

jal moreugeseoyo> (*jal-mo-reu-get-ssuh-yo;* I'm not sure?)

mollayo? (*mol-la-yo;* I don't know?)

"Where Are You From?"

After you **kkeunnae** (*kkeun-nae;* finish) introductions (see Chapter 3), people tend to first ask where you're from and what **gukjeok** (*gook-juhk;* nationality) you are. Are you from Korea? America? Canada?

If you want to ask where someone is from, ask using the following sentence:

eodieseo osyeoseoyo? (*uh-dee-ae-suh oo-syut-ssuh-yo;* Where are you from?)

The usual **daedap** (*dae-dap;* answer) to this question would be something like:

jeuneun . . . eseo waseoyo. (*juh-neun [your country] ae-suh wa-ssuh-yo;* I'm from [your country].)

If you want to ask someone whether she's from a particular **nara** (*na-ra;* country), you can ask:

eoneu naraeseo osyeoseoyo? (*uh-neu-na-ra-ae-suh oo-syut-ssuh-yo;* Which country are you from?)

When someone asks whether you're from a particular country, you can answer "Yes, I'm from [country]" or "No, I'm from [country]."

Ye, jeoneun [country] eseo waseoyo. (*ye, juh-neun, [country] ae-suh wa-seo-yo;* Yes, I'm from [country].)

Aniyo, jeoneun [country] eseo waseoyo. (*a-ni-yo, juh-neun, [country] ae-suh wa-seo-yo;* No, I'm from [country].)

Table 4-1 contains a short list of countries and their names in Korean.

Table 4-1	Country Names
Korean Name and Pronunciation	*English Name*
dogil (*do-gil*)	Germany
gana (*ga-na*)	Ghana
hoju (*ho-joo*)	Australia
ilbon (*il-bon*)	Japan
indo (*in-do*)	India
itaeri (*ee-tae-ree*)	Italy
jungguk (*joong-goog*)	China
kaenada (*kae-na-da*)	Canada
miguk (*mee-goog*)	USA
nyujillaend (*new-jil-lan-deu*)	New Zealand
peurangseu (*peu-rang-sseu*)	France
rebanon (*re-ba-non*)	Lebanon
reosia (*ruh-shi-a*)	Russia
sseuwiseu (*seu-wi-sseu*)	Switzerland
yeongguk (*young-goog*)	England

Describing your home community

What **sinae** (*shi-nae;* city), **dongne** (*dong-nae;* town), district, or country are you from? People will probably want to know, and you should be prepared to answer. First, familiarize yourself with the Korean words for these types of residential communities. Table 4-2 gives you a useful list of community words.

Table 4-2	Residential Communities
Korean Words and Pronunciations	*English Words*
do (*do*)	Province
dong (*dong*)	Neighborhood, area
eup (*eup*)	Town

Korean Words and Pronunciations	English Words
gu (*goo*)	District
gun (*goon*)	County
gwangyeoksi (*gwang-yuhk-shi*)	Metropolitan area
myepn (*myun*)	Township
ri (*ree*)	Village
seoul teukbyeolsi (*suh-ool teuk-byul-shi*)	Seoul City (example)
si (*shi*)	City

Koreans **sijak** (*shi-jak;* start) from large and move to small, so if you want to be more specific and talk about what city you're from, be sure to first say the state or country where you're from. For example:

> **jeoneun** Pennsylvaniae **inneun** Punxsutawney**eseo waseoyo.** (*juh-neun Pennsylvania-ae in-neun Punxsutawney-ae-suh wa-ssuh-yo;* I'm from Punxsutawney, Pennsylvania.)

> jeoneun [town] e inneun [city] eseo waseoyo. (*juh-neun [town]-ae in-neun [city]-ae-suh wa-sseo-yo;* I'm from [city], which is in [town].)

If you're talking about a non-Korean location, use the English name for the place as you usually say it. For example, if you come from Indianapolis, Indiana, say it as you would in English.

If you're talking about a Korean city, or a district, give the name of the larger area, and then the smaller area. For example, you can say **gangnamgu** (*gang-nam-goo;* Gangnam district), **sinsadong** (*shin-sa-dong;* sinsa area) and not the other way around.

If you don't know where a particular city is, ask "Where is that place?" Note that **geogi** (*guh-gee;* that), **geugot** (*geu-got;* that place), **yeogi** (*yuh-gee;* this) and **igot** (*ee-got;* this place):

> **geogiga eodi iseoyo?** (*guh-gee-ga uh-dee ee-ssuh-yo;* Where is that?)

> **geugosi eodieyo?** (*geu-go-shi uh-dee-ae-yo;* Where is that place?)

> **yeogiga eodieyo?** (*yuh-gee-ga uh-dee-ae-yo;* Where is this?)

> **igosi eodieyo?** (*ee-go-shi uh-dee-ae-yo;* Where is this place?)

The answer to this question always takes the **iseoyo** (*ee-ssuh-yo;* to exist).

[some word] **e iseoyo** ([some word]-*ae ee-ssuh-yo;* It's at [some word]). Substitute [some word] for locations or directions.

For example, you can say

new yorki boston wie iseoyo. (*new-york-ee bos-ton wee-ae ee-ssuh-yo;* New York is above Boston.)

indianapolisga indianae iseoyo. (*indianapolis-ga indiana-ae ee-ssuh-yo;* Indianapolis is in Indiana.)

Now remember that **–i** and **ga** is a location marker or particle. Add **i** after the location if it ends with a consonant and add **ga** if it ends with a vowel. (In Korean pronunciation, New York ends with a consonant, but Indianapolis end with a vowel). **wie** (*wee-ae;* above), means "above."

Table 4-3 gives you a list of common location and directional words.

Table 4-3	Locations and Directions
Korean Words and Pronunciations	*English Words*
bukjjok (*book-jjok*)	North
dongjjok (*dong-jjok*)	East
gakkai (*ga-kka-ee*)	Nearby
geuncheo (*geun-chuh*)	In the proximity of
meolli (*mul-li*)	Far
mit (*mit*), **area** (*a-rae*) interchangeable	Below
namjjok (*nam-jjok*)	South
seojjok (*suh-jjok*)	West
wi (*wee*)	Above
yeop (*yuhp*)	Next to

Talking about where someone lives

Where you're from and where you live now can be two different things, of course. If you want to ask where someone lives, use the following:

eodiseo saseyo? (*uh-dee-ae-suh sa-sae-yo;* Where do you live?)

Some other questions you may ask are:

jusoga eodieyo? (*joo-so-ga uh-dee-ae-yo;* What is your address?)

jibi eodieyo? (*jee-bee uh-dee-ae-yo;* Where is your house?)

jeonhwabeonhoga mwoeyo? (*juhn-hwa-bun-ho-ga mwo-ae-yo;* What is your telephone number?)

You may answer by using the following:

sigoreseo sarayo. (*shi-go-rae-suh sa-ra-yo;* I live in the countryside.)

sinaeeseo sarayo. (*shi-nae-ae-suh sa-ra-yo;* I live in the city.)

apateueseo sarayo. (*a-pa-teu-suh-ae sa-ra-yo;* I live in the apartment.)

What if you know someone who's staying in the town or country on business for an extended period of time? If you want to ask her where she lives at the moment, add **jigeum** (*jee-geum;* now) in front of **eodisu** (*uh-dee-suh;* where).

The answers to "Where do you live?" can look like

jeoneun [some word] eseo sarayo (*juh-neun [some word] ae-suh sa-ra-yo;* I live at [some word]). Substitute [some word] for location.

Discussing ethnicity and citizenship

Some people are born in one country but hold **simingwon** (*shi-nim-gwon;* citizenship) in another. Saying that you're from a single country may not be enough when you want to explain who you are, so I'll show you few more expressions.

Asking for someone's nationality in Korean is a broad question. It implies ethnicity, or a sense of belonging that you identify with. Although Korean does have the explicit **injong** (*in-jong;* race), people will simply ask you one of the following:

eodieseo waseoyo? (*uh-dee-ae-suh wa-ssuh-yo;* Where are you from?)

eoneunara saramieyo? (*uh-neu-na-ra sa-ram-ee-ae-yo;* What country are you from?/What nationality are you?)

You simply answer the questions as follows:

jeoneun [some word] eseo waseoyo. (*juh-neun [some word] ae-suh wa-sseo-yo;* I'm from [some word].)

jeoneun [some word] saramieyo. (*juh-neun [some word] sa-ram-ee-ae-yo;* I am [some word] person [usually answer with your nationality].)

The above forms of questions can have two types of answers. 1) You can answer the question to mean that you're from the location/country where you were born, or 2) that you feel like you're a part of the place, much like how John F. Kennedy wanted to express that he was a person of Berlin in his 1963 speech. For many Koreans living in U.S., people ask them "Where are you from?" Second generation Koreans born in US will answer, for example, "I'm from Boston or I'm an American." Then the immediate next question is "I mean, where are you (or your parents) originally from?/Which country are you originally from?" You may face some similar situations in Korea.

Suppose that in an introduction, the other person says that he or she is Korean, and you want to say that you're a Korean as well. Say so by replacing the **neun** in **jeoneun** with **do** (do; also).

jeodo [some word] eseo waseoyo. (juh-do [some word] ae-suh wa-ssuh-yo; I'm also from [some word].)

jeodo [some word] saramieyo. (juh-do [some word] sa-ram-ee-ae-yo; I am also [some word] person [usually answer with your nationality].)

Talkin' the Talk

Grace is lost in Seoul. She is asking Sung Jin where she can find a train station.

Grace: (holding a map) **sillyehamnida. jeo jom doajusilsu iseuseyo?**
shil-lae-ham-ni-da. juh-jom do-wa-joo-shil-soo ee-sseu-sae-yo?
Excuse me. Can you please help me?

Sung Jin: **a gireul ireo beorisyeotgunyo.**
a, gi-reul ee-ruh buh-ree syut-goon-yo.
Oh, you are lost.

Grace: **ye. gichayeogeul chatgo iseoyo.**
ye. gi-cha-yuh-geul cha-go-ee-ssuh-yo.
Yes, I'm looking for a train station.

Sung Jin: **eotteon gichayeogeul chajeuseyo?**
uh-ttun gi-cha-yuh-geul cha-jeu-sae-yo?
Which train station are you looking for?

Grace: **seoul yeogeul chatgo iseoyo.**
suh-ool yuh-geul cha-go ee-ssuh-yo.
I'm looking for Seoul station.

Sung Jin:	**bukjjogeuro 15bunman gasimyeon doeyo.**
	book-jjok–eu-ro 15-boon-man ga-shi-myun dwae-yo.
	Just go in North direction for about 15 minutes.

Grace:	(bowing) **jeongmal gamsahamnida.**
	jung-mal gam-sa ham-ni-da.
	Thank you very much.

Sung Jin:	(bowing) **cheonmanhaeyo.**
	chun-man-hae-yo.
	You are welcome.

Words to Know

agi	a-gi	Baby
chatgo iseoyo	cha-go-ee-ssuh-yo	Looking for
gichayeok	gi-cha-yuhk	Train station
gyeongchalseo	gyung-chal-so	Police station
hotel	ho-tel	Hotel
hwajangsil	hwa-jang-shil	Bathroom
injong	in-jong	Race
ireobeorisyeotgunyo	ee-ruh-buh-ree-syut-goon-yo	You are lost
jeoncheoryeok	juhn-chul-yuhk	Underground subway
jeongmal	jung-mal	Really
jeonhwabeonho	juhn-hwa-bun-ho	Telephone number
juso	joo-so	Address
nara	na-ra	Country

The Weather, the Seasons, and Everything in Between

Talking about the **nalssi** (*nal-sshi;* weather) is a staple of small talk. When you first get to know someone, she may ask what the weather is like where you come from (see Table 4-4 for some ideas on how to discuss weather). In this section, I go over a few expressions about the weather, and then **yeongyeol** (*yuhn-gyul;* connect) them to a conversation about what the weather is like where you come from. The general question used to ask about the weather is:

> **nalssiga eottaeyo?** (*nal-sshi-ga uh-ttae-yo;* What is the weather like?)

To this question, you can add **oneul** (*o-neul;* today), **naeil** (*nae-il;* tomorrow), **achim** (*a-chim;* morning), **jeonyeok** (*juh-nyeok;* evening) and **bam** (*bam;* night). For example: **oneul achim nalssiga eottaeyo?** (*o-neul a-chim nal-shi-ga uh-ttae-yo;* What is the weather like this morning?)

You will answer the questions as per examples below.

> **nalssiga.** (*nal-sshi-ga* [**good, bad, sunny, cloudy, etc.**]. Weather is [good, bad, sunny, cloudy, etc.].)

You can fill in the end of these sentences with the following weather-related adjectives.

For example:

> **nalssiga chuwoyo.** (*nal-sshi-ga choo-wo-yo;* The weather is cold.)

> **oneul jeonyeok nalssiga joayo.** (*o-neul juh-nyeok-nal-sshi-ga jo-a-yo;* The weather this evening is good.)

Table 4-4	Weather Conditions
Korean Words and Pronunciations	*English Words*
anjoaya (*an-jo-a-yo*)	Not good
chuwoyo (*choo-wo-yo*)	Cold
deowoyo (*duh-wo-yo*)	Hot
geonjohaeyo (*gun-jo-hae-yo*)	Dry
heuryeoyo (*heu-ryo-yo*)	Cloudy

Korean Words and Pronunciations	English Words
joayo (*jo-a-yo*)	Good
malgayo (*mal-ga-yo*)	Clear
mudeowoyo (*moo-duh-wo-yo*)	Hot and humid
nappayo (*na-ppa-yo*)	Bad
seonseonhaeyo (*seon-seon-hae-yo*)	Cool and refreshing
seupaeyo (*seu-pae-yo*)	Humid
siwonhaeyo (*shi-won-hae-yo*)	Cool
ttatteutaeyo (*tta-tteut-hae-yo*)	Warm

If you want to talk about precipitation, you need to say [some word] **i/ga** (depending on the ending: [some word] **i** for vowel and [some word] **ga** for consonant) **wayo** (*wa-yo:* [some word] coming) or [some word] **i/ga naeryeoyo** ([some word] *i/ga nae-ryuh-yo;* [some word] falls). **wayo** and **naeryeoyo** are interchangeable in Korean. Either one is fine. Here, I have already added the appropriate subject markers ([some word] **i/ga**) to the nouns for your convenience (see Table 4-5 for more on weather and seasons).

> **bi** (*bee;* rain) or **bi<u>ga</u>** (*bee-ga;* rain)
>
> **nun** (*noon;* snow) or **nun<u>i</u>** (*noo-nee;* snow)
>
> **ubak** (*ubak;* hail) or **uba<u>gi</u>** (*oo-ba-gee;* hail)

Using these words, you can say things like: **biga wayo** (*bee-ga wa-yo;* It's raining) or **nuni naeryeoyo** (*noo-nee nae-ryuh-yo;* It's snowing).

Table 4-5	Seasons and Months
Korean Words and Pronunciations	**English Words**
bom (*bom*)	Spring
yeoreum (*yuh-rum*)	Summer
gaeul (*ga-eul*)	Fall
gyeoul (*gyuh-ool*)	Winter
irwol (*ee-rwol*)	January
iwol (*ee-wol*)	February

(continued)

Table 4-5 *(continued)*

Korean Words and Pronunciations	English Words
samwol (*sam-wol*)	March
sawol (*sa-wol*)	April
owol (*o-wol*)	May
yuwol (*yoo-wol*)	June
chirwol (*chi-rwol*)	July
parwol (*pa-rwol*)	August
guwol (*goo-wol*)	September
siwol (*shi-wol*)	October
sibirwol (*shi-ee-rwol*)	November
sibiwol (*shi-ee-wol*)	December

You have probably noticed that each month consistently ends with the word **wol** (*wol;* month). The word that precedes **wol** is a Sino-Korean number, such as **il** (*il;* one), **i** (*ee;* two), **sam** (*sam;* three) and so on. You're actually saying month one, month two, month three, and so on. Pretty easy to remember, right?

You combine Sino-Korean numbers by saying **sibil** (*shi-bil;* eleven; *Literally:* ten one), **sibi** (*shi-bee;* twelve; *Literally:* ten two), and so on. Another example is **isipgu** (*ee-ship-goo;* twenty-nine; *Literally:* two ten nine). See Chapter 2 for more information on Korean numbers.

> In English, your answer to such a question would be, "The weather here is . . . ." but in Korean, you say, "**biseuthada** (*bee-seut-ha-da;* Similar to here" or "**deo deopda** (*duh duhp-da;* Hotter than here." For example: **nalssiga yeogihago biseuthaeyo.** (*nal-sshi-ga yuh-gee-ha-go bee-seut-hae-yo;* The weather is similar to here.)

If you want to compare two things, use the particle **boda** (*bo-da;* than/compared to). **boda** is a peculiar fellow, because it works quite differently from the English "than." When used at the beginning of a sentence "bo-da" means "compared to." Check out this example:

> **virginiaboda hangugi deoweoyo.** (*virginia-bo-da han-goo-gi duh-wo-yo;* <u>Compared to</u> Virginia, Korea is hotter.)

> **hangugi virginia boda deowoyo.** (*han-goo-gi virginia-bo-da duh-wo-yo;* Korea is hotter <u>than</u> Virginia.)

Talking About Jobs and Occupations

Another favorite topic of conversation is **jigeop** (*jee-guhp;* occupation). If you want to ask what someone does for a living, start off with this question:

museun ireul haseyo? (*moo-seun ee-reul-ha-sae-yo;* What do you do?)

The answer to this is very simple:

jeoneun [your occupation] eyo. (*juh-neun [your occupation] ae-yo;* I'm [your occupation].)

All you have to do is fill in your job description using the list of words in Table 4-6.

Table 4-6	Occupations
Korean Word and Pronunciation	*English Word*
hoegyesa (*hwae-gae-sa*)	Accountant
yorisa (*yo-ree-sa*)	Chef
daehaksaeng (*dae-hak-saeng*)	College student
keonseolteonteu (*kuhn-ssul-tuhn-teu*)	Consultant
oegyogwan (*wae-gyo-gwan*)	Diplomat
uisa (*ui-sa*)	Doctor
pyeounjipja (*pyun-jeep-ja*)	Editor
seungmuwon (*seung-moo-won*)	Flight attendant
gongmuwon (*gong-moo-won*)	Government official
daehakwonsaeng (*dae-hak-won-saeng*)	Graduate school student
godeunghaksaeng (*go-deung-hak-saeng*)	High school student
jubu (*joo-boo*)	Housewife
byeonhosa (*byun-ho-sa*)	Lawyer
gijang (*gee-jang*)	Pilot
gyosu (*gyo-soo*)	Professor
peurogeuraemeo (*peu-ro-geu-rae-muh*)	Programmer

(continued)

Table 4-6 *(continued)*

Korean Word and Pronunciation	English Word
gija (*gee-ja*)	Reporter
yeonguwon (*yuhn-goo-won*)	Researcher
gunin (*goo-nin*)	Soldier
haksaeng (*hak-saeng*)	Student
seonsaeng (*sun-saeng*)	Teacher
mujik (*moo-jik*)	Unemployed
weiteo (*wei-tuh*)	Waiter
jakga (*jak-ga*)	Writer

If you want to further ask where another person works, try this question:

eodieseo ilhaseyo? (*uh-dee-ae-suh il-ha-sae-yo;* Where do you work?)

The answer to this question will look like this:

jeoneun [some word] eseo ilhaeyo (*juh-neun [some word] ae-suh il-hae-yo;* I work at/from/for [some word]). Substitute [some word] with your work place, such as the name of your company. Please note that **eseo** (*ae-suh*) can mean "at," "from," and "for" when used in this context. An example of this would be something like: **jeoneun seoul daehakgyoeseo ilhaeyo** (*juh-neun seoul dae-hak-gyo-ae-suh il-hae-yo;* I work at/for/from Seoul national university).

The previous section gives you the word for **haksaeng** (*hak-saeng;* student), but if you want to be more specific and tell people about where you study, what you study, and what year you are, keep reading.

If you want to know where another person is studying, ask:

eodieseo gongbuhaseyo? (*uh-dee-ae-suh gong-boo-ha-sae-yo;* Where are you studying?)

The answer will look like:

jeoneun [some word] eseo gongbuhaeyo (*juh-neun [some word] ae-suh gong-boo-hae-yo;* I study at/from [some word]). Substitute the name of your school/college for [some word].

If you want to ask what the person is studying, ask:

> **museun gongbu hasaeyo?** (*moo-seun gong-boo ha-sae-yo;* What are you studying?)

The answer looks something like:

> **jeoneun [some word] gongbu haeyo.** (*juh-neun [some word] gong-boo-hae-yo;* I study [some word]). Substitute [some word] for your field of study/major.

Table 4-7 contains a list of things you could be studying.

Table 4-7	Areas of Study
Korean Words and Pronunciations	*English Words*
illyuhak *(il-lyu-hak)*	Anthropology
misulhak *(mee-sool-hak)*	Art History
keompyuteo gonghak *(keom-peu-tuh-gong-hak)*	Computer Science
gyeongjehak *(gyoung-jae-hak)*	Economics
yeongmunhak *(young-moon-hak)*	English Literature
sahak *(sa-hak)*	History
beopak *(buh-pak)*	Law
gyeongyeonghak *(gyoung-young-hak)*	Management
suhak *(soo-hak)*	Mathematics
uihak *(ui-hak)*	Medicine
cheolhak *(chul-hak)*	Philosophy
mullihak *(mool-lee-hak)*	Physics
sahoehak *(sa-hwae-hak)*	Sociology

If you want to ask someone in what year of **hakgyo** (*hak-gyo;* school) he/she is, you say:

> **myeot hangnyeoniseyo?** (*myeot hak-nyeon-ee-sae-yo;* What year/grade are you?)

An answer to this question may be:

jeoneun [some word] hangnyeonieyo. (*juh-neun [some word] hak-nyeon-ee-ae-yo;* I'm in year [some word]). Substitute your level or year of study with [some word]. Koreans use Sino-Korean numbers when they are speaking of the level of study in school. Please see Chapter 2 for more information on counting in Korean. For elementary school through college, say the **hangnyeon** (*hak-nyeon;* year) you are in that institution. Some examples follow:

jeoneun chodeunghakgyo sa hangnyeonieyo. (*juh-neun cho-deung-hak-gyo sa hak-nyeon-ee-ae-yo;* I'm in fourth year elementary school.)

jeoneun junghakgyo i hangnyeonieyo. (*juh-neun joong-hak-gyo ee hak-nyeon-ee-ae-yo;* I'm in second year middle school.)

jeoneun godeunghakgyo sam hangnyeonieyo. (*juh-neun go-deung-hak-gyo sam hak-nyeon-ee-ae-yo;* I'm in third year high school.)

jeoneun daehakgyo il hangnyeonieyo. (*juh-neun dae-hak-gyo il hak-nyeon-ee-ae-yo;* I'm in first year college.)

Note: For college, **il hangnyeon** (*il hang-nyeon*) is Freshman, **i hangnyeon** (*ee-hak-nyeon*) is Sophmore, **sam hangnyeon** (*sam hak-nyeon*) is Junior, and **sa hangnyeon** (*sa hak-nyeon*) is Senior.

In Korea, age groups are assigned to different levels of study in elementary, junior high, and high school. There are six years of **chodeunghakgyo** (*cho-deung-hak-gyo;* elementary school; grade 1 through 6), 3 years of **junghakgyo** (*joong-hak-gyo;* middle school; grade 7 through 9), 3 years of **godeunghakgyo** (*go-deung-hak-gyo;* high school; grade 10 through 12) and 4 years of **daehakgyo** (*dae-hak-gyo;* college/university). So if someone tells you that they are in 2nd year middle school, that means that they are in 8th grade, if they are in 3rd grade high school, they are in 12th grade and so on. However, in the U.S., grades 1 through 5 usually fall into elementary school, grades 6 through 8 fall into middle school, and grades 9 through 12 fall into high school.

hakbu (*hak-boo*): Undergraduate

seoksagwajeong (*suk-sa-gwa-jung*): Master's

baksagwajeong (*bak-sa-gwa-jung*): Ph.D.

You can also say:

jeoneun hakbu il haknyeonieyo. (*juh-neun hak-boo il hak-nyeon-ee ae-yo*: I'm in first year undergraduate course.)

jeoneun seoksagwajeong i haknyeonieyo. (*juh-neun suk-sa-gwa-jung ee hak-nyeon-ee-ae-yo;* I'm in 2nd year Master's degree.)

Jeoneun baksagwajung sam haknyeonieyo. (*juh-neun bak-sa-gwa-jung sam-hak-nyeon-ee-ae-yo;* I'm in 3rd year Ph.D.)

Cram schools and tutoring

In Korea, there are many cram or tutoring schools. After school, Korean students will go to these schools to learn mainly math, Korean, and English, which are the three main subjects that Korean students focus on. However, they also have tutoring schools and private tutors for social studies, physics, chemistry, biology, calculus, and so on. Tutoring schools have buses going around each apartment town, picking up and dropping off students at specfied times. So there is no need for the parents to be the drivers. Korean students will usually come home after dark. Especially for students in **godeunghakgyo** (*go-deung-hak-gyo;* high school), they'll be coming home (after many tutoring schools) around 11pm.

Describing the Members of Your Family

The use of **chinjok** (*chin-jok;* kinship) terms is a fascinating part of Korean **munhwa** (*moon-hwa;* culture). The kinship is a very **jungyohan** (*joong-yo-han;* important) part of Korean culture. Koreans have several dozen **daneo** (*da-nuh;* words) for family members, which may not exist in English. And a few family words have rules that the English language doesn't; for example, sometimes you choose a word depending on your **seongbyeol** (*sung-byul;* gender) and whether or not the person you're talking about is your family member or someone else's. Table 4-8 presents just a few words for immediate family that are hard to go wrong with.

Table 4-8	Own Family Members
Korean Word and Pronunciation	*English Word*
gomo (*go-mo*)	Aunt from dad's side (dad's sisters)
imo (*ee-mo*)	Aunt from mom's side (mom's sisters)
hyeongje (*hyoung-jae*)	Brothers
janyeo (*ja-nyuh*)	Children
ttal (*ttal*)	Daughter
abeoji (*a-buh-ji*)	Father
sonnyeo (*son-nyuh*)	Granddaughter
chinharabeoji (*chin-ha-ra-buh-ji*)	Grandfather from dad's side
oeharabeoji (*wae-ha-ra-buh-ji*)	Grandfather from mom's side

(continued)

Table 4-8 *(continued)*

Korean Word and Pronunciation	English Word
chinhalmeoni (*chin-hal-muh-ni*)	Grandmother from dad's side
oehalmeoni (*wae-hal-muh-ni*)	Grandmother from mom's side
jobumonim (*jo-boo-mo-nim*)	Grandparents
sonja (*son-ja*)	Grandson
nampyeon (*nam-pyun*)	Husband
bakkatyangban (*ba-kkat-yang-ban*)	Husband (when a wife refers to her husband); literal translation: outside person
eomeoni (*uh-muh-ni*)	Mother
hyeong (*hyoung*)	Older brother (used by males only)
oppa (*o-ppa*)	Older brother (used by females only)
nuna (*noo-na*)	Older sister (used by males only)
eonni (*un-ni*)	Older sister (used by females only)
bumonim (*boo-mo-nim*)	Parents
jamae (*ja-mae*)	Sisters
adeul (*a-deul*)	Son
samchon (*sam-chon*)	Uncle from dad's side (dad's brothers)
oesamchon (*wae-sam-chon*)	Uncle from mom's side (mom's brothers)
namdongsaeng (*man-dong-saeng*)	Younger brother
dongsaeng (*dong-saeng*)	Younger sibling
yeodongsaeng (*yuh-dong-saeng*)	Younger sister

In Korea, even if you are not blood-related, if you see an old man or woman, your should call them **harabeoji** (*ha-ra-buh-ji;* grandfather) and **halmeoni** (*hal-muh-ni;* grandmother). Also many Korean call their mother's friends **imo** (*ee-mo;* aunt, mom's sisters).

Now I take a look at a few expressions that have to do with family. I start off with "Do you have a [some word] ?" There are two ways to ask this question in Korean:

Ask someone if they have people more senior than the person you are speaking to, such as parents and grandparents: **[some word] kkesu gyeseyo?** (*[some word] kkae-suh gae-sae-yo;* Do you have a [some word]?) Replace "[some word]" with: parent/s, grandparent/s, uncle/s, and aunt/s. Or **bumonimkkaeseo gyeseyo?** (*boo-mo-nim-kkae-suh gae-sae-yo;* Do you have parents?)

Ask a general question about whether the person you are speaking to has brothers, sisters, or children: **[some word] i/ga iseoyo?** (*[some word] i/ga ee-ssuh-yo;* Do you have [some word]?), replacing "[some word]" with: brothers, sisters, or children. Or you may ask **eonniga iseoyo?** (*un-ni-ga it-ssuh-yo;* Do you have an older sister?). This is a question you ask females only, since you have used the word **eonni** (*un-ni;* older sister) which is used for females only.

Answers to the question about parents may be something like:

ye, bumonimi gyeseyo. (*ye, bu-mo-nim-ee gye-sae-yo;* Yes, I have parents.)

or

aniyo, bumonimi angyeseyo. (*a-ni-yo, bu-mo-nim-ee an-gye-sae-yo;* No, I don't have parents.)

Answers to the question about brothers/sisters/children may be something like:

ye, eonniga itseoyo. (*ye, un-ni-ga ee-ssuh-yo;* Yes, I have an older sister.)

aniyo, eonniga eobseoyo. (*a-ni-yo, un-ni-ga uhb-ssuh-yo;* No, I don't have an older sister.)

Talkin' the Talk

Hong Ser meets Matt on a date and she asks about Matt's family.

Hong Ser:	hyeongje jamaega iseoyo? *hyung-jae ja-mae-ga ee-ssuh-yo?* Do you have brothers and sisters?
Matt:	ne, hyeongi han myeong itgo, yeodongsaengi han myeong iseoyo. *ne, hyung-ee han-myung-it-go, yuh-dong-saeng-ee han-myung-ee-ssuh-yo.* Yes, I have one older brother and one younger sister.
Hong Ser:	hyeongnimeun myeot sarieyo? *hyung-nim-eun myuht-sal-ee-ae-yo?* How old is your older brother?

Matt:	**hyeongeun 32sarieyo**
	hyung-eun sam-shi-bee-sal-ee-ae-yo.
	My older brother is 32 years old.

Hong Ser:	**bumonimeun mwohaseyo?**
	boo-mo-nim-eun mwo-ha-sae-yo?
	What do your parents do?

Matt:	**bumonimeun seonsaengnimiseyo.**
	boo-mo-nim-eun sun-saeng-nim-ee-sae-yo.
	My parents are teachers.

Hong Ser:	**a, geuraeyo. cham jaldoenneyo**
	a, geu-rae-yo. cham-jal-dwet-nae-yo.
	Oh, that is really great.

Words to Know

cham	cham	Really
mwohasaeyo?	mwo-ha-sae-yo	What do you/they do?
jeonyeok	juh-nyuk	Dinner
deiteu	dae-ee-teu	Date
jeorang sagwillaeyo?	juh-rang-sa-gwil-lae-yo	Do you want to go out with me?

Exchanging Contact Information

Giving and receiving contact information is important if you want to keep in touch with someone. You may want to ask for the other person's **imeil juso** (*ee-mae-il joo-so;* e-mail address), **jeonhwabeonho** (*juhn-hwa-bun-ho;* phone number), **paekseubeonho** (*paek-seu-bun-ho;* fax number), or **juso** (*joo-so;* mailing address). And if you think that the other person may become an important part of your social or professional life, make sure to give him your **myeongham** (*myoung-ham;* business card). In Korean, when you have met someone for the first time and you are asking for their contact information, you need to ask them in a formal polite form. When you are asking for contact information of someone you have met before, informal polite form is enough.

Formal polite: **yeollakcheoga eotteoke doesimnikka?** (*yuhl-lak-chuh-ga uh-ttuh-kkae-dwae-shim-ni-kka;* What is your contact information?) You can substitute **yeollakcheo** (*yuhl-lak-chuh;* contact information) with **jeonhwabunho** (*juhn-hwa-bun-ho;* phone number) or some other specific contact information.

Informal polite: **yeollakcheoga eotteoke dwaeyo?** (*yuhl-lak-chuh-ga uh-ttuh-kkae-dwae-yo;* What is your contact information?)

Formal polite: **hoksi myeongham hanjang iseumnikka?** (*hok-shi myoung-ham han-jang-ee-sseum-ni-kka;* Do you have a business card?) *Literal translation:* Do you have one business card?

Informal polite: **hoksi myeongham hanjang iseoyo?** (*hok-si myoung-ham han-jang-ee-ssuh-yo;* You have a business card?) *Literal translation:* Do you have one business card?

Some answers to these questions may include the following:

Formal polite: **je myeonghamimnida.** (*jae myoung-ham-im-ni-da;* Here's my business card.)

Informal polite: **je myeonghamieyo.** (*jae myoung-ham-ee-ae-yo;* Here's my business card.)

Formal polite: **kkok yeollakhaejusipsio.** (*kkok yuhl-lak-hae-joo-ship-shi-yo;* Please make sure to contact me.)

Informal polite: **kkok yeollakhaejuseyo.** (*kkok yuhl-lak-hae-joo-sae-yo;* Please make sure to contact me.)

Formal polite: **kkok yeollakhagetseumnida.** (*kkok yuhl-lak-ha-get-ssum-ni-da;* I'll make sure to contact you.)

Informal polite: **kkok yeollakhalkkaeyo.** (*kkok yuhl-lak-hal-kkae-yo;* I'll make sure to contact you.)

Use the formal polite form to answer if you have met the person you are speaking to for the first time. Informal polite form can be used at any other times.

Formal Korean is fine for professional and business settings, but for parties and bars, it's a bit too formal. So if you need to ask someone for her number or e-mail address at a party or bar, choose the following informal polite sentences.

yeollakcheoga mwoeyo? (*yuhl-lak-chuh-ga mwo-ae-yo;* What's your contact information?)

imeil jusoga mwoeyo? (*ee-mae-il joo-so-ga mwo-ae-yo;* What's your e-mail address?)

jeonhwabeonhoga mwoeyo? (*juhn-hwa-bun-ho-ga mwo-ae-yo;* What's your number?)

kkok yeollakhaeyo. (*kkok yuhl-lak-hae-joo-sae-yo;* Contact me, please.)

Fun & Games

Fill in the blanks with equivalent English/Korean words.

1. Older sister for a female

_____

2. Younger brother

_____

3. Grandfather on mother's side

_____

4. Aunt on dad's side

_____

5. Oppa

_____

6. Eomoni

_____

7. Samchon

_____

8. Yeodongsaeng

_____

Chapter 5

Eating and Drinking

. . . .

In This Chapter

▶ Discovering Korean food

▶ Practicing good table manners

▶ Ordering food and conversing at a restaurant

▶ Cooking Korean food

. . . .

The culinary arts, history, and traditions in Korea are ancient ones that predate refrigeration and electricity. Exploring a culture through its culinary tradition is a great and delicious way to get to know more about the culture. This couldn't be truer with Korean cooking because the dining experience embodies the sense of community, tradition, and history of an ancient culture. Everyone can find something to eat at a Korean table. The variety of Korean food ranges from fresh spring greens tossed in sesame seed oil, soy sauce, and vinegar — for the timid, savory grilled meats wrapped in vegetables, and for the most daring, even live baby octopi dipped in red pepper paste!

This chapter elaborates on the Korean dining experience and how it differs from the dining experience of the West. This chapter also helps you to communicate when you're hungry or thirsty, sitting down to eat, as well as show you the proper table manners, how to order at a restaurant, buy groceries, and proper drinking and dining etiquette. I've also included a few authentic Korean recipes that can be made easily with items available in most grocery stores.

Dig In! Let's Eat!

The variety of side dishes gives each and every Korean meal a very subtle difference in the dining experience. The biggest difference in Korean dining obviously comes from the main dish, which varies and is shared by everyone on the table. Regardless of how the meal is set up, you will encounter many reasons to talk about food, and the sections that follow tell you how to let others know that you're hungry, different words and phrases related to cuisine, as well as the proper table manners you should be using.

Understanding meal time

The Korean word for a meal is **bap** (*bab; meal, rice*). In a broad sense, it simply means, meal. However, when Koreans refer to as **bap** usually, it is a bowl of steamed rice. When sitting at a table, each person is given a bowl of rice, and many side dishes are shared between the people sitting with you at the table, which enhances the sense of community and family in the dining experience. These side dishes are known as **banchan** (*ban-chan; side dishes*), and it's the variety of these side dishes that create the liquid, ever-changing format of a Korean table. The whole meal itself, **bap** and **banchan,** is also referred to as **bap**.

The verb "to eat," is **meokda** (*muhk-da*). The phrase **bap meogeoseoyo?** (*bap muh-guh-ssuh-yo; Have you eaten food?*) is a common, casual greetings between friends and family. If you want to ask someone if they would like to eat with you, you would ask **jeorang gachi bap meogeullaeyo?** (*juh-rang ga-chi bap muh-geul-lae-yo; Would you like to eat with me?*)

Another verb "to eat" is **deusida** (*deu-shi-dal*). This verb is usually used with more formal form of the word meal, which is **jinji** (*jin-ji; respectful way of saying meal*). Use the phrase **jinji deuseyo** (*jin-ji deu-sae-yo; Please eat your meal*) with foreign dignitary or your elders when you are asking them to eat their meal. In addition, when you are asking them if they have eaten already, use the phrase **jinji deusyeoseoyo?** (*jin-ji deu-syuh-ssuh-yo; Have you eaten?*) instead.

Other times, the meals are referred to according to the time of day. Achim (*-a-chim; morning, breakfast*), **jeomsim** (*jum-shim; lunch time, lunch*), and **jeonyeok** (*juh-nyeok; evening, dinner*), which means morning, afternoon and evening, respectively, can be replaced with the word **bap** to refer to the meals. So, **achim meogeotseoyo?** (*a-chim muh-guh-ssuh-yo?*) translates into, "Have you eaten breakfast?" and **jeomsim deusyeosseoyo?** (*jum-sim deu-seot-syuh-yo?*) into "Have you had lunch?" and **jeonyeok deuseyo** (*juh-nyeok deu-sae-yo*) means, "let's have dinner" and so forth.

Another word for a meal, a more respectful is **siksa** (*shik-sa; meal*). You use this term when you're in a more formal setting, like addressing your elders, or people you are not yet familiar with. Siksa hasyeosseoyo? (*Shik-sa ha-syuh-ssuh-yo?*) is a proper and more respectful way of asking, "have you eaten?" These are commonly used when you are asking your parents, in-laws, teachers, and business partners, if they have eaten already. Another phrase **siksa haseoyo** (*shik-sa ha-sae-yo; please eat*) is a proper way to ask some one to eat.

Satisfying your hunger

Gopayo (*go-pa-yo*) means to yearn, or to crave. So, **bae gopayo** (*bae go-pa-yo*),means, "I'm hungry." In the case of **bae gopayo**, the inflection can change the meaning of the phrase. What I mean by this is, if you say **bae gopayo?** (*bae-go-pa-yo?*), that means, "Are you hungry?", whereas if you were to say **bae gopayo** (*bae go-pa-yo*)," that means, "I'm hungry." **bae gopuseyo?** (*bae go-peu-sae-yo*) means are you hungry? in a more respectful way.

Asking someone whether they have eaten or not is more than just a greeting in Korea. It shows consideration of others, which is a quality highly regarded by Koreans. Remember the phrase, "**siksa hasyeosseoyo?** (*shik-sa ha-syuh-ssuh-yo;* have you eaten?" and it will serve you well if you want a Korean person to take you out to eat.

Your **mok** (*mok*) is your neck, or your throat. **mallayo** means dry, or parched. So, put those two together, and you get, **mok mallayo** (*mok mal-la-yo*), which are translated into "My throat is parched," or "I'm thirsty."

In Korean, your **bae** (*bae*) is your stomach. Putting all this together, you can come up with many different ways to suggest to go and eat somewhere. For instance, you could say, "**bae gopayo. bap meogeureo gayo** (*bae go-pa-yo. bab muh-geu-ruh ga-yo*)," which translates into "I'm hungry, let's have lunch." A variation of this, in a more formal tone, would be, "**bae gopayo. siksa hareo gasijyo.** (*bae go-pa-yo. shik-sa ha-ruh ga-shi-jyo*)," which translates into, "I'm hungry, let's go have a meal."

unje (*un-jae*) means, "sometime or when." **hanbeon** (*han-bun*) means, "once." **Siksa** (*shik-sa*) means "meal." **hapsida** (*hap-shi-da*) means, "let's do." **gachi** (*ga-chi*) means, "together." Literally translated, **unje hanbeon gachi siksa habsida!** (*un-jae han-beon ga-chi shik-sa hap-shi-da*) means, "let's share one meal sometime." In casual Korean usage, it's an expression that is used to stay in touch with acquaintances without actually committing to a plan. An English equivalent would be, "we should get together for dinner sometime." If you get rid of the word **unje**, which means "sometime," and **hanbeon**, which means, "once," and **gachi**, which means, "together," the phrase **siksa hapshida** (*shik-sa hap-shi-da*) becomes more like a request.

Sitting down to eat

The first thing you may notice about a Korean table is that it looks quite busy. You have a bowl of rice in front of you, possibly a small bowl of soup, a pair of chopsticks, and a spoon sits to your right. Surrounding your bowls of rice and soup are these little plates containing various vegetables and meats and eggs which are called **banchan** (*ban-chan;* side dishes). A staple sidedish, or **banchan** in Korean cooking is **gimchi** (*gim-chi*), which is pickled cabbage. A meal without **gimchi** is unthinkable for most Koreans.

If you and a friend were to go to a Korean restaurant, you would have your bowl of rice, and a small bowl of soup. The main dishes would be put between the two of you, surrounded by little side dishes, which you two share. This is quite different from the Western dining experience where everyone gets their own portion and eats from their own plates. This sharing of meals and mixing of utensils may turn off some Westerners overly concerned with germs.

In every Korean household the whole family shares meals every day at the dinner table. Even at Western restaurants, you may see Koreans sharing meals by swapping halves of their dishes, as sharing a meal is an important aspect of Korean dining.

sutgarak (*soo-ga-rak*), **sutgal** (*soot-gal*), or **sujeo** (*soo-juh*) means a spoon, and **jeotgarak** (*juh-ga-rak*), or **jeotgal** (*jut-gal*) means chopsticks. These two utensils are all you ever need in eating Korean food, but if you're not familiar with using chopsticks, feel free to ask for a fork and knife, which most restaurants will be happy to provide for you.

I've included a few vocabulary terms in Table 5-1 so that you may familiarize yourself with various Korean terms used in and around the kitchen.

Table 5-1	Culinary Terms	
Korean Word	*Pronunciation*	*Translation*
keop	*kup*	Cup
jeopshi	*jup-shi*	Plate
jaengban	*jaeng-ban*	Tray
gonggi	*gong-gi*	Bowl
sogeum	*so-geum*	Salt
seoltang	*suhl-tang*	Sugar
huchu	*hoo-choo*	Black pepper
sikcho	*shik-cho*	Vinegar
chamgireum	*cham–gi-reum*	Sesame seed oil
seupageti	*seu-pa-gae-tee*	Spaghetti
ppang	*ppang*	Bread
pija	*pee-ja*	Pizza
saelleodeu	*sael-uh-deu*	Salad

Korean Word	*Pronunciation*	*Translation*
saendeuwichi	*saen-deu-wee-chi*	Sandwich
seuteikeu	*seu-tae-ee-keu*	Steak
pa	*pa*	Green onions
yangpa	*yang-pa*	Onions
tomato	*to-ma-to*	Tomato
beurokeolli	*beu-ro-col-li*	Broccoli
yangbaechu	*yang-bae-choo*	Cabbage
gamja	*gam-ja*	Potato
gogi	*go-gee*	Meat
sogogi	*so-go-gee*	Beef
dakgogi	*dak-go-gee*	Chicken
dwaejigogi	*dwae-jee-go-gee*	Pork
saengseon	*saeng-sun*	Fish
gyeran	*gae-ran*	Egg
maneul	*ma-neul*	Garlic
danggeun	*dang-geun*	Carrot
dubu	*doo-boo*	Tofu
mandu	*man-doo*	Dumpling, pot sticker
subak	*soo-bak*	Watermelon
sagwa	*sa-gwa*	Apple
orenji	*o-ren-jee*	Orange

You will find very little difference between breakfast, lunch, and dinner in Korean cooking. Many Koreans eat a bowl of rice for breakfast, lunch, and dinner. The difference is that the breakfast tends to be a bit lighter with soups in light broth and maybe some fish. Lunch is a robust affair, with a variety of choices, and dinner usually consists of a main dish which is either fish or some kind of meat. A drink after work is a temptation that many working Koreans find hard to resist. Especially during dinner with friends or co-workers, liquor often finds its way onto the table. This is also a great way to build relationships between people and co-workers. (See the section, "Drinking, Korean Style," later in this chapter for more on drinking alcohol.)

Practicing good table manners

Due to its Confucian background and history, honoring elders is an important aspect in Korean culture. Even the eating habits of Koreans exhibit this. But there is more to table manners than simply honoring your elders. In fact, in Korea, the following slight gestures and mannerisms will show the people you are dining with that you took the time to learn the proper etiquette and will go a long way in impressing them:

- Your spoon should never be picked up until the elder at the table picks up his spoon.

- Don't talk loudly during meals or make slurping or smacking sounds while eating.

- After finishing your meal, you should put the spoon and chopsticks back to their original setting, and not leave them in the bowl.

- You should not rise from the dining table before other members have finished their meal.

- Before the meal, you always thank your host by saying, **"jal meokget-seumnida"**(*jal muh-get-sseum-ni-da;* I will eat it well).

- After the meal, it is customary to compliment the cook or the host, often-times by saying, **"jal meogeotseumnida"**(*jal muh-guh-sseum-ni-da;* I have eaten it well).

- You should always offer to pour a drink for your elders, and you should pour with the right hand, as you support your right wrist with your left hand.

- In receiving a drink, the hand positions should be the same, with your right hand holding the cup and your left hand supporting your right wrist, with your head slightly bowed.

Getting to Know Korean Cuisine

Because the country is situated in a peninsula, the Koreans eat a lot of seafood. Though their staple is rice and vegetables, meats, poultry, and fish are enjoyed in moderation, cooked with seasonal vegetables. Korean culinary history predates electricity and refrigeration, and if you ever travel to the countryside in Korea, you can still see how the food was kept before the days of electricity. In front of many houses in the countryside, you can see rows and rows of wide, earthenware crock jars that sit on nice, well-ventilated stands. These jars contain everything from soy sauce, hot pepper paste, soybean paste, to all different kinds of **gimchi** (*gim-chi;* pickled cabbage), and the biggest one usually contains rice.

Popular dishes

One cannot discuss Korean cuisine without mentioning **gimchi** and here's why: while the term **gimchi** is generally used to describe **tongbaechu gimchi** (*tong-bae-choo gim-chi;* whole Chinese cabbage gimchi), **gimchi** is made with many different vegetables and varies from region to region. For example, **chonggak gimchi** (*chong-gak gim-chi*) uses a similar fermentation technique on small turnips instead of cabbage. Other types of **gimchi** include **oi sobaegi** (*o-ee so-bae-gi;* **gimchi** made withcucumbers, **baek gimchi** (*baek-gim-chi;* white **gimchi** where no red pepper flakes are added), **mul gimchi** (*mool gim-chi;* water **gimchi** which has a refreshing broth), **dongchimi** (*dong-chi-mi;* watery radish **gimchi**), **bossam gimchi** (*bo-ssam gim-chi;* wrapped **gimchi**), and **kkakdugi** (*kkak-doo-gi;* diced radish **gimchi**) just to name a few. **gimchi** is now worldly known to have curative properties, aids in proper digestion, and even prevents various types of cancers. **gimchi**, as well as **doenjang** (*dwen-jang;* soy bean paste), **ganjang** (*gan-jang;* soy source), and **gochujang** (*go-choo-jang;* red pepper paste) are kept in earthenware jars so that the cabbage can ferment and breathe through the jars. Plus, these hardy jars also kept out pests, vermin, and insects.

These earthenware, crock jars that **gimchi** and other foods and sauces are kept in aid in the natural fermentation process of foods by keeping the temperature consistent and absorbing toxins that are innocuous to humans. In order to keep these jars at a consistent temperature, some of the jars are kept in caves or brooks during the summer time, and during the winter time, some of these jars are buried in the ground to prevent the contents from freezing. The items stored in these jars sometimes takes months, or years to cure properly, and many hours of care and dedication go into taking care of these jars. Indeed, the secret to great cooking is passed down through generations, with one generation teaching the other this very method of keeping food. The spirit of Korean culture is embedded in **gimchi** and the care and devotion it takes to make this tasty dish is an embodiment of the soul of Korea. Even in the city, many families have a **gimchi naengjanggo** (*gim-chi naeng-jang-go*), a special refrigerator dedicated to keeping home-made **gimchi** in their apartments and high-rises.

Enough about **gimchi**, as there are plenty of other things to try in Korean cooking than just pickled vegetables. A very popular dish in Korea is **bulgogi** (*bool-go-gi;* marinated beef), when translated literally means, "fire meat." This generally refers to strips of beef, marinated in various sauces and grilled over an open flame. There's also **dwaeji bulgogi** (*dwae-ji bool-go-gi;* marinated pork), and **dak bugogi** (*dak bool-go-gi;* marinated chicken), which are marinated pork and chicken, respectively. The marinades for the different kinds of meat are different, and the pork and chicken variation of **bulgogi** tend to be a bit more spicy, whereas the traditional beef **bulgogi** is sweet and savory.

Koreans are big on soup, too. Soup usually falls under one of these two categories:

- **guk** (*gook;* soup): Tends to be lighter and has almost a clear broth.

- **jjigye** (*jji-gae;* stew): A soup rich and strong in flavor, and much thicker in consistency.

guk and **jjigye** rarely share a table, but an important distinction is still made between the two. Usually, **guk** is served in a small bowl next to your bowl of rice, whereas a big bowl of **jjigye** sits in the middle of the table and is shared by all. Here's a little trick to know what's **jjigye** and what's **guk**. If you see people spooning the soup into their bowl of rice, chances are, they're eating **jjigye**. If you see the person dump their bowl of rice into the soup, chances are they're eating **guk**.

Setting time for a meal

Once you agree to a set time for a meal, it is considered rude to be late. Especially if the person you are meeting is someone older than you, you are expected there beforehand to greet the elder when they arrive. As a matter of fact, it's considered good manners to arrive early regardless of your age, but it is considered incredibly rude to keep an elder waiting. If you do see the person you are to meet already at the location, you can say, "**oraetdongan gidarisyeosseoyo?** (*o-raet-dong-an gi-da-ri-syuh-ssuh-yo*)," which means, "Did you wait long?" They will usually say, "**aniyo, onji eolma andoeyo**" (*a-ni-yo, on-ji ul-ma an-dae-yo;* No, I've just arrived), even if they had been there a while. You can also say, "**neujeoseo joesonghaeyo**" (*neu-juh-suh jwae-song-hae-yo;* I'm sorry I'm late), then bow, if you were late. Not to say that you should be early to every meeting, but punctuality is a sign of your consideration of others, and therefore a value highly regarded among Koreans.

Liking and disliking with adjectives

Do you like what you're eating? Perhaps you don't care much for it. Well, if you want to communicate that, check out Table 5-2 for some examples.

Table 5-2 Words and Phrases to Describe Liking Food ... Or Not!

Korean Word/Phrase	Pronunciation	Translation
mat	*mat*	Flavor
aju	*a-joo*	Very
neomoo	*nuh-moo*	Really

Korean Word/Phrase	Pronunciation	Translation
eopseoyo	*uhp-ssuh-yo*	It's not there or not exist
iseoyo	*ee-ssuh-yo*	Is there or does exist
mat eopseoyo	*mat uhp-ssuh-yo*	Flavor is not there, it is not tasty
aju mat iseoyo	*a-joo ma shi-ssuh-yo*	Flavor is there very much, it is very delicious
darayo	*da-ra-yo*	It's sweet
aju darayo	*a-joo da-ra-yo*	It's very sweet
jjayo	*jja-yo*	It's salty
neomoo jjayo	*nuh-moo jja-yo*	It's really salty
syeoyo	*syuh-yo*	It's sour

Dining Out

The service mentality in the Korean food and service industry is second to none. You can easily get the attention of the waitstaff by making eye contact with them, but you can simply call them over to your table as well, by saying, **yeogiyo** (*yuh-gi-yo;* here), or **sillye hamnida** (*shil-lae-ham-ni-da;* excuse me). **jumoon badajuseyo** (*joo-moon ba-da-joo-sae-yo*) means, "please take our order," or "we're ready to order," and **gyesan haejuseyo** (*gae-san hae-joo-sae-yo*) means, "can I have the check, please."

The sections that follow give you the info you need to successfully and confidently navigate public eateries in Korea.

Understanding what's on the menu

At most restaurants, the menu explains in English what the dishes are all about. If the menu contains only Korean words, feel free to ask the person you're with, or the waitstaff and they will be more than happy to help you. A thing to remember about Korean cooking is that there are no set courses. A meal is a continuous process that begins with the main course and ends with fruit, or a sweet drink. It is considered bad manners to leave rice in the bowl, so do try to finish. It is generally a good idea to take a look around the restaurant to see what other people are eating. If you feel a little daring, you can always point at another table and say, **jeogeo juseyo** (*juh-guh joo-sae-yo;* give me that one), or **jeobuni deusineungeo juseyo** (*juh-boon-ee deu-shi-neun-guh joo-sae-yo;* I'll have what that person's having).

Looking at a menu at a Korean restaurant, you may feel a little lost, because the words seem so foreign. Don't be afraid to ask questions, as Koreans are most proud of their foods and recipes and will go great lengths in describing what it is that you're about to order. You will find that they will be quick to accommodate you if you show a little daring and inquisitiveness. You can ask your waiter the following phrases. Point to an item on the menu and say **igeoneun eottaeyo** (*ee-guh-neun uh-ttae-yo*) which means "how about this?" or **eotteon eumsigi masiseoyo** (*uh-tteon eum-shi-gi ma-shi-ssuh-yo*) which means "what food is good here?"

Ordering at a restaurant

Because the word **juseyo** (*joo-sae-yo*) means, "please give to me," you can use this phrase to ask for many things, not just at a restaurant, but around town. To start with a couple of simple ones, you can say, **mul hanjanman juseyo** (*mool han-jan-man joo-sae-yo*), which means, "please give me one glass of water." If you want another bowl of rice at the restaurant, say **bap hangongi deo juseyo** (*bab hangongi duh jou-sae-yo;* please give me one more bowl of rice)? Table 5-3 gives you some more words you may want to use at a restaurant.

Table 5-3	Words to Use at a Restaurant	
Korean Word	*Pronunciation*	*Translation*
bap	*bab*	Rice
han (in both **han-gongi** and **han-geureut**)	*han*	One
gongi and **geureut**	*gong-gi, geu-reut*	Bowl or container
deo	*duh*	More
juseyo	*joo-sae-yo*	Please give to me
jusillaeyo?	*joo-shil-lae-yo*	Will you give it to me?

You can ask for many other items that you may want when you're dining at a Korean restaurant. **keopi hanjanman jusillaeyo** (*kuh-pee han-jan-man joo-shil-lae-yo*)? Translates into, "May I have a cup of coffee?" You can also say, **yeogi banchan jom deo juseyo** (*yuh-gi ban-chan jom duh joo-sae-yo*), which translates into, "please give us some more side dishes here." A simple way to ask for things is to say, **igeo jusillaeyo** (*ee-guh joo-shil-lae-yo*)? (Will you please give me this one?), or **jeogeot jom deo jusillaeyo** (*juh-guh jom duh joo-shil-lae-yo*)? (can I please have some more of that?)

When the person brings you whatever that you're looking for, you should always say, **gamsahamnida** (*gam-sa-ham-ni-da*), which simply means, "thank you." Another way of saying thanks is to say, **gomapseumnida** (*go-map-sseum-ni-da*). They're both acceptable ways of saying thanks and be polite at the same time, but **gamsahamnida** is the more formal of the two.

Smoking in front of an elder before he has lit up himself is considered a great faux pas in Korean culture. If the elder does not smoke, you shouldn't smoke in front of him, either. If the elder does smoke, you should wait until he lights the first cigarette and have it not facing the elder, preferably down wind. And of course, blowing smoke in someone's face is considered rude in any given culture, but much more so and disrespectful if you do it to an elder in Korea.

Ordering at a roadside shop

The streets of Korea are filled with these little roadside shops that sell everything from puffed rice snacks, to ramen, to sweet cakes, to rice cakes and all other kinds of food you can think of. Sometimes they're called, **pojang macha** (*po-jang ma-cha*), which means, "a covered wagon." Many of these roadside shops are open well into the night and you can see a myriad of people frequent these places, oftentimes leaving a bar or a club late at night. These "covered wagons" usually are quite specific in what they offer, and their choices are rather slim. A **pojang macha** could specialize in ramen noodles only, or rice cakes only. You rarely see a variety of menu items because of its smaller size, but each wagon will at least offer you one or two similar types of items. Depending on what you feel like, you can go and hunt out the right **pojang macha** to fit your taste. They're usually parked close together, so you wouldn't have to walk far to find what you're looking for.

Simply go into the one that you desire, and most of the time, you will find a long bench and a table across from the owner. Whatever it is that you're looking for, just add **"juseyo"** to it and they'll be happy to give it to you. For example, **tteokbokgi juseyo** (*dduk-bok-gi joo-sae-yo;* please give me rice cakes in red pepper sauce) and **odeng juseyo** (*o-daeng joo-sae-yo;* please give me fish cakes). Remember to thank the owner when your food arrives, and also remember to say, **jal meogeotseumnida** (*jal muh-guh-sseum-ni-da;* I've eaten well) when you're done. After a satisfying late night snack, you can say, **gyesan haejuseyo** (*gae-san hae-joo-sae-yo;* I would like to pay now). And the owner will tell you how much you owe for the food you've eaten.

As you leave the roadside shop, or any restaurant for that matter, you can say, **annyeonghi gyeseyo** (*an-young-hee gye-sae-yo;* be well here, stay in peace), or **sugo haseyo** (*soo-go ha-sae-yo;* work hard or keep up the good work). They're both acceptable forms of greeting when you're departing. They'll most likely say **annyeonghi gaseyo** (*an-young-hee ga-sae-yo;* be well leaving or go in peace). **annyeonghi gyeseyo** is a greeting that can be used for everyone when you're leaving, and **sugo haseyo** is usually said to people who are working, as in the waitstaff, the cook, the owner of the restaurant, and so forth. You can say **sugo haseyo** to anybody that works when you leave their place, be they a barber, a tailor, a lawyer, and so on.

Talkin' the Talk

James and Peter meet at a street and decide to go out to eat.

James: **peter ssi! oraenmanieyo!**
pete-sshi! o-raen-man-ee-ae-yo!
Peter! Long time no see!

Peter: **james ssi! jal iseoseoyo?**
james-sshi! jal-ee-ssuh-ssuh-yo?
James! Have you been well?

James: **ne ne. siksa hasyeoseoyo?**
ne ne. shik-sa ha-syuh-ssuh-yo?
Yes, yes. Have you eaten?

Peter: **aniyo. ajik an meogeoseoyo. gachi siksa halleyo?**
a-ni-yo. a-jik an muh-guh-ssuh-yo. ga-chi shik-sa hal-lae-yo?
No. I haven't eaten yet. Shall we eat together?

James: **joayo. eodiro gasillaeyo? jungguk sikdang? miguk eumsik?**
jo-a-yo. uh-dee-ro ga-shil-lae-yo? joong-goog shik-dang? mi-gook eum-shik?
Good. Where shall we go? Chinese restaurant? American food?

Peter: **miguk sigdangeuro gayo. yeogi geuncheoe manninneun daega iseoyo.**
mi-goog shik-dang-eu-ro ga-yo. yuh-gi geun-chuh-ae ma-shim-neun-dae-ga ee-ssuh-yo.
Let's go to an American restaurant. There is a good one right around here.

James: **hanguk eumsigeun eottaeyo? yeogi geuncheoe bulgogi jipi hana** inneundae. mannitge jalhaeyo.
han-goog eum-shik-eun uh-ttae-yo? yuh-gi geun-chuh-ae bool-go-gi jeep-ee ha-na-in-neun-dae. ma-shi-ge jal-hae-yo.
How about Korean food? There's one boolgogi place around here. They're very good.

Peter: **joayo! gasijyo!**
jo-a-yo! ga-shi-jyo!
Good! Let's go!

Words to Know

siksa	*shik-sa*	Meal
sikdang	*shik-dang*	Restaurant
sutgarak, sutgal, sujeo	*soo-ga-rak, soot-gal, soo-juh*	Spoon
jeotgarak, jeotgal	*juh-ga-rak, jut-gal*	Chopsticks
pokeu	*po-keu*	Fork
kal	*kahl*	Knife
ajik	*a-jik*	Not yet
gachi	*ga-chi*	together
miguk sikdang	*mi-goog shik-dang*	American restaurant
geuncheo	*geun-chuh*	Nearby
masitneun	*ma-shin-neun*	Delicious, tasty
maseomneun	*ma-dum-neun*	Not tasty
bulgogijip	*bool-go-gi-jeep*	Marinated beef house
oraenmanineyo	*o-ran-man-ee-nae-yo*	It's been a long time
jal iseoseoyo	*jal ee-ssuh-ssuh-yo*	Have you been well?

Chatting with the waitstaff

A good phrase to know in Korean when ordering at a restaurant would be, **ige mwoeyo** (*ee-gae mwo-ae-yo*)? This phrase translates into, "What's this?" Point at an item on the menu and ask this question, and most of the time, the waitstaff will explain to you the ingredients and preparations of the dish. **igeoneunyo** (*ee-guh-neun-yo*)? Means, "What about this one?" You can also ask, **yeogi mwoga masisseoyo** (*yuh-gi mwo-ga ma-shi-ssuh-yo*)?, which translates into, "What's good here?" You can also ask, **yeogi jeonmuni mwoeyo** (*yuh-gi juhn-moo-nee mwo-ae-yo*), which translates into, "What's the specialty here?" You may also hear the waiter or waitress say, **mwo deusillaeyo** (*mwo deu-shil-lae-yo*)?, which means, "What would you like to eat?" They may also ask you, **jumun hasillaeyo** (*joo-moon ha-shil-lae-yo*)?, which means, "Are you ready to order?"

Many Koreans are happy to suggest something for you, but be aware of what you're about to eat, and you should always ask what's in it before you venture into a wild, culinary experience. You could be leaving the restaurant with your mouth on fire because of the spices, or be staring at a plate of raw fish wondering where you went wrong.

Finding restrooms

hwajangsil (*hwa-jang-shil*) is the Korean word for a bathroom/restroom. **eodieyo** (*uh-dee-ae-yo*)? and **eodi iseoyo** (*uh-dee ee-ssuh-yo*)? are two variations on the question, "Where is [some word]?" If you want to ask "Where is the bathroom?" use the phrase **hwajangsiri eodieyo** (*hwa-jang-shi-ree uh-dee-ae-yo*)? Of course, you should never walk up to a stranger and just blurt out, "Where's the bathroom?" You should approach people with the phrase, **sillyehamnida** (*shil-lae-ham-ni-da*), which means, "excuse me." So, you get someone's attention by saying, **sillyehamnida, hwajangsiri eodi iseoyo** (*shil-lae-ham-ni-da. hwa-jang-shi-ree uh-di-ee-ssuh-yo*)? Which is translated, "Excuse me, but where is the bathroom?" This question can be asked in any public buildings where there are washrooms, not just in restaurants. Remember to say, **gamsahamnida** (*gam-sa-ham-ni-da;* thank you) when they direct you to the washroom.

Paying for your meal

If you're with company, you should always offer to pay, even though it will usually be met with fierce resistance. Paying for others not only shows your generosity, it will advance your acquaintanceship with a Korean person because the next time, they will surely pay. Paying for other's meal will guarantee a continuation in friendship because the other person will feel indebted to your sense of generosity and will try to reciprocate.

The phrase to say is, **yeogi gyesan haejuseyo** (*yuh-gi gae-san hae-joo-sae-yo*), which translates into, "I would like to pay now." Another commonly used phrase is **yeogi eolmaeyo** (*yuh-gi ul-ma-ae-yo*)? Which means "How much is it here?" Korean use the word **yeogi** (*yuh-gi;* here) when they are referring to themselves very often.

Drinking, Korean style

When a friend asks you to go bar hopping, or clubbing, or when you're entertaining a business partner, you'll run into situations when alcoholic beverages are in the mix. Generally, Koreans raise their glass and say, "**geonbae**" (*guhn-bae*) before drinking. It simply means, "cheers!" Remember these drinking etiquette tips:

- It's customary for the younger to pour the drink for the elder.
- There is proper etiquette for pouring as well. If you are the younger, you should hold the bottle with your right hand, while supporting your right wrist with the left hand as you pour.
- The younger should not drink until the elder takes the first sip, and the younger usually turns away from the elder to take a drink with both hands.

Koreans will forgive lapses in etiquette amongst foreigners, as it is not expected of them. Between Koreans, however, these drinking rituals are usually kept. Keep up with these little rituals and you'll impress the Koreans you drink with, which will go a long way in cementing your relationship with that person.

Table 5-4		Lists of Drinks
sul	*sool*	Alcoholic beverage
maekju	*maek-joo*	Beer
qain	*wah-een*	Wine
yangju	*yang-joo*	Foreign alcoholic beverages in general (e.g., whisky, vodka, and so on)
wiseuki	*wee-seu-kee*	Whiskey
bodeuka	*bo-deu-ka*	Vodka
soju	*so-joo*	Distilled Korean rice wine
mul	*mool*	Water

(continued)

Table 5-4 *(continued)*

keopi	kuh-pee	Coffee
uyu	oo-yoo	Milk
juseu	joo-sseu	Juices
sagwa juseu	sa-gwa joo-sseu	Apple juice
orenji juseu	o-ren-jee joo-sseu	Orange juice
cha	cha	Tea
nokcha	nok-cha	Green tea
insamcha	in-sam-cha	Ginseng tea

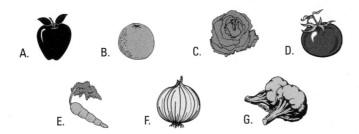

Identify these fruits and vegetables and write their Korean names below.

A. _____

B. _____

C. _____

D. _____

E. _____

F. _____

G. _____

Chapter 6

Shopping Made Easy

· ·

In This Chapter

▶ Going to stores

▶ Comparing merchandise

▶ Shopping for clothes and groceries

▶ Identifying bargains and haggling

· ·

*T*outing the 12th largest economy in the world, and being about the size of Indiana, one can find just about anything they're looking for in South Korea. Whether it's imported goods, consumer electronics, local flavors or treasures, there is something for everyone in South Korea. This chapter will help you find those items that you seek, allow you to navigate from the smallest shops to the largest department stores, help you navigate through prices, colors, quantity, and merchandise. This guide will also help you get the better deal, should a situation arise.

You can find many designated shopping areas for tourists in many parts of South Korea with well-lit, huge department stores that feature not only authentic Korean goods and wares but also Western wares. You can best find Western wares at these large commercial areas. Whether you're looking for souvenirs like a pair of **jangseung** (*jang-seung;* wooden guardians, protectors of villages), or a fancy **yangbok** (*yang–bok;* Western-style suit, business suit), this chapter shows you how to pick out the right one as well as haggle over the price.

Navigating Stores

If you ever find yourself in Seoul, and feel the need to shop, you can find several places that you should definitely look into. Inside the four main gates vicinity, are **myeongdong** (*myoung-dong*; city of Myeongdong), **dongdaemun sijang** (*dong-dae-moon shi-jang;* East gate market), and **namdaemun sijang** (*nam-dae-moon si-jang*; South gate market). **itaewon** (*ee-tae-won*; city of Itaewon) is a shopping and dining district that is very popular with the foreigners, and you can find great bargains here as well. The following sections give you the ins and outs of what type of stores you can find as well as how to shop in them.

Visiting department stores, markets, and small shops

You can always find a shopping district no matter what province you find yourself in Korea. **baekhwajeom** (*baek-hwa-jum;* department store) are everywhere in major urban areas, displaying items from all over the world. Especially near tourist attractions, you can always find a shopping complex nearby, usually within walking distance. Whether you're looking for **hyangsu** (*hyang-soo;* perfume), **hwajangpum** (*hwa-jang-poom;* cosmetics), **ot** (*ot;* clothes), or **jangnangam** (*jang-nan-gam;* toys), you can find them all in a **baekhwajeom.**

Although these large department stores are usually the best places to get what you're looking for, if you have the spirit of adventure in you and are dying to get some more local flavor, you can try going out into the city and walking into a small **gage** (*ga-gae;* store). You can find these little shops everywhere, with their windows displaying their merchandise facing the street. Although their selections are limited due to their size, you can find something authentic or genuinely Korean better in these stores rather than at big department stores.

If you crave the hustle and bustle of a market, you may try to look for a **sijang** (*shi-jang;* market), or a **byeoruk sijang** (*byuh-rook-shi-jang;* flea market). Flea markets tend to pop up mostly during weekends at designated locations, and usually are held for that day only. A myriad of humanity sell and push their wares here, and occasionally, people have been known to find the bargain of a lifetime at these places. **sijang** is more like an outdoor market, where fresh foods and produce are bought and sold at a lively pace.

The hustle and bustle of these open air markets cannot be beat. Whether you're looking for fabric, used books, dried fish, cooking utensils, watches, electronic equipment, or clothes, there is an open market for just about anything that you're looking for. If you're looking for that one bargain of a lifetime, you may be able to find it in any one of these open air markets. You can also find those rare and unusual items at these markets. **Dongdaemun sijang** (*dong-dae-moon shi-jang*; East gate market), for example, is the "Total Bazaar Fair" of Seoul, with everything from books to records to tools to shoes to clothes to musical instruments and antiques. You can normally handle the items, and the good-natured merchants won't snub you. This is also an excellent place to haggle and negotiate for the best price, as prices vary from one merchant to the next.

Merchants won't like it if you take pictures of their merchandise. Some of them won't like you handling either, especially if you don't buy the item afterwards, but this depends on the individual merchants.

Talkin' the Talk

Jane and Mona decide to go shopping for the day. They decide where to go.

Jane:	**jeo oneul sijange gayadoeyo.**
	juh oh-neul shi-jang-ae ga-ya-dwae-yo.
	I have to go to the market today.

Mona:	**jeoduyo. ga-chi gal-lae-yo?**
	juh-doo-yo. ga-chi gal-lae-yo?
	Me, too. Shall we go together?

Jane:	**joayo. uri sijange gatdaga baekhwajeomdo gayo. jega hwajangpumi piryohaeyo.**
	jo-a-yo. oo-ree shi-jang-ae gat-da-ga baek-hwa-jum-do ga-yo. jae-ga hwa-jang-poom-ee pi-ryo-hae-yo.
	Good. Let's go to the department store after the market. I need some make-up.

Mona:	**geuraeyo. jeodu ot hanbeol saibeullyeoguyo.**
	geu-rae-yo. juh-do ot han-bul sah-ee-beul-yuh-goo-yo.
	Let's do that. I want to buy new clothes.

Jane:	**ppalli gayo. sijange ppalli gaya baekhwajeome gajyo.**
	ppal-li ga-yo. shi-jang-ae ppal-li-ga-ya baek-hwa-jum-ae ga-jyo.
	Let's hurry. The faster we go to the market, the sooner we can go to the department store.

Words to Know

baekhwajeom	baek-hwa-jum	Department store
sijang	shi-jang	Market/Grocery store
byeoruk sijang	byuh-rook—si-jang	Flea market
seonmul	suhn-mool	Present/gift
chaek	chaeg	Book
eumban	eum-ban	Music record
jangnangam	jang-nan-gam	Toys
sinbal	shin-bal	Shoes
undonghwa	oon-dong-hwa	Gym shoes
ot	ot	Clothes
hanbok	han-bok	Traditional Korean clothes
yangbok	yang-bok	Western style suit
baji	ba-ji	Pants
chima	chi-ma	Skirt
boseok	bo-suk	Jewelry
banji	ban-ji	Ring
mokgeori	mok—guh-ri	Necklace

Browsing around

When you're in a store, the owner or the employee will come up to you to ask you if you need any help. In the large department stores, you'll most likely find an employee who speaks English, but at the smaller locations, or mom-and-pop establishments, you may not. Most often, you'll hear the owner or employee say, "**mueoseul chajeuseyo?**"(*moo-uh-seul cha-jeu-sae-yo?;* what are you looking for?) or "**eotteoke dowadeurilkkayo?**"(*uh-ttuh-kae do-wa deu-ril-kka-yo?; how can I help you?*). If you're just browsing, you can say, "**gugyeonghareo wasseoyo**" (*goo-gyoung-ha-ruh-wa-ssuh-yo; I'm just here to browse*). **gugyeong** (*goo-gyoung*) means to browse, or to spectate, so when you tell the employee that you're just here to browse, most of the time, they will let you undisturbed.

Asking for help

If you decide that you do need some help, you can always flag down the employee by saying, "**sillyehamnida**"(*shil-lae-ham-ni-da; Excuse me*). When you're looking for something, you can ask by saying, "**eodi itjyo?** (*uh-dee it-jyo?*) or **eodi isseoyo?** (*uh-dee ee-ssuh-yo,*" which both means, "where is it?" If you know what the item is called in Korean, you can just add the phrase, "**eodi itjyo** (*uh-dee it-jyo*) or **eodi isseoyo?**"(*uh-dee ee-ssuh-yo?*) after the thing you are looking for to ask for the location of it. For example, if you are looking for some toys, you can ask **jangnangamee eodi itjyo?** (*jang-nan-gam-ee uh-dee it-jyo; where are the toys?*). If you're looking for a suit, you can ask the employee, "**yangbogi eodi isseoyo?**"(*yang-bo-gee uh-dee ee-ssuh-yo?*). If you're looking for a souvenir, you can ask, "**ginyeompumi eodi isseoyo?**"(*gee-nyum-poom-ee uh-dee ee-ssuh-yo?*). Another useful phrase might be "**jeojom dowajusillaeyo?**" (*juh-jom do-wa joo-shil-lae-yo?*) which means "Can you please help me?"

Talkin' the Talk

Jane asks an attendant for help at a department store.

Jane: sillyehamnida. jeo jom dowajusillaeyo?
shil-lae ham-ni-da. juh jom do-wa-joo-shil-lae-yo?
Excuse me. Can you help me?

Attendant: ye sonnim. eotteoke dowadeurilkkayo?
ye son-nim. uh-tuh-kae do-wa-deu-ril-kka-yo?
Yes patron (customer). How can I help you?

Jane: yeoja ot hago hyangsuga eodi itjyo?
yuh-ja ot ha-go hyang-soo-ga uh-dee it-jyo?
Where are women's clothes and perfume?

Attendant: ye. samcheunge itseumnida.
ye. sam-cheung-ae ee-sseum-ni-da.
Yes, They are on the third floor.

Jane: **gomawoyo. aideul jangnangameun eodi itjyo?**
go-ma-wo-yo. a-ee-deul jang-nan-gam-eun uh-dee it-jyo?
Thank you. Where are the children's toys?

Attendant: **ye. jangnangameun sacheunge itseupnida.**
ye. jang-nan-gam-eun sa-cheung-ae ee-sseum-ni-da.
Yes, the toys are on the fourth floor.

Jane: **gomawoyo**
go-ma-wo-yo.
Thank you.

Words to Know

sonnim	son-nim	Customer/guest
jiha	jee-ha	Underground/basement
ilcheung	il-cheung	1st floor
icheing	ee-cheung	2nd floor
samcheung	sam-cheung	3rd floor
sacheung	sa-cheung	4th floor
itseupnida	ee-sseup-ni-da	It's there/it's at [some word]
eotteoke	uh-ttuh-kae	How
eodi	uh-dee	Where

Comparing Merchandise

You should familiarize yourself with several words if you want to compare one item with another. **ige** (*ee-gae*), or **igeo** (*ee-guh*) means "this one," **jeoge** (*juh-gae*) or **jeogeo** (*juh-guh*) means "that one." **igeo** (*ee-guh*; this one) and **jeogeo**(*juh-guh*; that one) are two good words to know. **joayo** (*jo-a-yo*) means "good." You can add the prefix **an-** in front of the word **joayo** and its variation **anjoayo** (*an-jo-a-yo*) denote something that is "not good." Other useful words to know will be **ssada** (*ssa-da;* cheap, good bargain) and **bissada** (*bi-ssa-da;* expensive).

nappayo,(*na-ppa-yo*) means "bad," and should never be used when comparing goods in Korea. When comparing items, Koreans generally use the phrase "**anjoayo** (*an-jo-a-yo*; not good)" opposed to "**nappayo** (*na-ppa-yo*; bad)." Try not to insult the shopkeeper by insinuating that his wares are "bad." Generally, you want to state what you prefer, or what you like better, than what you don't like, or what you consider bad.

Comparing several items

When you find that one item that you like out of many, you can point to an item and say, "**igeotdeul junge jeil joayo**" (*ee-guht-deul joong-ae jae-il jo-a-yo;* I like this one out of all these.) If you want to know which item between the two is cheaper, you can ask, "**igeorang igeo saie eotteonge deo ssayo?**"(*ee-guh-rang ee-guh sa-ee-ae uh-ttuhn-gae duh ssa-yo?;* between this item and this, which one is cheaper?). If you're having a hard time deciding between the two items, you can always ask the attendant, "**eotteonge deo joayo?**" (*uh-ttuhn-gae duh jo-a-yo?;* which one is better).

Pointing out the best item

If and when you decide on the item that you like, you can say, "**igeo hana juseyo**" (*ee-guh ha-na joo-sae-yo;* Please give me one of these.) "**ige jeil joayo**"(*ee-gae jae-il jo-a-yo;* I like this one the best.) **jeil** (*jae-il*) means "the best," or "number one," so when you say, "**jeoge jeil joayo**" (*juh-gae jae-il jo-a-yo*), translated literally means, "I like that one the best." **joayo** (*jo-a-yo*) means "good," or "I like." When you're shopping for clothes, you can substitute the word **ippeoyo** (*ee-ppuh-yo*; pretty) instead of the variations of **joayo** or you can also use **meosisseoyo** (*muh-shi-ssuh-yo*; handsome, fashionable). **ippeoyo** is usually used to describe feminine or children's clothing, while the term **meosisseoyo** is used globally in describing clothing.

Shopping for Clothes

Many fashion and clothing shops litter the shopping areas in Korea. **Mokdong** (*mok-dong*) Rodeo street for one, has over 150 stores that carry domestic and international brand name clothing at a discounted price. **Munjeongdong** (*moon-jung-dong*) Fashion Street also has over 200 clothing shops that sell all kinds of clothes from formal wear to sports wear, and **Guro** (*goo-ro*) Fashion Valley is another area that sells a wide variety of clothes. There are many shops in these areas that cater specifically to male clientele, as there are many that cater specifically to females and children. There are specialty shops that focus only on Western style and some that concentrate on just traditional Korean clothing. You can also visit **itaewon** (*ee-tae-won*), for Western, brand-name shops, or **namdaemun sijang** (*nam-dae-moon shi-jang*; South gate market) and **dongdaemun sijang** (*dong-dae-moon shi-jang*; East gate market) for the hustle and bustle of a wholesale market, where the items are sold at an incredibly affordable price. Regardless of where you decide to shop, you need to familiarize yourself with specific terms that I discuss in the following sections, such as those regarding size and color, so that you can be sure you get what you want.

Checking for sizes

Many formalwear shops will have a tailor on hand to measure you and make you a custom made suit, or a dress, but when you're shopping for clothes on the rack, it's nice to know a few words and phrases that will help you navigate through the desired size. You can grab an attendant and ask, "**igeoboda han ssaijeu deo keungeo isseoyo?**"(*ee-guh-bo-da ha n sa-ee-zeu duh keun-guh ee-ssuh-yo;* Do you have one a size bigger than this one?)". If the item is too big, you can ask, "**igeoboda han ssaijeu deo jageungeo isseoyo?**" (*ee-guh bo-da han ssa-ee-zeu duh ja-geun-guh ee-ssuh-yo*; Do you have one a size smaller than this one?).

In Korea, sizing units are very different than the sizing units used in the U.S. For example, for shoes, Koreans use centimeters to measure their feet and for bottoms (for example, pants, skirts, jean) they use the waist sizes. So it might be a good idea to measure the size of your waist before you go shopping in Korea. Following are comparison of Korean and U.S. sizes in various clothing.

- **Underwear:**

    Korea: 75A/75B/80A/80B/85A/85B

    U.S.: 32A/32B/34A/34B/36A/36B
- **Tops:**

    Korea (1): 44/55/66/77

    Korea (2): 85/90/95/100

    U.S.: XS/S/M/L
- **Bottoms**

    Korea (1): 44/55/66/77

    Korea (2): 23–24; 25–26; 27–29; 30–32 (waist sizes in inches)

    U.S. (1): XS/S/M/L

    U.S. (2): 0–2; 4–6; 8–10

✔ **Shoes**

> **Korea:** 230/235/240/245/250 (feet sizes in centimeters)
>
> **U.S.:** 6/6.5/7/7.5/8

Asking about colors

If you find a shirt that you like, but would like it in blue, you can ask the attendant, "**igeorang gateungeo paransaegeuro isseoyo?**" (*ee-guh-rang ga-teun-guh pa-ran-sae-geu-ro ee-ssuh-yo?;* Do you have same one as this one in blue?). If you're looking for it in green, you can ask, "**igeo choroksaek isseoyo?**" (*ee-guh cho-rok-saek ee-ssuh-yo?;* Do you have this in green?). **saek** (*saek*), or **saekgal** (*sae-kkal*) is the Korean word for color, so if you know what color you want, you can add **isseoyo** (*ee-ssuh-yo;* Do you have it) after the color. For example, **norangsaek isseiyo?** (*no-rang-saek ee-ssuh-yo?;* Do you have it in yellow?). Check out Table 6-1 to discover how you say your favorite color in Korean.

Table 6-1	Terms for Colors	
Korean Word	*Pronunciation*	*Translation*
hayansaek	*ha-yan-saek*	White
noransaek	*no-ran-saek*	Yellow
juhwangsaek	*joo-hwang-saek*	Orange
ppalgansaek	*ppal-gan-saek*	Red
choroksaek	*cho-rok-saek*	Green
parangsaek	*pa-rang-saek*	Blue
borasaek	*bo-ra-saek*	Purple
geomjeongsaek	*gum-jung-saek*	Blank
bamsaek	*bam-saek*	Brown
hoesaek	*hwae-saek*	Grey

Trying on clothes

When you try something on, you can ask the attendant, or the person you're with the question, "**eottaeyo?** (*uh-ttae-yo*)." "**eottaeyo?**" means "How is it?" or "what do you think?" In the interest of being polite, they will most likely say, "**meosisseoyo** (*muh-shi-ssuh-yo*; you look fashionable, it looks good). The "you" in that last phrase is assumed. **meot** (*muht*) in Korean means a lot of different things. It can mean sophistication, taste, and class, among other things. **isseoyo** (*ee-ssuh-yo*) means "to be present." So, when someone says **meoshisseoyo** (*muh-si-ssuh-yo*), it means "you look good," or "you look classy," or sophisticated, or tasteful, and so on.

Talkin' the Talk

 Natalie and Kate are at a department store shopping for clothes.

Natalie:	**yeogiyo. jeohui jom dowajuseyo.** *yuh-gi-yo! juh-hee jom do-wa-joo-sae-yo.* Excuse me/here please. Please help us.
Attendant:	**ne, mueoseul chajeuseyo?** *ne. moo-uh-seul cha-jeu-sae-yo?* Yes, what are you looking for?
Kate:	**yeoja bajirang chimaga eodi itjyo?** *yuh-ja ba-ji-rang chi-ma-ga uh-dee it-jyo?* Where are women's pants and skirts?
Attendant:	**ye. boyeodeurilkkaeyo? jeoreul ttaraoseyo.** *ye. bo-yuh-deu-ril-kka-yo? juh-reul tta-ra-o-sae-yo.* Yes, do you want me to show you? Please follow me.
Natalie:	(Holding up a skirt) **igeoneun eottaeyo?** *ee-guh-neun uh-ttae-yo?* How's this one?
Kate:	**meosisseoyo. paransaegeun innayo?** *muh-shi-ssuh-yo. pa-ran-saek-eun in-na-yo?* It's pretty. Do they have it in blue?
Attendant:	**ye. jamshiman gidariseyo. jega gatda deurilkkeyo** *ye. jam-shi-man gi-da-ree-sae-yo. jeh-ga gat-da deu-ril-kkae-yo.* Yes. Wait here a moment. I'll bring it for you.

Words to Know

yeogiyo	yuh-gi-yo	Here please
chajeusaeyo	cha-jeu-sae-yo	Looking for
boyeodeurilkkaeyo	bo-yuh-deu-ril-kka-yo	Would you like to see it
meosisseoyo	muh-shi-ssuh-yo	It looks good/ it's fashionable
jamsiman	jam-shi-man	A moment
gidariseyo	gi-da-ree-sae-yo	Please wait
paransaek	pa-ran-saek	Blue color
saek	saek	Color
boseoksang	bo-seuk-sang	Jewellery store
kkotgagye	kkot-ga-gae	Flower shop
supeomaket	su-puh-ma-ket	Super market
yakguk	yak-gook	Pharmacy/drug store
munbanggu	moon-bang-goo	Stationary/toy store

Shopping for Specific Items

Korea is very well known for its textile industry, but there are other popular buys in Korea. Besides clothing, Korea is also well known for leather and fur goods, antiques and replicas, electronic equipment, jewelry, ginseng, folk arts and crafts, traditional liquors and teas, **gimchi** (*gim-chee*), and other foods. Many of these items are readily available in duty-free shops and large department stores, but some of the treasures require a bit of hunting. A word of caution for the antique collectors is necessary here, though. Any antique items over 50 years old, including chests, calligraphy works and pottery, are not allowed to be taken out of the country, so if in doubt, you should check with the Art and Antiques Assessment Office.

Groceries

Many large, chain grocery stores carry international goods should you feel homesick, and you can find many Western eateries as well. If you're looking for an authentically Korean experience, you might want to visit a **sijang** (*shi-jang*), which is like a farmer's market. Here, you'll find many different varieties of **gimchi** being sold out of gigantic tubs, and these people are more than happy to give you a taste. While the large grocery stores have prices clearly labeled on the items, you can haggle for prices at these farmer's markets. Koreans are big on fresh food items, so you can find live fish and extremely fresh vegetables in these markets.

If a price is not clearly labeled on an item, you can ask, "**igeo eolmajyo?**" (*ee-guh ul-ma-jyo?*), which means, "How much is this?" "**igeo eolmaeyo?** (*ee-guh ul-ma-ae-yo*; How much is this?)" is also acceptable. **gagyeok** (*ga-gyuhk*) is the Korean word for price, so if you want to, you can also ask, "**igeo gagyeogi eolmaeyo?**" (*ee-guh ga-gyuh-gee ul-ma-ae-yo?*), which is translated, "What is the price of this item?"

Electronics

A good place to find state of the art electronic equipment is the COEX mall, or the Techno Mart. COEX mall is a huge underground labyrinth of shops, with all different kinds of amenities and facilities. COEX mall also houses a Cineplex, and the COEX Aquarium, which displays more than 40'000 fish of over 600 species and dozens of large sharks. Techno Mart is housed in a high rise building with an 11-screen multiplex theater, game rooms, restaurants and more. Techno Mart has hundreds of stores specializing in electronic and computer-related goods.

Antiques and souvenirs

There are many things Korea is known for when it comes to items of this nature. Dolls in splendid traditional costumes, fans, wooden masks, delicate and colorful embroidery, painted wedding ducks, kites, intricate mother-of-pearl lacquerware, ceramic pieces like white porcelain, and blue-jade celadon are readily available in many gift shops and duty-free shops. If you're searching for something a little more authentic, you should look into the **jangan-pyeong** (*jang-an-pyoung*) Antique Market, Cultural Property Artisan's Hall, or the Korea House Handicraft Shop. Many of these stores carry items that cannot be found anywhere else.

All About Buying: Pricing, Bargaining, Purchasing, Refunding

Once you find the item that you're looking for, and once you find out how much the item costs, you can start haggling over the price. Like I mentioned earlier, you'll probably have better luck at haggling over the price of an item at one of those open air markets as opposed to a large department stores, as the prices tend to be more fixed at these locations. It makes sense, however, when you think of it this way. The stalls in the open air markets are owned by individuals, and when you haggle over the price of an item at those shops, chances are, you are talking to the owner of the shop. In large department stores, you're probably talking to one of many employees, who have very little control in setting the price of the items. If and when you find yourself in one of these open air markets, you can begin by telling the shop owner, **"neomu bissayo"** (*nuh-moo bee-ssa-yo;* It's too expensive.) You can also say, **"jom kkakkajuseyo** (*jom kka-kka-joo-sae-yo;* Lower the price a little bit.) Literally translated, it means, "shave off a little bit (on the price)."

If and when you and the shop owner have agreed on a price, you can go ahead and pay for your purchase. **"eolmaeyo?** (*ul-ma-ae-yo?;* How much is it?) or **"eolmajyo?"** (*ul-ma-jyo?;* How much is it?). If you decide that you don't want the item after you've purchased it, bring it back to the store and say, **"banhwan haejuseyo"** (*ban-hwan hae-joo-sae-yo;* please give me a refund). You can also say, **"igeo jega eoje satgeodeunyo, yeongsujeung yeogi isseoyo** (*ee-guh jae-ga uh-jae sa-guh-deun-yo, young-soo-jeung yuh-gi ee-ssuh-yo;* I bought this item yesterday, here is the receipt). **banhwan haejuseyo** (*ban-hwan hae-joo-sae-yo;* Please give me a refund.) At large department stores, you shouldn't have any trouble getting a refund, but in one of those open air markets, you'd be hard pressed to find someone that will give you a refund. Such is the risk you run for searching out a bargain. While you may find items at a lower cost at these markets, getting your money back may be harder than it is if you were to purchase the item at a large, reputable department store.

Fun & Games

Please match the type of store with the items you would find in these stores shown in the illustration below.

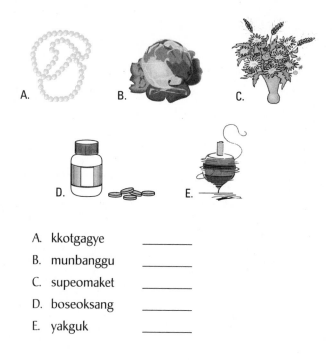

A.

B.

C.

D.

E.

A. kkotgagye   _____

B. munbanggu   _____

C. supeomaket   _____

D. boseoksang   _____

E. yakguk   _____

Chapter 7

Exploring the Town

. . . .

In This Chapter

▶ Knowing the time and day

▶ Exploring museums and galleries

▶ Taking in a movie

▶ Dealing with invitations

. . . .

Instead of being stuck in your hotel on a beautiful day, wouldn't you much rather hit the town? Wouldn't you rather visit a **bakmulgwan** (*bak-mool-gwan;* museum) and learn about Korean history and culture, or go see a **yeonghwa** (*young-hwa;* movie)? Perhaps you'd like to see a performance of **gugak** (*goo-gak;* traditional Korean music), **jung-ak** (*joong-ak;* music of the upper classes/court music), **nong-ak** (*nong-ak;* farmer's music/folk music), or **pansori** (*pan–so-ree;* epic solo song). If you want to catch any of these shows, you have to know when and where the shows are happening, of course. You have to know how to read a **jido** (*jee-do;* map), hail a **taeksi** (*taek-shi;* taxi), or take a **beoseu** (*buh-sseu;* bus) a **gicha** (*gee-cha;* train), or **jihacheol** (*jee-ha-chul;* subway). You also need to know the **naljja** (*nal-jja;* date) and **sigan** (*shi-gan;* time) to be there on time. If you check out the sections in this chapter, you can find out exactly what you need to make a date and keep it!

Knowing the Time and Day

yoil (*yo-il*) is a Korean word that means "day of the week." The prefix determines which day of the week it is. So **mogyoil** (*mo-gyo-il*) means Thursday, **toyoil** (*to-yo-il*) means Saturday, **woryoil** (*wo-ryo-il*) means Monday and so forth. Notice the word "**yoil**" that is present in all of those days. **si** (*shi*) is hour and **boon** (*boon*) is minutes. So, if someone asked you to meet at a **geukjang** (*geuk-jang;* theatre) on **suyoil** (*soo-yo-il;* Wednesday), **ohoo** (*o-who;* afternoon) **neshi** (*nae-shi;* 4 o'clock) **siboboon** (*shi-bo-boon;* 15 minutes), you'll have to meet that person at a theatre on Wednesday, at 4:15 pm. In this section, I will teach you how to say the day of the week, what months it is, and also how to tell times in Korean.

Days, weeks, months

The Korean word for a week is **ju** (*joo*). **juil** (*joo-il*) is a weekday, and **jumal** (*joo-mal*) means weekend. The Korean week begins on a Monday and ends on Sunday. **juil** is from Monday through Friday, and **jumal**, being the weekend, is Saturday and Sunday. For those who live for the weekend, **jumal** is the time when all the fun takes place. These are the days you go bar hopping; these are the days you go catch a movie. You can talk about what happened **jeobeonju** (*juh-bun-joo*; last week) or **jinan-ju** (*jee-nan-joo*; a week that had already passed), or **jeobeonjumal** (*juh-bun-joo-mal*; last weekend) or **jinanjumal** (*jee-nan-joo-mal*; a weekend that had already passed), or if this week's no good you can make plans for **daeumju** (*da-eum-joo*; next week). If it's a plan that cannot be postponed, you'll have to meet **ibeonju** (*ee-bun-joo*; this week). See Table 7-1 for how to spot and pronounce days of the week.

Table 7-1	Days of the week	
Korean Word	*Pronunciation*	*English Word*
woryoil	*wuh-ryo-il*	Monday
hwayoil	*hwa-yo-il*	Tuesday
suyoil	*soo-yo-il*	Wednesday
mogyoil	*mo-gyo-il*	Thursday
geumyoil	*geum-yo-il*	Friday
toyoil	*to-yo-il*	Saturday
iryoil	*ee-ryo-il*	Sunday

Telling time

After you are familiar with numbers in Korean, telling the time becomes a pretty easy thing to do. The only thing that you have to remember is **si** (*shi*; hour), **boon** (*boon*; minutes) and **cho** (*cho*; seconds). It is also helpful to know **ojeon** (*o-juhn*; morning, am) and **ohu** (*o-who*; afternoon, pm). If you have an important meeting at **ojeon ahopsi** (*o-juhn a-hop-shi*), then you know the meeting starts at 9:00 am. If the meeting starts at **ojeon ahopsi ban** (*o-juhn-a-hop-shi-ban*), that means your meeting starts at 9:30 am. **ban** (*ban*) means half, so translated literally, **ahopsi ban** means nine hours and a half, or half past nine. Remember, punctuality is a quality that is valued highly, so if you want to make a good impression, be sure to make it to your meeting a little early. To keep you on track and on time, just check out Table 7-2.

Table 7-2	Time-Related Terms	
Korean Word	*Pronunciation*	*English Word*
hansi	*han-shi*	1:00
dusi	*doo-shi*	2:00
sesi	*sae-shi*	3:00
nesi	*ne-shi*	4:00
daseotsi	*da-suh-shi*	5:00
yeoseotsi	*yuh-suh-shi*	6:00
ilgopsi	*il-gop-shi*	7:00
yeodeolsi	*yuh-duhl-shi*	8:00
ahopsi	*a-hop-shi*	9:00
yeolsi	*yuhl-shi*	10:00
yeolhansi	*yuhl-han-shi*	11:00
yeoldusi	*yuhl-doo-shi*	12:00
ojeon	*o-juhn*	Before noon, am.
ohu	*o-hoo*	After noon, pm.

Telling time relative to now

oneul (*o-neul*) is the Korean word for today. **eoje** (*uh-jae*) is yesterday, and **naeil** (*nae-il*) is tomorrow. **jigeum** (*jee-geum*) is the Korean word for right now. **najunge** (*na-joong-ae*) means later. One shouldn't do **naeil** what can be done **oneul**, right? But it's so much easier to say **najunge**. You can also say, **jom itdaga** (*jom ee-dda-ga*), which means, "in a little while, little later." **eonje** (*un-jae*) is the Korean word for when. So the question, **eonje hasilgeoeyo?** (*un-jae ha-shil-guh-ae-yo?;* when will you do it?) can be answered, **oneul halkkeoeyo** (*o-neul hal-kkuh-ae-yo;* I will do it today).

Other examples of using these words are: **naeil halkkeoeyo** (*nae-il hal-kkuh-ae-yo;* I will do it tomorrow), **jigeum halkkayo?** (*jee-geum hal-kka-yo;* Should I do it right now?), **najunge galkkeyo** (*na-joong-ae gal-kkae-yo;* I will go later) and **jom itdaga jeonhwa haseyo** (*jom ee-dda-ga juhn-hwa ha-sae-yo;* Please call in a while or please call little later.) If you have done it already, you can say, **"eoje haeseoyo"** (*uh-jae-hae-ssuh-yo;* I did it yesterday.) Then again, you may need to list the month in which you've done or plan to do something.

Seasonal terms can be helpful when making plans or discussing things you've done. Use Table 7-3 as your guide.

Table 7-3		Seasonal Terms
gyejeol	*gae-juhl*	The seasons
bom	*bom*	Spring
yeoreum	*yuh-reum*	Summer
gaeul	*ga-eul*	Fall
gyeoul	*gyuh-wool*	Winter

Talkin' the Talk

Sarah asks Tom about his birthday.

Sarah: **tomssi saengiri eonjeeyo?**
tom-shi, saeng-ee-ree un-jae-ae-yo?
Tom, when is your birthday?

Tom: **je saengilreun samwol isipsamirieyo. sarahssi saengireun eonjeeyo?**
jae saeng-ee-reun sam-wol ee-ship–sam-il ee-ae-yo. sarah-sshi saeng-ee-reun un-jae-ae-yo?
My birthday is March 23. When's your birthday, Sarah?

Sarah: **je saengireun sawol siboirieyo.**
jae saeng-ee-reun sa-wol-ship-o-il-ee-ae-yo.
My birthday is April fifteenth.

Tom: **jinanjuyeonaeyo? neujeotjiman saengil chukhahaeyo! jal bonaeseoyo?**
jee-nan-joo-yuhn-nae-yo? neu-juh-jee-man saeng-il chook-ha-hae-yo! jal bo-nae-ssuh-yo?
Then it was last week? Happy birthday! Did you spend it well?

Sarah: **ne. gajogirang gachi bonaeseoyo. jeonyeok gachi meogeoseoyo**
nae. ga-jo-gi-rang ga-chi bo-nae-ssuh-yo. juh-nyuhk ga-chi muh-guh-ssuh-yo.
Yes. I spent it with family. We had dinner together.

Words to Know

Months of the Year and Related Terms

irwol	ee-rwol	January
iwol	ee-wol	February
samwol	sam-wol	March
sawol	sa-wol	April
owol	o-wol	May
yuwol	yoo-wol	June
chirwol	chi-rwol	July
parwol	pa-rwol	August
guwol	goo-wol	September
siwol	shi-wol	October
sibirwol	shi-bee-rwol	November
sibiwol	shi-bee-wol	December
ibeondal	ee-bun-dal	This month
daeumdal	da-eum-dal	Next month
jeobeondal	juh-bun-dal	Last month
saengil	saeng-il	Birthday
seollal	sul-nal	New Year's day

Exploring Fun Places

From culture to clubs, Korea has a variety of places to check out for nightlife. The sections that follow not only introduce you to these places, but also, the following sections help you to navigate these places as well.

Visiting museums and galleries

Korea boasts of a long history and museums can be found not just in Seoul, but in other cities and areas. **gyeongju** (*gyoung-joo*) area, in the south east corner of the peninsula has many historical sites and museums for you to check out as well. You can also take in a lot of Korean history and culture in many of the Buddhist temples scattered throughout the countryside. **haeinsa** (*hae-in-sa*; Buddhist temple Haein) in particular, which is a UNESCO World Heritage Site, is the home of Tripitaka Koreana, or **palmandaejanggyung** (*pal-man-dae-jang-gyoung*), which is the world's oldest and most complete Buddhist canon, carved in wooden blocks around the 13th century. The wooden blocks which were used to print Tripitaka, predate the Gutenburg press by almost 400 years, are the oldest set of prints in the world.

Aside from temples and museums, you might also be interested to visit one of many palaces still remaining from the previous dynasties. Many of them have been renovated into parks and historical sites and guided tours are available. For example, **changdeokgung** (*chang-duhk goong*) palace, built in 1405, lends a glimpse into the beauty of traditional architecture and landscape of Korea.

Going to concerts, theatres, and performances

Korea has more than just museums and temples. The entertainment industry, and Korean pop culture has been exported to many different countries in the world, and the phenomenon has even given birth to a term, **hallyu** (*han-ryu*), meaning the "Korean Wave." Television dramas and films have been translated into many different languages and exported, and Korean music and the stars have been received very well by other Asian nations. While there are many entertainment venues that focus primarily on traditional Korean entertainment, more venues showcase modern Korean entertainment, and are easily accessible through ticket brokers. The front desk at the hotel, or a phone call to any tourism offices should make it easier for you to catch a glimpse of the "Korean Wave" and its stars.

Korean films

A large part of **hallyu** (*han-ryu*; Korean wave) is in its film industry. In the last few years, Korean films have been noticed by various international film festivals and a few of them have even made it into Hollywood as remakes. For example, *The Lake House* (2006) starring Keanu Reeves and Sandra Bullock is a remake of a Korean film titled *Il Mare*. *Il Mare* means the "sea" in French. In this movie, the building where the female character lived was called *Il Mare*. In Korea, this movie was called *Siwore*, which means "in the month of October." Korean films have been recognized in international film festivals as well. In 2002, the movie *Chihwaseon* (*chi-hwa-sun*) was awarded the best director prize at the Cannes Film Festival, and in 2004, the Grand Prix award from the same festival was given to a film titled *Old Boy*, and a film titled *Spring, Summer, Fall, Winter . . . and Spring* was given three different awards at the 2003 Locarno International Film Festival. A film titled *The Brotherhood of War* received critical acclaims, with limited release in the United States, and most recently, a film titled *The Host* enjoyed a limited release and rave reviews in the United States.

Talkin' the Talk

Peter and Janet decide to go see a movie together.

Peter: **oneul jeonyeoge yeonghwa boreo gallaeyo?**
           o-neul juh-nyuh-gae young-hwa bo-ruh gal-lae-yo?
           Do you want to go see a movie this evening?

Janet: **geuraeyo. museun yeonghwa bollaeyo?**
           geu-rae-yo. moo-seun young-hwa bol-lae-yo?
           Sure. What kind of movie should we watch?

Peter: **museoun yeonghwaga bogo sipeoyo. gongpo yeonghwaneun eottaeyo?**
           moo-suh-woon young-hwa-ga bo-go-shi-puh-yo. gong-po young-hwa-neun uh-ttae-yo?
           I want to watch a scary movie. How about a terror film?

Janet: **museoun yeonghwaneun sireoyo. jaemiinneun yeonghwaga bogosipeoyo.**
           moo-suh-oon young-hwa-neun shi-ruh-yo. jae-mee-in-neun young-hwa-ga bo-go-shi-puh-yo.
           I don't like scary movies. I want to watch a funny movie.

Peter: **joayo. uri gachi komedireul boreogayo.**
           jo-a-yo. oo-ree ga-chi ko-me-dee-reul bo-ruh-ga-yo.
           Good. Let's go and watch a comedy together.

Words to Know

geukjang	geuk-jang	Theater
bakmulgwan	bak-mool-gwan	Museum
misul	mee-sool	Art
eumak	eum-ak	Music
jeol	juhl	Temple
gongweon	gong-won	Park
gongpoyeonghwa	gong-po-young-hwa	Horror movie
komedi	ko-me-dee	Comedy
uri	oo-ree	We, us
gachi	ga-chi	Together
jeonyeoge	juh-nyuh-gae	Tonight
sireoyo	shi-ruh-yo	I don't like it, I don't want to
jaemiinneun	jae-mee-in-neun	Funny, entertaining
bogosipeoyo	bo-go-shi-puh-yo	I want to see
eottaeyo	uh-ttae-yo	How about
museoun	moo-suh-woon	Scary

Korean noraebang

noraebang (*no-rae-bang*; song room, karaoke room), when translated literally, means "song room." **noraebang**, or a karaoke room, is one of the most popular destinations for Koreans of all ages. Unlike karaoke in the West, where the karaoke machine is set up next to an event, **noraebang** is a room specifically designed for karaoke. Koreans like to go to the **noraebang** to unwind from their hard work week and to belt out a tune to relieve their stress. In certain areas, you'll see a **noraebang** on every street corner, as it is a very popular pastime for Koreans.

When a Korean suggests this activity, don't shy away from it, even if you're not a good singer. Even though it could potentially be embarrassing for the both of you, it can be a disarming event, bringing you closer to your friend or partner.

Talkin' the Talk

Maria, Katherine, and Adam discuss plans for the evening.

Maria: **simsimhaeyo. uri gachi nagaseo norayo.**
shim-shim-hae-yo. oo-ree ga-chi na-ga-suh no-ra-yo.
I'm bored. Let's all go out and have fun.

Katherine: **geuraeyo. jeodu simsimhaeyo. mwol hallaeyo?**
geu-rae-yo. juh-doo shim-shim-hae-yo. mwol hal-lae-yo?
Let's. I'm bored, too. What shall we do?

Adam: **noraebange gayo!**
no-rae-bang-ae ga-yo!
Let's go to a karaoke room!

Maria: **geukjange aju jaemiinneun yeonghwa haneunde. geugeo boreo gaji aneullaeyo?**
geuk-jang-ae a-joo jae-mee-in-neun young-hwa ha-neun-dae. geu-guh bo-ruh ga-jee an-eul-lae-yo?
There's a good movie playing in the theatre. Wouldn't you like to go and see it?

Katherine: **yeonghwaneun ibeonjumalkkaji hajiman noraebangeun eonjena galsu iseunikka yeonghwaboreo gayo.**
young-hwa-neun ee-bun-joo-mal-kka-jee ha-jee-man no-rae-bang-eun un-jae-na gal-soo ee-sseu-ni-kka yeong-hwa-bo-ruh ga-yo.
The movie's playing until this weekend, but the karaoke place is always open. Let's go see the movie.

Adam: **geuraeyo, yeonghwa boreo gayo. yeonghwa bogijeone siksa halkkayo?**
geu-rae-yo, young-hwa bo-ruh ga-yo. young-hwa-bo-gi-juhn-ae shik-sa hal-kka-yo?
Okay, let's go and see a movie. Should we eat before the movie?

Katherine: **jeon jigeum bae gopayo. jigeumgaseo jeomsim meokgo yeonghwa boreo gayo.**
juhn–jee-geum bae-go-pa-yo. jee-geum-ga-suh jumshim-muk-go young-hwa bo-ruh ga-yo.
I'm hungry now. Let's have lunch and then go see the movie.

Maria: **joayo. gasijyo.**
jo-a-yo. ga-shi-jyo
Good. Let's go.

Words to Know

simsimhaeyo	shim-shim-hae-yo	I'm bored
bae gopayo	bae go-pa-yo	I'm hungry
norayo	no-ra-yo	Let's have fun, let's play
geuraeyo	geu-rae-yo	Okay, me too
noraebang	no-rae-bang	Song room, karaoke room
ibeonjumal	ee-bun-joo-mal	This weekend
eonjena	un-jae-na	Always, anytime
boreogayo	bo-ruh-ga-yo	Let's go see it
siksa	shik-sa	Meal, food
jigeum	jee-geum	Right now

Bar- and club-hopping

There are many weekend warriors in Korea who enjoy going from one bar to another until sunrise. You could start from the **itaewon** (*ee-tae-won*) area and end up near the **gangnam** (*gang-nam*) Station area, famous for their bars and clubs. **itaewon** is a shopping area popular among foreigners, but if you want a real taste of Korean nightlife, you may want to end up near **sinchon** (*shin-chon*) on a late Saturday night. **sinchon** is a very popular shopping and entertainment district among the young people, and you'll find many cafes, clubs and beer houses in that district. Due to its popularity with the young people, you'll have little problem finding people who speak English as well.

Giving and Receiving Invitations

Politeness and good manners go a long way in Korea, and of course, part of good manners is knowing how to invite other people as well as accept invitations. You also have to know how to respectfully decline an invitation if you can't attend. So you can navigate social situations with ease, the following sections provide the ins and outs of invitations — both respectably giving and accepting.

A Korean generally asks you more than once to attend something, even if you decline. The generous nature of most Koreans may seem like persistence to Western eyes, and it is generally a good idea to accept an invitation unless you absolutely cannot make it. If you decide not to attend, just make sure you decline consistently. It is considered bad manners to say you'll attend and not show up.

Getting something started

You can suggest something by using the phrase, **eottaeyo?** (*uh-ttae-yo?; how about it? or How is it?*). You can use this phrase when running an idea by someone, and it can also be used to solicit an opinion from someone. For example, one can say, "**nesie mannayo. eottaeyo?**"(*nae-shi-ae man-na-yo. uh-ttae-yo?; Let's meet at 4 o'clock, how about it?*). You can also hold a shirt or a dress up against you and ask, "**eottaeyo?**" translated, "How do you like it?" When suggesting something to do, you can say, "**uri noraebange gachi gayo. eottaeyo?**"(*oo-ree no-rae-bang-ae ga-chi ga-yo. uh-ttae-yo?; Let us go to a karaoke room. How about it?*).

If you want to agree to do something, try using **joayo** (*jo-a-yo; good, okay*). It's used when you agree to something, or when something particularly grabs your fancy. For example, you can take a drink from your glass and say, "**joayo!**" meaning, "It's good!" When someone invites you to an event, you can say, "**joayo. gasijyo** (*jo-a-yo. ga-shi-jyo; Okay. Let's go*)." **gayo**, and **gasijyo** all mean "Let's go." The word **gasijyo** is little more formal than **gayo**. You can use **gayo** in everyday setting, but you should always say **gasijyo** in a more formal setting, or when you are speaking to your senior. A common phrase that is used is **gachi gayo** (*ga-chi ga-yo*), or **gachi gasijyo** (*ga-chi ga-shi-jyo*), meaning, "Let's go together." "**uri yeonghwa boreo gachi gayo. eottaeyo?**"(*oo-ree young-hwa bo-ruh ga-chi ga-yo. uh-ttae-yo?*) is translated, "Let us go watch a movie together. How about it?"

Inviting your friends to your house

jip (*jeep*) is the Korean word for "house or home." More commonly, the phrase **uri jip** (*oo-ree jeep*) is used, which means, "our house". Another more polite form of our house is **jeohui jip** (*juh-hee jeep*). Use **jeohui jip** when you are speaking to someone your senior, or to your boss. This implies that you want to show them respect. If you want to invite someone over to your house, you can say, **uri jibe nolleo oseyo** (*oo-ree jee-bae nol-luh o-sae-yo*; please come over to our house; literal translation is come play at our house) or **jeohui jibe nolleo oseyo** (*juh-hee jee-bae nol-luh o-sae-yo*; please come over to our house, literal translation is come play at our house). If you want to invite someone over for a meal, you can say, "**uri jibe siksahareo oseyo**" (*oo-ree jee-bae shik-sa-ha-ruh o-sae-yo*).

If someone asks for you to come over, you can say, **joayo. jigeum gasijyo** (*jo-a-yo. jee-geum ga-shi-jyo*; That sounds good. Let's go right now). or **joayo. eonje galkkayo?** (*jo-a-yo. uh-jae gal-kka-yo*; Sure, when should I go?).

Talkin' the Talk

Tony invites Samantha to his house for dinner.

Tony: samantha ssi. eonje urijibe waseo jeoyeok gachi meogeoyo. eottaeyo?
samantha-sshi. un-jae oo-ree-jee-bae wa-suh juh-nyuk ga-chi muh-guh-yo. Uh-ttae-yo?
Samantha, come over and have dinner at my house sometime. How about it?

Samantha: eonjeyo? mwol mandeusilkkeoeyo?
un-jae-yo? mwol man-deu-shil kkuh-ae-yo?
When? What will you make?

Tony: geulsseyo. ajik gyeoljeongeun anhaenneundeyo. eotteon eumsigeul joahaseyo?
geul–ssae-yo. a-jik gyul-jung-eun an-haen-neun-dae-yo. uh-ttun-eum-shi-geul jo-a-ha-sae-yo?
Well, I haven't quite decided yet. What kind of food do you like?

Samantha: **jeoneun hanguk eumsigi jeil joayo. doenjang jjigye, bibimbap, tteokbokgi gateungeo.**
juh-neun han-goog-eum-shi-gi jae-il jo-a-yo. dwen-jang jji-gye, bee-bim-bap, ttuhk-bo-ki ga-teun-guh.
I like Korean food the best. Doenjang soup, mixed rice, spicy rice cakes and such.

Tony: **geureomyeon, naeil jeoe jibe oseyo. yeoseotsi jjeume. jega doenjang jjigyerang tteokbokgi masitge mandeureo deurilkkeyo.**
geu-ruh-myun nae-il juh-ae jee-bae o-sae-yo. yuh-suh-shi–jjeum-ae. jae-ga dwen-jang jji-gye-rang ttuhk-bok-gi ma-shi-gae man-deu-ruh deu-ril-kkae-yo.
In that case, come to my house tomorrow. Around six o'clock. I'll make you a delicious doenjang soup and spicy rice cakes.

Words to Know

uri jip	*oo-ree-jeep*	Our house, our home
jeohui jip	*juh-hee jeep*	Our house, our home (more polite)
eottaeyo	*uh-ttae-yo*	How about it
geulsseyo	*geul-ssae-yo*	Well, um
eumsik	*eum-shik*	Food
doenjangjjigye	*dwen-jang-jji-gae*	Soy bean paste soup with vegetables/seafood
bibimbap	*bee-bim-bap*	Rice mixed with various vegitables
tteokbokgi	*ttuhk-bok-ki*	Rice cake in chili paste
oseyo	*o-sae-yo*	Please come
jjeume	*jjeum-ae*	About
masitge	*ma-shi-gae*	Delicious, yummy

Fun & Games

Draw a line to match the English words to their Korean equivalents.

Next week	ojeon yeolsiban
10:30 am	jumal
Afternoon	ohu
Last month	jinandal
Monday	ohu ahopsi
Weekend	woryoil
9:00 pm	daeumju

Chapter 8

Enjoying Yourself: Recreation and Sports

In This Chapter

▶ Talking about your hobbies

▶ Exploring nature

▶ Talking about the arts

▶ Playing sports and games

Korean people are generally known for their industrious and hard-working nature. That in itself is hardly surprising, considering the country has made quite a turn around from a war-torn nation to an economic powerhouse in less than 50 years. Koreans work hard, but they play hard, too. And the Korean people choose to relax and have fun in several different ways. Koreans have many different **chwimi** (*chwee-mee;* hobbies), ranging from **eumak** (*eum-ak;* music) and **misul** (*mee-sool;* art), to **chukgu** (*chook-goo;* soccer) and **sanchaek** (*san-chaek;* a stroll). You may also find the younger people at nightclubs and **PC bang** (*PC* bang; PC room, cyber café), many of which are open all night.

To make the most of your time in Korea, try not just sharing your hobbies and favorite pastime with other Koreans, but also be sure to take part in some of their favorites as well. This chapter provides you with the info you need to not only discuss your interests, but to also engage in other activities that Koreans enjoy, which you may not be familiar with.

Naming Your Hobbies

Are you the kind of person that enjoys watching **deulsae** (*deul-sae;* wild birds)? Do you collect **inhyeong** (*een-hyung;* dolls)? Perhaps you like more physical activities, like **yagu** (*yah-goo;* baseball) or **nonggu** (*nong-goo;* basketball). Perhaps you like to sit and read a great **chaek** (*chaeg;* book). Whatever your hobby may be, the most important aspect is that you have **jaemi** (*jae-mee;* fun) while you're involved in your hobby. Otherwise, it's not a hobby, right? Having a **chwimi** (*chwee-mee;* hobby) is important in a person's well being, of course, and you'll find that if you share a hobby with another person, it's much easier to make a connection and speak with them.

Talkin' the Talk

Carl and Amy discuss their hobbies.

Carl: **amyssi. gunggeumhange inneundeyo.**
amy-sshi. goong-geum-han-gae in-neun-dae-yo.
Amy, I'm curious about something.

Amy: **ye. mureoboseyo.**
ye. moo-ruh-bo-sae-yo.
Yes. Go ahead and ask.

Carl: **chwimiga mueojyo? simsimhalttae mwo haseyo?**
chwee-mee-ga mwo-jyo? shim-shim-hal-ttae mwo-ha-sae-yo?
What are your hobbies? What do you do when you're bored?

Amy: **jeoyo? jeon eoryeoseulttae buteo upyoreul moaseoyo. carlssineunyo?**
juh-yo? juhn uh-ryuh-sseul-ttae-boo-tuh oo-pyo-reul mo-a-ssuh-yo. carl-sshi-neun-yo?
Me? I've collected stamps ever since I was little. And what about you, Carl?

Carl: **jeoneun eoryeoseulttae buteo undongeul joahae-seoyo. yosaeneun nonggureul mani hajyo.**
juh-neun uh-ryuh-sseul-ttae boo-tuh oon-dong-eul jo-a-hae-ssuh-yo. yo-sae-neun nong-goo-reul ma-nee ha-jyo.
I've liked physical exercise since little. Lately I've been playing a lot of basketball.

Carl: **upyo moeuneungeo waeroneun tto mwo joahaseyo?**
oo-pyo mo-eu-neun-guh wae-ro-neun tto mwuh jo-a-ha-sae-yo?
What else do you like to do besides collecting stamps?

Amy: **gongwoneuro sanchaekhareo gakkeum nagayo.**
gong-won-eu-ro san-chaeg-ha-ruh ga-kkeum-na-ga-yo.
I go for a walk in the park sometimes.

Carl: **eonje jeorang gachi gallaeyo?**
un-jae juh-rang ga-chi gal-lae-yo?
Would you like to go with me sometime?

Amy: **joayo. eonje gachi hanbeon gayo.**
jo-a-yo. un-jae ga-chi han-bun ga-yo.
Great. Let's go together sometime.

Words to Know

baegu	*bae-goo*	Volleyball
chaegikgi	*chae-gil-kki*	Reading books
chejo	*chae-jo*	Calisthenics
chukgu	*chook-goo*	Soccer
chwimi	*chwee-mee*	Hobbies
deungsan	*deung-san*	Mountain climbing
eoryeoseulttae	*uh-ryo-sseul-ttae*	Since little
eumakdeutgi	*eum-ak-deut-kki*	Listening to music
geurimgeurigi	*geu-rim-geu-ree-gee*	Drawing pictures
golpeu	*gol-peu*	Golf
gongwon	*gong-won*	Park
shaendeubol	*haen-deu-bol*	Handball
misik chukgu	*mee-sik chook-goo*	American football

mureoboseyo	moo-ruh-bo-sae-yo	Please ask me
nonggu	nong-goo	Basketball
peullut yeonju	peu-leut yuhn-joo	Playing flute
piano yeonju	pee-a-no yuhn-joo	Playing piano
sanchaek	san-chaek	Stroll
simsimhalttae	shim-shim-hal-ttae	When bored
sipjasu	ship-ja-soo	Cross stitch
suyeong	soo-young	Swimming
taegwondo	tae-gwon-do	Tae-kwon-do
takgu	tak-goo	Table tennis
undong	oon-dong	Exercise
upyo	oo-pyo	Stamps
yagu	ya-goo	Baseball
yosaeneun	yo-sae-neun	Now days, lately

Exploring Nature

Korea is very well known for its natural beauty. The eastern half of the peninsula, with its mountain range, has undisturbed **pokpo** (*pok-po;* waterfalls), peaks of **san** (*sahn;* mountains), dense **sup** (*soop;* forests), rare exotic **sae** (*sae;* birds) and **yasaeng dongmul** (*ya–saeng dong-mool;* wildlife) not seen anywhere else in the world. The western part of the peninsula is well known for the beautiful **haebyeon** (*hae-byun;* beaches), great spots for **naksi** (*nak-shi;* fishing), and thousands of little **seom** (*suhm;* island) to enjoy **baenori** (*bae-no-ree;* boating). The DMZ (demilitarized zone) is said to have rare species of flora and fauna, and is even rumored to have a tiger or two! This section provides you with the info you need to wander the wonderful nature that Korea has in store for you.

Talkin' the Talk

 Jason buys train tickets to see the country.

Jason: **annyeonghaseyo. busaneuro ganeun gichapyo han-jang juseyo.**
an-nyoung-ha-sae-yo. boo-san-eu-ro ga-neun gee-cha-pyo han-jang joo-sae-yo.
Hello. Can I have one ticket to Busan please.

Attendant: **ye. myeotsie tteonaneun gichareul tasigetseumnika?**
ye. myuh-shi-ae ttuh-na-neun gee-cha-reul ta-shi-gae-ssum-ni-kka?
Yes. What time would you like the train you're on to depart at?

Jason: **sesibane tteonaneun gichapyo hanjang juseyo. gagi-jeone siksahago gallaeyo. yeogi geuncheoe masit-neun sikdang iseoyo?**
sae-shi-ban-ae ttuh-na-neun gee-cha-pyo han-jang joo-sae-yo. ga-gee-jun-ae shik-sa-ha-go gal-lae-yo. yuh-gi geun-chuh-ae ma-shin-neun shik-dang ee-ssuh-yo?
I would like the ticket for the train leaving at three thirty. I'd like to eat before I leave. Is there a good restaurant nearby?

Attendant: **ye. I gichayeok yeopeinneun junggukjibi yorireul jal-handago deureotseumnida.**
ye. ee gee-cha-yuk yuh-pae-in-neun joong-gook-jee-bee yo-ree-reul jal-han-da-go deu-ruh-sseum-ni-da.
Yes, I heard that the Chinese restaurant next to the train station has excellent food.

Jason: **gomawoyo. eolmaeyo?**
go-ma-wo-yo. ul-ma-ae-yo?
Thank you. How much is it?

Attendant: **sammanwon imnida.**
sam-man-won im-ni-da.
That will be 30000 won.

Jason: **yeogi iseoyo. gomawoyo.**
yuh-gi ee-ssuh-yo. go-ma-wo-yo.
Here it is. Thank you.

Words to Know

bada	bada	Sea
deulpan	deul-pan	Fields
gang	gang	River
gichapyo	gee-cha-pyo	Train ticket
haebyeon	hae-byun	Beach
hosu	ho-soo	Lake
myeotsi	myeot-shi	What time
pokpo	pok-po	Waterfalls
san	sahn	Mountain
sup	soop	Forests
tteonaneun	ttuh-na-neun	Leaving
yeonmot	yuhnmot	Pond

Admiring and discovering the landscape

A great way of enjoying the landscape of Korea is to take a train ride around the peninsula. As a matter of fact, a train ride from Seoul to Busan will give you a pretty good view of the rest of the **nara** (*na-ra;* country) because you must travel from the north-western part of South Korea to the south-eastern corner. As you travel, you slowly move away from the hyper-modern, **dosi** (*do-shi;* urban) cityscape to the countryside, with majestic **san** (*sahn;* mountains) and pristine **bada** (*ba-da;* beaches). Different parts of the country offer different scenery of course, some known for their **areumdaum** (*a-reum-da-oom;* beauty) during the summer, some during autumn, and so on.

Different areas of Korea are well known for different types of scenery. The Seoul metropolitan area is obviously well known for its amazing cityscape, but if you want to see the natural beauty of Korea, you'll have to travel a bit outside of the city. The eastern side of the peninsula is well known for its beautiful mountains and **sup** (*soop;* forests), the western side of the peninsula is well known for its little islets and **seom** (*suhm;* islands). The south eastern part of the peninsula is known for its well preserved historical artifacts and monuments. Don't be afraid to travel outside of the city. You will find the locals to be very warm, inviting, and very helpful.

Korean seasons

Korea lies in the temperate zone and has four clearly defined, distinct seasons. The monsoon season brings quite a bit of rainfall between late June and mid-July, and the **yeoreum** (*yuh-reum;* summers) are quite hot and humid. The winters are quite cold and there is a fair amount of **nun** (noon; snow). **gaeul** (*ga-eul;* fall) months are probably the most pleasant, as the continental winds bring cool, clear, and dry weather. When the leaves turn, the whole country turns red, orange, and vibrant yellow to create a beautiful panorama of fall colors. **bom** (*bom;* spring) is also very nice, as the weather is quite pleasant and mostly sunny days are expected from March to May. Each season has its own beauty, of course, spring with flowers blooming, summer with its warm pleasant days (however it can get quite hot and muggy in summer), fall and its beautiful foliage, and **gyeoul** (*gyuh-ool;* winter) and its white calm. Each season can be enjoyable for its own beauty.

Talkin' the Talk

Carol and Diane discuss the seasons in Korea.

Diane: **carolssi, gaeuri doemyeon uri nagyeop gugyeong-hareo sane gayo.**
carol-sshi ga-eul-ee dwae-myun oo-ree na-gyup goo-gyoung-ha-ruh sa-nae ga-yo.
Carol, let's go to the mountain and see the leaves change color when autumn comes.

Carol: **joeun saenggagieyo. gyeongchiga cham meosit-seulkkeoeyo. gyeoureuneun nungugyeonghareo gachi gayo.**
jo-eun saeng-ga-gee-ae-yo. gyoung-chi-ga cham muh-shi-sseul-gguh-ae-yo. gyuh-oo-rae-neun noon-goo-gyoung-ha-ruh ga-chi ga-yo.
That's a good idea. The scenery will be beautiful. Let's go together to look at the snow in the winter time, also.

Diane: **joayo. uri yaksokhaeyo. gaeureuneun nagyeop gugyeong, gyeoureuneun nungugyeong. eottaeyo?**
jo-a-yo. oo-ree yak-sok-hae-yo. ga-eul-ae-neun na-gyup goo-gyoung, gyuh-oo-rae-neun noon-goo-gyoung. uh-ttae-yo?

Good. Let's make a promise together. Go see the leaves turning in the fall, see the snow in the winter time. How about it?

Carol: **joayo. geureom bomirang yeoreumeneun mweo hajyo?**
jo-a-yo. geu-rum bo-mee-rang yuh-reum-ae-neun mwuh-ha-jyo?
Good. Then what do we do during spring and summer?

Diane: **gandanhaeyo. bomeneun kkot gugyeonghareo gago, yeoreumeneun haesuyokjange gachi gayo.**
gan-dan-hae-yo. bom-ae-neun kkot goo-gyung-ha-ruh ga-go, yuh-reum-ae-neun hae-soo-yok-jang-ae ga-chi ga-yo.
It's simple. During spring, we go watch the flowers, during summer, we go to the beach together.

Carol: **geuraeyo. geureom haesuyokjangeun eonje gallaeyo?**
geu-rae-yo. geu-rum hae-soo-yok-jang-eun un-jae gal-lae-yo?
Let's. When should we go to the beach then?

Diane: **ibeon jumareneun eottaeyo?**
ee-bun joo-ma-rae-eun uh-ttae-yo?
How about this weekend?

Carol: **ibeon jumal jochyo. geureom toyoil achime bwayo.**
ee-bun joo-mal jo-chyo. geu-rum to-yo-il a-chim-ae bwa-yo.
This weekend's good. I'll see you Saturday morning, then.

Words to Know

achim	a-chim	Morning, a.m.
bom	bom	Spring
gyejeol	gye-juhl	Seasons
gaeul	ga-eul	Fall, autumn

gyeoul	*gyuh-ool*	Winter
haesuyok swimming	*hae-soo-yok*	Going to the beach,
kkotgugyeong	*kkot-goo-gyoung*	Watching flowers
nagyeopgugyeong	*na-gyup-goo-gyoung*	Watching leaves turn
nungugyeong	*noon-goo-gyoung*	Watching snow
nyeoreum	*yuhreum*	Summer
ohu	*o-who*	Afternoon, p.m.

Talking about the Arts

Recently, **hallyu** (*han-nyu*), or the "Korean Wave" has heightened the interest the world has in Korean arts and **munhwasenghwal** (*moon-hwa-saeng-hwal;* entertainment). However, Korea also boasts of a rich history of culture and arts that can be enjoyed in many different places. The various **bangmulgwan** (*bak-mool-gwan;* museums) throughout the country catalog the arts and crafts of the Korean people throughout **yeoksa** (*yuhk-sa;* history) of course, but there are street festivals, musicians, and artists that embody this tradition and perform daily on the streets as well. In some of the historical and folk villages, you can still see traditional **eumak** (*eum-ak;* music) and **chum** (*choom;* dance) performed, and in various **gongwon** (*gong-won;* parks) and pavilions, more modern musicians and artists are showcased. You can find many galleries that house valuable **geurim** (*geu-rim;* paintings) from Korea's history as well as street artists that sell their wares at open-air markets and street festivals as well.

Korea has its own unique types of music. Many traditional sounds can be heard in pavilions and festivals nation wide. However, Korean music, popular music, to be exact, has been growing and evolving into a powerhouse of entertainment by its own right. Largely responsible for **hallyu** (*han-nyu;* Korean wave), Korean-pop and the stars who perform them have received international recognition and have achieved international stardom through the Korean Wave. Many celebrities in Korea enjoy fame in other countries like Taiwan, **jungguk** (*joong-gook;* China), **ilbon** (*il-bon;* Japan), and Thailand to name a few.

The term *hannyu* or Korean wave is a new term that Koreans and other Asian countries kind of "made up." It means any kind of music, movies, drama, etc., that are "made in Korea" (for example, sang by Korean artists in Korean). People from China, Japan, Thailand, etc., are learning Korean songs in Korean and also coming to Korea to see the live concerts of the singers. If the singer stars in a movie, they will definitely go and see that movie no matter what the cost. And the fans will do anything to get the star/singer's autograph. Korean wave is huge in Korea.

Playing Sports and Gaming

Koreans enjoy sports of many kind. One sport that has risen in popularity since Korea and Japan jointly hosted the World cup in 2002 is **chukgu** (*chook-goo;* soccer). Koreans also enjoy **yagu** (*ya-goo;* baseball), **nonggu** (*nong-goo;* basketball), and many other sports, like **golpeu** (*gol-peu;* golf). Tae kwon do is the national martial art, and a sporting version of the discipline has been popular for some time now as well. Koreans also excel in archery and are active participants in international sports competitions like the Olympics, the Asian Games, the World Cup, and so on. **ssireum** (*sshi-reum;* wrestling) is also big in Korea, which is a traditional Korean wrestling. The champion is given the title **cheonhajangsa** (*chun-ha-jang-sa*), which means, "the strongest under the heaven."

Playing games

Korea is known for its advances in computer and electronics technology, and it's no surprise that gaming culture has developed accordingly. There are televised **gyeonggi** (*gyoung-gee;* tournaments) of **geim** (*gae-im;* games) and gamers achieve celebratory status in some circles. Many Koreans take their gaming quite seriously and some have even turned it into a **jigeop** (*jee-gup;* career). The computer game Starcraft, in particular, has a professional competition circuit, and two major game channels run a Starleague, which is viewed by millions of fans. They have garnered support and sponsorships from major Korean corporations and they participate in World Cyber Games **maenyeon** (*mae-nyeon;* annually).

Gaming at a Korean PC bang

PC bang, literally translated "PC room," is a cyber café. It resembles an internet café, which is easy enough to find in any metropolitan area. It's a place where people gather to play multiplayer games online. It has become a cultural phenomenon in Korea with some controversy. It seems that people

jungdok (*joong-dok;* addicted) to gaming will often forget to drink **mul** (*mool;* water) or eat **eumsik** (*eum-shik;* food) and end up damaging their **geongang** (*guhn-gang;* health) sometimes, with severe consequences. The gaming industry is indeed a huge industry, poised to surpass Hollywood, and one can find a **PC bang** in just about every corner in a large metropolitan area. These rooms are usually filled at all times of the day and are very **ingi** (*in-gee;* popular) spots for **jeolmeun saram** (*juhl-meun sa-ram;* young people) to hang out. If you have a particular knack for computer games, or if you have a desire to be humbled by a pre-pubescent Korean kid, I recommend you visit one of these places and engage one of them in an online game of sorts.

Fun & Games

Below are few hobbies people like to do. Please write the Korean word for each of the hobbies illustrated below.

A.

B.

C.

D.

E.

A. _____
B. _____
C. _____
D. _____
E. _____

Chapter 9

Making Connections: Phone, Mail, Fax, and Internet

In This Chapter

▶ Making a phone call

▶ Sending a fax or a letter

▶ Getting online

*J*eonhwa (*juhn-hwa;* telephones) and the Internet have become a part of the daily grind. Whether you need to make a quick call, or satisfy your **imeil** (*ee-mae-il;* e-mail) **jungdok** (*joong-dok;* addiction) here are a few lines to help you get in **yeollak** (*yuhl-lak;* contact) with your friend, that **sojunghan saram** (*so-joong-han-sa-ram;* special person) of yours, or with people related to your upcoming business deal.

Although we are so familiar with getting connected with telephones or e-mails, there are also the "old ways" of getting connected: snail mails and faxes. For those of you who are more familiar with the old ways, I will also teach to how to get connected using these means. I personally get sentimental with old ways, and prefer writing to my loved ones a snail mail. When I receive one of these, that really makes my day!!

Phoning Made Easy

When Koreans pick up the phone they'll almost always answer with **yeoboseyo** (*yuh-bo-sae-yo;* Who is this?) You should, too. If your pronunciation is good enough, you're bound to surprise a few of your friends in the process. You might occasionally hear people use the formal greeting **annyeonghasimnikka** (*an-nyoung-ha-shim-ni-kka;* Hello/How are you?) after **yeoboseyo** to begin a phone conversation, but it's usually used in a telemarketer/sales representative kind of way.

In this section, I assume that you're not going to try and sell something or close a multimillion-dollar contract deal in Korean (Therefore, does not need the formal polite form of Korean.). Instead, I will show you how to get in touch with someone that you need to talk to, leave them a message or simply leave a callback number, send a fax, send a letter or a postcard from the post office, or how to find PC rooms to "surf the net."

Finding a phone

If you don't have access to a phone at the moment, look over these phrases to ask where a public phone is (please look at Chapter 12 if you need help with directions), or ask your host if you can use their phone.

> **geuncheoae ssuelssuinneun jeonhwagiga eodi iseoyo?** (*geun-chuh-ae sseul-soo-in-neun juhn-hwa-gee-ga uh-dee ee-ssuh-yo?;* Is there a phone I can use around here?)

> **geuncheoae goongjung jeonhwagiga eodi iseoyo?** (*geun-chuh-ae gong-joong-juhn-hwa-gee-ga uh-dee ee-ssuh-yo;* Where is there a pay phone around here?)

> **jeonhwa hantong jom sseodo doelkkayo?** (*juhn-hwa han-tong jom ssuh-do dwel-kka-yo;* Can I please make a phone call?)

This expression can be used when you have to make a call on your own phone, but it can also be used to ask if you can use someone else's phone. Asking someone if you can make a phone call using your own phone might seem really weird, but if you are with someone and you need to make a call, it's better to ask them for permission. This is the polite thing to do in Korea. Similar situations in U.S. might be something like this. You are in a middle of a conversation with someone, and you just remembered that you needed to make a really important phone call. Then you'll ask the person sitting next to you, "Do you mind if I make a quick call? or Can I please make a quick phone call?" In those cases, you need to say:

> **jeonhwa hantong jom haedo doelkkayo?** (*juhn-hwa han-tong jom hae-do dwel-kka-yo;* May I please make a phone call?)

Making the call

Korean phone numbers can be seven to eight digits long, and are preceded by a two- to three-digit **jiyeok beonho** (*jee-yuhk-bun-ho;* area code). **Hyudaepon** (*hyoo-dae-pon:* cellular phones. Literal translation: Carry around phone.) or haendeupon (*han-deu-pon;* cellular phone. Literal translation: Hand phone, that is phone for your hand) in Korea have separate **jiyeok beonho** from regional area codes such as 011, 010, and 016. If you can't quite figure out how to use the phone, you might want to ask your host, **jeonhwareul eottoeoke georeoyo?** (*juhn-hwa-reul uh-ttuh-kae guh-ruh-yo;* How do I make a phone call?) or **oebu jeonhwaneun eottoke georeoyo?** (*wae-boo-juhn-hwa-neun uh-ttuh-kae guh-ruh-yo;* How do I make phone calls to external numbers?) When you hear a dial tone and hear another voice at the end of the line, you might hear one of the following lines if the other person is unable to pick up the phone:

> **jamsihue dasi georeojuseyo.** (*jam-shi who-ae da-shi guh-ruh joo-sae-yo;* Please call me back little later.)

> **yeoboseyo, [some word] eyo/ [some word] ieyo.** (*yuh-bo-sae-yo, [some word] ae-yo/ [some word] ee-ae-yo;* Hello, this is [some word] .) Substitute [some word] with your name/title. **[some word] eyo** (*[some word] ae-yo;* It's [some word]) for names ending with vowels, **[some word] ieyo** (*[some word] ee-ae-yo;* It's [some word]) for names ending with consonant. For example: **yeobosaeyo, Rusaeyo.** (*yuh-bo-sae-yo, Rusa-ae-yo;* Hello, this is Rusa.)

> **yeoboseyo, jasonieyo.** (*yuh-bo-sae-yo, Jason-ee-ae-yo;* Hello, this is Jason.)

> **sillyejiman nuguseyo?** (*shil-lae-ji-man-noo-goo-sae-yo;* I beg your pardon, but who is this?)

> **jal andeullyeoyo.** (*jal-an-deul-lyuh-yo;* I can't hear you well.)

> **dasi malsseum hae juseyo.** (*da-shi mal-sseum-hae-joo-sae-yo;* Could you say that again?)

> **cheoncheonhi malsseumhae juseyo.** (*chun-chun-hee-mal-sseum-hae-joo-sae-yo;* Please speak slowly.)

> **joesonghaeyo. jega beonhoeul jalmot georeoseoyo.** (*jwae-song-hae-yo. jae-ga bun-ho-reul jal-mot guh-ruh-ssuh-yo;* I'm sorry. I dialed the wrong number.)

Talkin' the Talk

Will Rogers is at a shopping mall trying to make a call to his brother-in-law, Mr. Kim. He is looking for a phone.

Will:	**jeonhwa hantong jom sseodo doelkkayo?**
	juhn-hwa han-tong jom ssuh-do dwel- kka-yo?
	May I please make a phone call?

Sales clerk: **ye, i jeonhwareul sseuseyo.**
ye, ee-juhn-hwa-reul sseu-sae-yo.
Yes, you can use this phone.

Will: **oebu jeonhwaneun eotteoke georeoyo**
whae-boo-juhn-hwa-neun uh-ttuh-kae guh-ruh-yo?
How do I make phone calls to external numbers?

Sales clerk: **tonghwaeumi deullisimyeon gubeoneul nureun-daeum tonghwa hasigo sipeusin beonhoreul nureuseyo.**
tong-hwa-eum-ee deul-li-shi-myeon goo-bun-eul noo-reun-da-eum, tong-hwa-ha-go shi-peu-shin bun-ho-reul noo-reu-sae-yo.
After you hear the dial tone, press 9; then dial the number you want to call.

Will: **a, gamsahamnida.**
a, gam-sa-ham-ni-da.
Ah, thank you.

Will dials the number, and Mr. Kim picks up the phone.

Mr. Kim: **yeoboseyo.**
yuh-bo-sae-yo.
Hello.

Will: **yeoboseyo, Will Rodgers imnida. Jigeum heonhwa tonghwaga ganeunghaseyo?**
yuh-bo-sae-yo, Will Rodgers-im-ni-da. jee-geum juhn-hwa-tong-hwa-ga ga-neung-ha-sae-yo?
Hello, this is Will Rogers. Can you take a call right now?

Mr. Kim: **jigeum jeonhwareul batgiga jom gollanhaeyo. jamsi hue jega dasi geolkkeyo.**
jee-geum juhn-hwa-reul bat-gee-ga jom gol-lan-hae-yo. jam-shi who-ae jae-ga da-shi guhl-kkae-yo.
I'm a bit preoccupied at the moment. I'll call you back in a little bit.

Will: **a ye, annyeonghi gyeseyo.**
a ye, an-nyoung-hi gye-sae-yo.
Oh, okay, have a nice day.

Words to Know

gukjejeonhwa	guk-jae-juhn-hwa	International call
gyohwanwon	gyo-hwan-won	Operator
jamkkanman gidariseyo	jam-kkan-man gee-da-ree-sae-yo	Just a moment please.
jeonhwa	juhn-hwa	Telephone
jeonhwa hantong	juhn-hwa-han-tong	One call
jigeumeun jom bappayo	jee-geum-eun jom ba-ppa-yo	I'm little busy right now.
jiktongjeonhwa	jik-tong-juhn-hwa	Direct call
keuge malsseumhae juseyo	keu-gae-mal-sseum-hae-joo-sae-yo	Please speak louder.
nugureul chajeuseyo?	noo-goo-reul cha-jeu-sae-yo	Who are you looking for?
susinjabudam jeonhwa	soo-shin-ja-boo-dam juhn-hwa	Collect call
teullinbeonho	teul-lin-bun-ho	Wrong number
yeoboseyo	yuh-bo-sae-yo	Hello

Asking for someone

If the person who **daedap** (*dae-dap;* answered) the phone isn't the person you need to talk to, you need to ask for your party. The way that you ask for a person differs, depending on who you're **malhada** (*mal-ha-da;* talking) to and who you're asking for. I organized these sections according to a few possible scenarios you may encounter.

Calling business contacts

When you are calling business contacts, it is best to use the formal polite forms, rather than the informal polite forms you use in **maeil** (*mae-il;* everyday) conversation. If you do this, Koreans will be very impressed with your understanding of their culture; respecting your business **sangdae** (*sang-dae;* partner) is a big thing in Korea. Therefore, the following section will use the formal polite forms.

Koreans use two words to show whether or not someone is there. They are **iseoyo** (*ee-ssuh-yo;* He/she is here. Informal polite) and **gyesimnida** (*gye-shim-ni-da;* He/she is here. Formal polite). **iseoyo** is an informal polite way of saying someone is there whereas **gyesimnida** is an formal polite honorific way of saying that someone is there. For example, you'd use **gyesimnida**, when you're talking about someone in a higher position in your company and your grandparents and **iseoyo**, when you're talking about a peer, sibling, or a subordinate.

Some phrases which might be useful are as follows. You can replace "<u>Smith</u>" with the name/job title of the person you are looking for.

<u>smith</u>ssikkeseo jarie gyesimnikka? (*<u>Smith</u>-sshi-kke-suh ja-ree-ae gye-shim-ni-kka;* Is Smith there? Literal translation: Is Smith at his place?)

If Smith is not present:

aniyo, <u>smith</u>ssikkeseo jarie angyesimnida. (*a-ni-yo, <u>Smith</u>-sshi-kke-suh ja-ree-ae an-gye-shim-ni-da;* No, Smith is not here. Literal translation: Smith is not at his place.)

najunge jeonhwa georeo jusipsiyo. (*na-jung-ae juhn-hwa guh-ruh joo-ship-shi-yo;* Please call later.)

If Smith is present:

ye, <u>smith</u>ssikkeseo jarie gyesimnida. (*ye, Smith-sshi-kkae-suh ja-ree-ae gye-shim-ni-da;* Yes, Smith is here.)

jigeum bakkwo deurilkkayo? (*jee-geum ba-kkwo deu-ril-kka-yo;* Do you want me to put Smith on the phone now?)

Calling acquaintances at home

Calling your friends, classmates, and general acquaintances is pretty simple in Korean. Basically you make a call and ask **[some word] iseoyo?** ([some word] *ee-ssuh-yo;* Is [some word] there?). For example, **aliceiseoyo?** (*Alice-ee-ssuh-yo;* Is Alice there?). However, when you are calling for your teachers, Professors, or grandparents (basically someone older than you), it's a little different. You want to ask using **[some word] gyeseyo?** (*[some word] gye-sae-yo;* Is [some word] there?). For example, **harabeoji gyeseyo?** (*ha-ra-buh-ji gye-sae-yo;* Is grandfather there?).

Usual answers to these questions would be: **ye, iseoyo** (*ye, ee-ssuh-yo;* yes, he/she is here) or **aniyo, eopseoyo** (*a-ni-yo, uhp-ssuh-yo;* no, he/she is not here) and **ye, gyeseyo** (*ye, gye-sae-yo;* yes, he/she is here) or **aniyo, angyeseyo** (*a-ni-yo, an-gye-sae-yo;* no, he/she is not here). **gyeseyo** is little more respectful than **iseoyo**. But in most instances, **iseoyo** is fine.

It might further help you to know that **jip** (*jeep*) and **daeg** (*daeg*) both mean *house;* however, you use **daeg** when you want to show more respect toward the person you are talking about or talking to. Usually **daeg** is used when the person you are talking to or talking about has seniority over you. For example, grandparents, professors and teachers.

Leaving a message

If the person that you wanted to talk to isn't there, you might want to leave a message so that they can get back to you. When you are leaving any kind of a message, either on an answering machine or with someone else, you need to make sure that the message is very clear. Otherwise, the person you have left the message for, will not know what to do.

Leaving messages at businesses

Please be very clear when leaving a message for someone at a business setting. Also, you need to make sure that you are using formal polite form of Korean. Some useful phrases are:

> **meseji jeonhae deurilkkayo?** (*mae-sae-jee juhn-hae-deu-ril-kka-yo;* Do you want me to take a message?)

> **aniyo, gwaenchansseumnida.** (*a-ni-yo, gwaen-chan-sseum-ni-da;* No, that's all right.)

> **najunge dasi yeollakhagetseumnida.** (*na-jung-ae da-shi yuhl-lak-ha-get-sseum-ni-da;* I'll call again later.)

> **meseji namgyeodo doegetseumnikka?** (*mae-sae-jee nam-gyuh-do dwae-get-sseum-ni-kka;* Would it be all right if I leave a message?)

> **jega jeonhwa haeseotdago jeonhaejusipsiyo.** (*jae-ga juhn-hwa hae-ssuh-da-go juhn-hae-joo-ship-shi-yo;* Please say that I called.)

Leaving messages at someone's home

When leaving a message at someone's home, just make sure to be very polite. Remember, Koreans are very big on being polite and respectful.

> **mesejireul namgyeodo doelkkayo?** (*mae-sae-jee-reul nam-gyuh-do dwel-kka-yo;* May I leave a message?)

> **jega jeonhwa haeseotdago jeonhaejuseyo.** (*jae-ga juhn-hwa hae-ssuh-da-go juhn-hae-joo-sae-yo;* Could you please tell [some word] that I called?)

> **je yeollakcheoga [some word] imnida.** (*jae yuhl-lak-chuh-ga [some word] im-ni-da;* I can be reached at [some word].)

> **Je jeonhwabeonhoga imnida.** (jae-juhn-hwa-bun-bo-ga [some word] im-ni-da; My phone number is [some word].)

seonghami eotteoke doeseyo? (*suhng-ham-ee uh-ttuh-kae dwae-sae-yo;* What is your name?)

seonghamreul dasihanbeon bulleojuseyo. (*suhng-ham-eul da-shi han-bun bul-luh-joo-sae-yo;* Could you tell me your name again?)

yeol-lak-cheo/jeonhwabeonhoreul dasi hanbeon bulleojuseyo. (*yuhl-lak-chuh/juhn-hwa-bun-ho-reul da-shi-han-bun bul-luh-joo-sae-yo;* Could you please repeat your contact information/phone number for me?)

Leaving a recorded message

If you don't feel like leaving an awkward silence on someone's voice mail or answering machine, try using the following phrases:

annyeonghaseyo [some word] imnida. (*an-nyoung-ha-sae-yo, [some word] im-ni-da;* Hello, this is [some word].) substitute [some word] for your name.

[some word] euro yeollakhae juseyo. (*[some word] eu-ro yuhl-lak-hae-joo-sae-yo;* Please contact me at [some word]). Substitute [some word] for your contact information, usually a phone number.

Jega dasi yeollakdeurilkkeyo. (*jae-ga da-shi yuhl-lak-deu-ril-kke-yo;* I'll contact you again later.)

Talkin' the Talk

 Greg Moore decides to call Ms. Han, a close friend, at her home, but Ms. Han's daughter, Judy, picks up the phone. Greg asks Judy to put her mother on the line.

Greg:	**yeoboseyo?** *yuh-bo-sae-yo?* Hello?
Judy:	**yeoboseyo? nuguseyo?** *yuh-bo-sae-yo? noo-goo-sae-yo?* Hello? Who's this?
Greg:	**gregeyo, eomeoni jibe gyeseyo?** *greg-ae-yo, uh-muh-ni jee-bae gye-sae-yo?* Oh, is this Judy? I'm your mom's friend Greg. Is your mother home?
Judy:	**ye, gyeseyo.** *ye, gye-sae-yo.* Yes, my mom's home.

Greg: **geureom eomeoni jom bakkwojuseyo.**
geu-reom uh-muh-ni-jom bak-kwo-joo-sae-yo.
Oh, really? Could you put your mom on the line for me?

Judy: **ye. jamkkanman gidariseyo.**
ye. jam-kkan-man gee-da-ree-sae-yo.
Yes. Please hold on.

Words to Know

angyeseyo	*an-gye-sae-yo*	[some word] is not here (formal polite)
bakkwojuseyo	*ba-kkwo-joo-sae-yo*	Please put [some word] on the phone
bbyeongwon	*byoung-won*	Hospital
eopseoyo	*uhp-ssuh-yo*	[some word] is not here (informal polite)
gyeseyo	*gye-sae-yo*	[some word] is here (formal polite)
isseoyo	*ee-ssuh-yo*	[some word] is here (informal polite)
jamkkanman gidariseyo	*jam-kkan-han gee-da-ree-sae-yo*	Please hold on/ please wait
jip	*jeep*	House/home
nuguseuo	*noo-goo-sae-yo*	Who's this?
sijang	*shi-jang*	MarketSending a Letter or Postcard

Nobody likes waiting in long lines at post offices, and few people like making other people wait. When you go to the post office, it pays to know a few phrases to make everything go smoothly. If you want to send a **pyeonji** (*pyuhn-jee;* letter) or a **yeopseo** (*yuhp-ssuh;* postcard), use the phrases described in the following sections to get in and out of the **ucheguk** (*oo-chae-goog;* post office).

Buying stamps

If you want to buy some **upyo** (*oo-pyo;* stamps) for your parcel but don't know how many stamps you need, ask:

> **igeol [some word] ro bonaego sipeunde, upyoreul eolma eochireul buchyeoyahaeyo?** (*ee-geol [some word] ro bo-nae-go shi-peun-dae, oo-pyo-reul uhl-ma uh-chi-reul boo-chuh-ya-hae-yo;* I want to ship this off to [some word], how much in stamps do I need?). Substitute [some word] with the place you want to send parcel/letter/postcard.

Once you hear the amount, you can say:

> **[some word] won eochi upyoreul juseyo.** ([some word] *won uh-chi oo-pyo-reul joo-sae-yo;* Please give me [some word] 's worth of stamps.)

Asking for special services

If you need to send anything via express certified mail or whatnot, the following phrases may come in handy:

> **i soporeul [some word] ro buchineunde eolmaeyo?** (*ee-so-po-reul [some word] ro boo-chi-neun-dae uhl-ma-ae-yo?* (How much would it cost to ship this via [some word]?)

> **i soporeul [some word] ro buchyeojuseyo.** (*ee-so-po-reul [some word] ro boo-chuh-joo-sae-yo;* Please send this package for me via.)

You can fill in the blanks above with the following methods of shipment:

> **gajang ssan upyeon** (ga-jang ssan oo-pyeon; cheapest mail)

> **gajang ppareun upyeon** (ga-jang ppa-reun oo-pyeon: fastest mail)

> **hanggong upyeon** (hang-gong oo-pyeon; air mail)

> **jisang upyeon** (jee-sang oo-pyeon; surface mail)

> **deunggi upyeon** (deung-gee oo-pyeon; registered mail)

And you may need to know the following phrases:

> **Bonaeneuni jusoga mwoeyo** (*bo-nae-neun-ee joo-so-ga mwo-ae-yo;* What is the sender's address?)

> **Banneuni jusoga mwoeyo** (*ban-neun-ee joo-so-ga mwo-ae-yo;* What is the recipient's address?)

Sending a Fax

If you need to fax something but don't have a fax machine handy, most hotels and office-supply stores in Korea will let you send a fax for a fee: sometimes reasonable, sometimes not so reasonable. Walk up to the desk and say:

> **yeogiseo paekseureul bonaelsu iseoyo?** (*yuh-gi-suh pek-sseu-reul bo-nael-soo-ee-ssuh-yo;* Is it possible to send a fax from here?)

They might say **yeogiseoneun paekseureul mot bonaeyo** (*yuh-gi-suh-neun pek-sseu-reul mot bo-nae-yo;* You can't send a fax from here), in which case you'll have to look for another place. But if they say **ye** (*ye:* yes), they'll most likely point you over to **chaeksang** (*chaeg-sang;* desk) or a **kaunteo** (*ka-oo-tuh;* counter) that takes care of faxes.

The assistant or clerk will almost always ask you for a number, so do yourself a favor and write it down on a piece of paper before you go so you can coolly hand over the number. Even if sending the fax is important, you might want to find out the price *before* you get charged an arm and a leg by asking **paekseureul i beonhoro bonaego sipeunde, bonaeneunde eolmayeyo?** (*paek-sseu-reul ee-bun-ho-ro bo-nae-go-shi-peun-dae, bo-nae-neun-dae uhl-ma-ae-yo;* I want to send the fax to this number. How much will it cost?)

It's a good idea to inform the recipients that you are faxing them some material by saying **jaryoreul got paekseuro bonae deurigetseumnida.** (*ja-ryo-reul got pek-sseu-ro bo-nae-deu-ree-get-sseum-ni-da;*) I'll be sending some material by fax in a moment.)

Looking for an Internet Connection

Korea is an Internet junkie's dream come true. You can find an incredibly high density of PC rooms per square block in Korea, all equipped with excellent network connection speeds. Usually each of these **PC bang** (*PC-bang;* PC rooms) charge about one or two dollars by the hour, but if you're at a hotel or a ritzy part of town, you'll be charged an absurd price per hour, so make sure to ask **eolma** (*uhl-ma;* how much) it is.

There are many hundreds and thousands of PC rooms in Korea. PC rooms are rooms full of state of the art PC's (at least 20 to 30 PC's per room) that all have extremely high speed Internet connection. Usually they are even highly populated around universities to enable students to do their work and "play." You can just walk in, pay per hour usage (usually really cheap) and check your e-mails or surf the net to kill time before your date.

You can find a PC room by asking: **geuncheoe pisibangi eodie iseoyo?** (*geun-chuh-ae pee-see-bang-ee uh-dee-ae ee-ssuh-yo;* Is there a PC room nearby?)

If you want to know how to ask for directions, look at Chapter 12 for further reference.

But don't forget to find out what the price is first. Just ask: **sigandang yogeumi eolmaeyo?** (*shi-gan-dang yo-geum-ee uhl-ma-ae-yo;* How much is the price per hour?)

Often, PC rooms have numbers above the computers so that they can track how long you've used the computer. If the assistant wants to tell you to sit at some particular number, he or she might say:

[some word] beon jarieseo keompyuteoreul sseuseyo. (*[some word] bun ja-ree-ae-suh keom-pyu-tuh-reul sseu-se-yo;* Please use computer number [some word].)

Talkin' the Talk

Sean is in Seoul, looking for a computer so he can check his email and play some games.

Sean: geuncheoe pisibangi eodie iseoyo?
geun-chuh-ae pee-see-bang-ee uh-dee-ae ee-ssuh-yo?
Is there a PC room around here?

Stranger: jeo jjoge hana iseoyo
juh-jjok-gae ha-na ee-ssuh-yo.
There's one over there.

Sean walks over to the PC room, which looks full, and approaches the attendant.

Sean: jigeum bin jari iseoyo?
jee-geum been-ja-ree ee-ssuh-yo?
Do you have an empty seat now?

Attendant: **ye, sip chil beon keompyuteoga jigeum biyeo iseoyo.**
Jeo jjoge iseoyo.
*ye, ship chil bun keom-pyu-tuh-ga jee-geum bee-yuh
ee-ssuh-yo. juh-jjo-gae ee-ssuh-yo.*
Yes, seat seventeen 17 is empty. It's over there.

Sean: **cham, yeogineun sigandang eolmayeyo?**
cham, yuh-gi-neun shi-gan-dang uhl-ma-ae-yo?
Oh, what is the rate per hour here?

Attendant: **sigandang cheon obaegwonieyo**
shi-gan-dang chun o-baeg-won-ee-ae-yo.
It's 1,500 won per hour.

Sean: **gamsahamnida.**
gam-sa-ham-ni-da.
Thank you.

Words to Know

bin	been	Empty
cham	cham	By the way
eolmayeyo	uhl-ma-ae-yo	How much is it?
jari	ja-ree	Seats
keompyuteo	keom-pyu-tuh	Computer
pisibang	pee-see-bang	PC pc-rooms, internet cafés
sigandang	shi-gan-dang	Per -hour

Fun & Games

Draw a line between the matching pair.

House   jip (*jeep*)

Phone number   nuguseyo (*noo-goo-sae-yo*)

Hello   jeonhwabunho (*jeon-hwa-bun-ho*)

Friend   yeollakcheo (*yuhl-lak-chuh*)

Contact information   yeoboseyo (*yuh-bo-sae-yo*)

Who are you?   chingu (*chin-goo*)

Chapter 10

At the Office and Around the House

In This Chapter

▶ Doing business at the office and at dinner

▶ Going to meetings

▶ Finding your way around home

▶ Being a good houseguest

*W*hether you spend most of your time at the **samusil** (*sa-moo-shil;* office) or at **jip** (*jeep;* home, house), you'll want to know a word or two about **samu yongpum** (*sa-moo-yong-poom;* office supplies) and **gajeong yongpum** (*ga-jeong-yong-poom;* household goods). Especially, if you know few phrases in Korean, it'll be very handy at business settings to impress your business partner or your clients. They'll think that you have taken that "extra step" to make themselves "at home" with your new found knowledge of Korean language.

In this chapter, I will teach you how to say few handy phrases to use at work, such as asking for where things are and how to use office machinery. Also included in this chapter are phrases and words to use when you are staying at your Korean friend's house. I will also teach you some Korean customs so that your host/hostess will think you are very well informed about the Korean culture.

In this chapter, I stick mostly to formal polite form of Korean speech, when doing business at the office and when going to the meetings. At other times, I will use informal polite Korean, which was the form used throughout this book.

Getting Down to Work

Whether you're working at a **hoesa** (*hwae-sa;* company), or teaching at a **hakgyo** (*hak-gyo;*school), **il** (*il;* work) is **il**. In this section, I'll teach you some useful words and phrases to use while getting to and from workplace and also while working at the office.

Finding things at the office

For starters, you need to know at least one of the following crucial phrases you cannot live without:

> **keopi gigyega eodie itseumnikka?** (*kuh-pee-gee-gye-ga uh-dee-ae ee-sseum-ni-kka;* Where is the coffee machine?) and

> **hwajangsiri eodie itseumnikka?** (*hwa-jang-shi-ree uh-dee-ae ee-sseum-ni-kka;* Where's the restroom?)

Notice that both sentences end identically:

> **[some word] *i/ga* eodie itseumnikka?** ([some word] *i/ga-uh-dee-ae ee-sseum-ni-kka;* Where's [some word] ?)

If you want to specifically ask for men's or women's restrooms, substitute *[some word]* with **namja hwajangsil** (*nam-ja hwa-jang-shil;* men's restroom) and **yeoja hwajangsil** (*yuh-ja hwa-jang-shil;* women's restroom):

> **Namja hwahangsiri eodie itseumnikka?** (*nam-ja hwa-jang-shi-ree uh-dee-ae ee-sseum-ni-kka;* Where is men's restroom?)

> **Yeoja hwahangsiri eodie itseumnikka?** (*yuh-ja hwa-jang-shi-ree uh-dee-ae ee-sseum-ni-kka;* Where is women's restroom?)

You use **i** or **ga,** depending on whether the word ends in a consonant or a vowel. The rule is similar to how you choose *an* or *a,* but in Korean, you place the marker at the end of the word and add it as a suffix.

Office supplies

If you need to make some finishing touches on a **bogoseo** (*bo-go-suh;* report), send off a **paekseu** (paek-sseu; fax) or sign a document, you need to know a few words for **samuyongpum** (*sa-moo-yong-poom;* office supplies).

In Table 10-1, you can find a few things found in, on, or around a **chaeksang** (*chaeg-sang;* desk):

Hanging out at the water purifier

In Korea, it's hard to find water fountains. Instead, you'll find water purifiers with **jongikeop** (*jong-ee-keop;* paper cups). Most water purifiers dispense **tteugeoun mul** (*tteu-guh-oon-mool;* hot water) and **chan mul** (*chan-mool;* cold water). Sometimes, though, you may find instant **keopi** (*kuh-pee;* coffee) and/or **cha** (*cha;* tea) next to or near the water purifiers. If you do, feel free to help yourself.

Table 10-1	Things Around the Office	
Korean Word	*Pronunciation*	*Translation*
bolpen	*bol-pen*	Ballpoint pen
chak	*chaeg*	Books
gomubaendeu	*go-moo-baen-deu*	Rubber band
gongchaek	*gong-chaeg*	Notebooks
hochikiseu	*ho-chi-ki-sseu*	Stapler
hyeonggwangpen	*hyoung-gwang-pen*	Highlighter
jongi	*jong-ee*	Paper
keullip	*keul-lip*	Clip
munseo	*moon-suh*	Documents
pyeonjibongtu	*pyuhn-jee-bong-too*	Envelope
seoryu	*suh-ryoo*	Papers
seukachi teipeu	*tae-ee-peu*	Scotch tape
sseuregitong	*sseu-rae-gee-tong*	Wastebasket
syapeu	*sya-peu*	Mechanical pencils
upyo	*oo-pyo*	Stamp
yeonpil	*yuhn-pil*	Pencils

If you need any of these items, you may want to ask [some word] **eul/reul eodieseo guhalsu itseumnikka?** ([some word] *eul/reul uh-dee-ae-suh goo-hal-soo ee-sseum-ni-kka;* Where may I get a/some[some word]?). Substitute [some word] with the office supplies you need (see Table 10-1).

If you want to borrow something, ask [some word] **eul/reul jom billilsu itget-seumnikka?** (*[some word] eul/reul bil-lil-soo it-get-sseum-ni-kka;* May I borrow a/some [some word]?). Substitute [some word] with the office supplies you need (see Table 10-1).

Office machines

If you want to use communal office equipment, you need to ask where it is and how to use it. Most of the time, the menus and user instructions are in Korean.

Use the following phrases to ask about office equipment:

> **[some word] i/ga eodie itseumnikka?** (*[some word] i/ga uh-dee-ae ee-sseum-ni-kka;* Where is [some word]?)

> **[some word] eul/reul jom sseodo doegetseumnikka?** (*[some word] eul/reul jom ssuh-do dwae-get-sseum-ni-kka;* May I use [some word]?)

> **[some word] eul/reul bonaego sipeunde, jom dowa jusigetseumnikka?** (*[some word] eul/reul bo-nae-go shi-peun-dae, jom do-wa joo-shi-get-seum-ni-kka;* I want to send a [some word], can you please help me?)

> **[some word] eul/reul boksahago sipeunde, jom dowa jusigetseumnikka?** (*[some word] eul/reul bok-sa-ha-go shi-peun-dae, jom do-wa-ju-si-get-sseum-ni-kka;* I want to copy [some word], can you please help me?)

If you're pressed for time, the most important phrase is **jom dowa jusigetseumnikka?** (*jom do-wa joo-shi-get-sseum-ni-kka;* Can you please help me?). Just point to a thing and say it. Then the person you're speaking to will pick up on what you need.

If you need help with using certain office equipments, use the phrase **eul/reul sseuneungeoseul jom dowa jusigetseumnikka?** (*[some word] eul/reul sseu-neun-guh-seul jom do-wa-joo-shi-get-sseum-ni-kka;* Can you please help me to use [some word] ?). Table 10-2 lists some office equipments you may need to use to get your work done. Substitute [some word] with the office equipment you need to use.

Table 10-2	Office Equipment	
Korean Word	*Pronunciation*	*Translation*
boksagi	*bok-sa-gee*	Copier
jeonhwa	*juhn-hwa*	Telephone
keompyuteo	*keom-pyu-tuh*	Computer

Korean Word	Pronunciation	Translation
paekseu	*paek-sseu*	Fax
peurinteo	*peu-rin-tuh*	Printer
peurojekteo	*peu-ro-jek-tuh*	Projector

Using computers

Whether you have to print out a report, read up on company updates, or check your e-mail, computers will most likely play an integral part of your work at the office. Sure, you may be a computer guru, but when you ask to use someone's computer and find that everything is in Korean, you may want to know how to ask for a little assistance.

The following phrases may help you get help:

keompyuteoreul jom sseulsu itgetseumnikka? (*keom-pyu-tuh-reul jom sseul-soo it-get-sseum-ni-kka;* May I please use a/the computer?)

yeongeo japaneuro jom bakkwo jusilsu itgetseumnikka? (*young-uh-ja-pan-eu-ro jom ba-kkwo joo-shi-get-sseum-ni-kka;* Could you please change the keyboard input into English?)

imeileul jom hwaginhalsu itgetseumnikka? (*ee-mae-il-eul jom hwa-gin-hal-soo it-get-sseum-ni-kka;* May I check my e-mail?)

inteonet beuraujeoreul jom ttuiwojusigetseumnikka? (*in-tuh-net beu-ra-oo-juh-reul jom ttui-wo-joo-shi-get-sseum-ni-kka;* Could you open up a Web browser for me?)

i munseoreul chullyeokhae jusilsu itgetseumnikka? (*ee moon-seo-reul chul-lyeok-hae-joo-shil-soo it-get-sseum-ni-kka;* Could you print out this document for me?)

paireul ryeoreo jusilsu itgetseumnikka? (*pa-ee-reul yuh-ruh joo-shil-soo it-get-sseum-ni-kka;* Could you open this file for me?)

pail jom bonae jusilsu itgetseumnikka? (*pa-il yom bo-nae joo-shil-soo it-get-sseum-ni-kka;* Could you send this file for me?)

Afterward, use this phrase to thank the person who helped you:

keompyuteoreul jal sseotseumnida, gamsahamnida. (*keom-pyu-tuh-reul jal-ssut-sseum-ni-da, gam-sa-ham-ni-da;* Thanks for letting me use the computer.)

What to call your peers and superiors

For someone of equal or lower position, use that person's full name or family name, followed by his or her position. For someone named Son Jihoon, for example, the syllable that comes first, Son, is the family name, and Jihoon is the first name. Hence, you address him as Son Jihoon *position,* Son *position,* or just *position.*

Never address a **sangsa** (*sang-sa;* superior) by his or her first name. Korean society follows a strict hierarchy that requires you to address superiors with their job title as well as their family name or full name. If your boss is vice president of the company, and her name is Erica Choi, you should call her Erica Choi **busajang-nim** (*boo-sa-jang-nim;* vice president), Choi **sajangnim** (*sa-jang-nim;* president), or even just

sa jang nim. The **nim** placed after a person's position is a sign of further respect.

Here are a few common business titles:

✔ **sajang**	*sa-jang*	President
✔ **busajang**	*boo-sa-jang*	Vice president
✔ **gwang**	*gwa-jang*	Section chief
✔ **bujang**	*boo-jang*	Department chair
✔ **chajang**	*cha-jang*	Vice chief
✔ **daeri**	*dae-ree*	Representative/assistant
✔ **timjang**	*tim-jang*	Team leader

Remember to add **nim** after each of these words when you are addressing a superior.

or in general, you can say:

dowa jusyeoseo jeongmal gamsahamnida. (*do-wa-joo-syuh-suh jeong-mal gam-sa-ham-ni-da;* Thank you so much for helping me.)

Finding people at the office

If you need to track someone down, the following passages may be of help:

[some word] jariga eodi imnikka? ([some word] *ja-ree-ga uh-dee-im-ni-kka;* Where is [some word] 's seat?)

[some word] kkeseo jarie gyesimnikka? ([some word] *kke-suh ja-ri-ae gye-shim-ni-kka;* Is [some word] in the office?)

jamsiman gidaryeo jusipsiyo. (*jam-shi-man gee-da-ryuh-joo-ship-shi-yo;* One moment please.)

jarie gyesinji hwagin haedeurigetseumnida. (*ja-ree-ae gye-shim-jee hwa-gin-hae-deu-ree-get-seum-ni-da;* I'll check if he/she is there.)

ye, jeogi imnida. (ye, juhgi im-ni-da; Yes, it's over there.)

ye, jarie gyesimnida. (ye, ja-ree-ae gye-shim-ni-da; Yes, his/her seat is over there.)

jigeum jarie an gyesimnida. (jee-geum ja-ree-ae an gye-shim-ni-da; No, he/she isn't here.)

meseji namgyeo deurilkkayo? (mae-sae-jee nam-gyuh-deu-ril-kka-yo; Do you want to leave a message?)

Asking for directions

If you are looking for a office, meeting room, restroom, rest area, and so on, use the following phrase to ask for directions:

[some word] *i/ga* eodie itseumnikka? ([some word] *i/ga uh-dee-ae it-sseum-ni-kka;* Where is [some word] ?). Substitute [some word] for the office, meeting room, restroom, and so on. For example: **Hoeuisiri eodie itseumnikka?** (*hwae-ui-shi-ree uh-dee-ae ee-sseum-ni-kka;* Where is the meeting room?)

Answer to above question might be something like:

a, je samusil yeope itseumnida (*a, jae sa-moo-shil yuh-pae ee-sseum-ni-da;* Ah, it's next to my office.)

Some useful words to know might be: **ape** (*a-pae;* infront), **yeope** (*yuh-pae;* next to) and **dwie** (*dwee-ae;* behind).

Talkin' the Talk

Brian is looking for Mr Kim. He stops by his office to see whether Mr. Kim is in.

Brian: **gim timjangnimkkeseo jarie gyesimnikka?** *gim tim-jang-nim-kke-suh ja-ree-ae gye-shim-ni-kka?* Is Mr. Kim at his seat?

Secretary: **jamsiman gidaryeo jusipsiyo. jarie gyesinji hwagin-hae deurigetseumnida.** *jam-shi-man gee-da-ryuh joo-ship-shi-yo. ja-ree-e gye-shin-jee hwa-gin-hae-deu-ree-get-seum-ni-da.* One moment, please. I'll check to see if he's in.

Brian: **ye, gamsahamnida.**
ye, gam-sa-ham-ni-da.
Sure. Thank you.

Secretary: **ye, jigeum jarie gyesimnida. gim timjangnimkkeseo got naosilgeomnida.**
ye, jee-geum ja-ree-ae gye-shim-ni-da. gim tim-jang-nim-kke-suh got na-o-shil-gum-ni-da.
Yes, he's in his seat. He'll be coming out to see you in a moment.

Mr. Kim: **smith gwajangnim, waenirisimnikka?**
Smith gwa-jang-nim, waen-ee-ree-shim-ni-kka?
Hey, Mr. Smith, what are you doing round these parts?

Brian: **hoegye gwallyeon jaryoe gwanhae mureobolge iseoseoyo. hoeuiga kkeunnamyeon jamsi mannaseo yegihal su itgetseumnikka?**
hwae-gye gwal-lyeon-ja-ryo-ae gwan-hae moo-ruh-bol-gae ee-ssuh-suh-yo. hwae-ui-ga kkeun-na-myun jam-shi man-na-suh yae-gee-hal soo it-get-sseum-ni-kka?
I have few questions to ask you about the accounting information. Could we possibly meet and talk after the meeting?

Mr. Kim: **joseumnida. du sie jigwon hyugesireseo mannalkkayo?**
jo-sseum-ni-da. doo shi-ae jee-gwon hyoo-gae-shil-ae-suh man-nal-kka-yo?
Okay, how about if we meet at two o'clock in the employee lounge?

Brian: **ye, josseumnida. geureom sugohasipsiyo.**
ye, jo-sseum-ni-da. geu-rum soo-go-ha-ship-shi-yo.
Yeah, that sounds great. Have a nice day.

Words to Know

bokdo	bok-do	Hallway
chulgu	chul-gu	Exit
ellibeiteo	el-lee-bae-ee-tuh	Elevator
gyedan	gye-dan	Stairwell

ipgu	eep-gu	Entrance
japangi	ja-pan-gi	Vending machine
jeongsugi	jeong-soo-gi	Water purifier
robi	ro-bee	Lobby

Attending Meetings

Meetings are an inevitable part of the job. If you're doing business with Korean clients, they'll most likely bring their own interpreters. But saying a little Korean at the beginning of a meeting will leave a good impression and it may just give you an advantage over the competition.

Making introductions

For more on personal introductions, refer to Chapter 3 particularly to the section on bowing and shaking hands. Here are two common introductions used in meetings:

> **yeoreobun, annyeonghashimnikka.** (*yuh-ruh-boon an-nyoung-ha-shim-ni-kka;* Hello, ladies and gentlemen.)

> **yeoreobun, mannaseo bangapseumnida.** (*yuh-ruh-boon man-na-suh bang-gaap-sseum-ni-da;* It's a pleasure to meet you all.)

> **hoeuireul sijak hagetseumnida.** (*hwae-ui-reul shi-jak-ha-get-seum-ni-da;* Let's start the meeting.)

Speaking up in a meeting

The following phrases should come in handy during the meeting:

> **jilmuni itseumnida.** (*jil-moo-nee it-sseum-ni-da;* I have a question.)

> **geonuisahangi itseumnida.** (*guhn-ui-sa-hang-ee it-seum-ni-da;* I have a suggestion.)

siksa hue hoeuireul gyesok hagetseumnida. (*shik-sa hoo-ae hwae-ui-reul gye-sok ha-get-sseum-ni-da;* We'll continue after the meal.)

jamsi swieotda dasi sijakhagetseumnida. (*jam-shi swi-uht-da da-shi shi-jak-ha-get-seum-ni-da;* We'll take a quick break before continuing.)

[some word] bungan hyusigi itgetseumnida. (*[some word] boon-gan hyoo-shi-gee it-get-sseum-ni-da;* We will have a [some word] minute break.) Substitute [some word] with time.

pigonhasimnikka? (*pee-gon-ha-shim-ni-kka;* Are you tired?)

jeongmal pigonhamnida. (*jung-mal pee-gon-ham-ni-da;* I'm exhausted.)

gwaenchansseumnida. (*gwaen-chan-sseum-ni-da;* I'm all right.)

jom swieotda halkkayo? (*jom swi-uht-da hal-kka-yo;* Do you want to take a break?)

oneul hoeuireul iman machigetseumnida. (*o-neul hwae-ui-reul ee-man ma-chi-get-sseum-ni-da;* We'll finish today's meeting.)

Commenting about other people

This section is devoted to comments that Koreans make about other people, and possibly even you.

jom ginjanghangeot gatseumnida. (*jom gin-jang-han-guht gat-sseum-ni-da;* I/You/He/she looks a little nervous; formal polite). The sentence omits the subject, so you can use it depending on context.

mwonga jom misimjeokseumnida. (mwon-ga jom mee-shim-juhk-sseum-ni-da; It sounds questionable; formal polite)

jeongmal joeungeot gatseumnida. (*jung-mal jo-eun-guht gat-sseum-ni-da;* It sounds great; formal polite)

iri jal jinhaengdoeneun geot gatseumnida. (*ee-ree jal jin-haeng-dwae-neun-guht gat-sseum-ni-da;* It seems like everything is going well; formal polite)

Making the Rounds: Business Dinners

Many offices regularly go out to **hoesik** (*hwae-shik;* company dinners). **hoesik** are a regular part of Korean business culture, and although you can miss a few, it is best if you attend most them; they're are a good chance to meet people in your office and talk to them.

Sometimes after dinner, everyone goes to another restaurant or a bar. Each relocation is called a **cha** (*cha;* round). The **il cha** (*il cha;* first round) may be dinner at a nice restaurant; the **i cha** (*ee cha;* second round) may be a bar, followed by another bar, such a karaoke bar, and so on. It's not unheard of for a few members of the office to stay out the entire night and go straight back to work the next day.

If you're going out after your first day at the office, people will pour you many drinks so be aware.

Drinking politely

For the first shot of the night, it's a good idea to drink, or at least to raise your glass when everyone else does.

You may hear people ask **hanjan badeusijyo?** (*han-jan ba-deu-shi-jyo;* Would you like a shot?), offer one another drinks, and pass the shot glass around. This activity is called **janeul dollinda** (*jan-eul dol-lin-da;* passing the shot glass), and throughout the process, everyone shares a single glass. If you feel like it, you can take a shot and pour a shot for someone else (see the following section).

Pouring shots

In Korea, it's considered to be bad form to pour yourself a shot.

If you want to drink, hold up your empty shot glass with your right hand; use your left hand to prop up your right arm; and sway your shot glass from side to side while looking at someone. That person will pick up the cue and pour you a shot. Likewise, if you notice someone motioning for a shot, make sure that you help him or her out.

Serving (and being served by) superiors

Another thing you may want to keep in mind is to pour shots for seniors by using both hands. You can hold the bottle with both hands or support your right arm with the left one. When a senior is pouring you a shot, make sure you hold your shot glass with both hands.

You may want to look around and observe a few people doing this before doing it yourself. If you're drinking with peers, juniors, or friends, however, what you do usually doesn't matter.

When you drink in front of a senior, make sure to turn your head to the side (so that you are not facing the senior who poured you a drink) and drink. It is considered rude and disrespectful if you face the senior and drink facing them.

Declining drinks

If you don't drink, say **sureul anmasimnida** (*soo-reul an-ma-shim-ni-da;* I don't drink). If you don't think you can possibly drink anymore or reached your limit, say **sureul deo mot masimnida** (*soo-reul duh-mot ma-shim-ni-da;* I can't drink anymore). However, your co-workers, may not believe you and still keep pouring you the drink. This is the Korean drinking culture, so don't be surprised if people are forcing you to drink.

Making Yourself at Home

If you are staying at a Korean friend's house, they will go out of their way to make you feel welcome. Graciously accept their generosity, and in these instances, it is perfectly okay to use the informal polite form of Korean we have used in the previous chapters, rather than the formal polite form which was used at a business setting.

In this section, I will teach you basic phrases and words you need to make a good impression on your host, while staying at their house. I will cover the topics including various types of houses in Korea, using the bathroom, visiting Korean friend's house, taking tours, and also good manners for eating and drinking at someone's house.

The place where you live

Home can be an apartment, a condominium, or a single-family home. In Korea, people call their dwellings **jip** (*jeep:* home, house), which may be in any of the categories listed in Table 10-3.

Table 10-3		Housing Categories
Korean	*Pronunciation*	*English*
dandok jutaek	*dan-dok joo-taek*	Single-family house
yeollip jutaek	*yeol-lip joo-taek*	Row house
apateu	*a-pa-teu*	Apartment
wollum	*won-room*	One room

Trash talking: Getting rid of refuse

The Korean government enforces strict policies on trash. Every household is required to buy special **jongnyangje sseuregi bongtu** (*jong-nyang-jae sseu-rae-gee bong-too;* trash bags) from stores. As a result, most Koreans recycle everything they can.

If you need to take out the trash at your own place, make sure to separate paper, plastic, cans, and leftover food items. In Korea, separate bags are used for leftover food: **eumsing-mul sseuregibongtu** (*eum-sing-mool sseu-rae-gee-bong-too;* trash bag for leftovers).

If you decide to double-wrap a trash bag, make sure that the government-issued trash bag is clearly visible; otherwise, you'll be breaking the law.

To tell someone where you live, use this phrase:

> **jeoneun [some word] eseo sarayo.** (*juh-neun [some word] ae-suh sa-ra-yo;* I live in a ___). Substitute [some word] with the words for different housings above.

If you want to refer to your house in conversation, say **uri jip** (*u-ri jip;* My house).

Literally, **uri jip** (*oo-ree-jeep*) or **jeohui jip** (*juh-hee jeep*) means our house, but in conversational Korean, **uri** (*oo-ree;* our) or **jeohui** (*juh-hee*) is used instead of **nae** (*nae;* my).

The smallest room

A few things may catch you off guard when you try to take a shower in Korea. The first is that there are no shower curtains. You also won't find any fabric floor mats in contact with the floor. The reason is that Korean bathrooms have a drainage system built into the floor, so that it isn't a problem if a little water splashes around. Often, the floors in bathrooms get wet, and you need to buy yourself a pair of plastic slippers to wear in the bathroom.

The next thing that might take you off guard is that the bathtub might be full of random things. You might even wonder if Koreans ever use the bathtub. The answer is that they usually don't. Koreans may have showers in their bathtub (taking the shower head down from its holder) or bath children in there. However, for most Korean adults, rather than having a bath at home, they LOVE to go to the bath house instead. Now days, new apartments being built have showers but no bathtubs for this reason.

The last thing I'd like to mention is important, especially if you don't like taking showers with cold water. To have hot showers, you need to turn on the boiler system in the house manually. Make sure it's turned on several minutes before you turn on the hot water. Otherwise, you might begin your morning in a start. To prevent this from happening, ask your host **jigeum tteugeoun mul nawayo?** (*jee-geum tteu-guh-oon mool na-wa-yo;* Is the hot water running?).

Visiting Koreans at Home

In this section, I go over a few words for particular activities in the house, such as relaxing with friends and grabbing a bite to eat.

Koreans do not wear shoes in the house. So when visiting a Korean's house, be sure to take your shoes off. Taking shoes off shows that you respect the person's property and the person you are visiting. It is considered rude and dirty to wear the shoes in the house. Korean's house is like a sanctuary they come to relax after a day's hard work. You don't want to drag all the dirt from the street to the place that is supposed to be clean and relaxing. However, sometimes your host or hostess may tell you that its alright if you don't take your shoes off. But they are just trying to be polite, so that you feel more comfortable at their home. If I were you, I'd still take my shoes off.

Taking the tour

Is your chingu (*chin-goo;* friend) showing you around his house? The following phrases may come in handy:

> **yeogiga eoneu bangieyo?** (*yuh-gi-ga uh-neu bang-ee-ae-yo;* Which room is this?)

> **yeogiga nugu bangieyo?** (*yuh-gi-ga noo-goo bang-ee-ae-yo;* Whose room is this?)

> **bangi myeot gaeeyo?** (*bang-ee myuht gae-ae-yo;* How many rooms are there?)

Table 10-4 lists a few words for various parts of a house.

Table 10-4		Around the House
Korean	*Pronunciation*	*English*
daemun	*dae-moon*	Gate
hyeongwan	*hyun-gwan*	Entrance

Korean	Pronunciation	English
geosil	guh-shil	Living room
anbang	an-bang	Main room/master bedroom
chimsil	chim-shil	Bedroom
seojae	suh-jae	Study room
bang	bang	Room
bueok	boo-uhk	Kitchen
hwajangsil	hwa-jang-shil	Bathroom/restroom
beranda	bae-ran-da	Veranda, porch, or balcony
changgo	chang-go	Storage
byeokjang	byuhk-jang	Wall closet for storage (for anything)
otjang	ot-jang	Wardrobe closet (for clothes and blankets)

Chilling out

When you're hanging out in someone's yard or watching a film in the living room, these phrases should come in handy:

eumageul teulkkayo? (*eu-mak teul-kka-yo;* Should I put on some music?)

yeonghwareul bolkkayo? (*young-hwa-reul bol-kka-yo;* Do you want to watch a film?)

terebireul bolkkayo? (*tae-rae-bee-reul bol-kka-yo;* Do you want to watch some television?)

bureul kkeulkkayo? (*boo-reul kkeul-kka-yo;* Do you want to turn off the lights?)

bureul kilkkayo? (*boo-reul kil-kka-yo;* Do you want to turn on the lights?)

mwo piryohangeo iseuseyo? (*mwo pee-ryo-han-guh ee-sseu-sae-yo;* Do you need something?)

deouseyo? (*duh-oo-sae-yo;* Are you feeling hot?)

chuuseyo? (*chu-oo-sae-yo;* Are you feeling cold?)

Talkin' the Talk

Bill is visiting Christine in Seoul, and they are hanging out at Christine's place.

Bill:	**christine ssi, yeonghwana han pyeon bolkkayo?**
	Christine sshi, young-hwa-na han pyeon bol-kka-yo?
	Christine, would you like to watch a movie?
Christine:	**ye, monty python joahaseyo? takja wie dibidiga iseoyo.**
	Ye, Monty Python jo-a-ha-sae-yo? Tak-ja wee-ae dee-bee-dee-ga ee-ssuh-yo.
	Yes, do you like Monty Python? It's on top of the small table.
Bill:	**dangyeonhi joahajyo. jega jeil joahaneun yeonghwaeyo!**
	Dang-yuhn-hee jo-a-jyo. Jae-ga jae-il jo-a-ha-neun yeong-hwa-ae-yo!
	Of course I like it. It's my favorite film!
Christine:	**geureom uri geugeo bwayo. bill ssi, bul jom kkeojusillaeyo? najunge jeonyeogeun mwo sikyeo meogeulkkayo?**
	Geu-reom oo-ree geu-guh bwa-yo. Bill sshi, bool jom kkuh-joo-shil-lae-yo? na-joong-ae juh-nyuh-geun mwo shi-kyuh kka-yo?
	Then let's watch that. Bill, could you turn off the lights? And later on, do you just want to order out for dinner?
Bill:	**geureojyo mwo.**
	Geu-ruh-jyo mwo.
	Sure, let's do that.

Words to Know

achim	*a-chim*	Breakfast
bangseok	*bang-seok*	Floor cushions
bul	*bool*	Lights/fire (depend on the context)
dibidi	*dee-bee-dee*	DVD

dibidi peulleieo	dee-bee-dee peul-lae-ee-uh	DVD player
jeomsim	juhm-shim	Lunch
jeonyeok	juh-nyuk	Dinner
keopi teibeul	kuh-pee tae-ee-beul	Coffee table
radio	ra-dee-o	Radio
sopa	so-pa	Sofa
takja	tak-ja	Small table
terebi	tae-rae-bee	Television
yeong hwa	young-hwa	Movies

Eating and drinking

If you want more information about eating, refer to Chapter 5. Here, you'll find some words and phrases to use when you want to grab something to eat or do a little cooking at someone's house:

eumnyosu han jan masilleyo? (*eum-nyo-soo han-jan ma-shil-lae-yo;* Would you like a drink?)

eumnyosu han jan masilsu iseulkkayo? (*eum-nyo-soo han-jan ma-shil-soo ee-sseul-kka-yo;* May I have a drink?)

mwo masilleyo? (*mwo ma-shil-lae-yo;* What would you like to drink?)

baegopeuseyo? (*bae-go-peu-sae-yo;* Are you hungry?)

meogeul geot jom gatda deurilkkayo? (*muh-geul-guh jom gat-da deu-ril-kka-yo;* Do you want me to get you something to eat?)

mwo jom sikyeo meogeulkkayo? (*mwo jom shi-kyuh muh-geul-kka-yo;* Do you want me to order some food?)

[some word] piryohaseyo? (*[some word] pee-ryo-ha-sae-yo;* Do you need [some word] ?)

[some word] deusilleyo? (*[some word] deu-shil-lae-yo;* Do you want to eat [some word] ?)

[some word] masillaeyo? (*[some word] ma-shil-lae-yo;* Do you want to drink [some word] ?)

[some word] sseodo doelkkayo? (*[some word] ssuh-do dwel-kka-yo;* May I use [some word] ?)

[some word] iseoyo? (*[some word] ee-ssuh-yo;* Do you have [some word] ?)

You can substitute [some word] with the things you need, want to eat, want to drink, want to use, and so on.

Most Koreans have tables and chairs in their dining rooms, but not all do. Sometimes, you'll sit on the floor and have your food served to you on a folding table. However, this can have quite an effect on your legs. If the pain in your legs is too much for you to bear, you can excuse yourself and ask if you can sit on the sofa for a while or stand and walk around. Koreans will totally understand.

Talkin' the Talk

Later in the evening, Doug feels a little peckish and wants to have a snack.

Doug:	(rubbing his stomach) **june, hoksi gansikgeori eopseoyo?** *June, hok-shi gan-shik-guh-ree uhp-ssuh-yo?* June, do you have something to nibble on?
June:	**eojjeojyo? gansikgeoriga eomneundeyo. tongdalgi-rado sikilkkayo?** *uh-jjuh-jyo? Gan-shik-guh-ree-ga uhm-neun-dae-yo. tong-da-gee-ra-do shi-kil-kka-yo?* Guess what? I don't have any nibblies. Should I order a roast chicken?
Doug:	**jega sikilkkeyo. jeonhwabeonhoga mwojyo?** *jae-ga shi-kil-kke-yo. juhn-hwa-bun-ho-ga mwo-jyo?* I'll order it. What is their phone number?
June:	**032-933-7495eyo.** *gong-sam-ee-ae goo-sam-sam chil-sa-goo-o-ae-yo.* It's 032-933-7495.
Doug:	(picking up the phone and dialing the numbers) **yeo-boseoyo, yeogi ABC apateu 9 dong 102 ho indeyo tongdak hanmarirang maekju dubyeong gatda-juseyo. gomawoyo.** *yuh-bo-sae-yo, yuh-gi ABC a-pa-teu 9 dong 102 ho in-dae-yo. tong-dak han-ma-ree-rang maek-joo doo-byoung gat-da-joo-sae-yo. go-ma-wo-yo.* Hello? This is ABC apartment building 9, household number 102. Please bring 1 roast chicken and 2 bottles of beer. Thank you.

Words to Know

banchan	ban-chan	Side dishes
bap	bap	Rice
bapgonggi	bap-gong-gi	Rice bowl
doma	do-ma	Cutting board
eummyosu	eum-nyo-soo	Soft drink
gansikgeori	gan-shik-guh-ree	Nibblies/snacks
geureut	geu-reut	Bowl
gwaja	gwa-ja	Crackers
jan	jan	Glass
jeonjareinji	ojuhn-ja-re-in-jee	Microwave oven
jeopsi	juhp-shi	Plate
kal	kal	Knife
maekju	maek-joo	Beer
keop	kuhp	Cup
naengjanggo	naeng-jang-go	Refrigerator
naengdonggo	naeng-dong-go	Freezer
reinji	re-in-jee	Range, stove
sikilkkayo?	shi-kil-kka-yo	Should I order it?
siktak	shik-tak	Dining table
soju	so-joo	Korean alcoholic drink
sul	sool	Alcoholic drink
tongdak	tong-dak	Roast chicken

Staying over

If you're sleeping over at a Korean friend's house, you may notice that the bedroom doesn't have a **chimdae** (*chim-dae;* bed). In traditional Korean homes, people put out thick blankets on the floor as opposed to setting up beds, as in Western culture.

If you want to know more about why Koreans do this, please look in Chapter 20 under "Don't walk in a house with your shoes on."

The following phrases may be helpful during your visit:

> **annyeonghi jumuseyo.** (*an-nyoung-hee joo-moo-sae-yo;* Sleep well. Used when saying "good night" to people older than you.)

> **jal jayo.** (*jal ja-yo;* Sleep well. Can be used at anyone besides person with seniority.)

> **pyeonhi swiseyo.** (*pyuhn-hee swi-sae-yo;* Rest well.)

> **eodiseo jal kkayo?** (*uh-dee-suh jal-kka-yo;* Where should I sleep?)

The next morning, it is a good idea to say the following phrases:

> **annyeonghi jumusyeoseoyo?** (*an-nyoung-hee joo-moo-syuh-ssuh-yo;* Did you sleep well?; used for people with seniority.)

> **jal jaseoyo?** (*jal ja-ssuh-yo;* Did you sleep well?; used for everyone else.)

Grooming and hygiene matters

You may want to brush your teeth before you go to sleep or ask for a towel before you go in to take a shower. These phrases may help:

> **sugeoi piryohaseyo?** (*soo-geon-ee pee-ryo-ha-sae-yo;* Do you need a towel?)

> **sugeoneul jom billilsu iseulkkayo?** (*soo-geon-eul jom bil-lil-soo ee-sseul-kka-yo;* May I borrow a towel?)

> **chitsori piryohaseyo?** (*chi-sol-ee pi-ryo-ha-sae-yo;* Do you need a toothbrush?)

> **chitsol han gae billil su iseulkkayo?** (*chi-sol han-gae bil-lil-su ee-sseul-kka-yo;* May I borrow a toothbrush?)

> **syawo jom haedo gwaenchanayo?** (*sya-wo jom hae-do gwaen-chan-a-yo;* Is it all right if I take a shower?)

> **syawo hasillaeyo?** (*sya-wo ha-shil-lae-yo;* Do you want to take a shower?)

If accidents happen

Sometime the toilets get clogged. Actually, in Korea, this happens quite a bit. It's probably best to confess if you've clogged the toilet, and ask for some help of your host/hostess.

If you insist on finding a plunger on your own (because you are too embarrassed to ask for help of your host/hostess), go to a **jeonpasa** (*juhn-pa-sa;* electronics/hardware store) and ask **byeongitong ttulleun geo jom salsu iseulkkayo?** (*byuhn-gee-tong ttul-leun-guh jom sal-soo ee-sseul-kka-yo;* May I buy a plunger?) or go to the neighbors and ask **byeongitong ttulleun geo jom billil su iseulkkayo?** (*byuhn-gee-tong ttul-leun-guh jom bil-lil-soo ee-sseul-kka-yo;* May I borrow a plunger?).

Korean doesn't really have a word that means *plunger,* so it's just called *the thing that unclogs toilets.* Some people might call it **ttureoppeong** (*ttu-ruh-ppung;* thing that unclogs). You may want to make a plunging motion while you ask.

Talkin' the Talk

Bill is sleeping over at Christine's for the evening. He wants to take a shower before he turns in.

Christine:	**sopae baegehago ibureul rollyeo nwaseoyo.**
	so-pa-ae bae-gae-ha-go ee-boo-reul ol-lyuh nwa-ssuh-yo.
	I've put a pillow and a blanket on the sofa.

Bill:	**gomawoyo Christine ssi. geureonde hoksi sugeon jom billilsu iseulkkayo?**
	go-ma-wo-yo Christine sshi. geu-ruhn-dae hok-shi soo-geon jom bil-lil soo ee-sseul-kka-yo?
	Thanks, Christine. But could I borrow a towel?

Christine:	**dangyeonhajyo. jamkkanmannyo.**
	dang-yuhn-ha-jyo. jam-kkan-man-nyo.
	Of course. One moment.

Bill:	**gomawoyo. (Bill takes the towel and walks into the bathroom.)**
	go-ma-wo-yo.
	Thank you.

Words to Know

begye	be-gae	Pillow
binu	bee-noo	Soap
chitsol	chi-ssol	Toothbrush
chiyak	chi-yak	Toothpaste
damnyo	dam-nyo	Thick blankets
ibul	ee-bool	Blankets
jjl	jel	Gel
mogyok	mo-gyok	Bath
renjeutong	ren-jeu-tong	Contact-lens case
rosyeon	ro-syuhn	Lotion
semyeondae	se-myuhn-dae	Washbasin
sigyeomsu	shi-gyuhm-soo	Lens fluid
siteu	shi-teu	Sheets
sugeon	soo-geon	Towel
syawo	sya-wo	Shower
yo	yo	Quilt
yokjo	yok-jo	Bathtub

Cleaning up

If you're staying at someone's house for more than just a night, you may want to help a little around the house. Ask where the vacuum cleaner is and even help do the dishes. Your hosts will be impressed not only by your fluent Korean, but also by your considerate behavior.

Some useful phrases might be:

Jega cheongsoreul dowadeurilkkeyo. (*jae-ga chung-so-reul do-wa-deu-ril-kke-yo;* I'll help with cleaning the house.)

Jega seolgeosireul dowadeurilkkeyo. (*je-ga sul-guh-jee-reul do-wa-deu-ril-kke-yo;* I'll help with doing the dishes.)

Jega ppallaereul dowadeurilkkeyo. (*je-ga ppal-lae-reul do-wa-deu-ril-kke-yo;* I'll help with the laundry.)

The words in Table 10-5 may come in handy.

Table 10-5	Cleaning	
Korean	*Pronunciation*	*English*
cheongso	*chung-so*	clean
jeongni	*jung-nee*	organize
seolgeoji	*sul-guh-jee*	wash dishes
gomujanggap	*go-moo-jang-gap*	rubber gloves
haengju	*haeng-joo*	dishcloth
geollae	*guhl-lae*	rags for wiping the floor
rakseu	*rak-seu*	bleach
bitjaru	*bit-ja-roo*	broom
sseurebaji	*sseu-rae-ba-gi*	dustpan
daegeollae	*dae-guhl-lae*	mop
meonji	*muhn-jee*	dust
ppallae	*ppal-lae*	laundry
setakgi	*sae-tak-gee*	washing machine
geonjogi	*geon-jo-gee*	dryer
sejae	*sae-jae*	detergent

Fun & Games

Match corresponding Korean and English phrases and words.

cheongso	Should I order it?
mogyok	kitchen
sikilkkayo?	Can you please help me?
jom dowa jusigetseumnikka?	copier
jeongmal pigonhamnida	I'm exhausted
syawo hasillaeyo?	clean
bueok	bath
boksagi	Do you want to take a shower?

Part III
Korean on the Go

The 5th Wave   By Rich Tennant

"Remember, this is Korea. If you're swearing in Korean at someone older than you, be sure to do it in the more polite and formal form."

In this part . . .

Okay, you won't have any fun if you just go to Korea and sit in your hotel room. Of course, to get out of your hotel room and around town, you have to know some specific expressions as well as where to find things you need, like taxis, a place to eat, and so on. If you're traveling, use this part to make your experience more enriching as well as make your traveling easier. If you need to exchange currency, book a hotel room, or ask for directions, the chapters in this part provides you with all you need to know.

Chapter 11

Money, Money, Money

In This Chapter

▶ Getting familiar with Korean won

▶ Exchanging currency

▶ Handling ATM transactions

▶ Paying with cash, plastic, and checks

*d***on** (*don;* money), in its multitude of denominations and currencies, shapes and forms, helps us supply and demand products, goods, and services. If you want to, you can use it to buy a car, caviar, a four star day-dream, or maybe even a football team. But regardless of what you do with your money, it's hard to imagine going a day without it.

In this chapter, you enter the fray by learning how to get the money from the **eunhaeng** (*eun-hang;* bank), how to exchange it, and how to pay with **hyeongeum** (*hyun-geum;* cash) or **kadeu** (*ka-deu;* credit card).

Knowing Korean Currency

In South Korea, the local currency is the **won**. The **won** is pronounced like the *won* in "The Sox won the Series."

Korean currency is roughly 1,000 won to the dollar. So every penny is worth about 10 won. Here are the denominations to know:

✔ **il won** (*il–won;* 1 won): Worth a tenth of a penny. Although you can still use them to buy things, 1-won pieces are hard to come by nowadays.

✔ **sip won** (*ship-won;* 10 won) and **osip won** (*o-ship-won;* 50 won): The pennies and dimes of Korea. Most people find these coins a hassle to deal with. You can likely find **sip won** on the ground just like U.S. pennies.

✔ **baek won** (*baek-won;* 100 won): It has the same size and color as a quarter. These coins are used about as often as quarters but are actually worth about as much as a dime.

- **obaek won** (*o-baek-won;* 500 won): This coin has the size and shape of a 50-cent piece, but they are used much more extensively.

- **cheon won** (*chun-won;* 1,000 won): A white and light purple bill, is worth roughly $1.

- **ocheon won** (*o-chun-won;* 5,000 won): A white and brown bill, is worth roughly $5.

- **man won** (*man-won;* 10,000 won): A green bill, roughly worth about $10. The **man won** bill is the largest denomination printed by the Korean National Bank.

- **supyo** (*soo-pyo;* special bank check): Koreans do not use checks like we do. However, for denominations larger than **man won**, they have something called **supyo**. These **supyo** comes already printed with the amount. When you are using **supyo** in Korea, you need to show your identification and sign at the back of the **supyo**, just like endorsing checks. The most commonly used **supyo** is **sipman won** (*ship-man-won;* $100). Other amounts of **supyo** are **osipman won** (*o-ship-man-won;* $500) and **baekman won** (*baek-man-won;* $1000), but these are not very commonly used. You may need to pay a small fee if you want to go to a bank and take some money out using **supyo**.

It takes a while to get used to seeing so many zeroes behind the numbers, but it might help to know that Koreans usually put a comma after every three digits for easy reading. So you can think of the 1,000-, 5,000-, and 10,000-won bills as $1, $5, and $10 bills, respectively.

Changing Currency

Most banks in Korea exchange foreign currency at competitive rates, almost always better than those of hotels or kiosks, and almost all of them will exchange U.S. dollars for **won**. Even if you forgot to exchange your money before getting to Korea there are several banks at the airport that will exchange your dollars for **won**, so there's no need to sweat it. However, you may need to pay a small fee when you are exchanging currencies in Korea.

Some banks have their customers wait in line, but many of them require that you take a numbered ticket, take a seat somewhere and wait your turn. Once you see your number light up at one of the counters, walk towards the teller and be ready to take care of your business.

The phrases that I have included below are ones that you might hear the teller use, and ones that you might want to use yourself. I have listed the sentences roughly in the order of what words you may use during a visit to exchange currency. Although you can still use informal polite form of Korean to answer bank tellers, please note that at a bank setting, the tellers will usually use formal polite form of Korean, and they use Sino-Korean numbers. (For more information on Sino-Korean numbers, look in Chapter 2.)

[some word] beon sonnim [some word] [some word] beon changguro osipsiyo. *([some word] bun son-nim [some word] [some word] bun chang-goo-ro o-ship-shi-yo;* Will customer number [some word] please come to counter number [some word] [some word]?; formal polite). Substitute [some word] for the number ticket you are carrying, and [some word] [some word] for the number of the counter. For example:

sibobeon sonnim, gubeon changguro osipsiyo. *(ship-o-bun son-nim, goo-bun chang-goo-ro o-ship-shi-yo;* Will customer number 15 please come to counter number 9?; formal polite)

oneul mueoseul dowadeurilkkayo? *(o-neul moo-uh-seul do-wa-deu-ril-kka-yo;* How may I help you today? ; formal polite)

oneul museun illo osyeotseumnikka? *(o-neul moo-seun il-lo o-syuh-sseum-ni-kka;* What business brings you here today? ; formal polite)

Your answers to above questions might be something like below. However, you can either use formal polite or informal polite form to answer the teller. Either is just fine, although I think most Koreans will use the informal polite forms in this case.

hwanjeoneul hago sipseumnida. *(hwan-juhn-eul ha-go ship-sseum-ni-da;* I would like to exchange some currency; formal polite)

hwanjeoneul hago sipeoyo. *(hwan-juhn-eul ha-go shi-puh-yo;* I would like to exchange some currency; informal polite)

dalleoreul wonhwaro bakkwo jusipsiyo. *(dal-luh-reul won-hwa-ro ba-kkwo joo-ship-shi-yo;* I would like to exchange dollars for won; formal polite)

dalleoreul wonhwaro bakkwo juseyo. *(dal-luh-reul won-hwa-ro ba-kkwo joo-sae-yo;* I would like to exchange dollars for won; informal polite)

dalleo dae wonhwa hwannyuri eotteoke doemnikka? *(dal-luh dae won-hwa hwan-yoo-ree uh-ttuh-kae dwem-ni-kka;* How is exchange rate for the dollar to the won?; formal polite)

dalleo dae wonhwa hwannyuri eotteoke doeyo? *(dal-luh dae won-hwa hwan-yoo-ree uh-ttuh-kae dwae-yo? ;* How is the exchange rate for the dollar to the won?; informal polite)

yeohaengja supyoreul bakkulttaeneun hwannyuri eotteoke doemnikka? *(yuh-haeng-ja soo-pyo-reul ba-kkul-ttae-neun hwan-yoo-ree uh-ttuh-kae dwem-ni-kka?* What is the exchange rate, when you exchange traveler's checks? formal polite)

yeohaengja supyoreul bakkulttaeneun hwannyuri eotteoke doeyo? *(yuh-haeng-ja soo-pyo-reul ba-kkul-ttae-neun hwan-yoo-ree uh-ttuh-kae-dwae-yo;* What is the exchange rate, when you exchange traveler's checks? informal polite)

After you answer the teller's questions, the teller may say the following phrases.

ye sonnim, jamsiman gidaryeo jusipsiyo. (ye, son-nim, jam-shi-man gee-da-ryuh joo-ship-shi-yo; yes, sir/ma'am, one moment please; formal polite)

ye, wonhwa [some word] woneul junbihae deurigetseumnida. (*ye, won-hwa [some word] won-eul joon-bee-hae deu-ree-get-sseum-ni-da;* Yes, sir/ma'am, I'll get the [some word] won you asked for; formal polite)

Talkin' the Talk

Judy, an American tourist, goes to a bank teller to exchange some traveler's checks. She approaches counter number 3.

Teller: **oneul mueoseul dowadeurilkkayo?**
o-neul moo-uh-seul do-wa-deu-ril-kka-yo?
What can I help you with today?

Judy: **yeohaengja supyoreul hwanjeon hago sipseumnida. migukdalleo dae wonhwa hwannyuri eotteoke doeyo?**
yuh-haeng-ja soo-pyo-reul hwan-juhn ha-go ship-sseum-ni-da. mee-goog-dal-luh dae won-hwa hwan-yoo-ree uh-ttuh-kae dwae-yo?
I'd like to exchange traveler's checks. What is the U.S. dollar-to-won exchange rate?

Teller: **sasilttae hwannyureun ildalleoe cheonbaegwon-imnida, pasilttae hwannyureun ildalleoe cheonwon-imnida.**
sa-shil-ttae hwan-yoo-reun il-dal-luh-ae chun-bae-gwon-im-ni-da, pa-shil-ttae hwan-yoo-reun il-dal-luh-ae chun-won-im-ni-da.
It's $1 to 1,100 won when you buy and $1 to 1,000 won when you sell.

Judy: **geureom, yeohaengja supyo obaekdalleoreul won-hwaro bakkwo juseyo.**
geu-reom, yuh-haeng-ja soo-pyo o-baek-dal-luh-reul won-hwa-ro ba-kwo joo-sae-yo.
Then could you exchange $500 in traveler's checks to won for me?

Teller:	jamsiman gidaryeo jusipsiyo. osimmanwoneul jeonbu manwongwoneuro deurilkkayo?
	jam-shi-man gee-da-ryuh joo-ship-shi-yo. o-ship-man-won-eul juhn-boo man-won-gwon-eu-ro deu-ril-kka-yo?
	One moment, please. Do you want all of 500,000 won in 10,000-won bills?
Judy:	ocheonwongwon jipye dujanghago, cheonwongwon jipye yeoljang juseyo. nameojineun manwong-woneuro juseyo.
	o-chun-won-gwon jee-pye doo-jang-ha-go, chun-won-gwon jee-pye yuhl-jang joo-sae-yo. na-muh-jee-neun man-won-gwon-eu-ro joo-sae-yo.
	Please give me two 5,000-won bills and ten 1,000-won bills. I'd like the remainder in 10,000-won bills.

Words to Know

bakkwo jusipsiyo	ba-kkwo joo-ship-shi-yo	Please Exchange
eunhaengwon	eun-haeng-won	Bank teller
gidaryeo jusipsiyo	gee-da-ryuh joo-ship-shi-yo	Please wait
hwanjeon	hwan-juhn	Currency exchange
hwannyul	hwan-yuhl	Exchange rate
jamsiman	jam-shi-man	One moment
migukdalleo	mee-goog-dal-luh	U.S. dollar
pasilttae	pa-shil-ttae	When selling
sasilttae	sa-shil-ttae	When buying
wonhwa	won-hwa	Korean won
yeohaengja supyo	yuh-haeng-ja soo-pyo	Traveler's check
yeogwon	yuh-gwon	Passport

Working the ATM

If you're ever running low on cash in Korea, you might find it comforting to know that you can make quick withdrawal using your credit card, and sometimes debit card, at a Korean **hyeongeum jigeupgi** (*hyun-geum-jee-geup-gee;* ATM).

Just make sure to ask your bank or credit card company if its cards work in Korea. You might also want to ask whether your credit card company or bank takes a **susuryo** (*soo-soo-ryo;* surcharge) for every transaction made in Korea before you hop on to that plane.

ATMs are available at every corner in Seoul, and most places in Korea have ATMs within a walking distance. There is a negligible difference between the exchange rates at ATMs and banks so use whichever is most convenient.

Many ATMs in Korea have the option of displaying their menus in both English and Korean. However some of them will only display their menus in Korean. Even so you can usually make a deposit by clicking the top-right button. That's where the key for "yes" and the button for "make a with-drawal" usually are.

In this section I show you how to ask where the ATMs are, and then go over a few items on the menu that are usually read aloud by the ATM machine for users. Please look in Chapter 12 if you want to learn more about giving and receiving directions.

> **geuncheoe hyeongeum jigeupgiga eodie iseoyo?** (*geun-chuh-ae hyun-geum-jee-geup-gee-ga uh-dee-ae ee-ssuh-yo?;* Where is an ATM around here?: informal polite)

Directions to follow from the ATM may be as follows. However, these instruc-tions can be in English in some ATMs. In ATMs which only use Korean, follow-ing phrases might be written in Korean alphabet. In this case, you may need some help. ATMs in Korea will use formal polite form of Korean.

> **kadeureul neoheo jusipsiyo.** (*ka-deu-reul nuh-uh joo-ship-shi-yo;* Please insert your card.: formal polite)

> **ne jari bimilbeonhoreul imnyeok hasipsiyo.** (*nae-ja-ree bee-mil-bun-ho-reul im-nyuhk-ha-ship-shi-yo;* Please enter your four-digit secret numbers: formal polite)

> **wonhasineun sseobisseureul mongnogeseo seontaekhasipsiyo.** (*won-ha-shi-neun ssuh-bee-sseu-reul mong-no-gae-suh suhn-taek-ha-ship-shi-yo;* Please select your desired service from the menu: formal polite)

yegeumeul wonhasineun geumaegeul imnyeokhaejusipsiyo. (*yae-geum-eul won-ha-shi-neun geum-ae-geul im-nyuk-hae-joo ship-shi-yo;* Please enter the amount that you want to deposit to your account; formal polite)

chulgeumeul wonhasineun geumaegeul imnyeokhaejusipsiyo. (*chul-geum-eul won-ha-shi-neun geum-ae-geul im-nyuk-hae-joo-ship-shi-yo;* Please enter the amount that you want to withdraw from your account; formal polite)

Paying for Your Purchases

In Korea, after you've picked an item that you like from a store, the following phrases will be useful. You can point to the item that you want to buy and say **jeogeollo juseyo** (*juh-guhl-lo joo-sae-yo;* Please give me that one) or **ieogeollo juseyo** (*ee-guhl-lo joo-sae-yo;* Please give me this one). If you're settling a tab after a meal, you might want to say **gyesanseo jom juseyo** (*gye-san-suh jom joo-sae-yo;* Please bring me the bill).

When you're out at a bar or at a restaurant, don't be surprised if one of your friends or seniors in a company says he or she will cover the bill. It's customary for Koreans to treat one another to dinners and drinks. If you ever find out that someone has paid for you, don't forget to thank them by saying **gamsahamnida** (*gam-sa-ham-ni-da;* thank you; formal polite) or tell them that you had a great meal (see "Talkin' the Talk" in the next section). If you're feeling good, try surprising your seniors, clients, or business partners by saying **oneureun jega sagetseumnida** (*o-neu-reun jae-ga sa-get-sseum-ni-da;* I'll pay for it today; formal polite).What goes around comes around in Korean society, so try to pick up the tab occasionally.

After you've asked for the bill, look for a nearby counter to pay. Usually you don't have to specify whether or not you want to use cash or credit card if you have your preferred method of payment in one hand and the bill in the other. In this section, I go over a few expressions that may come in handy when you're using one method of payment or the other.

Using cash

Money talks. After you've received your bill and have walked up to the counter to pay, you might want to know the following sentences:

gyesan hwaginhaejuseyo. (*gye-san hwa-gin hae-joo-sae-yo;* Could you please see if the numbers [on the bill] are right?)

geoseureum doni bujokhaneyo. (*guh-seu-reum do-nee boo-jok-ha-nae-yo;* (I'm short on change.)

geoseureum doneul neomu mani jusyeoseoeyo. (*guh-seu-reum do–neul nuh-moo ma-ni joo-syuh-ssuh-yo;* You gave me too much change.)

jega doni jom bujokhaneyo. (*do-nee jom boo-jok-han-dae-yo;* I don't have enough money.)

eolmaga deo piryohaseyo? (*ul-ma-ga duh pee-ryo-ha-sae-yo;* How much more do you need?)

deochipei halkkayo? (*duh-chi-pae-ee hal-kka-yo;* Do you want to go Dutch?)

Talkin' the Talk

Jeongsu and Robert are co-workers who have just finished a meal at a restaurant.

Jeongsu:	**jeogiyo, yeogi gyesanseo jom jusillaeyo?** *juh-gee-yo, yuh-gi gye-san-suh jom joo-shil-lae-yo?* Excuse me, may we have the bill?
Waiter:	**ye sonnim. jamsiman gidaryeo jusipsiyo.** *ye son-nim. jam-shi-man gee-da-ryuh joo-ship-shi-yo.* Yes, sir. One moment, please.
Robert:	**oneureun jega naegetseumnida.** *o-neu-reun jae-ga nae-get-sseum-ni-da.* I'll pick up the tab for today's dinner.
Jeongsu:	**jeongmaryo? robeoteussi, oneul deokbune jal meo-geotseumnida.** *jeong-mal-lyo? Robert sshi, o-neul duhk-bun-ae jal muh-guh-sseum-ni-da.* Really? I really had a good meal, thanks to you, Robert.
Robert:	**byeol malsseumeuryo.** *byuhl mal-sseum-eul-yo.* Don't mention it.

The waiter brings back the bill. Robert pays.

Robert:	**hyeongeum nyeongsujeung jom butakhamnida. geurigo jandoneun an jusyeodo gwaenchanayo.** *hyun-geum young-soo-jeung jom boo-tak-ham-ni-da. geu-ree-go jan-don-eun an joo-syuh-do gwaen-chan-a-yo.* Please bring me a cash receipt. And don't worry about the change.

Jeongsu:	**Robertssi, ireonalkkayo?**
	Robert-shsi, ee-ruh-nal-kka-yo?
	Robert, do you want to get going?

Words to Know

byeol malsseumeuryo	byuhl mal-sseum-eul-yo	Don't mention it.
gyesanseo	gye-san-suh	Bill
hyeongeum nyeongsujeung	hyun-geum nyoung-soo-jeung	Cash receipt
ireonalkkayo	ee-ruh-nal-kka-yo	Shall we get going?
jandon	jan-don	Change
jeogiyo	juh-gee-yo	Hey there, but can also be used as excuse me
jeongmaryo	jeong-mal-yo	Really?
jigap	jee-gap	Wallet/purse (can be either depending on the person talking about it)
sillyehamnida	shil-lae-ham-ni-da	Excuse me
sonnim	son-nim	Guest, sir, ma'am
yeogi	yuh-gi	Over here

Using plastic

Before you can pay your bill using your credit card or debit card of choice, you may want to find out whether the merchant takes your credit card. Most shopping venues and restaurants have a display showing which cards they accept, so it's a good idea to look around for a sign before presenting your card.

CULTURAL WISDOM

Paying in installments

If the store accepts your type of card, the store clerk will almost always ask you if you want to charge the entire sum on your credit card statement, or if you want to make smaller installments. In Korea you don't need to be buying a car to have the option of making installments, you can make installments on things like the groceries. The cashier will ask you over how many months you'd like to make the installments.

ilsibullo haedeurilkkayo, (*il-shi-bool-lo hae-deu-ril-kka-yo;* Do you want the full amount charged at once?)

halburo haedeurilkkayo. (*hal-boo-ro hae-deu-ril-kka-yo;* Do you want to pay in installments?)

halburo myeot gaewollo haedeurilkkayo? (*hal-boo-ro myuh-gae-wol-lo hae-deu-ril-kka-yo;* How many monthly installments do you want to make?)

If you've looked around but can't find a sign, show the the card you want to pay with and ask **i kadeu badeuseyo?** (*ee ka-deu ba-deu-sae-yo;* Do you take this card?). If they don't, show them another card and ask, **i kadeuneunnyo?** (*ee ka-deu-neun-nyo;* What about this card?). When talking to a customer, waiters and person at the cash register will use formal polite form of Korean. However, it is perfectly fine for you to use the informal polite form.

Here are a few phrases you may hear or use when you pay with a credit card:

kadeuro jibul hasigetseumnikka? (ka-deu-ro jee-bool ha-shi-get-seum-ni-kka?: Do you want to pay by credit card?; formal polite)

jeohui eopsoeseoneun i kadeureul batji ansseumnida. (juh-hee uhp-so-ae-suh-neun ee ka-deu-neun bat-jee an-sseum-ni-da; Our business doesn't take this credit card.; formal polite)

jeohui eopsoeseoneun ___, __,___kadeuman batseumnida. (juh-hee uhp-so-ae-suh-neun ___, __, __ka-deu-man bat-sseum-ni-da: Our business takes only __, __, __ cards.; formal polite)

kadeu georaega seungini doeji ansseumnida. (*ka-deu guh-rae-ga seung-in-ee dwae-jee an-sseum-ni-da;* The transaction isn't going through.; formal polite)

hanbeon deo haebwajuseyo. (*han-bun duh hae-bwa-joo-sae-yo;* Please try it again: informal polite)

dareun kadeuneun eopseusimnikka? (*da-reun ka-deu-neun uhp-sseu-shim-ni-kka;* Do you have any other cards?; formal polite)

geuncheoe hyeongeum jigeupgiga innayo? (*geun-chuh-ae hyun-geum jee-geup-gee-ga in-na-yo;* Is there an ATM nearby?; informal polite)

i chingureul damboro matgyeonoko jamkkan don ppobeureo gatda olkkeyo. (*ee chin-goo-reul dam-bo-ro mat-gyuh-no-ko jam-kkan don ppo-beu-ruh gaht-get-da-ol-kkae-yo;* I'll leave my friend here as collateral while I go out to withdraw some money; informal polite)

Using personal checks

Using American personal checks in Korea is almost impossible, so make sure to leave your U.S. checkbooks at home. **Supyo** (*soo-pyo;* Korean personal checks) differ from U.S. ones in that they are bank issued and come in sums that you set at the bank. You can't sign the amount that you want to pay and sign at the bottom. You need to tell the teller how much you want the check to be; then he or she will print out a note with the agreed sum.

The most common denomination of personal checks is 100,000 won, which is roughly the equivalent of $100.

Most banks collect a fee for issuing checks, and if you want to spend the checks, it is necessary to provide photo ID. For this reason, in most cases, it's best if you stick to using cash and credit cards for most of your transactions in Korea.

Fun & Games

Please match the following illustrations with corresponding Korean words. See Appendix C for correct answers.

A.

B.

C.

D.

E.

F.

A. _____

B. _____

C. _____

D. _____

E. _____

F. _____

Chapter 12

Asking Directions

In This Chapter

▶ Asking and answering "where" questions

▶ Specifying which direction, how many, and how far

▶ Referring to locations, directions with actions

*E*veryone, even the most street wise, can get lost once in a while. Especially in a foreign country, this happens more often than one would like to admit. Then how do you get your bearing back? How do you continue on your trail, or continue your tour through a city? How do you ask someone where the nearest **sikdang** (*shik–dang;* restaurant) is, or **ucheguk** (*oo-chae-gook;* post office) is, or even a **hwajangsil** (*hwa-jang-shil;* bathroom)? If it is an emergency, you'll have to get to the nearest **byeongweon** (*byung–wuhn;* hospital), or **gyeongchalseo** (*gyung-chal-suh;* police station).

This chapter will give you a few handy tips that will make it easier to get back on the right track, get you to head in the right direction, even if it's just returning to the safety and comfort of your hotel, just by asking a few simple questions. After you learn a few, key phrases from this chapter, you should feel a bit more confident in venturing out.

When you are in the large metropolitan areas, the chances of you finding someone who speaks English is generally greater than you would if you were along the countryside. Try to pay particular attention to your surroundings in the more remote areas and the chances of you getting lost will be slightly slimmer.

Asking for Directions

Even the best map reader might need directions from time to time. You may discover yourself needing to find a particular location or needing to use transportation to get there. The following sections show you how to politely ask someone how to get to places or ask someone to take you somewhere.

Although it's perfectly acceptable to point in whichever direction you'd like to go to, it is considered extremely rude to point your finger at another person. Pointing your finger at someone is generally done in an accusatory manner, and it should never be done in polite company. If you would like to point someone out in a crowd, instead of pointing your finger at that person, point them out with an open hand.

Finding your way with "where?"

Before you approach a stranger to ask for directions, you have to know the proper way of addressing the person first. Start the conversation with **sillyehamnida** (*shil-lae ham-ni-da;* excuse me) or **sillyehajiman** (*shil-lae-ha-jee-man;* excuse me, but). A more direct, literal translation would be "begging your pardon," or "begging your pardon, but."

The key difference between the two phrases is that, **sillyehamnida** can be used as a phrase in itself, say, when you accidentally bump into someone. **sillyehajiman** is used when there's a request behind it. Such as, **"sillyehajiman, hwajangsiri eodi itjyo?"** (*shil-lae-ha-jee-man, hwa-jang-shi-ree uh-dee ee-jyo;* Excuse me, but/Begging your pardon, but can you tell me where the bathroom is?)

Next phrase you have to familiarize yourself with if you need to find where you're going to, is the phrase, **"eodi itjyo?"** (*uh-dee ee-jyo?;* Where is it?). **eodi** (*uh-dee*) is the Korean word for "where?", and **itjyo** (*ee-jyo?*) is the inquisitive version of the verb **itda** (*ee-da*), which means to exist, or to be. So, the question **"eodi itjyo?"** (*uh-dee ee-jyo?*), literally means, "Where is it?". Now all you have to do is to find the Korean word for the place you need to get to and add it in the front of the sentence.

Sounds simple enough, right? Well, this is where it gets a little tricky. You have to place one of the connecting syllables **ee** or **ga** between the object/destination of your choice and the question, "Where is it?" To understand which one to use, just follow these two simple rules:

✔ If the word or place you're looking for ends in a consonant, add **ee**.

✔ If the word or place you're looking for ends in a vowel, add **ga**.

Here are some examples:

- **hwajangsiri eodi itjyo?** (*hwa-jang-shil-ree uh-dee ee-jyo;* Where is the bathroom?)

- **gyeongchalseoga eodi itjyo?** (*gyung-chal-suh-ga uh-dee ee-jyo;* Where is the police station?)

- **doseosiri eodi itjyo?** (*doh-suh-shi-ree uh-dee ee-jyo?* Where is the library?)

- **suyeongjangi eodi itjyo?** (*soo-young-jang-ee uh-dee ee-jyo;* Where is the swimming pool?)

- **je keompyuteoga eodi itjyo?** (*jae kum-pyoo-tuh-ga uh-dee ee-jyo;* Where is my computer?)

- **chigwaga eodi itjyo?** (*chi-gwa-ga uh-dee ee-jyo;* Where is the dental office?)

Depending on how far the place you need to get to is, you may need to take a **jihacheol** (*jee-ha-chul;* subway), a **beoseu** (*buh-sseu;* bus), or a **taeksi** (*taek-shi;* taxi). Once again, in a large metropolitan area, the maps and guides will be easier to find in English, but out in the countryside, you'll have to remember how to ask directions in Korean. You may also want to learn how to say, **"yeogiseo meongayo?"** (*yuh- gee-suh mun-ga-yo;* Is it far from here?) or, **"yeogiseo gakgaungayo?"** (*yuh-gee-suh ga-gga-oon-ga-yo;* Is it near to here?) **yeogi** (*yuh-gee*) in Korean means "here." **meoreoyo** (*muh-ruh-yo*) means far, **gakkawoyo** (*ga-kka-wo-yo*) means near.

Talkin' the Talk

Jim is lost and trying to get back to his hotel. He walks to a gas station to ask for directions.

Jim:	sillyehamnida. jeo jom dowajusigeseoyo? *shil-lae-ham-nee-da. juh jom do-wah-joo-shi-get-ssuh-yo?* Excuse me. Can you please help me?
Attendant:	ne, eotteoke dowadeurilkkayo? mweo piryohaseyo? *ne, uh-ttuh-kae do-wa-deu-ril-kka-yo? moo-uh pee-ryo-ha-sae-yo?* Yes, How can I help you? What do you need?
Jim:	jega gireul ireobeoryeoseoyo. kalteun hoteri yeogiseo meongayo? *jae-ga geel-eul ee-ruh-buh-ryuh-ssuh-yo. kal-teun ho-te-ree yuh-gee-suh mun-ga-yo?* I've lost my way. Is the Carlton Hotel far from here?

Attendant: **aniyo. byeollo an meoreoyo. jeogi boineun beoseu jeongnyujang baro oreunjjoge iseoyo.**
a-ni-yo. byul-lo an-muh-ruh-yo. juh-gee bo-ee-neun buh-sseu jeong-nyu-jang ba-ro o-reun-jjo-gae ee-ssuh-yo.
No. It's not that far. It's immediately to the right of the bus stop you see over there.

Jim: **ye. gamsahamnida.**
ye. gam-sa-ham-ni-da.
Yes. Thank you very much.

Attendant: **mot chajeusimyeon dasi iriro oseyo. jega taeksireul bulleo deurilkkeyo.**
mot cha-jeu-shi-myun da-shi ee-ree-ro o-sae-yo. jae-ga taek-shi-reul bool-luh-deu-ril-kkae-yo.
If you can't find it, come back over here. I will call you a taxi.

Words to Know

an meoreoyo	*an muh-ruh-yo*	Not far
beoseu jeongnyujang	*buh-sseu jung-nyu-jang*	Bus stop
gakkawoyo	*ga-kka-wo-yo*	Near
iriro oseyo	*ee-ree-ro o-sae-yo*	Come back, come here
meoreoyo	*muh-ruh-yo*	Far
mwo piryohaseyo	*muh pee-ryo-ha-sae-yo*	What do you need?
oenjjok	*wen-jjok*	Left
oneuljjok	*o-reun-jjok*	Right

Specifying which direction

When you're giving or receiving direction through a language barrier, pointing and body language will go a long way in getting you on your way. However, you may want to remember a few of these words to help you along the way. An important word to know regarding direction is the word, **jjok,** (*jjok;* side), as in left side, right side, and such (see Table 12-1). You can also use **jjok** when talking about a "way," such as **ijjok** (*ee-jjok;* this way) and **jeo-jjok** (*juh-jjok;* that way). You will hear a Korean person use *jjok* a lot when giving you directions. Table 12-1 gives you some more directional words you may need to know.

Table 12-1	Terms for Direction and Location	
Korean Word	*Pronunciation*	*Translation*
apjjok	*ahp-jjok*	front side
bandaejjok	*ban-dae-jjok*	opposite side
bukjjok	*book-jjok*	north side
dongjjok	*dong-jjok*	east side
dwijjok	*dwee-jjok*	back side
gakkawoyo	*ga-kka-wo-yo*	near
jeogi	*juh-gee*	there
meoreoyo	*muh-ruh-yo*	far
namjjok	*nam-jjok*	south side
oenjjok	*wen-jjok*	left side
oreunjjok	*o-reun-jjok*	right side
seojjok	*suh-jjok*	west side
yeogi	*yuh-gee*	here

Talkin' the Talk

Pam is trying to get to the British Embassy. She asks Jerry for directions to the Embassy.

Pam: **jerryssi, jega naeil yeongguk yeongsagwane gaya doegeodeunyo. yeongsagwan kkaji eotteoke gajyo? yeogiseo meongayo?**
jerry-sshi. jae-ga nae-il young-gook young-sa-gwan ae ga-ya dwae-guh-deun-yo. young-sa-gwan-kka-jee uh-ttuh-kae ga-jee-yo? yuh-gee-suh mun-ga-yo?
Jerry. I have to go to the British Embassy tomorrow. How do I get to the Embassy? Is it far from here?

Jerry: **ye. jom meoreoyo. geureochiman taeksireul tago gamyeon jom bissado sigando jeoryakdoego pyeollihaeyo.**
ye. jom muh-ruh-yo. geu-ruh-chi-man taek-shi-reul ta-go ga-myun jom bee-ssa-do shi-gan-do juh-ryak-dwae-go pyul-lee-hae-yo.
Yes, it's quite far. However, if you take a taxi, although a little more expensive, you'll save a lot of time and it'll be more comfortable.

Pam: **taeksi unjeonsadeuri yeongguk yeongsagwani eodi inneunji alkkayo?**
taek-shi oon-jun-sa-deu-ree young-gook young-sa-gwa-nee uh-dee in-neun-jee al-kka-yo?
Do you think the taxi driver will know where the British Embassy is?

Jerry: **ama alkkeoeyo. hajiman eodi intneunji moreundamyeon Seoul sicheonge deryeoda dallago haseyo. yeongguk yeongsagwaneun Seoul sicheong baro yeope iseoyo.**
a-ma al-kkuh-ae-yo. ha-jee-man uh-dee in-neun-jee mo-reun-da-myun suh-ool shi-chung-ae dae-ryuh-da dal-la-go ha-sae-yo. young-gook young-sa-gwan-eun suh-ool shi-chung ba-ro yuh-pae ee-ssuh-yo.
They probably know. If they don't, ask them to take you to Seoul city hall. The British Embassy is right next to the Seoul city hall.

Pam: **gomawoyo jeryssi. naeil yeongsagwane gatda omyeon siksa gachi hallaeyo?**
go-ma-wo-yo jerry-sshi. nae-il young-sa-gwan-ae ga-tta-o-myun shik-sa ga-chi-hal-lae-yo?
Thank you, Jerry. When I come back from the Embassy tomorrow, would you like to grab a bite to eat?

Jerry: **joayo. geureom naeil bwayo.**
jo-a-yo. geu-rum nae-il bwa-yo.
Good. Then I'll see you tomorrow.

Words to Know

bissayo	bee-ssa-yo	Expensive
dogil	do-gil	Germany
miguk	mee-gook	U.S.
peurangseu	peu-rang-sseu	France
pyeollihaeyo	pyul-lee-hae-yo	Comfortable, convenient
sicheong	shi-chung	City hall
ssayo	ssa-yo	Cheap, not expensive
unjeonsasa	oon-juhn-sa	Driver
yeongguk	young-gook	England, UK
yeongsagwan	young-sa-gwan	Ambassy

Specifying distance

When asking someone how far somewhere is, they may answer you in meters or kilometers in Korea. Koreans do not use miles when they are talking about distance. So if you want to ask someone how far somewhere is, ask them **yeogiseo eolmana meoreoyo** (*yuh-gee-suh ul-ma-na muh-ruh-yo;* How far is it from here)? when asking them how near somewhere is, ask **yeogiseo eolmana gakkawoyo** (*yuh-gee-suh ul-ma-na ga-kka-wo-yo;* How close it from here)? When talking about distance, Koreans will use Sino-Korean numbers for meters and kilometers. However, when telling time to specify the distance, remember that the hours are in native Korean numbers and minutes are in Sino-Korean numbers. Typical answers to these questions might be something like:

> **oreunjjogeuro baek miteo gaseyo** (*o-reun-jjok-eu-ro baek mee-tuh ga-sae-yo;* Please go 100 meters to the right)

> **yeogiseo charo o killomiteo deo gayahaeyo** (*yuh-gee-suh cha-ro o kee-ro-me-tuh ga-ya-hae-yo;* From here you need to go 5 kilometers by car)

yeogiseo oenjjogeuro georeoseo obunjeongdo gaseyo (*yuh-gee-suh wen-jjo-geu-ro guh-ruh-suh o-boon-jung-do ga-ya-hae-yo;* From here you need to walk to your left for about five minutes)

Giving Directions

If you have to give directions to the hotel you're staying at, or if you want to give directions to a nice little restaurant you've found off the beaten path, you have to learn how to give directions to that person. When giving someone directions, you need to know more words than just **yeogi** (*yuh-gee;* here) and **jeogi** (*juh-gee;* there).

Referring to locations on the street

Usually, when referring to locations on the street, you would use the term "**ape**"(*a-pae*), which means "in front of." You would use this term with various landmarks as well. For example, you could say, "**namdaemun apeseo mannayo**" (*nam-dae-moon a-pae-suh man-na-yo*), which is translated, "Let's meet in front of Namdaemun." **namdaemun** (*nam-dae-moon*), which literally translated means, " the South Gate", was one of the four entry points into the capital city of the old **joseon** (*jo-suhn*) dynasty. The city of Seoul has grown way past the four gates marking the boundaries of the old capital, but **namdaemun** stood as a landmark and a thriving commercial district surrounds the landmark until recently. On Feb 10th 2008, **namdaemoon** was burnt down by an arsonist. This day, a great national treasure of Korea was lost. It was a very sad day.

Providing actions with directions

When you ask a Korean person for directions, most of the time, he/she will get right next to you and point at the direction you need to go. What they're trying to accomplish by standing right next to you is they're trying to give you directions from your perspective. Hand motions and body gestures are very important as indicators of directions. For example, if you need to turn **oenjjok** (*wen-jjok;* left) at the **sinhodeung** (*shin-ho-deung;* traffic light), he/she will make a wave in that direction after they point at the light. Pay particular attention to their hand signals (gestures) if you have trouble understanding their verbal directions. Learning to read body language is an important aspect in communication. When you're giving directions to someone, try standing next to the person and give them directions from their perspective.

Making directions flow

A good word to know in making directions flow is the word **daeume** (*da-eu-mae;* afterward or and then). So you can say

> **jeogi itneun shinhodeungeuro gan daeume oenjjogeuro gaseyo** (*juh-gee in-neun shin-ho-deung-eu-ro gan da-eu-mae wen-jjo-geu-ro ga-sae-yo;* after going to that traffic light over there, then go left).

> **geu hayansaek jip apeseo sesibane mannayo** (*geu ha-yan-saek jeep a-pae-suh sae-shi-ba-nae man-na-yo;* Let's meet in front of that white house at 3:30).

Talkin' the Talk

Patrick is trying to get Anita to try a new restaurant in town.

Patrick: **anitassi, aju masitneun sikdang hana chajanneunde jeorang gachi gallaeyo?**
aa-nee-ta-sshi, a-joo ma-shi-in-neun shik-dang ha-na cha-jah-neun-dae juh-rang ga-chi gal-lae-yo?
Anita, I found a great restaurant. Would you like to go with me?

Anita: **eodi inneundeyo?**
uh-dee in-neun-dae-yo?
Where is it?

Patrick: **yeogiseo byeollo meolji anayo. beoseu jeongryujang ape inneun sinhodeungeseo oenjjogeuro gamyeon golmok baro yeope iseoyo.**
yuh-gee-suh byul-lo mul-jee-a-na-yo. buh-sseu jung-ryoo-jang a-pae in-neun shin-ho-deung-ae-suh wen-jjo-geu-ro ga-myun gol-mog ba-ro yuh-pae ee-ssuh-yo.
It's not that far from here. If you go left at the traffic light in front of the bus stop, it's right next to the alley.

Anita: **eotteon eumsik jeonmunjib ingayo?**
uh-ttun eum-shik jun-moon-jeep in-ga-yo?
What kind of food do they specialize in?

Patrick: **iteri eumsik jeonmunjibieyo. guksureul geujibeseo jikjeop mandeulgeodeunnyo. neomu masiseoyo.**
ee-tae-ree eum-shik jun-moon-jeep-ee-ae-yo. gook-soo-reul geu-jeep-ae-suh jik-juhb man-deul-guh-deun-yo. nuh-moo ma-shi-ssuh-yo.
They specialize in Italian food. They make the noodles there themselves. It's so tasty.

Anita: **geuraeyo? geureom gachigayo. waenji gidaega doeneungeoryo?**
geu-rae-yo? geu-rum ga-chi-ga-yo. waen-jee gee-dae-ga dwae-neun-gul-ryo?
Really? Then let's go together. I'm looking forward to it.

Words to Know

ape	a-pae	Front
dwie	dwee-ae	Back
gidae	gee-dae	Expect
gil	gil	Road
golmok	gol-mok	Alley
guksu	gook-soo	Noodles
jeongryujang	jung-ryoo-jang	Bus stop
jeonmunjip	jun-moon-jeep	Specialty house
jikjeop	jik-juhp	Self
juyuso	joo-yoo-so	Gas station
sageori	sa-guh-ree	4-way intersection
sinhodeung	shin-ho-deung	Traffic light
sipjaro	ship-ja-ro	Cross road
yeope	yuh-pae	Side, next to

Fun & Games

According to the diagrams below, write down the cardinal direction these building are located in Korean. Answers can be found in Appendix C.

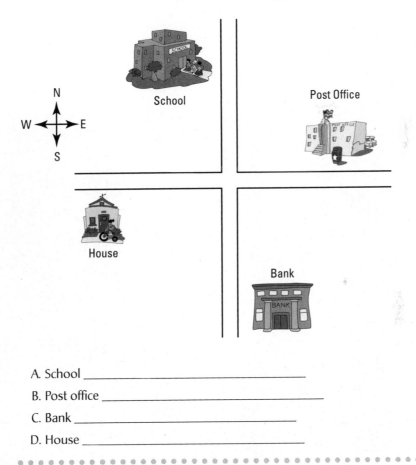

A. School _____

B. Post office _____

C. Bank _____

D. House _____

Chapter 13

Staying at a Hotel

* *

In This Chapter
▶ Checking out types of lodging
▶ Reserving a room
▶ Getting problems solved
▶ Settling the bill

* *

When you're visiting Korea, the chances are that you'll be staying at least for a while at a **hotel** (*ho-tel;* hotel), **yeoinsuk** (*yuh-in-sook;* Korean motel), or even a **minbak** (*min-bak;* bed and breakfast). You need to know the different accommodation options and the basic expressions so that you don't find yourself stuck with an unpleasant surprise.

This chapter gives you a brief overview of the accommodation options; some hints on proper etiquette; and expressions you need to reserve a room, check in, check out, and deal with any other issues in between.

Sorting Out the Accommodation Options

Just like anywhere else around the world, you can find the usual Western franchise hotels in Korea, mainly around the metropolitan areas like Seoul, Daegu, Daejeon, Busan (formerly spelled Pusan), and Gwangju. These hotels provide the usual, predictable amenities and services. If you are traveling on a fairly generous budget and are wary of trying new things, these places will be perfect for you. You can expect the staff to be fluent in English, and even if you're short on your Korean, that probably won't be a big problem at these places.

If you're willing to travel the less-beaten path and are looking for some more adventure, however, you can find numerous accommodation options, and they're usually more affordable than Western franchise hotels.

Traditional hotels

If you are used to sleeping on a soft surface, you may be in for a surprise: The traditional sleeping arrangement in Korea doesn't include a **chimdae** (*chim-dae;* bed). Instead, you find a **yo** (*yo;* a thick, heavy folding mattress) and **i-bul** (*ee-bool;* blanket) in the **jangnong** (*jang-nong;* closet) of your **bang** (*bang;* room). Spread the **yo** out on the floor, and use the **ibul** to keep yourself warm. This arrangement may sound uncomfortable, but it is softer than you think and actually better for your back than sleeping on a bed. The heat from the **ondol** (*on-dol;* heated floor) will keep you warm through a chilly winter night.

You won't find any sheets, but don't worry; the **yo** and **ibul** are covered with fitted sheets (think duvet covers). If the hotel is well maintained, housecleaning washes the covers after each guest.

When you wake up in the morning, you should make your bed or, more precisely, fold your bed. Fold the **yo** and **ibul** as you found them, and put them back in the closet or stack them in the corner of the room. This act is called **ibuleul gaeda** (*ee-bul-eul gae-da;* to fold the blanket), and proper etiquette is to take care of your bed yourself as soon as you wake up. The hotel staff won't be surprised if you don't, but if you do, you will be remembered as the well-mannered foreigner.

Motels

Next down the line after the hotel is the **yeogwan** (*yuh-gwan;* motel). These establishments are equivalent to motels in the United States and tend to be cheaper than hotels. You get what you pay for, so don't expect too much from these places.

Each room will have a separate **hwajangsil** (*hwa-jang-shil;* restroom), and you may or may not get a **chimdae** (*chim-dae;* bed). But you'll find a clean and affordable place with a friendly staff.

You can find **yeogwandeul** (*yuh-gwan-deul;* motels) are everywhere, usually near a **gichayeok** (*gee-cha-yuhk;* train station) or **beoseu jeongnyujang** (*beo-sseu-jung-nyoo-jang;* bus stop). Just look for a bright-red neon sign bearing the word **yeogwan** (*yuh-gwan*) or a ♨ symbol. The ♨ symbol means that the establishment has an **oncheon** (*on-chun;* hot spring). Interestingly, tons of **yeogwan**claim they have access to a natural hot spring that pumps out medicinal water.

You don't use an *s* after yeogwan like you would to change *motel* into *motels*. You should call it *yeogwandeul* when you are talking to someone about many motels. But usually even if there are more than one, Koreans usually use yeogwan instead of yeogwandeul.

Korean motels and B&Bs

Other options are **yeoinsuk** (*yuh-in-sook;* Korean motel) and **minbak** (*min-bak;* bed-and breakfast), which are homier and more informal than hotels and motels. Because these places tend to be small, you have the opportunity to interact with the staff members and other guests.

A **yeoinsuk** is a cheaper and smaller version of a **yeogwan**, and a **min-bak** is similar to a bed-and-breakfast. Both types of establishments tend to be family run and may be open only during the holiday seasons. In both places, you share a bathroom with other guests and sleep on a **yo** (*yo;* folding mattress) with an **ibul** (*ee-bool;* blanket).

Establishments in this category vary in terms of service and cleanliness. Some places include breakfast; others may charge you extra. You should call ahead and ask before you check in.

Hostels

Just like anywhere else you travel, you can find **yuseuhoseutel** (*yoo-sseu-ho-seu-tel;* youth hostel) in Korea. Youth hostels usually are more affordable than the other options. You share a room with other guests and have one or two communal showers and restrooms per floor.

A **yuseuhoseutel** may or may not have a cafeteria or a kitchen for meals.

Saunas and public baths

If you've been staying out till the wee hours of the morning and need a place to crash, or if you're stranded far from your hotel late at night, check out the ubiquitous **jjimjilbang** (*jjim-jil-bang;* large saunas). A **jjim-bang** can be considered as **mogyoktang** (*mo-gyok-tang;* public bath) that has several communal rooms (hot rooms, ice rooms, fire rooms, etc.) and an open area with heated floors where you can sleep or watch a TV. The public baths usually include pools of hot and cold water and individual showers.

jjimjilbang (*jjim-jil-bang*) are not your normal accommodation options. They're designed for people to take naps after a hot bath, but it's not uncommon for customers to stay overnight, since the owners of **jjimjilbang** do not keep tabs on you. Lodgings of this type are open 24 hours a day. If you want to try out one of them (I recommend that you visit at least one of these establishments), just buy a ticket, take a shower, change into the provided T-shirt and shorts, and visit the different communal rooms. When you find a spot with a thin mattress, you can sleep on them and no one will disturb you. A **jjimjilbang** costs much less than a normal motel would cost, and you don't have to check in or check out.

Always take a shower before you soak in the hot water. If you are familiar with the Japanese bathing style, you already know what to expect.

Finding Accommodations

Word of mouth is usually the best source of information you can get for a **yeogwan** (*yuh-gwan;* motel), **yeoinsuk** (*yuh-in-sook;* Korean motel), or **minbak** (*min-bak;* bed-and-breakfast). Ask around for recommendations before you start calling random places out of the **jeonhwabeonhobu** (*juhn-hwa-bun-ho-boo;* phone book). Also, narrow down your choices before you start roaming the streets so that you have a place to start.

The follow list gives you some descriptive words that you can use to ask your fellow travelers or friendly passers-by:

> **kkaekkeutan** (*kkae-kkeu-tan;* clean)
>
> **ssan** (*ssan;* cheap)
>
> **joeun** (*jo-eun;* nice)
>
> **gakkaun** (*ga-kka-oon;* nearby)

Talkin' the Talk

Dan is a college student who is backpacking through **Gyeongsangdo** (*gyoung-sang-do;* the southeastern region of Korea). He just arrived in a new town and needs a place to stay. He wants to stay in a **min-bak** (*min-bak;* bed-and-breakfast), but he doesn't know where to start looking, so he decides to ask Su-Jeong at the tourist information kiosk. Please note that Dan and Su-Jeong are speaking formal polite form of Korean because this is the first time they met.

Dan: **annyeonghasimnikka. geuncheoe kkaekkeutan min-bagi itseumnikka?**
an-nyoung-ha-shim-ni-kka. geun-chuh-ae kkae-kkeu-tan min-ba-gee ee-sseum-ni-kka?
Hello. Could you tell me where I can find a clean min-bak nearby?

Su-Jeong: **ye, gichayeok geuncheoe kkaekkeutago ssan min-bagi itseumnida**
ye, gee-cha-yuhk geun-chuh-ae kkae-kkeu-ta-go ssan min-ba-gee ee-sseum-ni-da.
Yes, you can find a clean and cheap minbak near the train station.

Dan: **gichayeogi eodie itseumnikka?**
gee-cha-yuh gee uh-dee-ae ee-sseum-ni-kka?
Where is the train station?

Su-Jeong: **jeojjogeuro baek miteo gamyeon oreunjjoge itseumnida. minbakjibeun gichayeok hago eunhaeng saie itseumnida.**
juh-jjo-geu-ro baek mee-tuh ga-myun o-reun-jjo-gae ee-sseum-ni-da. min-bak-jib-eun gee-cha-yuhk-ha-go eun-haeng-sa-ee-ae ee-sseum-ni-da.
The train station is on the right, a hundred meters from here to that direction. The minbak will be between the train station and the bank.

Dan: **a ye, gomapseumnida.**
a ye, go-map-sseum-ni-da.
Oh, okay, thank you.

Words to Know

ap	ap	Infront
eunhaeng	eun-haeng	Bank
gichayeok	gee-cha-yuhk	Train station
ijjok	ee-jjok	Over here
jeojjok	juh-jjok	Over there
jjimjilbang	jjim-jil-bang	Large sauna
kkaekkeutan	kkae-kkeu-tan	Clean
minbak	min-bak	Bed and breakfast
oenjjok	wen-jjok	Left
oreunjjok	o-reun-jjok	Right
sai	sa-ee	Between
ssan	ssan	Cheap
yeogwan	yuh-gwan	Motel
yeop	yuhp	Next to

Making Reservations

Now that you have an idea of where you want to stay, you should call ahead to make a reservation and ask some questions. If you are not planning to travel to the crowded coasts or popular mountains during holiday seasons, you probably won't have a problem finding accommodations. Nevertheless, you want to call ahead and figure out the rates and services offered.

These phrases can help you check on room availability and rates:

bangeul yeyakharyeogo haneundeyo. (*bang-eul yae-yak-ha-ryuh-go ha-neun-dae-yo;* I want to reserve a room.)

binbang iseoyo? (*bin-bang ee-ssuh-yo;* Do you have vacancies?)

harutbame eolmaeyo? (*ha-rut-ba-mae ul-ma-ae-yo;* How much is it for one night?)

sinnyongkadeu badayo? (*shin-nyong-ka-deu ba-da-yo;* Do you take credit cards?)

yeohaengja supyo badayo? (*yuh-haeng-ja soo-pyo ba-da-yo;* Do you take traveler's checks?)

Tell the clerk how long you plan to stay and the size of your party:

(number) bak iseul geoeyo. ([number] *bak ee-sseul guh-ae-yo;* I will be staying for (number) night([s]).)

For example: **sambak eseul geoyeyo.** (*sam-bak ee-sseul guh-ae-yo;* I will be staying for 3 nights.)

(number) myeong iseoyo. ([number] *myoung ee-ssuh-yo;* There are (number) people.)

For example: **dumyeong iseoyo.** (*doo-myoung ee-ssuh-yo;* There are two people.). Please see Chapter 2 for more information on numbers.

Talkin' the Talk

Dan walked to a nearby **gongjungjeonhwa** (*gong-jung-juhn-hwa;* public telephone, phone booth) to call ABC Hotel.

Clerk: **annyeonghasimnikka, ABC hotel imnida.**
an-nyoung-ha-shim-ni-kka, ABC ho-tel im-ni-da.
Hello, this is Hotel ABC.

Dan: **yeoboseyo. bang yeyakharyeogo haneundeyo. binbang iseoyo?**
yuh-bo-sae-yo. bang yae-yak-ha-ryuh-go ha-neun-dae-yo. bin-bang ee-ssuh-yo?
Hello. I want to reserve a room. Do you have any vacancies?

Clerk: **ye, binbang itseumnida. myeot bunisimnikka?**
ye, bin-bang ee-sseum-ni-da. myuh boon-ee-shim-ni-kka?
Yes, we have rooms available. How many people are there?

Dan: **han myeongiyo. harutbame eolmaeyo?**
han myoung-ee-yo. ha-rut-ba-mae ul-ma-ae-yo?
One person. How much is it for one night?

Clerk: **harutbame sibomanwon imnida. eolmana orae gye-sigetseumnikka?**
ha-rut-ba-me ship-o-man-won im-ni-da. ul-ma-na o-rae gye-shi-gae-sseum-ni-kka?
The rate is 150,000 won per night. How long are you planning to stay?

Dan: **sambak iseul geoeyo. sinnyoongkadeu badayo?**
sam-bak ee-sseul guh-ae-yo. shin-yong-ka-deu ba-da-yo?
I'm going to stay for three nights. Do you take credit cards?

Clerk: **ye, batseumnida. yeyak hasigetseumnikka?**
ye, ba-sseum-ni-da. yae-yak ha-shi-gae-sseum-ni-kka?
Yes, we do. Would you like to make a reservation?

Dan: **ye, josseumnida.**
ye, jo-sseum-ni-da.
Yes, that sounds good.

Words to Know

binbang	bin-bang	Empty room/vacancy
eolmaeyo?	ul-ma-ae-yo	How much is it?
eolmana orae	ul-ma-na o-rae	How long
gagyeok	ga-gyuhk	Price
haeyak	hae-yak	Cancellation
harutbam	ha-rut-ban	One night
hwiteuniseu keulleop	hwi-teu-ni-seu keul-luhb	Fitness club
iinsil	ee-in-shil	Double room
irinsil	il-in-shil	Single room
suyeongjang	soo-young-jang	Swimming pool
yeyak	yae-yak	Reservation

Asking for details

If you're planning to stay at a larger hotel with a good reputation, the expressions in the preceding section should be sufficient. But if you plan to stay at a **yeogwan** (*yuh-gwan;* motel), **yeoinsuk** (*yuh-in-sook;* Korean motel), or **minbak** (*min-bak;* bed-and-breakfast) and don't know what to expect, you may want to ask a couple more questions. The all-purpose question is **[some word] i/ga iseoyo?** (*[some word] i/ga i-seo-yo;* Do you have [some word]?) Some examples are:

> **chimdaega iseoyo?** (*chim-dae-ga ee-ssuh-yo;* Do you have a bed?)

> **inteoneti iseoyo?** (*in-tuh-net-ee ee-ssuh-yo;* Do you have an Internet connection?)

Just in case the transportation to the **yeogwan, yeoinsuk,** or **minbak** is inconvenient, you may also want to ask the following questions:

> **geogikkaji eotteoke chajagayo?** (*guh-gee-kka-jee uh-ttuh-kae cha-ja-ga-yo;* How do I find your place?)

> **museun gyotongeul iyonghaeya chatgi swiwoyo?** (*moo-seun gyo-tong-eul ee-yong-hae-ya chat-gee swee-wo-yo;* What transportation is most convenient to get there?)

Checking out the room

Don't forget to check out the room before you check in, because many smaller establishments require you to pay up front. These phrases may help:

> **bangi deobeul/singgeul ieyo?** (*bang-ee duh-beul/sing-geul ee-ae-yo;* Is the room a double/single?)

> **achim siksaneun nawayo?** (*a-chim shik-sa-neun na-wa-yo;* Is breakfast included?)

> **bang jom bol su iseoyo?** (*bang jom bol soo ee-ssuh-yo;* Can I take a look at the room?)

If you've checked out your room and don't like something about it, you can request a different room:

> **dareun bang iseoyo?** (*da-reun bang ee-ssuh-yo;* Is there another room?)

> **bangi jom jijeobun haneyo.** (*bang-ee jom ji-jeo-bun ha-ne-yo;* The room is a little dirty.)

Talkin' the Talk

Jessica is planning to stay in a small **minbak** (bed-and-breakfast) that Dan recommended. When she walks in, Mr. Park, the owner, greets her.

Jessica: **annyeonghaseyo. binbang iseoyo?**
an-nyoung-ha-sae-yo. bin-bang ee-suh-yo?
Hello. Do you have any vacancies?

Mr. Park: **ye itseumnida. harutbame sam manwonimnida.**
ye ee-sseum-ni-da. ha-rut-ba-mae sam man-won-im-ni-da.
Yes, we do. It will be 30,000 won per night.

Jessica: **bange yoksiri iseoyo?**
bang-ae yok-shi-ree ee-ssuh-yo?
Does the room have a private bath?

Mr. Park: **aniyo, eopseumnida. daesin gongdong hwajangsiri saegae itseumnida.**
a-ni-yo, uhp-sseum-ni-da. dae-shin gong-dong hwa-jang-shi-ree sae-gae ee-sseum-nida.
No, it does not. Instead, we have three communal bathrooms.

Jessica: **bang jom bol su iseoyo?**
bang jom bol soo ee-ssuh-yo?
Can I take a look at the room?

Mr. Park: **ye. ttara oseyo.**
ye. tta-ra o-sae-yo.
Yes. Follow me.

After seeing the room, Jessica is disappointed to find that the room was smaller and dirtier than she had expected.

Jessica: **bangi jom jijeobunhaneyo. dareun bang iseoyo?**
bang-ee jom jee-juh-boon-ha-nae-yo. da-reun bang ee-ssuh-yo?
The room is a little dirty. Do you have another room?

Mr. Park: **aniyo, eopseumnida.**
a-ni-yo, uhp-sseum-ni-da.
No, we don't have another room.

Jessica: **geureomyeon singyeong sseuji maseyo. annyeonghi gyeseyo.**
geu-ruh-myun shin-gyoung sseu-jee ma-sae-yo. an-nyoung-hee gye-sae-yo.
Then don't worry about it. Good bye.

Words to Know

chimdae	chim-dae	Bed
dareunbang	da-reun-bang	Different room
gongdong	gong-dong	Communal
hwajangjil	hwa-jang-shil	Restroom
inteonet	in-tuh-net	Internet
jeonhwa	juhn-hwa	Telephone
syawo	sya-wo	Shower
terebi	tae-rae-bee	TV
ttaraoseyo	tta-ra-o-sae-yo	Follow me
yoksil	yok-shil	Bathroom

Complaining 101

What would you do if you discovered that your toilet was hopelessly clogged? Or what if you lay down on your **yo** (*yo;* folding mattress) on a cold **gyeoulbam** (*gyuh-ool-bam;* winter night) expecting to doze off, only to find that the floor is ice cold? What if you expected a cool breeze of relief from the brutal August heat, only to be greeted by warm muggy air from your **eeokon** (*ae-uh-kon;* air conditioner)? These situations are only a sample of the problems you may run into during your stay in Korea, and you need to know how to deal with them.

Broken machinery

If some machinery in your unit is broken, and the problem is something relatively obvious and easily identifiable, the most efficient way to complain is to ask this:

[some word] jom gochyeo juseyo. (*[some word] jom go-chuh joo-sae-yo;* Please fix [some word] for me.)

eeokoon jom gochyeo juseyo. (*ae-uh-kon jom go-chuh joo-sae-yo;* Please fix the air conditioner for me.)

byeongitong jom gochyeo juseyo. (*byun-gee-tong jom go-chuh joo-sae-yo;* Please fix the toilet bowl for me.)

semyeondae jom gochyeo juseyo. (*sae-myun-dae jom go-chuh joo-sae-yo;* Please fix the basin for me.)

Some useful words are;

hiteo (*hee-tuh*) heater

naengjanggo (*naeng-jang-go*) refrigerator

mun (*moon*) door

sudokkokji (*soo-do-kkok-jee*) faucet

You may want to add a short description of the problem before you ask someone to fix it:

eeokoni annawayo. eeokon jom gochyeo juseyo. (*ae-uh-kon-ee an-na-wa-yo. ae-uh-kon jom go-chuho joo-sae-yo;* The air conditioner is not functioning. Please fix the air conditioner.)

byeongitong muri annaeryeogayo. byeongitong jom gochyeo juseyo. (*byun-gee-tong moo-ree an-nae-ryuh-ga-yo. byun-gee-tong jom go-chuho joo-sae-yo;* The water is not flushing. Please fix the toilet.)

If you don't think you can remember these expressions, just remember how to say **[some word] i/ga gojang naseoyo** (*[some word] i/ga go-jang na-ssuh-yo;* [some word] is broken). The management should come take care of the problem.

Noisy neighbors

If your next-door neighbors are too loud, you can't say **yeop bangi gojang-naseoyo. yeop bang jom gochyeo juseyo** (*yuhp bang-ee go-jang-na-ssuh-yo. yuhp-bang jom go-chuh-joo-sae-yo;* The next door [neighbor] is broken. Please fix the next door [neighbor].). Instead, you can say this:

yeop bangi neomu sikkeureowoyo. (*yuhp bang-ee nuh-moo shi-kkeu-ruh-wo-yo;* The next room is too loud.)

Other problems

Use the expression **bangi neomu** [some word]. (*bang-ee nuh-moo [some word];* The room is too [some word]) to describe what is wrong with your room, and fill in the blank with the appropriate word:

deowoyo (*duh-wo-yo*) hot

chuwoyo (*choo-wo-yo*) cold

deoreowoyo (*duh-ruh-wo-yo*) dirty

jagayo (*ja-ga-yo*) small

sikkeureowoyo (*shi-kkeu-ruh-wo-yo*) noisy/loud

If you are staying in a place that has **ondolbang** (*on-dol-bang;* Korean floor heating), you may be uncomfortable because the floor is too hot or too cold. If you want to be more specific, you can use the following expressions:

badagi neomu tteugeowoyo. (*ba-da-gee nuh-moo tteu-guh-wo-yo;* The floor is too hot.)

badagi neomu chagawoyo. (*ba-da-gee nuh-moo cha-ga-wo-yo;* The floor is too cold.)

Checking Out

Even if you fall in love with the place where you're staying, you can't stay there forever. After all, you have many other exciting places to visit. In this section, I show you how to find out your check-out time and how to pay the bill at the front desk.

If you're staying at a **yeoinsuk** (*yuh-in-sook;* Korean motel) or **minbak** (*min-bak;* bed-and-breakfast), you probably paid when you checked in. For those places, all you have to do is fold your bedding in the morning (refer to "Traditional hotels," earlier in this chapter), pack up, and leave.

To be polite, make sure to say goodbye to the owners if you're staying in a small facility.

You need some of these expressions when you are checking out:

myeotsie bangeul biwoya doeyo? (*myuh-shi-ae bang-eul bee-wo-ya dwae-yo;* What time do I need to check out?)

gyesan halkkeyo. (*gye-san hal-kkae-yo;* I would like to pay the bill.)

gyesanseoga jal mot doengeot gateunndeyo. (*gye-san-suh-ga jal mot dwen-geot ga-teun-dae-yo;* I think there is a mistake on the bill.)

Talkin' the Talk

Joshua is ready to leave the ABC Hotel after staying three nights. He walks up to the front desk to pay his bill and leave.

Clerk: **annyeonghasimnikka. pyeonan hasyeotseumnikka?**
an-nyoung-ha-shim-ni-kka. pyuhn-an ha-syuht-sseum-ni-kka?
Hello. Was your stay comfortable?

Joshua: **ye, joaseoyo. gyesanhalkkeyo.**
ye, jo-a-ssuh-yo. gye-san-hal-kke-yo.
Yes, it was great. I would like to pay the bill.

Clerk: **ye, chong hapaeseo osimmanwon nawatseumnida.**
ye, chong ha-pae-suh o-shim-man-won na-wa-sseum-ni-da.
Yes. The total is 500,000 won.

Joshua is slightly surprised, because he thought the bill would be 450,000 won. He wants to know where the extra 50,000 won came from.

Joshua: **ye? gyesanseoga jalmot doengeot gateundeyo. omanwon deo naongeot gatayo.**
ye? gye-san-suh-ga jal-mot dwen-guht ga-teun-dae-yo. o-man-won duh na-on-guht ga-ta-yo.
Excuse me? I think there is a mistake on the bill. I am charged 50,000 won additional.

Clerk: **a, ye, jamsimannyo.**
a, ye, jam-shi-man-nyo.
Ah, yes. Just a moment, please.

When the clerk checks, he discovers the hotel made a mistake and charged Joshua for room service that he didn't order.

Clerk: **a, joesonghamnida. chong sasip omanwon imnida.**
a, swae-song-ham-ni-da. chong sa-ship o-man-won im-ni-da.
Ah, I'm so sorry. The total is 450,000 won.

Joshua: **yeogi iseoyo.**
yuh-gee ee-ssuh-yo.
Here it is.

Clerk: **ye, gamsahamnida. annyeonghi gasipsiyo.**
ye, gam-sa-ham-ni-da. an-nyoung-hee ga-ship-shi-yo.
Thank you very much. Good bye.

Words to Know

bangbeonho	bang-bun-ho	Room number
bangyeolsoe	bang-yuhl-sae	Room key
chekeuout	che-keu-out	Check out
daeume tto olkkeyo	da-eum-ae tto-ol-kkae-yo	I'll come back next time.
gyesanhalkkeyo	gye-san-hal-kke-yo	I'd like to pay the bill.
gyesanseo	gye-san-suh	Bill
rumsseobiseu	room-ssuh-bee-sseu	Room service

Fun & Games

Fill in the blanks with the words from the following list (Appendix C reveals the correct answers):

jijeobunhaneyo

jeonhwa

gyesanseo

binbang

oneul

1. Bange _____ ga iseoyo? (Is there a telephone in the room?)

2. _____ chekeuautago sipeoyo. (I would like to check out today.)

3. Joesonghamnida, _____ i eopseumnida. (I'm sorry, we don't have vacancies.)

4. Bangi neomu _____. (The room is so dirty.)

5. Je _____ ga anieyo. (This is not my bill.)

Chapter 14

Transportation

. . . .

In This Chapter

▶ Getting around at the airport

▶ Getting around town

▶ Public transportation in Korea

▶ Renting a car

. . . .

*E*ven though Korea is a very small country, getting from one place to another can be quite a hassle. Because of the high population density, getting around can be more troublesome than a lot of other countries. Especially in urban areas, the rush hour traffic can last for hours, and a good part of your day may be ruined by being stuck in traffic. It can simply be a **nappeunkkum** (*na-ppeun-kkoom;* nightmare). However, even though Korea has a high population density, the country is quite modernized and has an excellent **daejung gyotong** (*dae-joong gyo-tong;* public transport) system that is very reliable. If you do visit the country, you should utilize the available public transit system to maximize your visit. By teaching you a few key phrases and sentences, this chapter can help you enjoy the country by minimizing the hassle that can be encountered in airports, bus terminals, train stations, and hailing cabs.

Getting Around at the Airport

Korea participates actively in the global economy. Due to the large amount of foreign investment in the country, many signs in **gonghang** (*gong-hang;* airports) and other transportation hubs have English written along side Korean on them. Initially, this will make your navigation through an airport much easier. You may also notice that the people working behind the information desk or the ticket counters all speak English as well. Korea is also a country that enjoys its technological advances and developments, so at Incheon International Airport, for example, you may even find a robot or two wandering around ready to call you a cab, make reservations at a hotel for you, recommend you fine shopping areas, or provide other amenities. It may even be able to recommend you a great restaurant, though what a robot knows about food, I haven't the slightest. Regardless of what the robot may tell you, the following sections can make your way through the airport easier.

Making it past the check-in counter

If you're ready to go on a **yeohaeng** (*yuh-haeng;* travel or trip), you need to be sure that you have everything so that you can get past the ticket counter with ease. Go over the following checklist of items to make sure you have everything you need for your journey:

✔ A **yeogwon** (*yuh-gwon;* a passport)

✔ A **yeohaeng gabang** (*yuh-haeng ga-bang;* a luggage or travel bag)

✔ Your **yeohaeng iljeong** (*yuh-haeng il-jung;* travel itinerary)

Talkin' the Talk

Brian is traveling from Chicago to Seoul. He is at the airport checking his bags in with the attendant.

Attendant:	**annyeonghaseyo. tiket jom boyeojusigetseumnikka?**
	an-nyoung-ha-sae-yo. tee-ket jom bo-yuh-joo-shi-get-sseum-ni-kka?
	Hello. May I please see your ticket?
Brian:	**ye. yeogi iseoyo.**
	ye. yuh-gee ee-ssuh-yo.
	Yes. Here it is.

Attendant: **seoule gasineyo. yeogwon jom boyeojusigetseum-nikka?**
seoul-ae ga-shi-nae-yo. yuh-gwon jom bo-yuh-joo-shi-gae-sseum-ni-kka?
I see you're going to Seoul. May I see your passport please?

Brian: **ne. yeogi iseyo.**
ne. yuh-gee ee-ssuh-yo.
Yes. Here it is.

Attendant: **eolmadongan hanguge gyesilgeomnikka?**
ul-ma-dong-an han-goo-gae gye-shil-gum-ni-kka?
How long are you planning on staying in Korea?

Brian: **sabak oil dongan iseul yejeongieyo.**
sa-bak o-eel dong-an ee-sseul yea-jung-ee-ae-yo.
I plan on staying four nights and five days.

Attendant: **yeohaeng gabangeun myeotgae gatgo gyesimnikka?**
yuh-haeng ga-bang-eun myut-gae gat-go gae-shim-ni-kka?
How many bags of luggage do you have?

Brian: **ye, segae gatgo iseoyo.**
ye, sae-gae gat-go ee-ssuh-yo.
Yes, I have three.

Attendant: **geujunge ginae gabangeun myeotgae gatgo gyesimnikka?**
geu-joong-ae gee-nae ga-bang-eun myut-gae gat-go gye-shim-ni-kka?
How many of those are carry-on luggage?

Brian: **i baenang hanamanyo.**
ee bae-nang ha-na-mahn-yo.
Just this backpack.

Attendant:	**changmun yeope inneun jwaseogeul deurilkkayo, animyeon tongno yeope inneun jwaseogeul deurilkkayo?**
	chang-moon yuh-pae in-neun jwa-suh-geul deu-ril-kka-yo, a-nee-myun tong-no yuh-pae in-neun jwa-suh-geul deu-ril-kka-yo?
	Would you like a seat next to the window, or would you like a seat next to the aisle?
Brian:	**doelsu iseumyeon changmun yeope inneun jwaseogeul juseyo.**
	dwel-soo ee-sseu-myun chang-moon yuh-pae in-neun jwa-suh-geul joo-sae-yo.
	If at all possible, I would like a seat next to the window, please.
Attendant:	**ye, algetseumnida. tapseunggwon yeogi itseumnida. pyeon beonho ibaek sipsam, jul isipsam, jwaseok "A" imnida.**
	ye, al-get-sseum-ni-da. tap-seung-gwon yuh-gi ee-sseum-ni-da. pyun bun-ho ee-baek ship-sam, jool ee-ship-sam, jwa-suk "A" im-ni-da.
	Yes, I understand. Here is your boarding pass. It's flight number two hundred and thirteen, row twenty three, seat "A."
Brian:	**gamsahamnida.**
	gam-sa-ham-ni-da.
	Thank you very much.
Attendant:	**ye, annyeonghi gasipsiyo.**
	ye, an-nyoung-hee ga-ship-shi-yo.
	Yes, please enjoy your journey.

Words to Know

baenang	*bae-nang*	Back pack
balcha	*bal-cha*	Departure (trains and buses)
bija	*bee-ja*	Visa
changmun	*chang-moon*	Window
chekeu in	*che-keu een*	Checking in
chulbal	*chul-bal*	Departure (flights)
chulgu	*chool-goo*	Exit
churipgu	*choo-rip-goo*	Entrance/exit/gate
dochak	*do-chak*	Arrival
doelsuiseumyeon	*dwel-soo-ee-sseu-myun*	If at all possible
eolmadongan	*ul-ma-dong-an*	For how long
gasineyo	*ga-shi-nae-yo*	You are going to
ginae gabang	*gee-nae ga-bang*	Carry on luggage
ipgu	*eep-goo*	Entrance
iseul yeojeongieyo	*ee-sseul yea-jung-ee-ae-yo*	Do you plan to stay?
jwaseok beonho	*jwa-suk bun-ho*	Seat number
mokjeokji	*mok-juk-jee*	Destination
myeotgae	*muht-gae*	How many
pyeon beonho	*pyun bun-ho*	Flight number
sojipum	*so-jee-poom*	Personal belongings
tapseunggwon	*tahp-seung-gwon*	Boarding pass/ticket
tiket	*tee-ket*	Ticket
tongro	*tong-no*	Aisle
yeohaengja supyo	*yuh-haeng-ja soo-pyo*	Traveler's check

Getting past Immigration and Customs

After you arrive at the airport, before you can go to the baggage claim, you have to go through the **ipgukja simsadae** (*eep-gook-ja shim-sa-dae;* Immigration) They check your **yeongwon** (*yuh-gwon;* passport) for your **bija** (*bee-ja;* visa). They also ask you if you're here on **il gwangye** (*il-gwan-gye;* work related), **gwangwang** (*gwahn-gwang;* sightseeing) or **chinji bangmun** (*chin-jee-bang moon;* visiting family & friends). After going through immigration, you need to pick up your bags and go through the customs. If you have anything to declare, especially meat, vegetables, seeds, fruits, dairy, anything made of fresh wood, etc. (just like in U.S.) you must declare those items. If you do not declare them and you get caught, you will have hefty fines and some good explaining to do. Due to the recent world affairs, security at the airport will be pretty tight and they will go through your luggage and such, but be patient and cooperative. You will have little trouble making it past the customs and you'll be out of the **gonghang** (*gong-hang;* airport) in no time.

Generally, from the United States, it takes at least ten to fourteen hours to get to Korea. Flying halfway around the world does take a bit of time and you may find yourself wanting something other than the in-flight movie that is provided. Many intercontinental flights do offer movies, blankets, pillows, and magazines to help pass the time, but you may grow tired of them rather quickly. Try to bring a book you enjoy, or a small handheld game device to make the time pass by much quicker.

Leaving the airport

Most airports have various means of travel available right as you leave the terminal. Many of them have **beoseu** (*buh-sseu;* bus) stops, **gicha** (*gee-cha;* train) stops, and **jihacheol** (*jee-ha-chul;* subway) stops all located within the airport. If you're not fond of mass transit or unsure as to how to get to your destination using them, you can always find a row of taeksi (*taek-si;* taxis) parked in front of the arrivals terminal as well. You can also find an **annaeweon** (*an-nae-won;* attendant/guide) who can hail a cab for you, make a reservation at a hotel, or whatever else you need done.

Hotels of every kind and quality are available in Korea, from the fanciest of world-class hotels, to more affordable, "efficient" motels. Instead of staying at hotels, you may also give hostels a try, or give temple stay a go. There are many Buddhist temples that offer temple stays and it's a completely different experience of the country than what a stay at a hotel can offer. If it is a genuine "Korean" experience you crave, these hostels or temple stays might just do the trick.

Getting Around Town

You've finally arrived at your hotel room, have unpacked, showered, and properly stretched out your **dari** (*da-ree;* legs). Now you're ready to hit the town. How do you go about doing it? Well, if you've arrived at a major metropolitan area like Seoul, or Busan, all the transportation options imaginable are available to you and can easily be found. The front desk at the hotel can be more than helpful in accomplishing this task. They may have a complimentary **jido** (*jee-do;* map) available for you, and because a **gichayeok** (*gee-cha-yuhk;* train stop) or a **beoseu jeongnyujang** (*buh-sseu jung-nyoo-jang;* bus stop) is usually right in front of the hotel or a short walk away, they will be more than happy to call you a **taeksi** (*taek-shi;* taxi, cab), or rent you a **jadongcha** (*ja-dong-cha;* car). If you're staying at a more rural area, some travel by foot may be necessary before you reach one of these transportation hubs. Acquiring a map of the area you're staying at, and circling out from your hotel as the central point is a good way to maximize your stay and enjoy the sights.

Hailing a cab

You'll find taxis all over the city. Parked in front of bus terminals, train stations, hotels, within a large, metropolitan area, you can find cabs pretty much anywhere. All you have to do is stand by the edge of the street and raise your **son** (*sohn;* hand), and a cab will pull up to pick you up eventually. However, if you're out in the country, or more rural areas, you have to call a taxi. This can be done by looking in a phone book, taking a phone number off the side of a cab, or you can ask someone to call a cab for you at any hotel or restaurant. Simply walk up to the front desk and say, "**jeo taeksi handaeman bulleo juseyo**" (*juh taek-shi han-dae-man bool-luh joo-sae-yo;* Please call me a taxi").

Once you're in the cab, remember to put on your **anjeon baelteu** (*an-jun belteu;* seat belt) and try using the following phrases:

- ✔ **yeogiseo jeil gakkaun baekhwajeome deryeoda juseyo.** (*yuh-gee–suh jae-il ga-gga-oon baek-hwa-jum-ae dae-ryuh-da joo-sae-yo;* Please take me to the nearest department store from here.)

- ✔ **i jusoe deryeoda juseyo.** (*ee joo-so-ae dae-ryuh-da joo-sae-yo;* Please take me to this address.). While saying this phrase, you need to show the driver the piece of paper with the address written down.

- ✔ *[some word]* **-e deryeoda juseyo.** (*[some word]* -ae dae-ryuh-da joo-sae-yo; Please take me to [some word].). You can substitute [some word] with the names of the places you need/want to go. For example, **yeongsagwan** (*young-sa-gwan;* embassy), **sicheong** (*shi-chung;* city hall), **gyeongbokgung** (*gyoung-bok-goong;* gyeong-bok palace), etc.

✔ **[some word]-kkaji ganeunde eolmaeyo?** (*[some word] -kka-jee ga-neun-dae ul-mh-ae-yo?* How much to go to [some word] ?). Substitute [some word] with the names of places you need/want to go.

✔ **eolmaeyo?** (*ul-ma-ae-yo?* How much is it?)

Taking a bus

At a major transportation hub, a **jido** (*jee-do;* map) of the bus **gyeongno** (*gyung-no;* routes) may be available, but at a bus stop, you may have to rely on the map that is against the wall. Taking some time to study the routes of buses is a good idea. Korea has a pretty extensive public transit system and you can take the buses pretty much to anywhere. Not only can you take a bus in and around a city, you can also take a **gosok beoseu** (*go-sok buh-sseu;* express bus) from one city to another. It's a pretty inexpensive way to travel and see the countryside as well. **gosok beoseu** usually does not stop at regular stops like the **sine beoseu** (*shi-nae buh-sseu;* city bus) does, and you can only ride the **gosok beoseu** at one of the **beoseu jeongnyujang** (*buh-sseu jung-nyoo-jang;* bus terminal) only. When getting on a bus, don't forget to ask the driver whether the bus is going to your destination. Ask the driver **i beoseuga [some word] euro gayo?** (*ee buh-sseu-ga [some word] eu-ro ga-yo;* Is this bus going to [some word]?). Substitute [some word] with your destination city/town. Usually the bus driver does not give change, so you need to have the correct amount of money to ride on the bus (even if you pay more than the bus fare, you won't get the change). Most Koreans use prepaid bus passes to ride the bus.

Riding the subway

A **jihacheol** (*jee-ha-chul;* subway) is a pretty efficient way to travel around the city. Seoul has an excellent subway system that will take you to just about any part of the city. However, during **chultoegeun sigan** (*chool-twae-geun shi-gan;* rush hour, time to get to and from work), the subway can be extremely crowded as people try to get to and from work. If you're the least bit claustrophobic, I strongly suggest you avoid the subways during rush hour. Another benefit of the subway system is that they run pretty late into the night. So, if you've had a late night drinking and singing with your friends at a **noraebang** (*no-rae-bang;* karaoke room), you can take advantage of any one of the public transit systems available in the city and save you the trouble of a DUI in a foreign country.

Talkin' the Talk

Ryan is talking to Eric on the phone about meeting up for drinks later tonight.

Eric: **yeoboseyo?**
yuh-bo-sae-yo?
Hello?

Ryan: **ericssi, ryan ieyo. jal iseoseoyo?**
eh-rik-sshi, ra-ee-un-ee-ae-yo. jal ee-ssuh-ssuh-yo?
Eric, this is Ryan. Have you been well?

Eric: **o raianssi, oraenmanieyo. anbonji han dudal jeongdo doeneungeo gateunde. geudongan jal iseotjiyo?**
oh ra-ee-un-sshi, o-raen-man-ee-ae-yo. an-bon-jee han doo-dal jung-do dwe-neun-guh ga-teun-dae. geu-dong-an jal ee-ssuh-jee-yo?
Oh Ryan, it's been a while. It's been about one or two months since the last time I saw you. Have you been well during then?

Ryan: **ye, ye. byeoril eopseoseoyo. yo dudal dongan yeol-lageul mothaeseo mianhaeyo.**
ye, ye. byul-il uhp-ssuh-ssuh-yo. doo-dal dong-an yuhl-la-geul mot-hae-suh mee-an-hae-yo.
Yes, yes. Not much has gone on. I'm sorry I haven't kept in touch with you for the last two months.

Eric: **geureochi anado jeodo ryan -ssi hante hanbeon yeol-lageul haetseoya doeneungeonde anhaeseo mian-haeyo. yosae il ttaemune neomu bappaseo bap meogeul sigando eomneungeo gateyo.**
geu-ruh-chi a-na-do juh-do ra-ee-un-sshi han-tae han-bun yuhl-la-geul hae-ssuh-ya dwe-neun-guhn-dae an-hae-suh mee-an-hae-yo. yo-sae il ttae-moon-ae nuh-moo ba-ppa-suh bab muh-geul shi-gan-do um-neun-guh ga-tae-yo.
I've been meaning to contact you as well, Ryan. Sorry I haven't done so. I've been so busy at work, it seems like I don't even have time to eat.

Ryan: **geuraeseo jega oneul jeonhwa deuringeoeyo. oneul jeonyeok jeorang gachi hasillaeyo?**

geu-rae-suh jae-ga o-neul jun-hwa deu-rin-guh-ae-yo. o-neul juh-nyuk juh-rang ga-chi ha-shil-lae-yo?

That's why I'm calling you today. Would you like to have dinner together?

Eric: **oneul jeonyeogeun jom gollanhaeyo. je yeoja chin-gurang jeonyeogeul gachi meokgiro yaksok hae-seoyo. jeonyeok meogeun daeume mannamyeon eottaeyo?**

o-neul juh-nyuh-geun jom gol-lan-hae-yo. jae yuh-ja chin-goo-rang juh-nyuh-geul ga-chi muk-gee-ro yak-sok-eul hae-ssuh-yo. juh-nyuk muh-geun da-eum-ae man-na-myun uh-ttae-yo?

Dinner this evening's not very good. I promised my girlfriend that I'd have dinner with her. How about we meet after dinner?

Ryan: **geureom uri ahopsie seoulyeok baro ape inneun suljibeseo mannaneunge eottaeyo? jeon geu jibeseo jeonyeok meokgo gidarigo iseulkkeyo.**

geu-rum oo-ree a-hop-shi-ae gee-cha-yuk ba-ro a-pae in-neun sool-jeep-ae-suh man-na-neun-gae uh-ttae-yo? jun geu jee-bae-suh juh-nyuk muk-go gee-da-ree-go ee-sseul-kkae-yo.

How about we meet at the bar right in front of the Seoul train station at nine o'clock? I'll have dinner there and just wait for you.

Eric: **joayo. doelsu iseumyeon ppalli gakkeyo. geureom oneul bame bwayo.**

jo-a-yo. dwel-soo ee-sseu-myun ppal-lee gal-kkae-yo. geu-rum o-neul ba-mae bwa-yo.

Great. I'll try to get there as soon as I can. Then I'll see you later tonight.

Words to Know

anbonji	*an-bon-jee*	Haven't seen
bappaseo	*ba-ppa-suh*	Been busy
byeoril	*byul-il*	Nothing much
geudongan	*geu-dong-ahn*	During those time
il	*il*	Work
jariseoseoyo	*jal-ee-ssuh-ssuh-yo*	Have you been well?
jeongdo	*jung-do*	About
jeonyeok	*juh-nyuk*	Dinner
jeorang	*juh-rang*	With me
jom gollanhaeyo	*jom gol-lan-hae-yo*	It's not good
mianhaeyo	*mee-an-hae-yo*	I'm sorry.
namjachingu	*nam-ja-chin-goo*	Boyfriend
oraenmanineyo	*o-raen-ma-nee-nae-yo*	It's been a while
ppalli	*ppal-lee*	Hurry, fast
suljip	*sool-jeep*	Bar, drinking house
yeojachingu	*yuh-ja-chin-goo*	Girlfriend
yeollak	*yuhl-lak*	Keep in touch
yosae	*yo-sae*	These days

Getting on the train

Railways cross all over the country. The rail system connects just about every city to each other. By as early as 2012, Korea plans to have a commercialized maglev train system up and running. This train will run at over 300 miles per hour and make the trip from Seoul to Busan in less than an hour. People will be able to travel further and cover greater distances in shorter amount of time, allowing people to work further away from their homes and get away quicker and easier and faster than ever before. When you buy your **pyo** (*pyo;* ticket) make sure you know what **peulaetpom** (*peul-laet-pom;* platform) your train leaves on, **myeot si** (*myuht-shi;* what time), whether it's a **pyundo** (*pyun-do;* one-way ticket), or a **wangbokpyo** (*wang-bok-pyo;* round-trip ticket) when you're at the **kaunteo** (*ka-oon-tuh;* counter). Some useful phrases are;

i gichaneun myeotsie tteonayo? (*ee gee-cha-neun myuht-shi-ae ttuh-na-yo;* What time is this train leaving?)

seoulganeun gichaneun myeotsie tteonayo? (*suh-ool-ga-neun gi-cha-neun myuht-shi-ae ttuh-na-yo;* What time is this train to Seoul leaving?). You can substitute Seoul with any other city you need/want to go.

i gichareul taryeomyeon eoneu peullaetpomeuro gayahaeyo? (*ee gee-cha-reul ta-ryuh-myun uh-neu peul-laet-pom-ae-suh ta-ya-hae-yo;* If I want to catch this train, which platform do I need to go to?)

seoureseo busankkai wangbokpyo juseyo. (*suh-oo-rae-suh boo-san-kka-jee wang-bok-pyo joo-sae-yo;* Please give me a round trip ticket from Seoul to Busan.). You can substitute Seoul and Busan with the destination cities of your choice.

Fun & Games

Please write down the following transports in Korean. (See Appendix C for the answers).

A. _____

B. _____

C. _____

D. _____

E. _____

Chapter 15

Planning a Trip

. . . .

In This Chapter

▶ Picking the right time for travel

▶ Choosing a destination

▶ Packing for the trip

▶ Dealing with the travel agency

. . . .

So you've decided to go to Korea. What should you bring? Will you be going for business, or pleasure? Is there a certain site you have to see, or a certain festival you have to attend? Careful planning and knowing exactly what you want out of your vacation will go a long way in maximizing your time and money during your trip. This chapter guides you through picking out what time of the year you may want to travel, where you may want to go to see what sites, what you may need to bring, and how to deal with the people that you may encounter. Got your passport and toothbrush ready?

Picking a Good Time for Travel

You obviously wouldn't want to take a trip to Korea in the middle of the winter time if you're interested in playing golf. Likewise, you wouldn't want to plan a trip to Korea in the middle of the summer if you're interested in skiing. The following sections show you not only what times might be good for travel, but also how to communicate your travel dates to someone else, by examining how to name days and months in Korean.

Checking out the seasons

Korea does have four very distinct seasons, so what ever type of weather you fancy, you can find it in Korea:

✔ From March to May, you can see a beautiful **bom** (*bom;* spring) with rare flowers in bloom, and trees burst into leafy splendor.

✔ During the hot and humid **yeoreum** (*yuh-reum;* summer), the vegetation is lush and you'll see many people escape the summer heat by going to the beaches.

✔ Monsoon rains begin usually in late June and last until mid-July, and August is hot and humid.

✔ **gaeul** (*ga-eul;* fall) begins as September brings in the cool continental winds and dry weather.

✔ October, when the leaves turn color, the whole countryside turns a vivid orange, red, and yellow.

✔ The winter is cold and generally dry with occasional snow. During the **gyeoul** (*gyuh-ool;* winter) months, three or four days of cold weather are often followed by a few warm days.

Naming months and counting days

If you want to ask someone when they're planning a trip to Korea, you can ask them, **"eonje hanguge gasilkkeoeyo?"** (*un-jae han-goo-gae ga-shil-kkuh-ae-yo?*), which is translated as, "When will you be going to Korea?" If someone asks you that very question, you can answer, **"ne, siwol isibsamilnal tteonaseo siwol samsibilnal olkkeoeyo"** (*ne, shi-wol ee-ship-sam-il-nal ttuh-na-suh shi-wol sam-ship-il-nal ol-kkuh-ae-yo*). You just told that person, "Yes, I will be leaving on the 23rd of October and I will be back on the 30th of October."

You have to substitute the days and months to tell someone when you're really planning on leaving and returning. To do that, you have to be able to name the days and months in Korean (see Table 15-1).

Conveniently enough, you don't have to remember separate names for all the months. If you can count up to twelve, just add the suffix **wol** (*wol;* month) behind the number and you have the corresponding month. For example, **samwol** (*sam-wol*) means the third month, which is the month of March. Similarly, if you just attach the suffix **–il** (*il;* day) to a number, you have the date. For example, **siboil** (*ship-o-il*) is the fifteenth. You may notice that the Korean word for "day" and the number "one" is the same (**il**). So the first day of the month becomes **ilil** (pronounced, *ee-ril*). The reason for the difference in pronunciation is because Koreans use the same consonant for the letters "r" and "l", and the pronunciation of that consonant changes depending on the position of that consonant. In general, the same consonant is pronounced as 'r' when it appears at the beginning and 'l' at the end. Chapter 7 has a table that lists all the months in the year, days of the week and time relative to now. In case you don't feel like going back to that chapter, I have reproduced it for you here.

Table 15-1	Months of the Year and Other Pertinent Travel-Planning Terms	
Korean Word	*Pronunciation*	*Translation*
irwol	ee-rwol	January
iwol	ee-wol	February
samwol	sam-wol	March
sawol	sa-wol	April
owol	o-wol	May
yuwol	yoo-wol	June
chirwol	chee-rwol	July
parwol	pa-rwol	August
guwol	goo-wol	September
siwol	shi-wol	October
sibirwol	ship-ee-rwol	November
sibiwol	ship-ee-wol	December
ibeondal	ee-bun	This month
daeumdal	da-eum-dal	Next month
jeobeondal	juh-bun-dal	Last month
saengil	saeng-il	Birthday
seollal	suhl-nal	New Year's day
woryoil	wo-ryo-il	Monday
hwayoil	hwa-yo-il	Tuesday
suyoil	soo-yo-il	Wednesday
mogyoil	mo-gyo-il	Thursday

(continued)

Table 15-1 (continued)

Korean Word	Pronunciation	Translation
geumyoil	geum-yo-il	Friday
toyoil	to-yo-il	Saturday
iryoil	ee-ryo-il	Sunday
hansi	han-shi	1:00
dusi	doo-shi	2:00
sesi	sae-shi	3:00
nesi	nae-shi	4:00
daseotsi	da-suh-shi	5:00
yeoseotsi	yuh-suh-shi	6:00
ilgopsi	il-gop-shi	7:00
yeodeolsi	yuh-dul-shi	8:00
ahopsi	a-hop-shi	9:00
yeolsi	yuhl-shi	10:00
yeolhansi	yuhl-han-shi	11:00
yeoldusi	yuhl-doo-shi	12:00
ojeon	o-juhn	Before noon, am.
ohu	o-hoo	After noon, pm.

Talkin' the Talk

 Jim is planning a trip to Korea. Heather is asking him about the trip.

Heather: **jimssi, annyeonghaseyo?**
jim-sshi, a-nyoung-ha-sae-yo?
Jim, have you been well?

Jim: **heatherssi! bangawoyo!**
heather sshi! ban-ga-wo-yo!
Heather! Glad to see you!

Heather   **hanguk gasindago deureosseoyo. eonje gaseyo?**
han-goog ga-shin-da-go deu-ruh-ssuh-yo. un-jae ga-sae-yo?
I heard you were going to Korea. When are you going?

Jim: **ne. daeumju suyoire tteonaseo iljuil jeongdo iseulkkeoeyo.**
ne. da-eum-joo soo-yo-ee-rae ttuh-na-suh il-joo-il jung-do ee-sseul-kkuh-ae-yo.
Yes. I leave next Wednesday and plan on staying for a week or so.

Heather: **daeumju suyoirimyeon guwol isib pparirineyo. hanguk gaeul punggyeongi cham meositdago deure-oseoyo. jaemi itgetneyo.**
da-eum-joo soo-yo-ee-ree-myun goo-wol ee-ship ppa-ril-ee-nae-yo. han-goog ga-eul poong-gyoung-ee cham muh-shi-da-go deu-ruh-ssuh-yo. jae-mee ee-get-nae-yo.
Next Wednesday is the September twenty-eighth. I heard that the fall scenery in Korea is very beautiful. It sounds like fun.

Jim: **ne. hanguge gabogo sipeunji oraedoeseoyo. sajin mani jjigeo olkkeyo.**
ne. han-goo-gae ga-bo-go shi-peun-jee o-rae-dwe-ssuh-yo. sa-jin ma-ni jjee-guh ol-kkae-yo.
Yes. I've wanted to go and see Korea for a long time now. I'll bring back lots of pictures.

Heather: **jeo ginyeompum hanaman gatda jusillaeyo?**
juh gee-nyum-poom ha-na-man gat-da joo-shil-lae-yo?
Will you bring me a souvenir?

Jim: **mullonijyo!**
mool-lo-nee-jyo!
Of course!

Words to Know

banggawoyo	ban-ga-wo-yo	Glad to see you
bidio	bee-dee-o	Video
daeumdal	da-eum-dal	Next month
daeumju	da-eum-joo	Next week
eonje gaseyo	un-jae ga-sae-yo	When are you leaving?
ginyeompum	gee-nyum-poom	Souvenir
mullonijyo	mool-lo-nee-jyo	Of course
punggyeong	poong-gyung	Scenery
sajin	sa-jin	Photo
seonmul	suhn-mool	Present
tteonaseo	ttuh-na-suh	Leaving

Korean holidays

Koreans officially follow the Gregorian calendar, though some holidays are observed on the lunar calendar of that year. On official holidays, offices and banks are closed, but palaces, museums, most restaurants, department stores, and amusement facilities are open. **seollal** (*suhl-nal;* New Year's day) and **chuseok** (*choo-suhk;* Korean harvest festival) are the most important traditional holidays for Koreans. Millions of people visit their **gohyang** (*go-hyang;* hometown, one's place of origin) to celebrate with their families during these periods. On **seollal**, Koreans hold a memorial service for their ancestors and perform **sebae** (*sae-bae;* a formal bow of respect to their elders) as a New Year's greeting. Table 15-2 lists Korean holidays.

On these holidays you never know if it's a good time to visit — it depends on how you feel about crowds. Although everyone visits their families, department stores and other businesses might be crowded. Of course, all the transport systems will be totally full and in total mess.

Table 15-2		Korean Holidays
Holiday	*Date*	*Description*
New Year's Day	January 1	The first day of the new year is recognized and celebrated.
Seollal, Lunar New Year's Day	January 28 to 30 (changes year to year)	Lunar New Year's Day (**Seollal**) is one of the most important traditional days of the year, still more recognized than January 1st. Most businesses are closed, and people take off several days to visit their hometowns to be with family.
Independence Movement Day	March 1	This day commemorates the Declaration of Independence proclaimed on March 1st, 1919, while under Japanese colonization. A reading of the declaration takes place in a special ceremony at Tapgol Park in Seoul, where the document was first read to the public.
Buddha's Birthday	May 5 (changes year to year)	It falls on the 8th day on the 4th lunar month. Elaborate, solemn rituals are held at many Buddhist temples across the county and lanterns are hung in the temple courtyards. On the Sunday evening before Buddha's birthday, these lanterns are lit and carried in parades.
Children's Day	May 5	On this day, parents dress up the little ones and take them to children's parks, amusement parks, zoos or the cinema for a full day of fun and games.
Memorial Day	June 6	Memorial Day is set aside to honor the soldiers and civilians who gave their lives in the service of their country. The largest ceremony is held at the National Cemetery in Seoul.
Constitution Day	July 17	This holiday commemorates the proclamation of the Constitution of the Republic of Korea on July 17th, 1948.

(continued)

Table 15-2 *(continued)*

Holiday	Date	Description
Liberation Day	August 15	This holiday commemorates the Japanese acceptance of the Allies' terms of surrender and the resulting liberation of Korea in 1945.
Chuseok, Korean Thanksgiving Day	October 5 to 7 (changes year to year)	**Chuseok** (*Choo-suhk*) is one of the year's most important traditional holidays. It is celebrated on the 15th day of the 8th lunar month. **Chuseok** is often referred to as Korean Thanksgiving Day. It's a celebration of the harvest and a thanksgiving for the bounty of the earth. Family members come from all parts of the country to visit their ancestral homes.
National Foundation Day	October 3	This holiday commemorates the founding of the Korean nation in 2333 BCE by the legendary god-king **Dangun** (*Dahn-goon*). A simple ceremony is held at an altar on top of Mt. Manisan, Ganghwa island. The altar is said to have been erected by Dangun to offer thanks to his father and grandfather in heaven.
Christmas Day	December 25	Christmas is observed as a national holiday in Korea.

Naming off the years

olhae (*ol-hae*) is the Korean word for "this year." **jaknyeon** (*jang-nyuhn*) is last year, and **naenyeon** (*nae-nyuhn*) is next year. **nyeon** (*nyuhn*) is the Korean word for "year," so add the appropriate numbers in front of the word and you have the given year. For example, **icheonpaillyeon** (*ee-chun-pall-lyuhn*) is the year 2008.

Koreans also adhere to the Chinese zodiac, though nowadays it's taken less seriously than in the past. Very much like Western astrology, people born under certain signs exhibit certain personality traits. The difference between the Chinese zodiac and the Western zodiac is that in Western zodiac changes monthly whereas the Chinese zodiac changes yearly. 2008 is the year of the rat, which marks the beginning of the twelve-year cycle. The Koreans add the word **-tti** (*ttee*) to the various animal names representing the year to describe what sign you are. So, if you were born in the year of the rat, you would be a **juitti** (*jwee-ttee*). Check out your sign in Table 15-3.

Table 15-3	The Animals of the Chinese Zodiac	
Korean Word	*Pronunciation*	*Translation*
baemtti	*baem-ttee*	Year of the Snake
daktti	*dahk-ttee*	Year of the Rooster
doejitti	*dwe-jee-ttee*	Year of the Pig
gaetti	*gae-ttee*	Year of the Dog
horangitti	*ho-rahng-ee-ttee*	Year of the Tiger
juitti	*jwee-ttee*	Year of the Rat
maltti	*mahl-ttee*	Year of the Horse
sotti	*so-ttee*	Year of the Ox
tokkitti	*to-ggi-ttee*	Year of the Rabbit
yangtti	*yahng-ttee*	Year of the Goat
yongtti	*yong-ttee*	Year of the Dragon
wonsungitti	*won-soong-ee-ttee*	Year of the Monkey

Specifying dates and times

Once you have your itinerary, bags packed and ready to go, you'll have to know your **sigan** (*shi-gan;* time). There is a 17-hour difference between Chicago and Seoul. When it is 6:30 pm on Thursday in Chicago, it is 9:30 am on Friday in Seoul. You have to remember that when you decide to **yeohaeng** (*yuh-haeng;* travel). You wouldn't want to call someone at three o'clock in the morning just to tell them what fun you had at the Gwangju Gimchi Festival, or how the visit to the Seokguram grotto was life changing.

You also want to know what time museums and shops open and close, at what time a show starts, what date and time to set your reservation at, and so forth. **"myeotsieseo myeotsikkaji yeollyeo itnayo?"** (*myuht-shi-ae-suh myuht-shi-kka-jee yuhl-lyuh eet-na-yo?*), which is translated, "From what time to what time are you open?", might be a good question to know to make sure to not find a "closed" sign in front of the attraction you might want to see. **yeyak** (*yae-yak; reservation*) is a good word to know if you want to make sure they save a seat for you. **yeyak** means reservation, and many attractions, especially during peak tourist seasons, have a tendency to sell out quickly, so calling ahead and making a **yeyak** is often good practice.

Trains and buses, as well as other means of mass transit move according to schedule, in a timely manner. Chances are, if you miss a train, one will be along very shortly. However, sitting in a bus stop, or a train station was not what you went to Korea to experience, right? Arriving a little early for departures and giving yourself a little time for boarding and such can save you missed rides, long delays, and needless **gidarim** (*gee-da-rim; waiting*).

Choosing Your Destination

If you're headed to Korea on business, chances are, you'll spend quite a bit of time in the capital city, Seoul, or perhaps one of the major port cities like Busan, or Ulsan. If you're there for pleasure, a vacation, or on a holiday, the whole country is available for your enjoyment. Well, then. Where to go? That depends entirely upon what your interests are. Even though Korea is a **jageun nara** (*ja-geun na-ra; small country*), it is a country with a rich history and culture that can take a lifetime or more to fully explore. Sights and delights of every kind are available for the pickiest of vacationers. Whether you're looking for world-class resort style pampering, or if you're ready to experience a monastic, contemplative and Spartan lifestyle at a Buddhist temple, Korea has all kinds of wondrous experiences for the **yeohaenggaek** (*yuh-haeng-gaek; visitor*). You can also find Koreans to be incredibly friendly and warm, inviting people with a giving nature, eager to lend a hand in enhancing your experience of the country.

If it is shopping you crave, staying near Seoul and vicinity is probably a good plan. Itaewon area, Gangnam district, Dongdaemun and Namdaemun markets have an almost inexhaustible supply of goods for the pickiest of consumers. If it is history you crave, you can take it all in near the Gyeongju area, where the remnants and artifacts of the Silla dynasty still survive in **bangmulgwan** (*bang-mool-gwan; museums*), ancient tombs and temples over a thousand years old. From bird watching and folk festivals, to nightclubs and cafes, whatever it is that you're looking for, you can probably find it in Korea. Immersing yourself in a foreign culture can be a great opportunity for you to discover something new, not just in that foreign culture, but something new in yourself as well.

Try to pick destinations with some of these sites and activities listed in Table 15-4, and you'll almost be guaranteed a good time on your travels.

Table 15-4	Sites and Activities	
Korean Word	**Pronunciation**	**Translation**
baekhwajeom	*baek-hwa-jum*	Department store
bangmulgwan	*bang-mool-gwan*	Museum
geukjang	*geuk-jang*	Theatre
gongweon	*gong-won*	Park
gungjeon	*goong-juhn*	Palace
haebyeon	*hae-byun*	Beach
jeol	*juhl*	Temple
misulgwan	*mee-sool-gwan*	Art gallery
san	*san*	Mountain
singmulgwan	*shik-mool-gwan*	Botanical garden

Is your trip to Korea a part of a travel package? Will you be going to other Asian countries before or after your visit to Korea? How about **jungguk** (*joong-gook;* China)? **ilbon** (*il-bon;* Japan), or **taeguk** (*tae-gook;* Thailand) perhaps? Whereever it is you decide to go, you may want to familiarize yourself with the terms **–eseo** (*ae-suh,* from) and **–ro** or **–euro** (to):

- ✔ "**jeoneun donggyeongeseo bukkyeongeuro gayo**" (*juh-neun dong-gyoung-ae-suh book-gyoung-eu-ro ga-yo*) is translated, "I am going from Tokyo to Beijing."

- ✔ "**jeoneun nyu yogeseo amseutereudameuro gayp**" (*juh-neun nyoo-yo-gae-suh am-seu-te-reu-da-meu-ro ga-yo*) is translated, "I am going from New York to Amsterdam."

- ✔ "**jeoneun hyuseutoneseo meksikoro gayo**"(*juh-neun hyoo-seu-ton-ae-suh mek-shi-ko-ro ga-yo*) is translated, "I am going from Houston to Mexico."

When do you use **-ro** and when do you use **-euro**? It's quite simple, actually. If the last syllable of the place name ends with a consonant, like, **ilbon**, or **taeguk,** you use the marker**-euro**, so you say **ilboneuro**, or **taegugeuro**. If the last syllable of the place name ends with a vowel like, **Hawai** (*ha-wa-ee;*

Hawaii) or **Pari** (*Pa-ree;* Paris), so you say **Hawairo**, or **Pariro**. Table 15-5 lists a few other places for you to practice "to" and "from" with.

Table 15-5		Places
Korean Word	*Pronunciation*	*Place*
hoju	*ho-joo*	Australia
areujentina	*a-reu-gen-ti-na*	Argentina
beurajil	*buh-ra-jil*	Brazil
kaenada	*kae-na-da*	Canada
jungguk	*joong-gook*	China
ijipteu	*ee-jeep-teu*	Egypt
yeongguk	*young-gook*	England
peurangseu	*peu-rang-sseu*	France
dogil	*do-gil*	Germany
gana	*ga-na*	Ghana
yeongguk	*young-gook*	Great Britain
indo	*in-do*	India
israural	*ee-seu-ra-ael*	Israel
itaeri	*ee-tae-ree*	Italy
ilbon	*il-bon*	Japan
rebanon	*rae-ba-non*	Lebanon
nyujillaend	*new-jil-lan-deu*	New Zealand
reosia	*ruh-shi-a*	Russia
seupein	*seu-pae-in*	Spain
seuweden	*seu-wae-den*	Sweden
seuwiseu	*seu-wee-sseu*	Switzerland
daeman	*dae-man*	Taiwan
miguk	*mee-gook*	USA
wollam	wol-nam	Vietnam

Packing for Your Trip

Well, now that you have the itinerary all ready, I think we're ready to pack. Make sure you have your **gabang** (*ga-bahng;* bag) ready, and let's start packing! Table 15-6 lists some items that you might need. Of course, if you can't find them, or forget to pack them, I'm sure you'll be able to pick it up at the nearest **gage** (*ga-gae;* store).

Table 15-6	Things to Pack	
Korean Word	*Pronunciation*	*Translation*
binu	*bee-noo*	Soap
bit	*beet*	Brush
chitsol	*chi-ssol*	Toothbrush
chiyak	*chi-yak*	Toothpaste
hwajangpum	*hwa-jang-poom*	Makeup, cosmetics
myeondogi	*myuhn-do-gee*	Razor
sajingi	*sa-jin-gee*	Camera
shinbal	*shin-bal*	Shoes
yangmal	*yang-mal*	Socks
yeogweon	*yuh-gwon*	Passport

Getting the Help of a Travel Agency

Don't think you can manage the countryside by yourself? A little timid? Could use a little help? Information and assistance are readily available at the Korean **yeohangja** (*yuh-haeng-ja;* Tourist) Organization's Tourist Information Center or at information counters in **gukjegonghang** (*gook-jae-gong-hang;* international airports) and at major tourist sites. They provide city maps, brochures and information on tours, shopping, dining, and accommodations. You can also visit www.tour2korea.com for more information on travel. You can find organized group tours to and guided tours to various sites you care to visit.

If you're having a real difficult time, you can also contact BBB (Before Babel Brigade), which has 2,400 volunteers fluent in 17 **oegugeo** (*wae-goo-guh;* foreign languages) who will help you with translation problems whenever and wherever via mobile phone. They can be reached by dialing 1588-5644 and pressing the number assigned for the language you need. Press 1 for English, 2 for Japanese, 3 for Chinese, 4 for French, 5 for Spanish, 6 for Italian, 7 for Russian, 8 for German, 9 for Portuguese, 10 for Arabic, 11 for Polish, 12 for Turkish, 13 for Swedish, 14 for Thai, 15 for Vietnamese, 16 for Malay, and 17 for Indonesian.

Korea Tourist Organization also offers Goodwill Guide Services, which provides **tongyeok** (*tong-yuhk;* interpretation) assistance as a part of its **gongjja** (*gong-jja;* free) tour guide service. Reservations are usually required, so it's best to check ahead first. You can go to www.goodwillguide.com for more information.

Having a tour guide is also a good way to practice and brush up on your Korean if you're a novice speaker. Listening to them, practicing words and phrases with them may be a bit less intimidating than trying to speak to a Korean who doesn't know a word of English. Finding a Korean who speaks English shouldn't be very difficult. Surprise your tour guide and others around you by saying some of the phrases and sentences you learned in this book. You will raise a few eyebrows and get a few **miso** (*mee-so;* smiles) when you do.

Fun & Games

Please write the equivalent Korean sentences/words below. See Appendix C for answers.

  1. I'm going to Korea next month. _____

  2. When are you leaving? _____

  3. Where is the bus stop? _____

  4. Glad to see you _____

  5. Train station _____

  6. Museum _____

  7. Department store_____

Chapter 16

Handling an Emergency

. . . .

In This Chapter

▶ Shouting for help

▶ Calling the police

▶ Getting medical help

▶ Getting legal help

. . . .

*E*ven though the chances of something happening on your trip to Korea is rather slim, you always run the chance of needing to call the **gyeongchal** (*gyung-chal;* police) or end up in a **byeongwon** (*byoung-won;* hospital) because something you ate didn't agree with you. One just never knows what may happen. This is why it is important to plan for the unforeseen. By teaching you a few phrases, this chapter gives you the info you need to handle **eunggeupsanghwang** (*eung-geup-sang-hwang;* emergencies) like calling for help, calling the authorities, medical attention, and **beopjeok doum** (*buhp-juhk do-woom;* legal help). Even if you remember just a few of these phrases you can get in contact with the appropriate people who can help you no matter the situation.

Shouting for Help

There are many ways to get someone's attention. Screaming at the top of your lungs is one way, though you'll more likely scare people away with a yell. Knowing what to yell depending on the situation comes in handy. The most important one you might want to remember is, "**saram sallyeo!**" (*sa-ram sal-lyuh!*). **saram** (*sa-ram*) means "person," and **sallyeo** (*sal-lyuh*) means "to save," or "rescue." Put the words together and "**saram sallyeo!**" is literally translated, "save this person!" or "rescue this person!" If you're stuck at a location and cannot move, you can say, "**yeogiyo!**" (*yuh-gee-yo!*), which means, "Over here!"

jeo jom dowajuseyo (*juh jom do-wa-joo-sae-yo*) is translated, "Please help me." **jeo jom dowajusillaeyo?** (*juh-jom do-wa-joo-shil-lae-yo?*) is translated, "Can you please help me?" When you request help from someone, you will most likely be asked, "**eotteoke dowadeurilkkayo?** (*uh-ttuh-kae do-wa-deu-ril-kka-yo*)" which is translated, "How can I help you?" or, "How do you need help?" You can probably start with the sentence, **keunil nasseoyo** (*keu-neel na-ssuh-yo*). This phrase means, "There is an emergency." Literal translation is "a big thing happened."

Calling the Police

What do you do if you realize only too late that you had encountered a **somaechigi** (*so-mae-chi-gee*; pickpocket)? What if you meet a **kkangpae** (*kkang-pae*; thug) or **doduk** (*do-dook*; thief)? You'll have to call the **pachulso** (*pa-chool-so*; police station) and talk to a **gyeongchalgwan** (*gyoung-chal-gwan*; police officer). You'll have to fill out a **bogoseo** (*bo-go-suh*; report) as well.

You will notice the police in Korea to be very helpful. If you flag a police officer down on the street, the chances of him speaking at least a limited amount of English is pretty good. At the police station, you will find that there are police officers who speak English very well, and can be very accommodating. **gwangwang munhwa** (*gwan-gwang moon-hwa*; tourism) is a very big industry in Korea, so the law enforcement is very **chinjeul** (*chin-juhl*; kind) in helping wayward tourists. Don't expect to retrieve the items you lose, though. Once something is stolen, it's probably gone for good. Crime is generally low in Korea, but it does happen. The best way to avoid getting taken is to be aware of your surroundings. Mind your belongings and they will stay yours.

Reporting an accident to the police

If you're involved in an **sago** (*sa-go*; accident), you'll have to report it to the police. The emergency number in Korea is 119. Most of the time, the **gyohwansu** (*gyo-hwan-soo*; operator) handling the emergency situation will speak English. In case the operator doesn't, you'll have to be able to give the operator **banghyang** (*bang-hyang*; directions) to your **witch** (*wee-chee*; location) in Korean. You'll also have to give some other details in Korean, such as, if anyone is injured, how many people or vehicles are involved, and possibly describe the accident in detail. The best **joeon** (*jo-uhn*; advice) I have for such difficult circumstance is to have **innaesim** (*in-nae-shim*; patience). The language barrier is something that can easily be overcome in Korea. The thing to remember is not to get too excited and not get too frustrated. You will be able to fill out your report on the accident.

Talkin' the Talk

 James calls the emergency number to report an accident.

Operator:	**irilgu imnida. eotteoke dowadeurilkkayo?** *il-il-goo im-ni-da. uh-ttuh-kae do-wa-deu-ril-kka-yo?* This is 119. How may I help you?
James:	**keunil naseoyo! cha sagoga naseoyo!** *keu-neel na-ssuh-yo! cha sa-go-ga na-ssuh-yo!* There is an emergency! There has been a car accident!
Operator:	**jinjeong haseyo. jigeum wichiga eodiingayo?** *jeen-jung ha-sae-yo. jee-geum wee-chee-ga uh-dee-in-ga-yo?* Please remain clam. Where is your location?
James:	**sicheong baro ape iseoyo. gugeupcha handae bonae juseyo. dachin sarami inneungeot gateyo.** *shi-chung ba-ro a-pae ee-ssuh-yo. goo-geup-cha han-dae bo-nae joo-sae-yo. da-chin sa-ram-ee in-neun-guh ga-tae-yo.* I'm right in front of the city hall. Please send an ambulance. I think someone's hurt.
Operator:	**jamsiman gidariseyo. gugeupchawa gyeongchal-gwani geumbang sicheong apeuro galgeosimnida.** *jam-shi-man gee-da-ree-sae-yo. goo-geup-cha-wa gyoung-chal-gwan-ee geum-bang shi-chung a-peu-ro gal-guh-shim-ni-da.* Please wait a moment. An ambulance and a police officer will be arriving in front of the city hall momentarily.
James:	**ye. ssaireni deullineyo. gomawoyo.** *ye. ssa-ee-rae-ni deul-lee-nae-yo. go-ma-wo-yo.* Yes. I can hear the siren now. Thank you very much.

Words to Know

chasago	cha-sa-go	Car accident
eunggeupsanghwang	eung-geup-sang-hwang	Emergency
geumbang	geum-bang	Soon, right away
gugeupcha	goo-geup-cha	Ambulance
gyeongchalgwan	gyoung-chal-gwan	Police officer
jamsiman gidariseyo	jam-shi-man gee-da-ree-sae-yo	Please wait a moment.
jinjeonghaseyo	jeen-jung-ha-sae-yo	Please calm down.
sago	sa-go	Accident
sobangcha	so-bang-cha	Fire truck
sobanggwan	so-bang-gwan	Fire fighter
witch	wee-chee	Location

Finding the lost and found

There is a chance that you might have misplaced your **gabang** (*ga-bang;* bag). It may not have been a thief after all. If you retrace your steps carefully, you may even think of where you might have left your bag. Many large **gonggong jangso** (*gong-gong jang-so;* public places), such as **yuwonji** (*yoo-won-jee;* amusement parks), **bakmulgwan** (*bak-mool-gwan;* museums), hotels, and **keun baekhwajeom** (*keun baek-hwa-jum;* large shopping malls, department store) have a lost and found that you can check for your lost items. Simply flag down an attendant and ask, **"yeogi bunsilmul bogwansiri iseyo?"** (*yuh-gee boon-shil-mool bo-gwan-shil-ee ee-ssuh-yo?;* Is there a lost and found here?). A lot of these major public locations will have a lost and found and the attendant will be more than happy to take you there, so don't completely give up hope on that lost item.

Getting Medical Help

Getting sick in a **oeguk** (*wae-gook;* foreign country) is never a good thing. In fact, an ill timed **gamgi** (*gam-gee;* cold) or **dokgam** (*dok-gam;* flu) can positively ruin a **yeohaeng** (*yuh-haeng;* vacation) that you've saved and planned for months. One can never know when one's going to come down with something, so it's generally a good idea to travel prepared. If you have prescription medication you're taking, bring it with you on the trip along with a copy of the **cheobangjeon** (*chuh-bang-juhn;* prescription). Also, keeping your **yang-mul** (*yang-mool;* medication) with your carry-on luggage is a good idea in case your checked luggage gets misplaced. If you do encounter a medical emergency, the best thing to do is to remain calm. **danghwangham** (*dang-hwang-ham;* panic) will not help the situation any. Most major hospitals will have English-speaking staff ready to help, and the following sections will help you navigate in finding your doctor and describing some of your symptoms.

Finding a doctor

If you're lucky, you'll never have to use any of the words or phrases I present to you here on this chapter. Most likely, your trip to Korea will be filled with life changing experiences and awe inspiring scenery. Should your luck run out, or encounter a string of bad ones, you'll have to go to a **byeongwon** (*byoung-won;* hospital) and see the **uisa** (*eui-sa;* doctor).

Talkin' the Talk

Jane has a stomach ache and Paul convinces her to go to the hospital.

Paul: **janessi, gwenchanayo? pyojeongi anjoeungeo gatayo.**
jane-sshi, gwen-cha-na-yo? pyo-jung-ee an-jo-eun-guh ga-ta-yo.
Jane, are you alright? You don't look so well.

Jane: **yosae sogi anjoayo. myeochil dongan baega apaseo gosaeng mani haeseoyo.**
yo-sae so-gee an-jo-a-yo. myuh-chil dong-an bae-ga a-pa-suh go-saeng ma-nee hae-ssuh-yo.
My guts have been hurting lately. I've been suffering from an upset stomach for the last few days.

Paul: **eolmankeum apayo? mani apeumyeon byeongwone gayadoeneungeo anieyo?**
ul-man-keum a-pa-yo? ma-nee a-peu-myun byoung-won-ae ga-ya-dwae-neun-guh a-ni-ae-yo?
How bad does it hurt? If you're in a lot of pain, shouldn't you go to the hospital?

Jane: **jom gidarimyeon gwenchaneulgeo gateyo. apatda anapatda hageodeunyo.**
jom gee-da-ree-myun gwen-cha-neul-gguh ga-tae-yo. a-paht-da an-a-paht-da ha-guh-deun-yo.
I think I'll be okay if I wait a little while. The pain comes and goes.

Paul: **byeongwone hanbeon gabwayo. jega gachi gajulkkeyo. itdaga byeongwone jeonhwa haeyo.**
byoung-won-ae han-bun ga-bwa-yo. jae-ga ga-chi ga-jool-kkae-yo. ee-tta-ga byoung-won-ae juhn-hwa hae-yo.
Let's go to the hospital. I'll go with you. Call the hospital later.

Jane: **joayo. kkok gachi gayadoeyo. jeoneun byeongwoni museowoseo silkeodeunnyo.**
jo-a-yo. kkok ga-chi ga-ya-dwae-yo. juh-neun byoung-wo-nee moo-suh-woh-suh shil-kuh-deun-yo.
Good. You have to come with me, though. I don't like hospitals because I'm afraid of them.

Paul: **geokjeong marayo. jega gachi gajultenikkayo. byeongwon museoulkkeo hanado eopseoyo.**
guk-jung ma-ra-yo. jae-ga ga-chi ga-jool-tae-nee-kka-yo. byoung-won moo-suh-wool-kkuh ha-na-do uhp-ssuh-yo.
Don't worry. I'll go with you. A hospital is nothing to be afraid of.

Words to Know

| an apayo | an-a-ppa-yo | It's not hurting, it doesn't hurt |
| apayo | a-ppa-yo | It's hurting, it hurts |

byeongwon	byoung-won	Hospital
cheobangjeon	chuh-bang-juhn	Prescription
dokgam	dok-gam	Flu
dudeuregi	doo-deu-ruh-gee	Rashes
gamgi	gam-gee	Cold
gichim	gee-chim	Cough
gosaeng	go-saeng	Suffering
hanbeon gabwayo	han-bun ga-bwa-yo	At least go once, please go
museowoyo	moo-suh-wo-yo	Afraid, scared
myeochildongan	myuh-chil-dong-an	Last few days
pyojeong	pyo-jung	Look, expression on the face
sok	sohk	Gut, inside the stomach
uisa	eui-sa	Doctor
yak	yak	Drugs
yeol	yuhl	Fever

Describing what ails you

When you go see the doctor, you'll of course have to tell him or her exactly what is bothering you. The verb **apeuda** (*a-peu-da*) means "to hurt," so you can use any of the words listed in Table 16-1 and Table 16-2, and say, "[some word]-**i or ga apayo** (*a-pa-yo*)" to say "[some word] hurts." When do you use -**i** and -**ga** as the connecting syllable? Use the following guidelines:

✔ If the word ends in a consonant, like **nun** (*noon;* eye) or **son** (*sohn;* hand), you use -**i.** For example, you'd say, "**nuni apayo**" (*noo-nee a-pa-yo;* my eye hurts) or "**soni apayo**" (*so-nee a-pa-yo;* my hand hurts).

    ✔ If the word ends in a vowel, like **meori** (*muh-ree;* head) or **ko** (*ko;* nose), you would use **-ga** as the connecting syllable. So you'd say, "**meoriga apayo**" (*muh-ree-ga a-pa-yo;* my head hurts) or "**koga apayo**" (*ko-ga a-pa-yo;* my nose hurts).

Table 16-1 lists ailments that you may encounter in your travels.

Table 16-1	Basic Body Parts	
Korean Word	*Pronunciation*	*English Word*
bae	*bae*	Stomach
bal	*bal*	Foot
balgarak	*bal-ga-rahk*	Toe
dari	*da-ree*	Leg
deung	*deung*	Back
eokke	*uh-kkae*	Shoulder
eolgul	*ul-gool*	Face
gan	*gahn*	Liver
gaseum	*ga-seum*	Chest
geunyuk	*geu-nyook*	Muscle
gwi	*gwee*	Ear
ip	*eep*	Mouth
jang	*jahng*	Intestines
ko	*ko*	Nose
meori	*muh-ree*	Head
mok	*mohk*	Neck
mom	*mohm*	Body
nun	*noon*	Eye
pal	*pal*	Arm
pe	*pae*	Lung
ppyeo	*ppyuh*	Bone
simjang	*shim-jahng*	Heart

Korean Word	Pronunciation	English Word
singyeong	shin-gyoung	Nerves
son	sohn	Hand
songarak	sohn-ga-rahk	Finger
wi	wee	Stomach (organ)

Table 16-2		Medical Ailments
Korean Word	**Pronunciation**	**English Word**
am	ahm	Cancer
boktong	bok-tong	Stomachache
byeonbi	byuhn-bee	Constipation
cheonshik	chun-shik	Asthma
dokgam	dok-gahm	Flu
dutong	doo-tong	Headache
gamgi	gahm-gee	Cold
gohyeorap	go-hyuh-rahp	High blood pressure
gwanjeolyeom	gwahn-juhl-lyuhm	Arthritis
A hyeong gannyeom	A hyoung ga-nyuhm	Hepatitis A
B hyeong gannyeom	B hyoung ga-nyuhm	Hepatitis B
C hyeong gannyeom	C hyoung ga-nyuhm	Hepatitis C
ijil	ee-jeel	Dysentery
jeohyeorap	juh-hyuh-rahp	Low blood pressure
kolera	kol-lae-ra	Cholera
momsal	mohm-sal	Fatigue
pyeryeom	pae-ryuhm	Pneumonia
seolsa	suhl-sa	Diarrhea
simjang mabi	shim-jahng ma-bee	Heart attack
yeol	yuhl	Fever

Discussing your medical history

When you go see the doctor, he or she will ask you several questions regarding you and your **gajik** (*ga-jok;* family)'s medical history. Like I mentioned earlier, most major hospitals will have staff that speak English, but in case you're at a hospital that doesn't have one, you'll have to remember a few sentences. As a **hwanja** (*hwan-ja;* patient), you'll have to describe your symptoms and medical history correctly. "**gajokbundeul junge [some word] areusinbun gyeshimnikka?**" (*ga-jok-boon-deul joong-ae [some word] a-reu-shin-boon gye-shim-nee-kka?,* Has anyone in your family ever suffered from [some word]?) might be a question that a doctor may ask you. "**eodiga eotteoke apeushimnika?**" (*uh-dee-ga uh-ttuh-kae a-peu-shim-nee-kka;* Where and how does it hurt?) might be another question a doctor may ask. You'll have to describe your symptoms correctly, and answer the questions your doctor asks you correctly. Don't be afraid to ask the doctor to repeat himself. He will be more than happy to slow things down and use hand signals and body language to ask you the questions again.

Making a diagnosis

Once you're in the doctor's office, he or she will want to run some tests on you. They may want your **pi** (*pee;* blood), your **sobyeon** (*so-byuhn;* urine), or your **daebyeon** (*dae-byuhn;* bowel movement). I'm sure they'll want to measure your **ki** (*kee;* height), your **chejung** (*chae-joong;* weight), and your **hyeorap** (*hyuh-rahp;* blood pressure). Depending on the situation, further tests may be required for the doctor to make a **jindan** (*jeen-dahn;* diagnosis). You may need a **simjeondo** (*shim-juhn-do;* electrocardiogram, EKG), or an **ekseurei gigye** (*ehk-sseu-rae-ee gee-gye;* X-ray machine) to correctly diagnose your ailment. Once your ailment is properly diagnosed, proper **yak** (*yahk;* medicine) will be prescribed. Then you'll have to go to the **yakguk** (*yahk-gook;* pharmacy) to get your **yak** so that you can take it. Table 16-3 gets you acquainted with medical-related terms that can you help in the face of an emergency.

Korea does have excellent hospitals and offer top notch medical care, so you need not be worried about the **wisaeng sangtae** (*wee-saeng sang-tae;* sanitary conditions) or the quality of care you'll be receiving should you find yourself there. Especially in large urban areas like Seoul or Busan, there are many reputable hospitals both independent and university affiliated, leading the world in research fields such as genetics and robotics. They are also very knowledgeable in Eastern medicine, such as **chim** (*cheem;* acupuncture), **hanyak** (*han-yahk;* herbal remedies), **buhang** (*boo-hwang;* cupping) and **ddeum** (*ddeum;* moxibustion) to name a few. Koreans are indeed quite fortunate in this manner that they receive best medical care from both the Western and the Eastern world.

Table 16-3	Medical and Emergency Terms	
Korean Word	*Pronunciation*	*English Word*
byeongwon	*byoung-won*	Hospital
cheon	*chae-on*	Body temperature
chim	*cheem*	Acupuncture
eunggeupsil	*eung-geup-shil*	Emergency room
gugeupcha	*goo-geup-cha*	Ambulance
hangsaengje	*hang-saeng-jae*	Antibiotics
hannyak	*han-yahk*	Herbal medicine
hyeorap	*hyuh-rahp*	Blood pressure
jusa	*joo-sa*	Syringe
maekbak	*maek-bak*	Pulse
ondogi	*on-do-gee*	Thermometer
pi	*pee*	Blood
susul	*soo-sool*	Surgery
uisa	*eui-sa*	Doctor
yak	*yahk*	Medicine
yakguk	*yahk-gook*	Pharmacy
yaksa	*yahk-sa*	Pharmacist

Following the prescription

Once you get your medicine, you'll have to know whether to take it once a day, or twice a day. You'll have to know which medicine is which also, so that you don't take the wrong **bogyongnyang** (*bo-gyong-yang;* dosage), or the wrong medication. The best thing to do is to find a person who can read Korean and have that person explain the proper dosage to you, write them down and put them on the bottles. If you're at a **yakguk** (*yahk-gook;* pharmacy) where the pharmacy tech speaks English, you can ask the tech and she will be more than happy to explain the proper dosage to you. She may even be able to print you out the drug information and dosage information in English. Don't be afraid to ask questions about your drug information regardless of what country you're in. You should always have as much information on the medication you take. **haru** (*ha-roo*) is the Korean word for a single day. **hwe** (*hwae*) or **beon** (*bun*) means the number of times. So, if the directions read, "**harue dubeon**" (*ha-roo-ae doo-bun;* twice daily), or "**harue 2hwe**" (*ha-roo-ae ee-hwae;* twice daily), then you know to take it twice daily.

Getting Legal Help

Unless you've done something terribly wrong, the chances of you needing legal help in Korea will be pretty rare. Koreans are genuinely friendly and helpful towards **yeohaengja** (*yuh-hang-ja;* tourists) and **oegugin** (*wae-goo-gin;* foreigners). It is precisely because tourism is such a big industry in Korea. However, if you do need a **byeonhosa** (*byuhn-ho-sa;* lawyer, legal council), you're probably better off finding your **daesagwan** (*dae-sa-gwan;* embassy), or **yeongsagwan** (*young-sa-gwan;* consulate). They will be able to provide you with all the legal council you need.

Fun & Games

Please identify following body parts in Korean. See Appendix C for answers.

1. Leg _____

2. Hand _____

3. Toes _____

4. Eyes _____

5. Ears _____

6. Nose _____

7. Mouth _____

8. Head _____

9. Chest _____

10. Foot _____

11. Fingers _____

12. Back _____

Part IV
The Part of Tens

In this part . . .

Take the time to check out this part because you can look and sound more like a Korean with the lists I've provided. You can discover ten ways to learn Korean quickly, ten phrases to make you sound more Korean, ten expressions that Koreans like to use, and ten things you shouldn't do in front of Koreans. Not only are these sections short, but they're also easy to remember. So they can be a big help to your understanding of Korean and Korean culture.

Chapter 17

Ten Ways to Get a Quick Handle on Korean

In This Chapter

▶ Using multimedia resources to learn Korean

▶ Visiting Korean restaurants

▶ Making Korean word lists

*W*hether you just started learning Korean, or can already speak a good amount, you may want a few pointers on how to further improve your Korean. In this chapter, I include ten tips on how you can do just that.

Find Koreans (or Other Korean Speakers) Near You

People say that to live a good life, all you really need is to converse with good people, eat in the company of good people, and of course sleep with a clear conscience. So go out and make some good Korean friends to converse and eat with; even if your friends can't help you much with the language, you still end up on the winning side. In general, though, Koreans are more than happy to explain parts of their culture and language to you. Some may even consider you one of theirs, meaning that they think you are as Korean as them, if you play the role of an entertaining peer, caring senior, and respectful junior.

Use Korean Language Tapes, CDs, and Other Multimedia Resources

When you learn Korean, immerse yourself in it, even when your friends aren't around. Pop in an audio CD on your way to work, or look up a few Web resources that you can download or listen to online. Be patient and go over them regularly and often. Although your progress may be a little sluggish at first, your efforts will pay off.

Visit Korean Restaurants and Bars

Getting people to open up and talk around strangers can be a little hard. But food and alcohol make people relax and open up a lot easier. The best place to learn about Korean customs is at a table, either over a meal or a drink. If you have trouble speaking in Korean, have a few shots of **soju** (*so-joo*; Korean rice wine), and you'll be speaking, crying, and laughing in Korean by the end of the night. Just be careful to not speak too much Korean to inanimate objects — you may scare your new Korean friends away.

Sing Korean Songs

When you're first learning a language, don't forget how helpful listening to songs can be. Songs are easier to remember than lists of vocabulary and pages of sentences. Although a lot of people start off by listening to modern pop music, you may want to start off with children's songs — they're catchier and easier to remember. If you do decide to listen to contemporary Korean pop, be prepared to find yourself singing about unrequited love and heartbreak in a very sappy way. But then again, if the people around you don't speak Korean, they won't know what you're singing about. You can find a few selections of Korean songs at www.amazon.com, especially the songs they played in Korean dramas and movies. You may also find some Korean songs from www.youtube.com.

Watch Korean Movies

Over the past few years, Korean movies have enjoyed a renaissance. On average, the quality of Korean movies has gone up, and several Korean films have received wide acclaim at international film competitions, such as the Cannes and Sundance film festivals. Korean movies cover a wide gamut of styles and offer something for everyone: art house flicks, thrillers, shockers, tear jerkers, and comedies. You may want to stop by a video store in your neighborhood that specializes in foreign films, or order a DVD online. Again, you can buy Korean movies from www.amazon.com. Although their selection is not large, amazon.com carries some very popular Korean movies. However, you may also find Korean movies from www.youtube.com.

Watch Korean Drama

The addictiveness of Korean drama has been likened to that of hard drugs. Korean dramas draw criticism with regard to unrealistic plots and repetitive story lines; every single one of them has to do with a love triangle of some sort. Even then, few people have the self-control to stop watching them. In fact, Korean drama has spread to the rest of Asia, and you can most likely talk about Korean dramas with your Chinese, Japanese, and Southeast Asian friends. www.amazon.com carries very popular Korean dramas with translations in English subtitles, which will be very helpful. Otherwise you can go to the individual Korean TV channels and watch pay per view. Some Korean TV channels are www.mbc.co.kr, www.sbs.co.kr, www.kbs.co.kr. From these, I recommend www.mbc.co.kr since their Web site can be read in English as well as Korean by press of a button on the Web site. You may also find Korean dramas from www.youtube.com.

Surf the Net for Korean Web Sites

Look online for a wealth of information regarding Korea and Korean language. Films, travel, language — the Internet has something for everyone. If you can read Korean script, you can make use of the excellent language materials offered by universities and colleges, and soon you may even be able to read bits and pieces of the Korean Web pages of your interest.

Look Up Words in a Korean Dictionary

Learning a language can be frustrating if you don't know many words. Paper dictionaries are great when you have the time to thumb through pages and circle random words you want to know, but electronic dictionaries have a clear advantage in terms of speed and convenience. You can even find several dictionaries online. Try http://www.zkorean.com/dictionary.shtml. Their dictionary is pretty good. If you have the time, check out the Web site itself. They have very useful information on learning Korean. Also try out http://www.ectaco.co.kr/English-Korean-Dictionary.

Make Korean Word and Phrase Lists

If you have trouble remembering words and phrases, use the information in this book to make lists of them. Then carry the lists around and look at them when you have an extra minute or two, or when you need them. Anticipate a particular activity for the day, and try writing down a few words or sentences at a time that you think you may need. For instance, write down sentences and words that have to do with types of clothing, sizes, and costs when you're going shopping; and write a list of tastes and colors when you're going out to eat. Then use the lists, or repeat the words to yourself when appropriate, regardless of where you are. Eventually, you should feel comfortable enough with the words to use them in front of Koreans.

Go to Korea!

Face it: No matter how many word lists you make or how diligently you surf the Net looking for online material, and no matter how hard you study or how much you try to imitate Korean, there's no immersion like total immersion. Buying a reasonably priced plane ticket to Korea and traveling for a short duration is possible. If you're strapped for cash, try going to Korea on an English-teaching program. Companies will often pay for your room and board, but make sure to check that the company is reputable, and stay safe.

Chapter 18

Ten Things to Avoid Doing in Korea

. . . .

In This Chapter

▶ Being humble

▶ Observing hierarchies

▶ Paying attention to your public behavior

. . . .

Acceptable public behaviors vary from country to country. For example, slurping your noodles and soup is considered rude in England, but you can do it in Korea without any worries of appearing rude. And you may be used to wearing your shoes in other people's houses where you live, but in Korea, it's a big no-no.

Perhaps you've seen foreigners make an occasional cultural mistake in your own country, and you've tried hard to muffle your laughter. This chapter aims to save you from making the same mistakes when you visit Korea!

Bragging or Accepting Compliments

Nobody likes listening to bragging, even if the person is good at what he or she claims. But in Korean culture, it's considered a virtue to go one step further and graciously decline any compliments. In Korea, self-deprecation is nearly an art form, and it's a good idea to train yourself to express yourself in a humble manner when speaking in Korean.

You often hear Koreans say **animnida, animnida** (*a-nim-ni-da, a-nim-ni-da;* No, no, not at all) after compliments they receive, and sometimes even mildly put themselves down. You may see people prepare food for you and say things like **maseun eopjiman** (*ma-seun uhp-jee-man;* although it doesn't taste good), **charingeon eopjiman** (*cha-rin-guhn uhp-jee-man;* although I haven't prepared anything much), and **bujok hajiman** (*boo-jok ha-jee-man;* although it [the food I've prepared for you] has many shortcomings). And sometimes Koreans may even actively bash themselves a little and say things like **yeongeoreul jal mot hajiman [some word]** (*young-uh-reul jal mot ha-jee-man [some word];* I'm not that good at English, but [some word]) or **meoriga nappayo** (*muh-ree-ga nappa-yo;* I'm not that smart). So don't worry if it seems like your friend or host has a self-esteem problem; it's just a cultural thing.

Making Someone Lose Face in Public

Koreans occasionally take to bashing themselves a little in front of other people. They do so to be humble, but that doesn't give you a right to bash them as well. Be careful that you don't make your friend or, especially a superior, lose face in front of other people by putting him down mildly or contradicting him in front of others. This behavior not only hurts the feelings of the other person, but also makes you seem inconsiderate to everyone who witnesses the event. If you want to point out something wrong, wait until you can speak to the other person alone. As unfair as this may seem, like Brussels sprouts and chicken liver, Koreans believe it helps you build discipline and character.

Something that you may particularly want to be wary of is raising your voice or showing contempt to your parents and older siblings in front of other people. This goes against the social hierarchy that Koreans impose upon themselves (look at Chapter 3 for more on hierarchy) and, as a result, Koreans may lose a significant amount of respect that they had for you.

Sitting or Eating Before the Seniors in the Group

In Korean culture, the senior is the leader of the group. He initiates handshakes, decides what to do, and agrees to suggestions. The people who are his juniors — be they juniors through age or through hierarchy on the job — play a more passive role and follow his lead. From the dinner table to the meeting room, the senior dictates when the meal or meeting begins.

Don't sit down or eat before the senior of the group. Although this rule isn't always observed in more informal settings (such as family dinners), it's a good idea to observe the hierarchy at meals and meetings. If you're unsure, watch what the people around you are doing so you can play it by ear. To put it another way, it might be a good idea to keep in mind the social relationship or distance you have to others.

Calling Your Boss or Teachers by Their First Names

A Korean name is usually three syllables long. Take, for example, Kim Jong-ll. The first syllable is the family name, and the remaining two are the first name. A few other examples are **Kong Sung-Joo** (*gong-sung-joo*) and **Choe Won-Nyeong** (*choe-won-young*). The last names in these examples, respectively, are **Kong** and **Choe.**

Calling someone by their last name alone isn't as polite as calling them by their full name. And by no means should you ever call your boss, your teacher, your parents, or anyone else who you consider your senior by their first names. Koreans think this is simply rude and can be compared to calling your judge by her first name during a court session.

Saying "Ssi" After Your Own Name

Koreans use the words **ssi** (sshi) and **nim** (nim) when they address people to show respect toward the people they're speaking with or about (see Chapter 3). It's a lot like saying Mr. or Mrs. But even if you hear a lot of people use these words when addressing you, don't use them when speaking about yourself. And similarly, don't use the honorifics, such as **kkeseo** (*kkae-suh;* No English translation; added after the person's name when you want to show respect towards the person you are speaking about) and **ssi** (*sshi;* Mr. or Mrs./Ms.) when speaking about yourself, unless you're trying to be sarcastic. **kkeseo** and **ssi** can be used for both males and females. However, **ssi** is used more frequently. **kkeseo** is usually used when the person in question is doing something or has said something. For example: **seonsaengnimkkeseo oneul jibe oseyo** (*suhn-saeng-nim-kkae-suh o-neul jee-bae o-sae-yo;* The teacher is coming to the house today).

Walking into a House with Your Shoes on

In the United States, you learn that you shouldn't slurp your food while you eat. However, you never really learn why. I could just tell you that walking into a house with your shoes on is rude, but instead I try to provide you with a bit of background as to why this is the case.

In Korea, the rooms of the house relied on a floor heating system called **ondol** (*on-dol;* warm stone), which involved heating a huge stone, or stones, underneath the room. The **ondol** is one of the main reasons why Koreans slept on the floor; sleeping on mattresses spread out on the floor allowed for the most efficient heat transfer. For the same reason, Koreans sit on cushions on the floor as opposed to sitting on chairs.

Koreans don't wear shoes in the house because floors used to serve as the surface upon which they slept and sat. Even though most Koreans nowadays live in westernized homes, the majority of Korean houses still rely on floor heating systems, just like **ondol**, although they do not use stone anymore. Nowdays, Koreans use copper wires for the floors, heating systems. Although many Koreans have started adopting westernized furniture, such as sofas and even beds, the custom of taking off your shoes when you enter a house still survives. Observe this custom because — if you don't, it'll bother your host about as much as it would if someone wore muddy shoes and walked around on your bed.

Sometimes, though, people just might allow you to wear shoes in the house, and, if that's the case, they let you know by saying, **sinbal an beoseodo doeyo** (*shin-bal an buh-suh-do dwae-yo;* You don't have to take your shoes off), **sinbal sineodo doeyo** (shin-bal shin-uh-do dwae-yo: You can wear your shoes), or **sinbal sineodo gwaenchanayo** (*shin-bal shin-uh-do gwaen-chan-a-yo;* It's okay to wear your shoes).

Crossing Your Legs When You Sit

Koreans are used to sitting **chaeksangdari** (*chaek-sang-da-ree;* sitting Indian style) on the floor. Even in modern society, when people sit on floors, they still sit this way. As uncomfortable as sitting **chaeksangdari** may seem, it's significantly more comfortable than kneeling. In a traditional formal gathering, the **chaeksangdari** was reserved for the seniors or elders of the group, and the juniors knelt on the floor until the elders suggested **pyeonhage anjayo** (*pyun-ha-gae an-ja-yo;* Please sit comfortably).

In contemporary society, most daily events take place in chairs, but the tradition of the juniors sitting in restricted positions remains. As a result, Koreans, especially in formal meetings, don't cross their legs while sitting in chairs. Instead, they keep their legs placed neatly, or side by side, in front of them.

Kissing in Public

Koreans aren't accustomed to public displays of affection. They bow to you, shake your hand, and — if they know you well enough — maybe even hug you. But don't expect to see anything beyond that in public, even if two people are happily engaged or married. Private displays of affection are fine, but public displays of affection aren't.

I'm not sure that there's one particular reason for this custom, but it may have come about because Korea was heavily influenced by Confucian ideals, which enforce segregation of males and females. And it may also be because of the strict codes of conduct enforced by Korean dictators in the 1970s. Those strict codes prohibited any "indecent activity." Regardless, you shouldn't publicly display affection. In fact, make sure you don't, lest you give granny a heart attack.

Taking the First "No, Thank You" Literally

One custom that's common for people from Asian cultures is to turn down a meal, drink, gift, or favor — even if the person is hungry, thirsty, in need of a ride home, or really wants that tea set you're offering. Korea is no exception to this custom. Don't worry — just because someone turns you down with a **gwaenchanayo** (*gwaen-chan-a-yo;* It's alright), it doesn't necessarily mean that they don't want what you have to offer.

There's a small cultural game going on here. The guest or gift receiver doesn't want to appear greedy, and the host or gift giver wants to seem generous. So be sure to make an offer more than once. And don't forget that you, too, should turn down an offer a few times before accepting.

Picking Up Your Rice Bowl and Using Your Spoon to Eat

A common custom of people from Asian cultures is to hold onto their rice bowls while they eat. In China and Japan, rice bowls are even rounded at the bottom to make holding them up easier. But in Korea, the bottoms of rice bowls are flat. They're meant to stay on the table during meals. Lifting a bowl up to polish off a little remaining soup or rice is all right, but otherwise keep your bowls on the table.

Another peculiarity of Korean culture is that Koreans eat their rice with a spoon rather than chopsticks. Although it isn't a hard and fast rule, you should usually use your chopsticks to pick up pieces of side dishes and use your spoon to eat your rice and communal soups.

Chapter 19

Ten Favorite Korean Expressions

In This Chapter

▶ Impressing Koreans with your language abilities

▶ Getting a handle on common terms from Korean speakers

Some Korean expressions are used more often then others, and here I present you with ten expressions that Koreans use all the time. By knowing them, not only can you talk like a native Korean, but you can also respond when someone uses them on you! Try listening for them in daily conversation, and don't forget to try using them yourself.

ppalli

ppalli (*ppal-li*) means *hurry or fast.* Common uses include **ppalli waseo meogeoyo** (*ppal-li wa-suh muh-guh-yo;* Hurry on over and eat), **ppalli gayo** (*ppal-li ga-yo;* Let's hurry up and go), **ppalli jom haeyo** (*ppal-li jom hae-yo;* Hurry up and do it), and **ppalli jom bikyeojuseyo** (*ppal-li jom bee-kyuh joo-sae-yo;* Hurry up and get out of the way). Koreans have a penchant for speed, so it's no surprise that the word **ppalli** is a part of everyday conversation.

gwaenchanayo

The term **gwaenchanayo** (*gwen-chan-a-yo*) is almost identical to the English *okay.* When you say **gwenchanayo**, it means "It's okay." When you raise the end of **gwenchanayo**, it becomes a question, so it means "Is it ok?" instead. You can use it to ask how someone feels or thinks about something, and to decline favors and state opinions.

jeongmal, jinjja, cham

jeongmal (*jung-mal*), **jinjja** (*jin-jja*), and **cham** (*cham*): All three mean *really*, but **cham** is very close to the English *sure*. You can use **jeongmal** and **jinjja** as sentences by themselves:

> **jeongmal.** (*jung-mal;* Really.)
>
> **jeongmal?** (*jung-mal?;* Really?)
>
> **jinjja.** (*jin-jja;* Really.)
>
> **jinjja?** (*jin-jja?;* Really?)

Or use them as adjectives, the way I do in this example: **jinjja, jeo anieyo. jinjja.** (*jin-jja juh a-ni-ae-yo. in-jja;* Really, it's not me. Really.)

Here are some examples of how these terms are used in conversation:

> **jinjja gyosunimkkeseo sukjega eopdago hasyeoseoyo!** (*jin-jja gyo-soo-nim-kke-suh sook-jae-ga uhp-da-go ha-syeo-ssuh-yo;* Really, the professor said there was no homework!)
>
> **jeongmal oneuldo yageunieyo?** (*jeong-mal o-neul-do ya-geun-ee-ae-yo;* Really, do I have to work a night shift again?)
>
> **oneul nalssiga cham deopneyo.** (*o-neul nal-ssi-ga cham deop-nae-yo;* My, the weather is really/surely hot today.)
>
> **jeo chimaga cham ippeoyo.** (*juh chi-ma-ga cham ee-ppuh-yo;* That skirt sure is pretty.)

a, geuraeyo

> **a, geuraeyo?** (*a, geu-rae-yo;* Ah, is that right?/Ah really?)
>
> **geuraeyo.** (*geu-rae-yo;* That's right/exactly.)

In Korean, you rarely use this expression to question anything the other person is saying. Instead, use it to show that you're following what the other person is saying. Often, people nod their head, and even make semi-surprised faces as they listen.

geuraeyo shows agreement with the speaker and indicates that the listener is paying attention. The technical term for this phenomenon is "backchannelling."

To get a feel for this phrase, imagine one friend saying **jinjja gyosunimkkeseo sukjega eopdago hasyeoseo!** (*jin-jja gyo-soo-nim-kke-suh sook-jae-ga uhp-da-go* *ha-syuh-syuh-yo;* Really, the professor said there was no homework!) and another friend saying **a geuraeyo?** (*a-geu-rae-yo;* Ah, is that right?).

jamkkanmanyo

jamkkanmanyo (*jam-kkan-man-nyo*) means *one moment please.*

Another word for **jamkkanmannyo** is **jamsimanyo** (*jam-shi-man-yo*). From the two, **jamsimanyo** is used in more formal occasions. For example, **jamsiman gidaryeo juseyo** (*jam-shi-man gee-ra-ryuh joo-sae-yo;* Please wait one moment.). However, if a colleague says **a ppalli jom haseyo** (*a ppal-li jom ha-sae-yo;* Hurry up, will you?), then you can say **a jamkkanmannyo, jamkkanmannyo** (*a jam-kkan-man-yo, jam-kkan-man-yo;* Hey, one moment, one moment).

mwo haeyo

When you say **mwo haeyo** (*mwo hae-yo*) you're asking, *what are you doing?* or *what's up?* You can expect a friend or colleague to ask you this question when you pass by. You can also use **mwo haseyo** (*mwo ha-sae-yo;* What are you doing?). **mwo haseyo** is little more formal than **mwo haeyo**.

mollayo

Use the word **mollayo** (*mol-la-yo*) to say *I don't know.*

This phrase is very commonly used in Korean conversation. If you listen carefully, you should be able to pick up this phrase very easily. Here's an example of using these terms in conversation

mwo meogeullaeyo? (*mwo muh-geul-lae-yo;* What do you want to eat?)

a, mollayo, amugeona meogeoyo. (*a, mol-la-yo, a-moo-guh-na muh-guh-yo;* Ah, I dunno, let's eat anything.)

joayo

You can use **joayo** (*jo-a-yo*) just like the statement *good* and the question *good?* in English. If you want to use this term to ask someone with seniority "Do you like it?" ask them using the phrase **joeuseyo?** (*jo-eu-sae-yo;* Do you like it?) instead of **joayo**?

jal doetneyo

Say **jal doetneyo** (*jal dwet-nae-yo;* That turned out well) when something good has happened. The phrase **jal doesseoyo** (*jal dwae-ssuh-yo;* That turned out well). Use **jal doetneyo** or **jal doesseoyo** whenever you're happy with a result.

The phrase **doetneyo** (*dwae-nae-yo*) or **doesseoyo** (*dwae-ssuh-yo*) without the **jal** infront of it, has somewhat negative meaning. It means *that's enough.* Do not use **doesseoyo** or **doetneyo** without the **jal** in front of it. Some people might get offended when they hear you say **doetneyo** or **doesseoyo** after they offer you something.

jeoreon, ireon

Koreans use **jeoreon** (*juh-ruhn;* Oh dear, Oh my or like that) or **ireon** (*ee-ruhn;* Oh dear, Oh my or like this) by itself when they hear or see something bad or harmful happen to another person. For example, **jeoreon, jeoreon, jeoreon** (Dear, oh dear, oh dear). **ireon** (Oh my). But each word has another meaning as well. **jeoreon** also means *like that,* and **ireon** also means *like this.*

Make sure you don't confuse **jeoreon** (Oh dear) and **ireon** (Oh my) with **jeoreon** (like that) and **ireon** (like this). To differentiate between which "Oh dear, Oh my" and "like this, like that" you need to know the context at which these words are being used. For example, **jeoreon ot hana juseyo** (*juh-ruhn ot ha-na joo-sae-yo;* Please give me a clothes like that one) and **jeoreon, sarami dachyeotneyo** (*juh-ruhn, sa-ram-ee da-chut-nae-yo;* Oh dear, someone got hurt).

Another way to use these words are: **ireon jeoreon ildo itjyo, mwo.** (*Literally:* Well, things like this and that happen. But a better translation is, Well, all sorts of things happen.)

Chapter 20

Ten Phrases That Make You Sound Korean

In This Chapter

▶ Expressing satisfaction

▶ Showing resignation

▶ Complaining about things

*I*n any language, people expect to hear certain common phrases, such as "Hello," "Nice to meet you," and, of course, "What's your name?" But Korean has some common expressions that are often hard for non-native speakers to understand. Using these expressions sometimes catches native speakers off guard and leads them to believe that you have a good understanding of both the language and the culture. So using these phrases is greatly to your advantage!

Here I present you with ten phrases that make you sound like you've been speaking Korean all your life. I hope you have fun using them on your unsuspecting Korean-speaking friends. Perhaps after they hear you using these expressions, they'll be a lot more careful about what they say in Korean around you! Please note that most of these phrases are in plain form, and should be only used among friends, unless noted otherwise.

akkapda

a-kkap-da: What a waste, that was close, what a pity; plain

This word means that you regret seeing something wasted. Perhaps you just saw someone throw out perfectly good food, or you lost a book you bought only five minutes before. Informal polite form of this word is **akkawoyo** (*a-kka-wo-yo;* informal polite) and **akkapnaeyo** (*a-kkap-nae-yo;* informal polite). Although **akkapda** is the plain form version of **akkapneyo** or **akka-woyo**, it is most commonly used among Koreans. You can also use this term to say *that was close.* In a golf match, for example, the announcer may say **ye, ujeu seonsuga banggeum peoteureul haetseumnida. ye a, a akkapnaeyo.** (*ye, u-jeu seon-soo-ga bang-geum peo-teu-reul haet-sseum-ni-da. ye a, a-kkap-nae-yo;* Yes, Woods has just taken a putter. Yes, oh that was so close.). However, the people listening to the announcer, will be saying "**akkapda** (*a-kkap-da*), **akkawo** (*a-kka-wo*)."

eojjeol su eopgun

uh-jjul-soo uhp-goon: It looks like I have no other choice; plain

Use **eojjeol su eopgun** when you want to show resignation, especially when you're given a choice that doesn't have an ideal outcome or that doesn't give you any advantage. For example, suppose you go to a bar to meet a friend, but then you get a call from your friend saying he can't make it. Of course, now you have no choice but to drink by yourself, so you mutter to yourself **eojjeol su eopgun, honjaseo surina masyeoyaji.** (*uh-jjul soo uhp-goon, hon-ja-suh soo-ree-na ma-syuh-ya-jee;* Looks like I have no other choice but to drink by myself.)

geureonde itjanayo

geu-ruhn-dae ee-ja-na-yo: By the way, you know; informal polite

Koreans often use **geuleonde** (*geu-ruhn-dae;* but, by the way; plain) and **itjanayo** (*ee-ja-na-yo;* hey, you know; plain) individually, and together as **geuleonde itjanayo** (*geu-ruhn-dae ee-ja-na-yo;* By the way, did you know; informal polite) to begin sentences. Using them makes sentences sound natural. People sometimes contract **geuleonde** to **geunde** (*geun-dae;* By the way; plain), and **itjanayo** (*ee-ja-na-yo;* hey, you know; informal polite) can take the plain form **itjana** (*ee-ja-na;* Did you know; plain), which is used very commonly.

Examples of these words include the following:

✔ **geuleonde itjanayo oneul nalssiga cham siwonhajyo?** (*geu-ruhn-dae ee-ja-na-yo o-neul nal-sshi-ga cham shi-won-ha-jyo;* Hey, by the way, isn't the weather cool today?)

✔ **geunde geuregeuneun eodi itjyo?** (_geun-dae geu-rae-geu-neun uh-dee ee-jyo;_ By the way, where's Greg?)

✔ **itjanayo, sigan jom iseoyo?** (_ee-ja-na-yo, shi-gan jom ee-ssuh-yo;_ Hey, do you have time?)

jom

jom: A little, please

Koreans use **jom** (_jom;_ a little, please) almost instinctively, so they may not notice at first that you're using it, but when they do notice, they'll be more than a little pleasantly surprised. **jom** (_jom;_ a little, please) is actually a contraction of the word **jogeum** (_jo-geum;_ a little). **jogeum** can mean only _a little,_ but **jom** can have different meanings depending on whether you're using it as an adjective or an adverb.

When the term is an adverb, it also means _a little._ Check out these examples:

✔ **eumsigi jom maewoyo.** (_eum-shi-gee jom mae-wo-yo;_ The food is a little spicy.)

✔ **jigeum jom neujeoseoyo** (_jee-geum jom neu-juh-ssuh-yo;_ It's a little late.)

✔ **iri yojeum jom manayo.** (_il-ee yo-jeum jom ma-na-yo;_ I have a bit too much work nowadays.)

But when you use the term as an adjective, it means _please._ Here's an example: **yeogiseo gyesan jom haejuseyo?** (_yuh-gee-suh gye-san jom hae-joo-sae-yo;_ Could you please take care of the bill here?)

jjajeungnanda

jja-jeung-nan-da: That's irritating, it's annoying; plain

At one point or another, you're bound to get into a situation that annoys you. Your flight may be delayed over and over again. Or your boss may give you too much grief at work. If you ever feel the need to express the frustration and annoyance that you feel, say **jjajeungnanda** (_jja-jeung-nan-da;_ it's irritating, it's annoying; plain). The informal polite form of this word is **jjajeungnayo** (_jja-jeung-na-yo;_ informal polite); however, Koreans don't usually use this form. The phrase **jjajeungnanda** is commonly used when you are talking to yourself or among close friends. Just make sure your boss doesn't hear you!

jukgetda

jook-get-da; I feel like dying; plain

English speakers often use the topics of death and dying as figures of speech in everyday conversation: "I was scared to death! I thought I was going to die!" And, occasionally, you may hear people say "This is to die for" or "I could die and go to heaven."

Koreans also use the plain form **jukgetda** (*jook-get-da;* to die) in a number of ways and forms, but if you ever listen to a group of Koreans, you can tell that they use it even more liberally than English speakers. Some of the expressions carry over in English better than others, but for some, you just have to use trial and error to figure out how and when to use them. Here's an example: In English, you may say, with plenty of sarcasm, "This tastes so good it makes me want to kill myself!" However, in Korean, you say **massiseo jukgetda, jugeo** (*ma-shi-ssuh jook-get-da, joo-guh;* This tastes so good it makes me want to kill myself! Kill myself!) with a look of genuine satisfaction on your face.

Other, similar expressions that translate more naturally from Korean to English include:

- **deowo jukgetda.** (*duh-wo jook-get-da;* It's so hot, I feel like dying.)
- **a pigonhae jukgetda.** (*a pee-gon-hae jook-get-da;* I'm so tired, I could die.)
- **baebulleo jukgetda.** (*bae-bul-luh jook-get-da;* I'm so full, I just might die.)
- **a, jukgo sipda.** (*a, jook-go ship-da;* I want to die.)

Informal polite form of this phrase is **jukgetseyo** (*jook-get-ssuh-yo;* I feel like dying). If you want to complain to another adult about your children, say **ai ttaemune jukgetseyo.** (*a-ee ttae-moo-nae jook-get-ssuh-yo;* My kid is killing me.)

When you're threatening someone, you don't have to use any polite forms. For that reason, here I use both **jugeo** (*joo-guh;* die) and **jugeullae?** (*joo-geul-lae;* Do you want to die?), which are in plain form.

Koreans also use **jukda** (*jook-da;* to die) as a threat. You may hear **jugeo** (*joo-guh;* die) or **jugeullae?** (joo-geul-lae; Do you want to die?). You may have heard **jugeullae?** in the Korean film *My Sassy Girl.* Often, it's used jokingly between friends.

jugeullae? (*joo-geul-lae;* Do you want to die?) is still a threat, even if you mean it as an idle one. Make sure you use this only with your close friends. When in doubt, wimp out and never use **jukda** (*jook-da;* to die) as a joke if the other person is your senior or is older than you.

kkeunnaejunda

kkeun-nae-joon-da: That's awesome; plain

Koreans often use **kkeunnaejunda** (*kkeun-nae-joon-da;* plain) to mean *awesome* or *amazing*. The informal polite form of this phrase is **kkeunnaejunaeyo** (*kkeun-nae-joo-nae-yo;* informal polite). However, this form is not very commonly used. Most commonly used phrase is **kkeunnaejunda**, which you will only use among your friends. You can also use it in sentences like these:

- ✔ **bunwigiga kkeunnaejunda.** (*boon-wee-gee-ga kkeun-nae-joon-da;* What an awesome atmosphere.)
- ✔ **oneul nalssi kkeunnaejunda.** (*o-neul nal-sshi kkeun-nae-joon-da;* What amazing weather.)
- ✔ **jeogeo jom bwa. jeongmal kkeunnaejunda.** (*juh-guh jom bwa. jung-mal kkeun-nae-joon-da;* Hey, look over there, that's really something.)

neukkihada

neu-kki-ha-da: Aftertaste of oily, greasy foods, or an action so overdone it makes you queasy; plain

The primary use of **neukkihada** (*neu-kki-ha-da;* oily, greasy, someone's actions makes you feel queasy; plain) is simple. Use it when you want to describe oily or greasy foods — think fast food or burgers. Informal polite form of this phrase is **neukkihaeyo** (*neu-kki-hae-yo;* It's oily, greasy or that person is making me queasy). You can use the word **neukkihaeyo** to describe that the food you are eating is way too greasy for you. It is commonly used among Koreans as well as **neukkihada**. You often hear Koreans say **neukkihangeo meokgosipda.** (*neu-kki-han-guh muhk-go-ship-da;* I feel like eating something greasy.) or **i eumsik neomu neukkihaeyo.** (*ee eum-shik nuh-moo neu-kki-hae-yo;* This food is too greasy.)

Koreans also use **neukkihada** to describe people and their actions. A similarity in English is using *saccharine* to describe people or actions that are overly nice to the point of being unnatural or uncomfortable. Koreans use **neukkihada** to exclusively describe men. They do not use **neukkihada** to describe women. Use it to describe the feeling you get when someone seems to be putting on airs to look more sophisticated or charming than they are.

Suppose your guy friend is trying to impress a girl he just met at a bar. He's being a perfect gentleman, which is completely out of character for him, and as a result you have a hard time suppressing your laughter. Here, you can use **neukkihada** (*neu-kki-ha-da*) to express the awkwardness that you feel. Perhaps you later tell your friend **akka neo neomu neukkihadeora.** (*a-kka nuh nuh-moo neu-kki-ha-duh-ra;* Man, you were being so uncharacteristically smooth back there that I felt queasy watching you.)

TIP You can also use **neukkihada** negatively. For example, you can use it if you see a female friend of yours dancing with a dude who looks and acts strangely like Fabio, and even talks like Fabio — and you really don't like Fabio. You may want to use **neukkihada** to describe that person. **jeo saram jom neukkihada** (*juh sa-ram jom neu-kki-ha-da;* That person looks like he's trying a little too hard, and it's making me uncomfortable.)

siwonhada

shi-won-ha-da: Cool, refreshing, or good; plain

You can use **siwonhada** (*shi-won-ha-da;* cool, refreshing) just as you do the English word *cool*. For Koreans, a cool breeze on a summer day is **siwonhada,** and a cup of cold lemonade is also **siwonhada**. Literally, **siwonhada** means *cool*, but Koreans use it to capture a much broader range of feelings. Koreans also use **siwonhada** to describe the sense of mental catharsis or refreshment that you feel after experiencing a happy event. Furthermore, although scratching an itch and drinking a hot cup of tea aren't literally cool, Koreans use the word **siwonhada** because it internalizes the feeling that you get from a breeze on a hot summer day. The informal polite form is **siwonhaeyo** (*shi-won-hae-yo*) and you can use this phrase to describe the drink you are drinking is cool or the weather is cool. **siwonhaeyo,** however, does not have as broad range of feeling as the **siwonhada**, since it's not used as much as **siwonhada**, and sounds kind of awkward.

Koreans use **siwonhada** to describe seeing a long-needed summer rainstorm, driving down an non-congested road, taking a shot of tequila, and seeing a person they don't like get into trouble. In this way, Koreans use the word **siwonhada** to describe a feeling of catharsis. It's like having a breeze lift your spirits.

You can also use **siwonhada** to describe the feeling of refreshment that you get from scratching an itch, stretching out, walking out of a sauna, or drinking a cup of tea.

sugohaeyo

soo-go-hae-yo: Keep up the good work; informal polite

This is a common expression in English, of course, but you should be especially certain to use it often when you're working with people who speak Korean. Using **sugohaeyo** (*soo-go-hae-yo;* Keep up the good work) is okay with people you know well or work with a lot. Make sure you use the formal polite form, **sugohasipsiyo** (*soo-go-ha-ship-shi-yo;* Keep up the good work) if you're going to use the expression around any seniors.

Part V
Appendixes

The 5th Wave   By Rich Tennant

"We're still learning the language and Martin tends to act out things he doesn't know the word for. He tried buying a toilet seat the other day and they almost threw him out of the store."

In this part . . .

In this part you can find several references that you may want to turn to while flipping through the rest of the chapters or while out on your own. You can find verb tables that show the conjugations of regular and irregular verbs, and a mini-dictionary for Korean-to-English and English-to-Korean words. Think you've mastered the Fun & Games sections? Well, check out the answers in this part as well as look for the list of tracks that appear on the audio CD.

Appendix A

Korean Verbs

*T*his section lists Korean verbs, in their dictionary forms. For proper use of Korean verbs, consult Chapter 2. Try to remember that the verb usually ends a Korean sentence, and you're off to a great start!

akkida/*a-kki-da*/to cherish

alda/*al-da*/to know

allyeojida/*al-yuh-jee-da*/to be known

anda/*an-da*/to sit

annaehada/*an-nae-ha-da*/to guide

apeuda/*a-peu-da*/to be hurt, to be ill, to be sick

baeuda/*bae-oo-da*/to learn

bakkuda/*ba-kkoo-da*/to change, to exchange

bappeuda/*ba-ppeu-da*/to be busy

batda/*bat-da*/to receive

beorida/*buh-ree-da*/to throw away, to discard

beotda/*buht-da*/to take off, to undress, to unburden

bichuda/*bee-choo-da*/to shine on, to shed a light on

bissada/*bee-ssa-da*/to be expensive, too costly

boda/*bo-da*/to look, to see

boyeojuda/*bo-yuh-joo-da*/to show

bureuda/*boo-reu-da*/to call, to summon, to be full

chada/*cha-da*/to be cold, to be full, to kick (For proper usage, please check the context in which the verb is used.)

chaengida/*chaeng-gi-da*/to gather together, to pack

chajihada/*cha-jee-ha-da*/to occupy, to possess

chamda/*cham-da*/to be patient, to persevere, to endure

chamgahada/*cham-ga-ha-da*/to participate, to join

charida/*cha-ree-da*/to prepare, to get ready

chatda/*chat-da*/to search, to look for

cheorihada/*chuh-ree-ha-da*/to take care of

chida/*chi-da*/to hit, to strike

chiida/*chi-ee-da*/to get hit (for example, in a car accident)

chinhada/*chin-ha-da*/to be intimate, to be close, to be friendly

chiuda/*chi-oo-da*/to put away, to clean up, to remove

chuda/*choo-da*/to dance

chupda/*choop-da*/to be cold

chwihada/*chwee-ha-da*/to be drunk, to be intoxicated

chwisohada/*chwee-so-ha-da*/to cancel

dahada/*da-ha-da*/to complete, to finish

dalda/*dal-da*/to hang, to put up

dallida/*dal-lee-da*/to run

danggida/*dang-gee-da*/to pull

danida/*da-nee-da*/to come and go, to go about

deonjida/*duhn-jee-da*/to throw

deopda/*duhp-da*/to be hot, warm

deullida/*deul-lee-da*/to be heard

deurida/*deu-ree-da*/to give

deutda/*deut-da*/to listen

dolboda/*dol-bo-da*/to look after

dollida/*dol-lee-da*/to turn, to spin

dowajuda/*do-wah-joo-da*/to help

duda/*doo-da*/to leave alone

eodupda/*uh-doop-da*/to be dark, to be dim

eolda/*uhl-da*/to freeze

eojireopda/*uh-jee-ruhp-da*/to be dizzy

eojireuda/*uh-jee-reu-da*/to make a mess

eopda/*uhp-da*/to not exist, to run out, to not have

eoryeopda/*uh-ryuhp-da*/to be difficult

gabyeopda/*ga-byuhp-da*/to be light, weighs little

gada/*ga-da*/to go, to come, to proceed, to travel

gajida/*ga-jee-da*/to have, to take

galda/*gal-da*/to exchange, to grind

gamchuda/*gam-choo-da*/to hide

garida/*ga-ree-da*/to cover up, to hide, to conceal

garyeopda/*ga-ryuhp-da*/to itch

gatda/*gat-da*/to be same

geotda/*guht-da*/to walk

gidarida/*gee-da-ree-da*/to wait

gilda/*gil-da*/to be long, lengthy

gireuda/*gee-reu-da*/to raise

gochida/*go-chee-da*/to fix

goreuda/*go-reu-da*/to choose

guhada/*goo-ha-da*/to save, to find

hada/*ha-da*/to do

himdeulda/*him-deul-da*/to be hard, to be difficult

igida/*ee-gee-da*/to win

ikda/*ilk-da*/to read

ipda/*eeb-da*/to wear

itda/*eet-da*/to exist, to be here, to be present

jada/*ja-da*/to sleep

jakda/*jahg-da*/to be small, doesn't fit

jallida/*jal-lee-da*/to be cut, to be laid off

japida/*ja-pee-da*/to be grabbed, to be captured

japda/*jap-da*/to grab, to capture, to grasp

jareuda/*ja-reu-da*/ to cut

jeopda/*juhp-da*/to fold

jeotda/*juht-da*/to stir, to be wet

jichida/*jee-chee-da*/to be exhausted

jida/*jee-da*/to lose

jubda/*joob-da*/to pick up

keuda/*keu-da*/to grow

kiuda/*kee-oo-da*/to nurture, to raise

makda/*mak-da*/to block

makhida/*mak-hee-da*/to be blocked, to be clogged

mandeulda/*man-deul-da*/to make

mannada/*man-na-da*/to meet

mareuda/*ma-reu-da*/to be dry, to be thirsty

masida/*ma-shi-da*/to drink

meogida/*muh-gee-da*/to feed

meokda/*muhk-da*/to eat

meokhida/*muk-hee-da*/ to be eaten

meolda/*muhl-da*/to be far away

mitda/*meet-da*/to believe

moeuda/*moh-eu-da*/to gather something (for example, berries)

moida/*mo-ee-da*/ to gather together (for example, people)

mollida/*mol-li-da*/to be cornered

moreuda/*moh-reu-da*/to not know

mulda/*mool-da*/to bite

naegihada/*nae-gee-ha-da*/to gamble

naerida/*nae-ree-da*/to get off, to get down

namgida/*nam-gee-da*/to leave behind

nanuda/*na-noo-da*/to divide

nareuda/*na-reu-da*/to carry, to deliver

neukkida/*neu-kki-da*/to feel

neurida/*neu-ree-da*/to be slow

nolda/*nol-da*/to play

nollada/*nol-la-da*/to be surprised

nollida/*nol-lee-da*/to tease

nota/*no-ta*/to release, to let go

nullida/*nool-lee-da*/to be pressed down, to be squashed

nureuda/*noo-reu-da*/to press down, to squash

oda/*o-da*/to come

pada/*pa-da*/to dig

palda/*pal-da*/to sell

pallida/*pal-lee-da*/to be sold

sada/*sa-da*/to buy

salda/*sal-da*/to live

sallida/*sal-lee-da*/to let live, to rescue

samkida/*sam-kee-da*/to swallow

saranghada/*sa-rang-ha-da*/to love

sogida/*so-gee-da*/to fool

sokda/*sog-da*/to be fooled

tada/*ta-da*/to get on, to ride

taeuda/*tae-oo-da*/to give a ride

ulda/*ool-da*/to cry

utda/*oot-da*/to smile, to laugh

Korean-English Mini-Dictionary

A

achim (a-chim) breakfast

adeul (a-deul) son

aein (ae-een) lover, significant other

aekche (aek-chae) liquid

aekja (aek-ja) picture frame

agi (a-gee) baby

ajik (a-jik) yet, still

akgi (ahk-gi) musical instrument

al (ahl) egg

alda (al-da) to know

an (an) interior, inside

anae (a-nae) wife

angae (an-gae) fog

aniyo (a-ni-yo) no

anjeon (ahn-jun) safety

ansim (an-shim) peace of mind

ap (ap) the front

apateu (a-pa-teu) apartment

apeuda (a-peu-da) painful

arae (a-rae) underneath

areumdabda (a-reum-dap-da) beautiful

B

bab (bab) cooked rice

bada (ba-da) the sea, the ocean

bae (bae) stomach or a boat

baedal (bae-dal) delivery

baji (ba-jee) pants, trousers

baksa (bak-sa) someone with a doctor of philosophy (PhD) degree, i.e., doctor with PhD not MD

balmok (bal-mok) ankle

ban (bahn) half

bang (bang) room

banghyang (bang-hyang) direction

bangmulgwan (bang-mool-gwan) a museum

bap (bab) cooked rice

baram (ba-ram) the wind

bawi (ba-wee) a rock

beob (buhb) the law

beolgeum (buhl-geum) a fine, penalty

beopjeong (buhp-jung) a (law) court

bi (bee) rain

bimil (bee-meel) secret

boda (bo-da) to see, to look

bok (bohk) blessings, good fortune

boksu (bohk-soo) revenge

bom (bom) spring

bori (bo-ree) barley

boseok (bo-suhk) jewels

bukjjok (book-jjok) north, northern side

bul (bool) fire

bun (boon) fraction, minute

byeong (byoung) sickness, disease

byeongweon (byoung-won) a hospital

C

cha (cha) a car, tea

chaegim (chae-gim) responsibility

chaek (chaeg) book

changmun (chang-moon) window

chejo (chae-jo) gymnastic exercises

chejung (chae-joong) weight

cheol (chuhl) iron, steel

cheoldo (chuhl-do) railroad

cheon (chun) a thousand, fabric

chigwa (chi-gwa) dentistry

chim (chim) spit, acupuncture needle

chima (chi-ma) skirt

chisol (chi-ssol) toothbrush

chiyak (chi-yak) toothpaste

cho (cho) second (time), candle

chodae (cho-dae) invite

chukha (choo-ka) congratulations

chwiso (chwee-so) cancellation

D

daeum (da-eum) next

dal (dal) moon, month

dari (da-ree) leg or bridge (depends on the context)

daseot (da-suht) five

dasi (da-shi) again

deulda (deul-da) to hold

deulida (deul-lee-da) to be heard

deungsan (deung-san) mountain climbing

deurida (deu-ree-da) to give, to offer

deutda (deut-da) to hear

dochak (do-chak) arrival

dok (dok) poison, earthenware pot

don (don) money

dongjeon (dong-jun) coins

dongjjok (dong-jjok) east, eastern side

dongmul (dong-mool) animal

dopda (dop-da) to help

dosi (do-shi) city

dul (dool) two

dutong (doo-tong) headache

E

eodi (uh-dee) where

eodum (uh-doom) darkness

eodupda (uh-doop-da) to be dark, obscure

eoje (uh-jae) yesterday

eojjeoda (uh-jjuh-da) by chance

eojireopda (uh-jee-ruhp-da) to be dizzy

eojireopida (uh-jee-ruh-pee-da) to mess up, disarrange

eojjeoda (uh-jjuh-da) by chance

eokkae (uh-kkae) shoulder

eolda (ul-da) to freeze, be frozen

eoleun (ul-leun) quickly, fast

eolgul (ul-gool) face

eolma (ul-ma) how much

eomeoni (uh-muh-ni) your own mother

eomeonim (uh-muh-nim) someone else's mother

eomji (uhm-jee) the thumb

eomma (um-ma) mommy

eondeok (uhn-duhk) a hill, a meadow

eoneu (uh-neu) which, what

eoneujjok (uh-neu-jjok) which direction

eoneuttae (uh-neu-ttae) what time, when

eongmang (uhng-mang) a mess

eonje (un-jae) when

eopda (uhp-da) doesn't exist, ran out

eopdeurida (uhp-deu-ree-da) to lie flat

eoreum (uh-reum) ice

eoreun (uh-reun) adult, elder

eorida (uh-ree-da) to be young

eoriseokda (uh-ree-suhk-da) to be foolish

eoryeopda (uh-ryuhp-da) hard, difficult

eotteoke (uh-ttuh-kae) how

G

gabyeopda (ga-byuhp-da) to be light, not heavy

gada (ga-da) to go

gaeul (ga-eul) autumn, fall

gage (ga-gae) a store, a shop

gagu (ga-goo) furniture

gagyeok (ga-gyuhk) price, cost

gajeong (ga-jung) household

gakkapda (ga-kkap-da) to be near, be close by

gakkeum (ga-kkeum) occasionally

gakkuda (ga-kkoo-da) cultivate, grow

galbi (gal-bee) ribs, also a Korean marinated beef dish

gan (gan) liver

ganeulda (ga-neul-da) to be thin, slender

gang (gang) river

ganjang (gan-jang) soy sauce

garo (ga-ro) width, breadth, across

garu (gh-roo) powder

garyeopda (ga-ryuhp-da) to itch

gaseum (ga-seum) the chest, the breast

gasi (ga-shee) a thorn, a bur

gaunde (ga-oon-dae) the middle

gawi (ga-wee) scissors, shears

gicha (gee-cha) a train

gil (gil) a road

gugyeong (goo-gyoung) browsing, looking

guksu (gook-soo) noodles

gwangwang (gwan-gwang) sightseeing, tour

gwi (gwee) ear

gyeongchal (gyung-chal) policing

gyeongchi (gyoung-chi) scenery

gyotong (gyo-tong) traffic

H

hada (ha-da) to do, to perform

haebyeon (hae-byun) the beach

hana (ha-na) one

hanguk (han-goog) Korea

heori (huh-ree) waist

heungmi (heung-mee) interest

him (him) strength

hongsu (hong-soo) a flood

hwajang (hwa-jang) make-up

hwajangsil (hwa-jang-shil) bathroom

hyuji (hyoo-jee) toilet paper

hyujitong (hyoo-jee-tong) wastebasket

hyusik (hyoo-shik) rest, repose

I

i (ee) two or tooth depending on the context

ibul (ee-bool) a quilt, a blanket

idal (ee-dal) this month

igeot (ee-guht) this one

igeotjeogeot (ee-guht-juh-guht) this and that

ijjok (ee-jjok) this side

il (il) a day or work or one depending on the context

ilgop (il-gop) seven

ima (ee-ma) forehead

inaljeonal (ee-nal-juh-nal) this day and that day

ip (eep) mouth

ipda (eep-da) put on, to wear

ipgu (eep-goo) entrance, entry way

ipsul (eep-sool) lips

ireon (ee-ruhn) like this, such

ireum (ee-reum) name

isa (ee-sa) to move, relocate

itda (eet-da) to connect, to be

iteul (ee-teul) two days

J

jagda (jak-da) small

jajeongeo (ja-juhn-guh) a bicycle

jal (jal) well, nicely, satisfactorily

jalmot (jal-mot) a fault, a mistake, an error

jam (jam) sleep, slumber

jandon (jan-don) loose change

jangbi (jang-bee) equipment, fitting, outfit

jangnangam (jang-nan-gam) toys

jangsa (jang-sa) trade, business, commerce

jangsik (jang-shik) ornament, decoration

jangso (jang-so) a place, a spot, a location

jayeon (ja-yuhn) nature

jeogeot (juh-guht) that one, that thing

jeol (juhl) a Buddhist temple or a formal bow depending on the context

jeolban (juhl-ban) a half

jeomsim (jum-shim) lunch

jeonbu (jun-boo) all parts, the whole

jeoncha (jun-cha) streetcar, a trolley, a tank

jeondeung (jun-deung) electric light, a lamp

jeongeojang (jung-guh-jang) a railroad station

jeongryujang (jung-ryoo-jang) a bus stop

jeonhwa (juhn-hwa) a telephone, a phone call

jeonja (juhn-ja) electronic

jeonyeok (juh-nyuhk) evening, dusk, dinner

jeotgarak (juht-ga-rak) chopsticks

jibul (jee-bool) payment, defrayment

jida (jee-da) to be defeated, to fade or cast a shadow depending on the context

jido (jee-do) a map, guidance, leadership

jigap (jee-gahp) a wallet, a pocketbook

jigeop (jee-guhp) one's occupation, a vocation

jihacheol (jee-ha-chul) the subway

jikjang (jik-jang) one's place of work

jikjeop (jik-juhp) direct, immediate

jinchal (jin-chal) medical examination

jinju (jin-joo) a pearl

jintongje (jin-tong-jae) an analgesic, painkiller

jip (jeep) a house, a home

jiuda (jee-oo-da) to erase

jiyeok (jee-yuhk) a region, an area, a zone

jjada (jja-da) salty, or to squeeze, press, extract

jjak (jjak) one of a pair, a side

jjitda (jjeet-da) tear, rend, rip

jjok (jjok) a piece, a slice, a plank

jongari (jong-a-ree) the calf of the leg

jongryu (jong-ryoo) a kind, a sort

jongyo (jong-gyo) a religion, a faith

jotda (jo-ta) to be good, to like

ju (joo) the main part, vermillion, a state, a province, a continent, a stock, a share, a week

juil (joo-il) weekday

jumal (joo-mal) the weekend

jumun (joo-moon) an order, ordering

jusa (joo-sa) an injection, a shot

juso (joo-so) one's address

K

kal (kal) a knife, a sword

kaljaru (kal-ja-roo) a knife handle

kaljip (kal-jeep) a scabbard, a sheath

kamkamhada (kahm-kahm-ha-da) to be dark

keodarata (kuh-da-ra-ta) very big, large

keojida (kuh-jee-da) to grow bigger

keopi (kuh-pee) coffee

keuda (keu-da) to grow

keugi (keu-gee) size, dimensions

keundon (keun-don) big money, a lot of money

keungil (keun-gil) a main road

keunil (keun-il) a great undertaking, emergency

ki (kee) a rudder, height of a person, a key

kiseu (kee-sseu) a kiss

ko (ko) a nose

kogamgi (ko-gam-gee) a cold in the head

kogolda (ko-gol-da) snore

kompyuteo (kuhm-pyoo-tuh) a computer

kong (kong) beans, soybeans, a pea

kyeolle (kyuhl-lae) a pair

M

mabi (ma-bee) paralysis, palsy

macha (ma-cha) a carriage, a coach

madi (ma-dee) a joint, a node, a segment

maekju (maek-joo) beer, ale

maeum (ma-eum) the mind, spirit

majimak (ma-jee-mahk) the last, the end

mal (mahl) a horse or language depending on the context

malhada (mahl-ha-da) talk, speak, converse

man (mahn) bay, gulf, or ten thousand depending on the context

mandeulda (mahn-deul-da) make, manufacture

mandu (mahn-doo) dumplings

maneul (ma-neul) garlic

mani (ma-ni) much, lots, plenty

manjok (mahn-jok) satisfaction, contentment

masida (ma-shi-da) drink, take, swallow

mat (maht) a taste, a flavor, savor

meokda (muhk-da) eat, take, have

meokhida (muh-kee-da) get eaten

meomchuda (muhm-choo-da) to stop, to cease

meoreojida (muh-ruh-jee-da) become more distant

meori (muh-ree) the head

minsok (meen-sok) ethnic customs

mirae (mee-rae) the future

mit (meet) the lower part, the bottom

mok (mok) the neck

muge (moo-gae) weight, heft, importance

mul (mool) water

mulgogi (mool-go-gee) fish

mun (moon) a gateway, a door

munje (moon-jae) a question, a problem

N

na (na) I, me, oneself

naebok (nae-bok) thermal underwear

nagada (na-ga-da) to go out

nakksi (nak-shi) fishing

nal (nal) a day

naljja (nal-jja) the date

nallo (nal-lo) a stove, a heater

nalssi (nal-sshi) the weather

namja (nam-ja) a man, a male

namjjok (nam-jjok) south, southern side

namu (na-moo) a tree

nanuda (na-noo-da) to divide, part

net (net) four

nolda (nol-da) to play

nongchon (nong-chon) a rural community

nongdam (nong-dam) a joke, a jest

nugu (noo-goo) who

nun (noon) eye, snow

O

o (o) five

oda (o-da) to come

oneul (o-neul) today, this day

orak (o-rak) amusement, recreation

oreunjjok (o-reun-jjok) the right side

osip (o-ship) fifty

P

pa (pa) green onion

pado (pa-do) waves, billows

pal (pal) eight

palda (pal-da) to sell, offer for sale

pallida (pal-lee-da) to be sold

panmae (pahn-mae) a sale, selling

parang (pa-rang) blue

peuro (peu-ro) a professional

pi (pee) blood

pibu (pee-boo) the skin

podo (po-do) grapes

pogi (po-gee) giving up, abandonment

pumjil (poom-jeel) a quality

pyeolli (pyuhl-lee) convenience, expediency

pyeonji (pyun-jee) a letter

pyo (pyo) a ticket, admission ticket, a vote, a ballot

pyosi (pyo-shi) an indication, a sign

R

radio (ra-dee-o) a radio

reida (re-ee-da) radar

reijeo (rae-ee-juh) a laser

rejeo (re-juh) leisure

resseulling (re-sseul-ling) wrestling

ripoteu (ree-po-teu) a report

robi (ro-bee) a lobby

S

sa (sa) four

sada (sa-da) to buy, to purchase

saenggak (saeng-gak) thinking, a thought

saeop (sa-uhp) an undertaking, an enterprise

sago (sa-go) an accident

sajin (sa-jin) a photograph, a picture

sam (sam) three

samusil (sa-moo-shil) an office

san (san) a mountain

sanchaek (san-chaek) a walk, a stroll

saneop (san-uhp) industry

saram (sa-ram) a person

sarang (sa-rang) love

sasil (sa-shil) a fact, a reality

seojjok (suh-jjok) west, western side

seolmyeong (sul-myoung) explanation

seonmul (sun-mool) a gift, a present

seonsaeng (suhn-saeng) a teacher, a master

seonsu (sun-soo) an athlete

seorap (suh-rahp) a drawer, a desk drawer

sigan (shi-gan) an hour, the time

sigye (shi-gae) a clock, a watch

sijang (shi-jang) a market

siksa (shik-sa) a meal

sinbal (shin-bal) shoes

sinmun (shin-moon) a newspaper

sip (ship) ten

son (son) hand

songarak (son-ga-rak) finger

sontop (son-top) fingernail

sosik (so-shik) news, tidings, word

ssada (ssa-da) to be inexpensive, to be cheap

sucheop (soo-chup) a pocketbook

suchul (soo-chool) export, exportation

sukje (sook-jae) homework

sul (sool) alcoholic drink, wine, booze

sum (soom) a breath, breathing

sungyeong (soon-gyoung) a police officer

sup (soop) a forest

T

tada (ta-da) to burn or to ride depending on the context

taeksi (taek-shi) a taxi

taeyang (tae-yang) the sun

tal (tahl) a mask

tamheom (ta-muhm) exploration, expedition

tap (tahp) a tower

tapseung (tahp-seung) boarding, riding

teok (tuhk) the jaws, the chin

tong (tong) a tube, a pipe, a barrel

ttaragada (tta-ra-ga-da) to follow

ttaro (tta-ro) separately

ttatteutada (tta-tteut-ha-da) to be warm

tteok (ttuhk) rice cake

tteonada (ttuh-na-da) to leave, to depart

tteugeopda (ddeu-guhp-da) be hot, to burn

tteut (ddeut) intent, meaning

tti (ttee) a belt, a sash, year of the zodiac

ttokgatda (ttok-gat-da) be exactly alike

ttokttokhada (ttok-ttok-ha-da) to be smart

ttwida (ttwee-da) to run

U

uju (oo-joo) the universe, the cosmos

umul (oo-mool) a well

undong (oon-dong) physical exercise

unjeon (oon-juhn) operation of machinery, driving

upyeon (oo-pyun) mail, post

upyo (oo-pyo) a postage stamp

usan (oo-san) an umbrella

useum (oo-seum) a laugh, a smile

W

wi (wee) the upside, the topside, the stomach

wichi (wee-chi) a position, a situation

wigi (wee-gee) a crisis, an emergency

wiheom (wee-hum) a danger, a peril

wihyeop (wee-hyup) intimidation, a threat

Y

yachae (ya-chae) vegetables

yagu (ya-goo) baseball

yak (yak) medicine, a drug

yakguk (yak-gook) a pharmacy

yaksok (yak-sok) a promise

yeodeol (yuh-duhl) eight

yeogi (yuh-gee) here, this place

yeogweon (yuh-gwon) a passport

yeohaeng (yuh-haeng) travel, a trip

yeoja (yuh-ja) a woman, a girl

yeok (yuhk) a railroad station

yeoksa (yuhk-sa) history

yeol (yuhl) ten, heat

yeolda (yuhl-da) to open, to unlock

yeolswe (yuhl-swae) a key

yeongeo (yeong-uh) english

yeonseup (yuhn-seup) practice

yeop (yuhp) next to, the flank, on the side

yeoreum (yuh-reum) summer

yetnal (yaen-nal) ancient times, old days

yeyak (yae-yak) a reservation

yogeum (yo-geum) the fee, a fare

yori (yo-ree) cooking, a dish

yuhok (yoo-hok) temptation, enticement

yuk (yook) six

yuksip (yook-ship) sixty

yumeo (yoo-muh) humor

yuri (yoo-ree) glass

English-Korean Mini-Dictionary

A

abandon: **beorida** (buh-ree-da)

ability: **neungryeok** (neung-ryuhk)

accident: **sago** (sa-go)

ache: **apeuda** (a-peu-da)

acknowledge: **injeonghada** (een-jung-ha-da)

acquisition: **chwideuk** (chwee-deuk)

act: **yeongi** (yuhn-gee)

action: **haengdong** (haeng-dong)

actually: **sasireun** (sa-shee-reun)

adapt: **jeogeung** (juh-geung)

add: **deohada** (duh-ha-da)

address: **juso** (joo-so)

adequate: **jeokdanghan** (juhk-dang-han)

admiration: **gamtan** (gahm-than)

admission: **ipjang** (eep-jang)

adult: **eoreun** (uh-reun)

adventure: **moheom** (mo-huhm)

advertisement: **gwanggo** (gwang-go)

advice: **chungo** (choong-gh)

affirm: **hwagin** (hwa-geen)

after: **daeume** (da-eu-mae)

afternoon: **ohu** (oh-hoo)

again: **dasi** (da-shee)

age: **nai** (na-ee)

agony: **gotong** (go-tong)

agreement: **gyeyak** (gae-yak)

ahead: **apseoseo** (ahp-suh-suh)

aid: **dopda** (dohp-da)

aim: **gyeonyang** (gyuh-nyang)

air: **gonggi** (gong-gee)

alarm: **gyeongbo** (gyung-bo)

alert: **gyeonggye** (gyung-gae)

algebra: **suhak** (soo-hak)

all: **jeonche** (jun-chae)

animal: **dongmul** (dong-mool)

apology: **sagwa** (sa-gwa)

automobile: **jadongcha** (ja-dong-cha)

ache: **apeuda** (a-peu-da)

adult: **eoreun** (uh-reun)

adventure: **moheom** (mo-huhm)

again: **dasi** (da-shi)

age: **nai** (na-ee)

agreement: **gyeyak** (gae-yak)

allow: **heorak** (huh-rak)

almost: **geoeui** (guh-eui)

alone: **hollo** (hol-lo)

also: **ttohan** (tto-han)

anger: **hwa** (hwa)

answer: **daedap** (dae-dahp)

apple: **sagwa** (sa-gwa)

arm: **pal** (pal)

arrival: **dochak** (do-chahk)

art: **misul** (mee-sool)

attorney: **byeonhosa** (byun-ho-sa)

audience: **gwangaek** (gwan-gaek)

autumn: **gaeul** (ga-eul)

B

baby: **agi** (a-gee)

back (body part): **deung** (deung)

back (direction): **dwi** (dweeb)

background: **baegyeong** (bae-gyung)

bad: **nappeun** (na-ppeun)

baggage: **suhwamul** (soo-hwa-mool)

ball: **gong** (gong)

bank: **eunhaeng** (eun-haeng)

bar: **suljip** (sool-jeep)

barber: **ibalsa** (ee-bal-sa)

barrel: **tong** (tong)

barrier: **jangbyeok** (jang-byuk)

baseball: **yagu** (ya-goo)

bat (baseball): **baeteu** (bae-teu)

bath: **mogyok** (mo-gyok)

battle: **jeontu** (juhn-too)

beach: **haebyeon** (hae-byun)

bead: **guseul** (goo-seul)

bean: **kong** (kohng)

bear (animal): **gom** (gom)

bear (carry): **nareuda** (na-reu-da)

beard: **teoksuyeom** (tuk-soo-yuhm)

beautiful: **yeppeun** (yae-ppeun)

because: **waenyahamyeon** (wae-nya-ha-myun)

bed: **chimdae** (chim-dae)

beef: **swegogi** (swae-go-gee)

beer: **maekju** (maek-joo)

before: **jeone** (juh-nae)

beggar: **geoji** (guh-jee)

behavior: **haengdong** (haeng-dong)

behind: **dwi** (dwee)

belief: **mideum** (mee-deum)

believe: **midda** (meet-da)

bell: **jong** (jong)

belly: **bae** (bae)

belt: **belteu** (bel-teu)

bend: **guburida** (goo-boo-ree-da)

benefit: **iik** (ee-eek)

bent: **gubeun** (goo-beun)

best: **jeil** (jae-il)

bet: **naegi** (nae-gee)

between: **saie** (sa-ee-ae)

beware: **josim** (jo-sim)

bicycle: **jajeongeo** (ja-juhn-guh)

bird: **sae** (sae)

blanket: **damyo** (dahm-nyo)

boat: **boteu** (bo-teu)

body: **mom** (mohm)

bone: **ppyeo** (ppyuh)

book: **chaek** (chaeg)

box: **sangja** (sang-ja)

boy: **sonyeon** (so-nyuhn)

brain: **new** (nwae)

bread: **ppang** (ppang)

bridge: **dari** (da-ree)

brother: **hyeongje** (hyoung-jae)

bubble: **geopum** (guh-poom)

budget: **yesan** (yae-san)

bug: **gonchung** (gon-choong)

bulk: **keugi** (keu-gee)

burn: **tada** (ta-da)

but: **hajiman** (ha-jee-man)

butterfly: **nabi** (na-bee)

buy: **sada** (sa-da)

by: **gyeote** (gyuh-tae)

C

cab: **taeksi** (taek-shi)

calendar: **dallyeok** (dal-lyuk)

call: **bureuda** (boo-reu-da)

camera: **sajingi** (sa-jeen-gee)

campsite: **kaempeujang** (kaem-peu-jang)

cancel: **chwiso** (chwee-so)

candle: **yangcho** (yang-cho)

candy: **satang** (sa-tang)

cap: **moja** (mo-ja)

capital: **sudo** (soo-do)

car: **jadongcha** (ja-dong-cha)

card: **kadeu** (ka-deu)

care: **geokjeong** (guk-jung)

carpenter: **moksu** (mok-soo)

carriage: **macha** (ma-cha)

carry: **unbanhada** (oon-ban-ha-da)

cartoon: **manhwa** (man-hwa)

carve: **saegida** (sae-gee-da)

cash: **hyeongeum** (hyun-geum)

cast: **deonjida** (dun-jee-da)

castle: **seong** (suhng)

cat: **goyangi** (go-yang-ee)

catch: **japda** (jap-da)

cause: **weonin** (wuh-neen)

caution: **josim** (jo-sheem)

cave: **dongul** (dong-gool)

cease: **meomchuda** (muhm-choo-da)

ceiling: **cheonjang** (chun-jang)

celebrate: **chukha** (choo-ka)

cell: **sepo** (sae-po)

cellar (basement): **jihasil** (jee-ha-shil)

cello: **chello** (chael-lo)

cemetery: **myoji** (myo-jee)

center: **jungsim** (joong-sim)

century: **segi** (sae-gee)

certificate: **jeungmyeongseo** (jeung-myung-suh)

certify: **bojeunghada** (bo-jeung-ha-da)

chain: **saseul** (sa-seul)

chalk: **bunpil** (boon-pil)

challenge: **dojeon** (do-jun)

chance: **gihwe** (gee-hwae)

change: **bakkuda** (ba-ggoo-da)

character: **teukseong** (teuk-sung)

charity: **jabi** (ja-bee)

charm: **maeryeok** (mae-ryuhk)

cheap: **ssada** (ssa-da)

cheat: **sogida** (so-gee-da)

chest (body part): **gaseum** (ga-seum)

chest (box): **sangja** (sang-ja)

chew: **ssipda** (ssip-da)

chicken: **dak** (dak)

chin: **teok** (tuhk)

China (country): **jungguk** (joong-goog)

china (plates): **dojagi** (do-ja-gee)

choice: **seontaek** (suhn-taek)

church: **gyohwe** (gyo-hwae)

cinema: **yeonghwagwan** (young-hwa-gwan)

city: **dosi** (do-shi)

clash: **chungdol** (choong-dol)

class: **deunggeup** (deung-geup)

claw: **baltop** (bal-top)

clean: **kkaekkeuthan** (kkaeae-kkeu-than)

cleaning: **cheongso** (chung-so)

climate: **gihu** (gee-hoo)

clock: **sigye** (see-gyae)

close (door): **datda** (dat-da)

close (near by): **gakkapda** (ga-kkap-da)

clothes: **ot** (ot)

cloud: **gureum** (goo-reum)

coat: **wetu** (wae-too)

coffee: **keopi** (kuh-pee)

cold: **chupda** (choop-da)

complex: **bokjaphan** (bok-ja-pahn)

computer: **keompyuteo** (kuhm-pyoo-tuh)

crash: **chungdol** (choong-dol)

cry: **ulda** (ool-da)

cure: **chiryo** (chi-ryo)

cut: **jareuda** (ja-reu-da)

D

dad: **appa** (a-ppa)

dark: **eoduun** (uh-doo-oon)

day: **nat** (nat)

dead: **jugeun** (joo-geun)

debate: **toron** (to-ron)

debt: **bit** (beet)

deception: **sagi** (sa-gee)

decition: **gyeolsim** (gyul-shim)

deep: **gipeun** (gee-peun)

definitely: **hwaksilhi** (hwak-shee-ree)

degree: **jeongdo** (jung-do)

delight: **gippeum** (gee-bbeum)

delivery: **baedal** (bae-dal)

demand: **yogu** (yo-goo)

dentist: **chigwaeuisa** (chee-gwa-eui-sa)

depart: **chulbal** (chool-bal)

depth: **gipi** (gee-pee)

description: **myosa** (myo-sa)

dice: **jusawi** (joo-sa-wee)

die: **jukda** (jook-da)

dinner: **jeonyeok** (juh-nyuk)

direction: **jido** (jee-do)

discount: **harin** (ha-reen)

disease: **byeong** (byung)

dish: **jeopsi** (juhp-shee)

distance: **geori** (guh-ree)

disturb: **banghae** (bang-hae)

do: **hada** (ha-da)

doctor: **euisa** (eui-sa)

dog: **gae** (gae)

door: **mun** (moon)

drama: **yeongeuk** (yuhn-geuk)

drug: **yak** (yak)

drum: **buk** (book)

E

each: **gakja** (gak-ja)

earth: **jigu** (jee-goo)

east: **dongjjok** (dong-jjok)

easy: **swiun** (swee-oon)

eat: **meokda** (muhk-da)

echo: **meari** (mae-ah-ree)

economy: **gyeongje** (gyung-jae)

editor: **pyeonjipja** (pyun-jip-ja)

education: **gyoyuk** (gyo-yook)

effect: **gyeolgwa** (gyul-gwa)

eight: **yeodeolb** (yuh-duhl)

elbow: **palkkumchi** (pal-kkoom-chi)

electric: **jeongi** (juhn-gee)

eleven: **yeolhana** (yuhl-ha-na)

emergency: **bisang** (bee-sang)

end: **kkeut** (kkeut)

enter: **deureogada** (deu-ruh-ga-da)

entrance: **ipgu** (eep-goo)

equal: **gateun** (ga-teun)

error: **silsu** (shil-soo)

escape: **talchul** (tal-chool)

estimation: **pyeongga** (pyung-ga)

evening: **jeonyeok** (juh-nyuhk)

event: **sageon** (sa-ggun)

ever: **eonjenga** (uhn-jaen-ga)

evidence: **jeunggeo** (jeung-guh)

exactly: **jeonghwakhage** (jung-hwa-ka-gae)

exchange: **gyohwan** (gyo-hwan)

expectation: **gidae** (gee-dae)

eye: **nun** (noon)

F

face: **eolgul** (ul-gool)

fact: **sasil** (sa-shil)

failure: **silpae** (shil-pae)

fake: **gajja** (ga-jj)

fall (autumn): **gaeul** (ga-eul)

family: **gajok** (ga-jok)

far: **meolli** (muhl-lee)

farm: **nongjang** (nong-jang)

fast (speed): **gosok** (go-sok)

father: **abeoji** (a-buh-jee)

fatigue: **piro** (pee-ro)

fault: **chaegim** (chae-geem)

fear: **duryeoum** (doo-ryuh-oom)

feast: **chukje** (chook-jae)

feather: **gitteol** (git-tuhl)

feed: **meogida** (muh-gee-da)

feel (touch): **manjida** (man-jee-da)

female: **yeoseong** (yuh-suhng)

fence: **dam** (dahm)

fever: **yeol** (yuhl)

few: **jogeum** (jo-geum)

fiction: **soseol** (so-suhl)

fiddle (violin): **baiollin** (ba-ee-ol-lin)

field: **deulpan** (deul-pahn)

fight: **ssaum** (ssa-oom)

fill: **chaeuda** (chae-oo-da)

final: **majimak** (ma-jee-mak)

find: **chatda** (chat-da)

finger: **songarak** (son-ga-rak)

finish: **kkeutnaeda** (kkeun-nae-da)

fire: **bul** (bool)

fire extinguisher: **sohwagi** (so-hwa-gee)

firefighter: **sobangsu** (so-bang-soo)

firetruck: **sobangcha** (so-bang-cha)

first: **jeil** (jae-il)

fish: **mulgogi** (mool-go-gee)

fishing: **nakksi** (nak-shi)

five: **daseot** (da-suht)

fix: **gochida** (go-chi-da)

flood: **hongsu** (hong-soo)

flour: **milgaru** (mil-ga-roo)

flower: **kkot** (kkot)

fluid: **aekche** (aek-chae)

fly: **nalda** (nal-da)

food: **sikpum** (shik-poom)

foot: **bal** (bal)

football: **chukgu** (chook-goo)

for: **wihayeo** (wee-ha-yuh)

forbid: **geumhada** (geum-ha-da)

force: **him** (heem)

fore: **ape** (ah-pae)

forest: **sup** (soop)

forget: **ijeobeorida** (ee-juh-buh-ree-da)

forgiveness: **yongseo** (yong-suh)

form: **moyang** (mo-yang)

formula: **gongsik** (gong-shik)

fortress: **yosae** (yo-sae)

four: **net** (net)

fourteen: **yeolnet** (yuhl-net)

friend: **chingu** (chin-goo)

from: **buteo** (boo-tuh)

frozen: **eoreun** (uh-reun)

fruit: **gwail** (gwa-il)

full: **chan** (chan)

fund: **jageum** (ja-geum)

funeral: **jangryesik** (jang-ryae-shik)

furniture: **gagu** (ga-goo)

future: **mirae** (mee-rae)

G

gain: **eodda** (uht-da)

gallery: **misulgwan** (mee-sool-gwan)

gamble: **dobak** (do-bak)

game: **nori** (no-ree)

gap: **gangyeok** (gan-gyuk)

garden: **jeongweon** (jung-won)

garnish: **jangsik** (jang-shik)

gas: **gaseu** (ga-sseu)

gate: **mun** (moon)

gather: **moeuda** (mo-eu-da)

generation: **sedae** (sae-dae)

genius: **cheonjae** (chun-jae)

germ: **segyun** (sae-gyoon)

get: **eotda** (uht-da)

girl: **sonyeo** (so-nyuh)

give: **juda** (joo-da)

glove: **janggap** (jang-gahp)

glue: **jeopchakje** (juhp-chak-jae)

go: **gada** (ga-da)

god: **sin** (shin)

goddess: **yeosin** (yuh-shin)

good: **joeun** (jo-eun)

goose: **geowi** (guh-wee)

government: **jeongbu** (jung-boo)

grade: **deunggeup** (deung-geup)

graduation: **joreop** (jo-ruhp)

grammar: **munbeop** (moon-bup)

grasp: **butjapda** (boot-jahp-dh)

grave: **mudeom** (moo-dum)

green: **choroksaek** (cho-rok-saek)

greet: **insahada** (in-sa-ha-da)

ground: **ttang** (ttang)

grow: **jarada** (ja-ra-da)

guess: **chucheukhada** (choo-cheuk-ka-da)

guide: **annaeja** (an-nae-ja)

H

habit: **seupgwan** (seup-gwan)

hack: **jareuda** (ja-reu-da)

hail (ice): **ubak** (oo-bak)

half: **ban** (ban)

halt: **jeongji** (jung-jee)

hand: **son** (sohn)

handle: **sonjabi** (sohn-ja-bee)

hang: **maedalda** (mae-dal-da)

hanger: **otgeori** (ot-guh-ree)

happy: **gippeun** (gee-ppeun)

have: **gajigoitda** (ga-jee-go-ee-tta)

head: **meori** (muh-ree)

health: **geongang** (guhn-gang)

hear: **deullida** (deul-lee-da)

heart: **simjang** (shim-jang)

heat: **deowi** (duh-wee)

heavy: **mugeoun** (moo-guh-oon)

here: **yeogi** (yuh-gee)

high: **nopeun** (no-peun)

hill: **eondeok** (uhn-duhk)

home: **gajeong** (ga-jung)

honest: **jeongjikhan** (jung-jee-kan)

honor: **myeongye** (myuhng-yae)

hoof: **balgup** (bal-goop)

hope: **heuimang** (heui-mang)

horizon: **supyeongseon** (soo-pyung-sun)

horn: **ppul** (ppool)

horse: **mal** (mahl)

hospital: **byeongweon** (byoung-won)

hotel: **hotel** (ho-tel)

hour: **hansigan** (han-shi-gan)

house: **jip** (jeep)

how: **eotteoke** (uh-ttuh-kae)

hundred: **baek** (baek)

I

ice: **eoreum** (uh-reum)

idea: **saenggak** (saeng-gak)

idol: **using** (oo-sang)

if: **manyage** (ma-nya-gae)

illness: **byeong** (byoung)

import: **suiphada** (soo-eep-ha-da)

impression: **insang** (in-sang)

improvement: **gaeryang** (gae-ryang)

incident: **sageon** (sa-gun)

include: **pohamhada** (poh-hahm-hah-da)

increase: **neullida** (neul-lee-da)

indeed: **chameuro** (cha-meu-ro)

independence: **dongnip** (dong-neep)

indirect: **ganjeop** (gan-jup)

industry: **saneop** (sa-nuhp)

influence: **yeonghyang** (young-hyang)

injury: **sangcheo** (sang-chuh)

insect: **gonchung** (gon-choong)

inside (inside of house): **anjjok** (an-jjok)

instead: **daesin** (dae-shin)

instinct: **bonneung** (bon-neung)

interfere: **ganseop** (gan-suhp)

internal: **naebu** (nae-boo)

international: **gukjejeok** (gook-jae-juk)

interview: **myeonjeop** (myun-jup)

intimate: **chinmilhan** (chin-mee-ran)

intoxication: **chwihada** (chwee-ha-da)

invention: **balmyeong** (bal-myung)

invest: **tujahada** (too-ja-ha-da)

invite: **chodaehada** (cho-dae-ha-da)

inward: **anjjogeul** (ahn-jjo-geul)

irregular: **bulgyuchikhan** (bool-gyoo-chee-kan)

it: **geugeot** (geu-guht)

J

jacket: **jaket** (ja-ket)

jail: **gyodoso** (gyo-do-so)

Japan: **ilbon** (il-bon)

jaw: **teok** (tuhk)

jealousy: **jiltu** (jeel-too)

job: **il** (il)

join: **gyeolhap** (gyuh-rahp)

joke: **nongdam** (nong-dam)

journey: **yeohaeng** (yuh-haeng)

judge: **pansa** (pahn-sa)

judgment: **jaepan** (jae-pahn)

juice: **jyuseu** (jyoo-sseu)

K

key: **yeolsoe** (yuhl-swae)

kick: **chada** (cha-da)

kill: **jugida** (joo-gee-da)

kind (many kinds of things): **jongryu** (jong-ryoo)

kind (person): **chinjeolhan** (chin-juh-rahn)

king: **wang** (wang)

kiss: **kiseu** (kee-sseu)

knee: **mureup** (moo-reup)

knife: **kal** (kal)

knight: **gisa** (gee-sa)

knock: **dudeurida** (doo-deu-ree-da)

know: **alda** (al-da)

knowledge: **jisik** (jee-shik)

Korea: **hanguk** (han-goog)

L

labor: **nodong** (no-dong)

laboratory: **yeonguso** (yeon-goo-so)

lack: **bujok** (boo-jok)

lamp: **deungbul** (deung-bool)

language: **eoneo** (uh-nuh)

large: **keun** (keun)

last (in line): **majimak** (ma-jee-mahk)

laugh: **utda** (oo-tta)

law: **beop** (bup)

leader: **jidoja** (jee-do-ja)

leak: **saem** (saem)

lean: **gidaeda** (gee-dae-da)

leather: **gajuk** (ga-jook)

leave: **ddeonada** (dduh-na-da)

left: **wenjjok** (wen-jjok)

leg: **dari** (da-ree)

legend: **jeonseol** (juhn-sul)

less: **jeogeun** (juh-geun)

letter: **pyeonji** (pyun-jee)

liberty: **jayu** (ja-yoo)

library: **doseosil** (do-suh-shill)

license: **myeonheo** (myun-huh)

lid: **ddukkeong** (ddoo-ggung)

lie (down): **nupda** (noop-da)

lie (untrue): **geojitmal** (guh-jeet-mal)

lift: **ollida** (ol-lee-da)

lightly: **gabyeopge** (ga-byup-gae)

like (alike): **biseuthan** (bee-seu-tan)

line: **jul** (jool)

lip: **ipsul** (eep-sool)

listen: **deutda** (deut-da)

little: **jageun** (ja-geun)

live: **salda** (sal-da)

liver: **gan** (gahn)

living: **saraitneun** (sa-ra-eet-neun)

load (baggage): **jim** (jeem)

lobby: **robi** (ro-bee)

location: **jangso** (jang-so)

lock: **jamulsoe** (ja-mool-swae)

lodge: **sukbak** (suhk-bahk)

lodging (homestay): **hasuk** (ha-sook)

log: **tongnamu** (tong-na-moo)

logic: **nolli** (nol-lee)

lone: **honja** (hon-ja)

long: **gin** (geen)

look: **boda** (bo-da)

loop: **gori** (go-ree)

loose: **pullin** (pul-leen)

lose: **ilta** (eel-ta)

loss: **ireum** (ee-reum)

loud: **sikkeureoun** (shee-kkeu-ruh-oon)

love: **sarang** (sa-rang)

lover: **yeonin** (yuh-neen)

low: **najeun** (na-jeun)

lower: **nachuda** (na-choo-da)

luck: **haengun** (haeng-oon)

lumber: **jaemok** (jae-mok)

lump: **deongeori** (dung-uh-ree)

lunch: **jeomsim** (juhm-shim)

lung: **pye** (pae)

M

machine: **gigye** (gee-gae)

mad: **michin** (mee-cheen)

made: **mandeureojin** (man-deu-ruh-jeen)

mail: **upyeon** (oo-pyun)

make-up: **hwajangpum** (hwa-jang-poom)

man: **namja** (nam-ja)

mandate: **myeongryeong** (myung-ryung)

mankind: **illyu** (eel-yoo)

manner: **yejeol** (yae-juhl)

many: **maneun** (ma-neun)

March (month): **samweol** (sam-wol)

marine: **haeyang** (hae-yang)

market: **sijang** (shi-jang)

marriage: **gyeorhon** (gyuh-ron)

marvel: **gyeongi** (gyoung-ee)

mask: **tal** (tal)

massive: **keun** (keun)

master: **juin** (joo-een)

mat: **maeteu** (mae-teu)

match: **sihap** (shi-hap)

mate: **jjak** (jjak)

material: **jaryo** (ja-ryo)

math: **suhak** (soo-hak)

matter: **muljil** (mool-jeel)

maturity: **seongsuk** (sung-sook)

May (month): **owol** (o-wol)

maybe: **ama** (a-ma)

meadow: **choweon** (cho-won)

meal: **siksa** (shik-sa)

meat: **gogi** (go-gee)

mechanic: **jeongbisa** (jung-bee-sa)

medicine: **yak** (yak)

medium: **junggan** (joong-gan)

meet: **mannada** (man-na-da)

melt: **nokda** (nok-da)

member: **hoeweon** (hwae-won)

memory: **gieok** (gee-uk)

mend: **gochida** (go-chee-da)

mention (talk): **malhada** (mal-ha-da)

merchant: **sangin** (sang-een)

mercy: **jabi** (ja-bee)

mess: **nanjap** (nan-jap)

message: **jeongal** (jun-gal)

metal: **geumsok** (geum-sok)

method: **bangbeop** (bang-bup)

middle: **gaunde** (ga-oon-dae)

milk: **uyu** (oo-yoo)

mind: **maeum** (ma-eum)

mine (dig): **gwangsan** (gwang-san)

mine (own): **naeggeo** (nae-gguh)

minimum: **choeso** (chwae-so)

miracle: **gijeok** (gee-juk)

mirror: **geoul** (guh-ool)

misery: **burhaeng** (boo-raeng)

misfortune: **burun** (boo-roon)

mistake: **jalmot** (jal-mot)

mitten: **jangap** (jang-gahp)

mix: **seokkda** (suk-da)

money: **don** (don)

monkey: **weonsungi** (won-soong-ee)

more: **deo** (duh)

morning: **achim** (a-chim)

mother: **eomeoni** (uh-muh-nee)

motion: **idong** (ee-dong)

mountain: **san** (san)

mouse: **jwi** (jwee)

mouth: **ip** (eep)

move: **umjigida** (oom-jee-gee-da)

movie: **yeonghwa** (yung-hwa)

murder: **sarin** (sa-reen)

muscle: **geunyuk** (geu-nyook)

museum: **bakmulgwan** (bang-mool-gwan)

music: **eumak** (eu-mak)

mystery: **sinbi** (shin-bee)

myth: **sinhwa** (shin-hwa)

N

nail: **mot** (mot)

naked: **beolgeobeoseun** (bul-guh-buh-seun)

name: **ireum** (ee-reum)

nap: **najjam** (na-jjam)

narrow: **jobeun** (jo-beun)

nation: **gukga** (gook-ga)

nationality: **gukjeok** (gook-juhk)

nature: **jayeon** (ja-yeon)

near: **gakkapda** (ga-kkap-da)

neck: **mok** (mok)

need: **piryo** (pee-ryo)

needle: **baneul** (ba-neul)

neighborhood: **iut** (ee-oot)

nephew: **joka** (jo-ka)

nerve: **singyeong** (shin-gyung)

net: **geumul** (geu-mool)

new: **saeroun** (sae-ro-oon)

news: **nyuseu** (nyoo-sseu)

next: **daeum** (da-eum)

nice: **joeun** (jo-eun)

night: **bam** (bam)

nine: **ahop** (a-hop)

nineteen: **yeolahop** (yuh-ra-hop)

ninety: **gusip** (goo-ship)

no: **aniyo** (a-ni-yo)

none: **eopda** (uhp-da)

north: **bukjjok** (book-jjok)

nose: **ko** (ko)

not: **anida** (a-nee-da)

note: **gakseo** (gak-suh)

novel: **soseol** (so-sul)

November: **sibirweol** (shi-bee-rwol)

now: **jigeum** (jee-geum)

number: **beonho** (bun-ho)

O

oath: **maengse** (maeng-sae)

obedience: **sunjong** (soon-jong)

object: **mulgeon** (mool-gun)

observation: **gwanchal** (gwan-chal.)

occupy: **chajihada** (cha-jee-ha-da.)

occurrence: **sageon** (sa-gun)

October: **siweol** (shi-wol)

odd: **isanghada** (ee-sang-ha-da)

odor: **naemsae** (naem-sae)

office: **samuso** (sa-moo-so)

often: **jaju** (ja-joo)

old (people): **naideusin** (na-ee-deu-shin)

old (things): **oraedoen** (o-rae-dwen)

once: **hanbeon** (han-bun)

one: **hana** (ha-na)

onion: **yangpa** (yang-pa)

only: **yuilhan** (yoo-ee-rahn)

open: **yeollin** (yuhl-lin)

opinion: **euigyeon** (eui-gyuhn)

opportunity: **gihoe** (gee-hwae)

oppose: **bandaehada** (ban-dae-ha-da)

oppress: **apbakhada** (ahp-ba-ka-da)

option: **seontaekgweon** (sun-taek-gwon)

order: **jeongdon** (jung-don)

ordinary: **botong** (bo-tong)

other: **dareun** (da-reun)

our: **uri** (oo-ree)

out: **bakkeuro** (bak-geu-ro)

P

package: **sopo** (so-po)

pain: **apeum** (a-peum)

paint: **mulgam** (mool-gam)

pair: **hanbeol** (han-buhl)

palm: **sonbadak** (son-ba-dak)

pan: **nimbi** (naem-bee)

pants: **baji** (ba-jee)

paper: **jongi** (jong-ee)

parallel: **pyeonghaeng** (pyung-haeng)

paralyze: **mabi** (ma-bee)

pardon: **yongseo** (yong-suh)

park: **gongweon** (gong-won)

part: **ilbu** (eel-boo)

participate: **chamga** (cham-ga)

particular: **teukbyeol** (teuk-byuhl)

parting: **ibyeol** (ee-byuhl)

party: **moim** (mo-im)

pass: **jinada** (jee-na-da)

passage: **tonghaeng** (tong-haeng)

passenger: **seungaek** (seung-gaek)

passion: **yeoljeong** (yuhl-jung)

past: **gwageo** (gwa-guh)

pasture: **mokjang** (mok-jang)

patent: **teukheo** (teu-kuh)

patience: **innae** (in-nae)

pay: **jibul** (jee-bool)

peace: **pyeonghwa** (pyoung-hwa)

pen: **pen** (pen)

pencil: **yeonpil** (yuhn-pil)

people: **saram** (sa-ram)

perfect: **wanjeonhan** (wan-jun-han)

performance: **yeonju** (yuhn-joo)

perhaps: **ama** (a-ma)

period: **gigan** (gee-gahn)

person: **saram** (sa-ram)

personality: **seonggyeok** (suhng-gyuk)

phone: **jeonhwa** (juhn-hwa)

photograph: **sajin** (sa-jin)

pick: **ppopda** (ppop-da)

picnic: **sopung** (so-poong)

picture: **geurim** (geu-reem)

piece: **jogak** (jo-gahk)

pig: **doeji** (dwae-jee)

pigeon: **bidulgi** (bee-dool-gee)

pilot: **jojongsa** (jo-jong-sa)

pin: **pin** (peen)

pitch: **deonjida** (duhn-jee-da)

pitcher (baseball): **tusu** (too-soo)

pitcher (container): **jujeonja** (joo-jun-ja)

place: **jangso** (jang-so)

plan: **gyehoek** (gyae-hwek)

plant: **sikmul** (shik-mool)

plate: **jeopsi** (juhp-shee)

play: **nolda** (nol-da)

pleasure: **gippeum** (gi-ppeum)

pledge: **seoyak** (suh-yak)

pocket: **jumeoni** (joo-muh-nee)

poem: **si** (shee)

poet: **siin** (shee-een)

police: **gyeongchal** (gyoung-chal)

pool: **suyeongjang** (soo-young-jang)

poor: **gananhan** (ga-na-nan)

popularity: **ingi** (een-gee)

porridge: **juk** (jook)

portrait: **chosanghwa** (cho-sang-hwa)

position: **wichi** (wee-chee)

possession: **jaesan** (jae-san)

pour: **butda** (boot-da)

power: **him** (heem)

practice: **yeonseup** (yuhn-seup)

prayer: **gido** (gee-do)

precious: **gwijunghan** (gwee-joong-han)

precise: **jeonghwak** (jung-hwak)

prepare: **junbi** (joon-bee)

present: **seonmul** (sun-mool)

pressure: **apryeok** (ahm-ryuk)

pretty: **yeppeuda** (yae-ppeu-da)

price: **gagyeok** (ga-gyuk)

print: **inswae** (in-swae)

prison: **gamok** (ga-mok)

prize: **sangpum** (sang-poom)

pro: **peu-roh** (peu-ro)

process: **jinhaeng** (jeen-haeng)

proclaim: **seoneon** (suh-nuhn)

product: **sanmul** (san-mool)

production: **saengsan** (saeng-san)

profession: **jigeop** (jee-guhp)

profit: **iik** (ee-eek)

program: **poeurogeuraem** (peu-ro-geu-raem)

progress: **baldal** (bal-dal)

prohibit: **geumji** (geum-jee)

promise: **yaksok** (yak-sok)

pronounce: **barium** (ba-reum)

proof: **jeungeo** (jeung-guh)

protect: **boho** (bo-ho)

pull: **danggida** (dang-gee-da)

push: **milda** (meel-da)

Q

qualification: **jagyeok** (ja-gyuk)

quality: **pumjil** (poom-jeel)

quantity: **bullyang** (bool-lyang)

queen: **yeowang** (yuh-wang)

quick: **bballi** (bbal-lee)

quiet: **joyong** (jo-yong)

quit: **geumanduda** (geu-man-doo-da)

R

radio: **radio** (ra-dee-o)

rain: **bi** (bee)

rainbow: **mujigae** (moo-jee-gae)

rat: **jwi** (jwee)

rate: **biyul** (bee-yool)

read: **ilgda** (eel-da)

ready: **junbi** (joon-bee)

real: **jinjja** (jeen-jja)

rear: **dwi** (dwee)

reason: **iyu** (ee-yoo)

receive: **batda** (bat-da)

recess: **hyusik** (hyoo-sheek)

recommend: **chucheon** (choo-chun)

record: **girok** (gee-rok)

recovery: **hoebok** (hwae-bok)

red: **ppalgan** (ppal-gan)

reduce: **jurida** (joo-ree-da)

refund: **banhwan** (ban-hwan)

refuse: **geojeol** (guh-jul)

region: **jibang** (jee-bang)

relationship: **gwangye** (gwan-gae)

religion: **jongyo** (jong-gyo)

remember: **gieok** (gee-uhk)

repair: **suri** (soo-ree)

report: **bogo** (bo-go)

require: **piryo** (pee-ryo)

research: **yeongu** (yuhn-goo)

resist: **jeohang** (juh-hahng)

resource: **jaweon** (ja-won)

respect: **jongyeong** (jon-gyung)

responsible: **chaegim** (chae-geem)

rest: **swida** (swee-da)

return (to home): **doragada** (do-ra-ga-da)

revenge: **boksu** (bok-soo)

rich: **buja** (boo-ja)

rid: **eobsaeda** (uhp-sae-da)

ride: **tada** (ta-da)

right (direction): **oreunjjok** (o-reun-jjok)

ring (jewelry): **banji** (ban-jee)

ring (bell): **ullida** (ool-lee-da)

ripe: **igeun** (ee-geun)

rise: **ireoseoda** (ee-ruh-suh-da)

risk: **wiheom** (wee-hum)

river: **gang** (gang)

road: **gil** (gil)

rock: **dol** (dol)

roof: **jibung** (jee-boong)

room: **bang** (bang)

root: **ppuri** (ppoo-ree)

rope: **jul** (jool)

rose: **jangmi** (jang-mee)

round: **dungeon** (doong-geun)

rubber: **gomu** (go-mo)

rude: **murye** (moo-rae)

ruin: **pamyeol** (pa-myuhl)

run: **dallida** (dal-lee-da)

S

sack: **jaru** (ja-roo)

sad: **seulpeuda** (seul-peu-da)

saddle: **anjang** (ahn-jang)

safe: **anjeon** (ahn-jun)

sale: **panmae** (pan-mae)

salt: **sogeum** (so-geum)

salvation: **gujo** (goo-jo)

same: **gateun** (ga-teun)

sand: **morae** (mo-rae)

save: **guhada** (goo-ha-da)

saving: **jeoryak** (juh-ryak)

say: **malhagi** (mal-ha-gee)

scale (balance): **cheonching** (chun-cheeng)

scale (fish): **bineul** (bee-neul)

schedule: **siganpyo** (shee-gan-pyo)

scheme: **gyehoek** (gyae-hwek)

scholar: **hakja** (hak-ja)

school: **hakgyo** (hak-gyo)

scissors: **gawi** (ga-wee)

scout: **jeongchal** (jung-chal)

scratch: **halkwida** (hal-kwee-da)

screw: **nasa** (na-sa)

sea: **bada** (ba-da)

search: **chatda** (chat-da)

season: **gyejeol** (gyae-juhl)

seat: **jari** (ja-ree)

see: **boda** (bo-da)

self: **jasin** (ja-shin)

sell: **palda** (pal-da)

send: **bonaeda** (bo-nae-da)

sense: **gamgak** (gam-gak)

sentence: **munjang** (moon-jang)

separate: **bunli** (bool-lee)

serious: **jinji** (jeen-jee)

servant: **hain** (ha-een)

service: **bongsa** (bong-sa)

seven: **ilgop** (il-gop)

shade: **geuneul** (geu-neul)

shadow: **geurimja** (geu-reem-ja)

shake: **heundeulda** (heun-deul-da)

shallow: **yateun** (ya-teun)

shame: **changpi** (cang-pee)

shape: **moyang** (mo-yang)

shave: **myeondo** (myuhn-do)

shoe: **sinbal** (shin-bal)

shop: **gage** (ga-gae)

shoulder: **eoggae** (uh-kkae)

sight: **sigak** (shi-gak)

sign: **giho** (gee-ho)

sit: **anda** (ahn-da)

six: **yeoseot** (yuh-suht)

size: **keugi** (keu-gee)

skin: **pibu** (pee-boo)

skirt: **chima** (chee-ma)

sky: **haneul** (ha-neul)

sleep: **jada** (ja-da)

slow: **neurin** (neu-rin)

small: **jageun** (ja-geun)

smell: **naemsae** (naem-sae)

snow: **nun** (noon)

soap: **binu** (bee-noo)

society: **sahoe** (sa-hwae)

socks: **yangmal** (yang-mal)

some: **jom** (jom)

song: **norae** (no-rae)

south: **namjjok** (nam-jjok)

spoon: **sutgarak** (soot-ga-rak)

spring: **bom** (bom)

square: **sagakhyeong** (sa-ga-kyung)

star: **byeol** (byuhl)

start (to start something): **sijak** (shee-jak)

station: **jeongeojang** (juhng-guh-jang)

stomach: **bae** (bae)

stop: **meomchuda** (muhm-choo-da)

storm: **pokpung** (pok-poong)

street: **geori** (guh-ree)

strength: **him** (heem)

strong: **ganghan** (gang-han)

student: **haksaeng** (hak-saeng)

study: **gongbu** (gong-boo)

submission: **bokjong** (bok-jong)

substitute: **daeyong** (dae-yong)

succeed: **seongong** (suhng-gong)

sugar: **seoltang** (suhl-tang)

suggest: **amsi** (ahm-shee)

sun: **taeyang** (tae-yang)

swear: **maengse** (maeng-sae)

sweat: **ttam** (ttahm)

swim: **suyeong** (soo-yuhng)

T

take: **gatda** (gat-da)

talk: **malhada** (mahl-ha-da)

taste: **mat** (maht)

taxi: **taeksi** (taek-shi)

tea: **cha** (cha)

teacher: **seonsaengnim** (sun-saeng-nim)

tear (cry): **nunmul** (noon-mool)

tear (rip): **jitda** (jjeet-da)

telephone: **jeonhwagi** (jun-hwa-gee)

telescope: **mangweongyeong** (mang-won-gyung)

television: **telebijyeon** (te-rae-bee-jyun)

temporary: **ilsi** (eel-shee)

ten: **yeol** (yuhl)

tent: **cheonmak** (chun-mak)

terminal: **jongjeom** (jong-jum)

territory: **yeongto** (young-to)

terror: **gongpo** (gong-po)

test: **siheom** (shee-hum)

that: **jeogeot** (juh-guht)

theater: **geukjang** (geuk-jang)

theme: **juje** (joo-jeh)

theory: **hakseol** (hak-sul)

there: **geogi** (guh-gee)

thick: **dukkeoun** (doo-gguh-oon)

thief: **doduk** (do-dook)

think: **saengak** (saeng-gak)

thirst: **galjeung** (gahl-jeung)

this: **igeot** (ee-guht)

thought: **saengak** (saeng-gahk)

threat: **hyeopbak** (hyup-bak)

three: **set** (set)

thumb: **eomji** (uhm-jee)

Thursday: **mogyoil** (mo-gyo-il)

ticket: **pyo** (pyo)

time: **sigan** (shi-gan)

toe: **balgarak** (bal-ga-rak)

together: **gachi** (ga-chee)

toilet: **hwajangsil** (hwa-jang-sil)

tomorrow: **naeil** (nae-eel)

tool: **dogu** (do-goo)

tooth: **ibbal** (ee-bbal)

touch: **manjida** (man-jee-da)

tower: **tap** (tahp)

toy: **jangnangam** (jang-nan-gam)

traffic: **gyotong** (gyo-tong)

train: **gicha** (gee-cha)

training: **hullyeon** (hool-lyun)

transform: **byeonhyeong** (byun-hyung)

translate: **beonyeok** (buh-nyuhk)

transport: **unban** (oon-ban)

tree: **namu** (na-moo)

trip: **yeohaeng** (yuh-haeng)

turn: **dollida** (dol-lee-da)

tutor: **gyosa** (gyo-sa)

two: **dul** (dool)

U

ugly: **chuhada** (choo-ha-da)

ultimate: **choehu** (chwae-hoo)

umbrella: **usan** (oo-san)

umpire: **simpan** (shim-pahn)

uncle: **samchon** (sam-chon)

uncomfortable: **bulpyeon** (bool-pyun)

under: **mite** (mee-tae)

underground: **jiha** (jee-ha)

understanding: **ihae** (ee-hae)

up: **wiro** (wee-ro)

urban: **dosi** (do-shei)

urgent: **wigeupan** (wee-geu-pahn)

use: **sayong** (sa-yong)

V

vacation: **hyuga** (hyoo-ga)

value: **gachi** (ga-chi)

vegetable: **yachae** (ya-chae)

vengeance: **boksu** (bok-soo)

verb: **dongsa** (dong-sa)

very: **maeu** (mae-oo)

vest: **joggi** (jo-ggee)

view: **gyeongchi** (gyuhng-chi)

vinegar: **sikcho** (shik-cho)

vision: **siryeok** (shi-ryuhk)

visit: **bangmun** (bang-moon)

voice: **moksori** (mok-so-ree)

vote: **tupyo** (too-pyo)

W

wait: **gidarida** (gee-da-ree-da)

walk: **gutda** (guht-da)

want: **weonhada** (won-ha-da)

warm: **dubda** (duhp-da)

wash: **ssitda** (sseet-da)

water: **mul** (mool)

wave: **pado** (pa-do)

way: **gil** (geel)

we: **uri** (oo-ree)

wear: **ipda** (eep-da)

weather: **nalssi** (nal-ssee)

wedding: **gyeolhonsik** (gyuh-ron-shik)

week: **ju** (joo)

weekday: **juil** (joo-il)

weekend: **jumal** (joo-mal)

weight: **muge** (moo-gae)

well (water): **umul** (oo-mool)

west: **seojjok** (suh-jjok)

what: **mueot** (moo-uht)

when: **eonje** (un-jae)

where: **eodi** (uh-dee)

which: **eoneu** (uh-neu)

while: **dongan** (dong-an)

who: **nugu** (noo-goo)

whose: **nugueui** (noo-goo-eui)

why: **wae** (wae)

wide: **neolbeun** (nuhl-beun)

win: **igida** (ee-gee-da)

wind: **baram** (ba-ram)

window: **changmun** (chang-moon)

wing: **nalgae** (nal-gae)

wisdom: **jihye** (jee-hae)

wish: **barada** (ba-ra-da)

with: **wagachi** (wa-ga-chee)

woman: **yeoja** (yuh-ja)

wood: **mokjae** (mok-jae)

word: **daneo** (da-nuh)

work: **il** (il)

write: **sseuda** (sseu-da)

wrong: **teullin** (teul-leen)

X

x-ray: **ekseurei** (ek-sseu-rae-ee)

xylophone: **silopon** (shi-lo-pon)

Y

year: **yeon** (yuhn)

yellow: **norang** (nohrahng)

yes: **ne** (ne)

yet: **ajik** (a-jik)

Z

zero: **yeong** (young)

zoo: **dongmulweon** (dong-moo-rwon)

Appendix C

Answer Key

. . . .

*T*he following are all the answers to the Fun & Games quizzes located at the end of each chapter.

Chapter 1

1. jejeongeo (*ja-jun-guh*)
2. chimdae (*chim-dae*)
3. insa (*in-sa*)
4. aksu (*ak-soo*)
5. mom (*mohm*)
6. wiheom (*wee-hum*)
7. chingu (*chin-goo*)
8. jeojjok (*juh-jjok*)
9. chitsol (*chi-ssol*)
10. ppang (*ppang*)

Chapter 2

1. Informal polite
2. Yes. It is a huge thing.
3. Two different ways: Native Korean and Chinese-based Sino-Korean
4. byeong (*byoung*)
5. mari (*ma-ree*)

Chapter 3

1. Hello/hi
2. Thank you
3. I'm sorry
4. Excuse me
5. Name
6. Mother
7. Father
8. Family
9. Teacher
10. Lawyer

Chapter 4

1. eonni (*un-ni*)
2. namdongsaeng (*nam-dong-saeng*)
3. oeharaboji (*wae-ha-ra-buh-ji*)
4. gomo (*go-mo*)
5. Older brother for a female
6. Mother
7. Uncle on dad's side (dad's brothers)
8. Younger sister

Chapter 5

A. sagwa (apple)
B. orenji (orange)
C. yangbaechu (cabbage)
D. tomato (tomato)
E. danggeun (carrot)
F. yangpa (onion)
G. beurokeolli (broccoli)

Chapter 6

kkotgagye; flower shop (C. bunch of flowers)

munbanggu; stationery/toy shop (E. a top)

supeomaket; supermarket (B. cabbage)

boseoksang; jewelry store (A. necklace)

yakguk; pharmacy/drugstore (D. drugs/medicine)

Chapter 7

Next week; daeumju

10:30 am; ojeon yeolsiban

Afternoon; ohu

Last month; jinandal

Monday; woryoil

Weekend; jumal

9:00 pm; ohu ahopsi

Chapter 8

A. takgu

B. piano yeonju

C. Tae kwon do

D. peullut yeonju

E. deungsan

Chapter 9

House; jip (*jeep*)

Phone number; jeonhwabunho (*juhn-hwa-bun-ho*)

Hello; yeoboseyo (*yuh-bo-sae-yo*)

Friend; chingu (*chin-goo*)

Contact information; yeollakcheo (*yuhl-lak-chuh*)

Who are you? nuguseyo (*noo-goo-sae-yo*)

Chapter 10

cheongso; clean

mogyok; bath

sikilkkayo? Should I order it?

jom dowa jusigetseumnikka? Can you please help me?

jeongmal pigonhamnida; I'm exhausted

syawo hasillaeyo? Do you want to take a shower?

bueok; kitchen

boksagi; copier

Chapter 11

A. hyeungeun jigeupgi (*hyun-geum jee-geup-gee*; ATM)

B. eunahaengwon (*eun-haeng-won*; bank teller)

C. eunhaeng (*eun-haeng*; bank)

D. yeogwon (*yuh-gwon*; passport)

E. sinnyongkadeu (*shin-yong-ka-deu*; credit card) Usually called "kadeu" for short

F. jigap (*jee-gap*; wallet/purse)

Chapter 12

A. hakgyoneun sageori bukjjoge iseoyo; The school is at the North of four-way intersection.

B. uchegugeun sageori dongjjoge iseoyo; The post office is at the East of four-way intersection.

C. eunhaengeun sageori namjjoge iseoyo; The bank is at the South of the four-way intersection.

D. jibeun sageori seojjoge iseoyo; The house is at the West of the four-way intersection.

Chapter 13

1. jeonhwa

2. oneul

3. binbang

4. jijeobunhaneyo

5. gyesanseo

Chapter 14

A. bihaenggi; airplane

B. gicha; train

C. jihacheol; subway

D. beoseu; bus

E. taeksi; taxi

Chapter 15

1. jeoneun daeum dare hanguge gayo. I'm going to Korea next month.

2. eonje gaseyo? When are you leaving?

3. beoseu jeongnyujangi eodi iseoyo? Where is the bus stop?

4. banggawoyo. Glad to see you.

5. gichayeok; train station

6. bangmulgwan; museum

7. baekhwajeom; department store

Chapter 16

1. dari

2. son

3. balgarak

4. nun

5. gwi

6. ko

7. ip

8. meori

9. gaseum

10. bal

11. songarak

12. deung

Appendix D

On the CD

• •

*I*n this appendix, you can thumb through the list of tracks recorded on the CD as well as check out the system requirements you need to run the CD. You can even find information on getting technical support.

Feel free to skip around the track list, and definitely take advantage of the accompanying Talkin' the Talk text in the chapters listed. Remember, you can find the sections that have been recorded on the CD by looking for the On the CD icon in each chapter.

Tracks on the CD

The following is a list of tracks that appear on the book's audio CD.

Track 1: Intro and Pronunciation Guide

Chapter 2

Track 2: Having a Korean conversation

Track 3: Discussing foods you like

Chapter 3

Track 4: Greetings in Korean

Track 5: Meeting people

Track 6: What's your name?

Track 7: Talking about the weather

Track 8: Saying goodbye

Chapter 4

Track 9: Getting directions

Track 10: Discussing family

Chapter 6

Track 11: Getting the attendant to help you

Track 12: Shopping for clothes

Chapter 7

Track 13: Let's go see a movie!

Chapter 8

Track 14: What are your hobbies?

Track 15: Buying tickets for a train

Chapter 9

Track 16: Making a phone call

Track 17: Talking on the phone

Track 18: Navigating the PC bang

Chapter 10

Track 19: Visiting a friend

Track 20: Taking a shower

Chapter 11

Track 21: Paying for your meal

Chapter 12

Track 22: Finding your way back

Chapter 13

Track 23: Reserving a room

Track 24: Looking at a room

Track 25: Checking out

Chapter 14

   Track 26: Checking your bag at the airport

Chapter 15

   Track 27: Planning a trip to Korea

Chapter 16

   Track 28: Calling for an emergency

System Requirements

You will need a CD player with audio capabilities in order to listen to this CD.

Customer Care

If you have trouble with the CD-ROM, please call the Wiley Product Technical Support phone number at (800) 762-2974. Outside the United States, call 1(317) 572-3994. You can also contact Wiley Product Technical Support at http://support.wiley.com. John Wiley & Sons will provide technical support only for installation and other general quality control items. For technical support on the applications themselves, consult the program's vendor or author.

To place additional orders or to request information about other Wiley products, please call (877) 762-2974.

Index

• A •

a little, expression, 295
acceptable behavior
  about, 283
  bragging, 283–284
  chopsticks, 288
  compliments, 283–284
  crossing legs while sitting, 286
  eating, 284
  first names, 285
  last names, 285
  losing face, 284
  no thank you, 287
  public displays of affection, 287
  rice bowls, 287–288
  self-deprecation, 283–284
  seniors, 284
  shoes in house, 285–286
  sitting, 284
  spoons, 287–288
  titles, 285
accidents at home, 185
accommodations
  about, 215
  bed and breakfast, 215, 217
  beds, 216
  broken machinery, 226–227
  check out rooms, 224–225
  checking out, 228–230
  cleanliness, 228
  complaints, 226–228
  details, 223–224
  finding, 218–220
  hostels, 217
  hotels, 216
  motels, 216–217
  noisy neighbors, 227

  public baths, 217–218
  reservations, 220–222
  saunas, 217–218
  temperature problems, 228
acquaintances at home, calling, 156–157
actions with directions, 210
activities, travel to Korea, 257
adjectives
  disliking with, 100–101
  with English verbs, 34–35
  like verbs, 36–37
  liking with, 100–101
  speech parts, 36–37
adverbs, 37–38
affection, public display, 287
affricates, 14
airports
  about, 233–238
  check-in, 234–235
  leaving, 238
animals of Chinese zodiac, 255
answer key, 331–335
Antique Market, 122
antiques shopping in Korea, 122
areas of study, conversation, 85
arts, 147–148
asking
  directions, 203–210
  directions in office, 170–172
  for help, shopping, 115–116
  names, introductions, 61–64
  for someone, 155–157
ATMs for money, 196–197
awesome expression, 297

• B •

banks for currency, 192–193
bargaining, shopping in Korea, 123

bars
  about, 134–135
  tips for improvement, 280
baseball, 148
basic phrases, fluency, 18–20
beaches, 142
beckoning, body language, 21
bed and breakfasts, 215, 217
beds in hotels, 216
Before Babel Brigade (BBB), 260
behavior, acceptable
  about, 283
  bragging, 283–284
  chopsticks, 288
  compliments, 283–284
  crossing legs while sitting, 286
  eating, 284
  first names, 285
  last names, 285
  losing face, 284
  no thank you, 287
  public displays of affection, 287
  rice bowls, 287–288
  self-deprecation, 283–284
  seniors, 284
  shoes in house, 285–286
  sitting, 284
  spoons, 287–288
  titles, 285
birds, 142
blank, 119
blue, 119
boating, 142
body language
  beckoning, 21
  bowing, 21–22
  elders, 21
  handshakes, 22
  nodding, 22
  respect, 21
body parts terminology, 270–271
bowing
  body language, 21–22
  introductions, 51
bragging, unacceptable behavior, 283–284
broken machinery in hotels, 226–227

Brotherhood of War, 131
brown, 119
browsing, shopping, 114–115
Buddha's Birthday, 253
Buddhist temples, 238
buses
  about, 238, 256
  transportation, 240
  travel to Korea, 256
business
  about, 165
  asking directions, 170–172
  calling contacts, 155–156
  commenting about other people, 174
  computers, 169–170
  finding items, 166–169
  finding people, 170
  introductions, 173
  leaving messages, 157
  meetings, 173–174
  peers and superiors, 172
  speaking up, 173–174
  travel to Korea, 256
business dinners
  about, 174
  declining drinks, 176
  drinking politely, 175
  pouring shots, 175
  serving superiors, 175
buying in Korea, 123
by the way expression, 294–295

• *C* •

calling
  acquaintances at home, 156–157
  business contacts, 155–156
  police in emergencies, 264–265
cash, 197–199
CDs
  about, 5
  contents, 337–339
  system requirements, 340
  technical support, 340
  tips for improvement, 280
changing currency, 192–195

check-in, airport, 234–235
checking
  hotel rooms, 224–225
  out, hotels, 228–230
  for sizes, shopping, 118–119
checks
  currency, 201
  fees, 201
  personal, 201
Chihwaseon, 131
Children's Day, 253
Chinese zodiac, 254–255
chopsticks, acceptable behavior, 288
Christmas Day, 254
Chuseok, 254
citizenship, 77–79
cleaning up homes, 186–187
cleanliness, accommodations, 228
clothes shopping in Korea, 117–121
clubs, 134–135
COEX mall, 122
colors, shopping in Korea, 119
commenting about other people,
    office, 174
common expressions
  about, 293
  awesome, 297
  dying, 296–297
  it's annoying, 295
  keep up good work, 299
  a little, 295
  queasy, 297–298
  refreshing, 298–299
  resignation, 294
  by the way, 294–295
  what a pity, 293–294
common particles, 40
communications
  about, 151
  asking for someone, 155–157
  calling acquaintances at home, 156–157
  calling business contacts, 155–156
  finding phones, 152
  Internet, 161–163
  leaving messages, 157–159
  leaving messages at businesses, 157

leaving messages at someone's home,
    157–158
leaving recorded messages, 158–159
mail, 160–161
making calls, 152–155
phone, 151–159
sending faxes, 161
comparing
  merchandise, shopping, 116–117
  several items, shopping, 117
complaints, accommodations, 226–228
compliments, acceptable behavior, 283–284
computers, office, 169–170
concerts, 130
Confucian ideals, 287
conjugating verbs, 32–33
consonants, pronunciation, 13–17
Constitution Day, 253
contact information, conversation, 90–91
contents, CD, 337–339
conversation
  about, 71
  areas of study, 85
  citizenship, 77–79
  contact information, 90–91
  country names, 74
  cram schools, 87
  essential words, 71–73
  ethnicity, 77–79
  formal usages, 71–73
  home community, 74–76
  jobs, 83–87
  locations and directions, 76
  members of family, 87–90
  months, 82
  occupations, 83–87
  questions, 71–73
  seasons, 80–82
  tutoring, 87
  weather, 80–82
  where are you from, 73–79
  where someone lives, 76–77
conversions, currency, 191–192
counters
  numbers, 44–46
  Sino-Korean, 45–46

country names, 74
cram schools, 87
credit cards, 199–201
crossing legs while sitting, 286
cuisine
  about, 93, 98–101, 174
  acceptable behavior, 284
  chopsticks, 288
  declining drinks, 176
  dining out, 101–107
  drinking politely, 175
  homes, 181–183
  hunger, 95
  liking and disliking with adjectives,
    100–101
  meal time, 94
  menus, 101–102
  ordering at restaurant, 102–103
  ordering at roadside shop, 103–104
  paying for meal, 106–107
  popular dishes, 99–100
  pouring shots, 175
  restrooms, 106
  rice bowls, 287–288
  serving superiors, 175
  setting time for meal, 100
  sitting down to eat, 95–97
  spoons, 287–288
  table manners, 98
  waitstaff, 106
Cultural Property Artisan's Hall, 122
currency
  about, 191
  ATMs, 196–197
  banks, 192–193
  cash, 197–199
  changing, 192–195
  checks, 201
  conversions, 191–192
  credit cards, 199–201
  debit cards, 199–201
  paying in installments, 200
  personal checks, 201
  types, 191–192
customs, going through, 238
cyber cafes, 148–149

• D •

Dangun, 254
dates, 255–256
days
  about, 125–126
  travel, 248–251
debit cards, 199–201
declining
  drinks, business, 176
Demilitarized Zone (DMZ), 142
demonstrative pronouns, 29
department store shopping, 112–114
describing
  ailments, emergencies, 269–271
  people, introductions, 62
destinations, Korea, 256–259
diagnosis, emergencies, 272
dictionaries
  about, 281
  Korean-English, 307–329
dictionary form, verbs, 32
dining out
  about, 101–107
  acceptable behavior, 284
  chopsticks, 288
  cuisine, 98–101
  declining drinks, 176
  drinking politely, 175
  hunger, 95
  liking and disliking with adjectives,
    100–101
  meal time, 94
  menus, 101–102
  ordering at restaurant, 102–103
  ordering at roadside shop, 103–104
  paying for meal, 106–107
  popular dishes, 99–100
  pouring shots, 175
  restrooms, 106
  rice bowls, 287–288
  serving superiors, 175
  setting time for meal, 100
  sitting down to eat, 95–97

spoons, 287–288
table manners, 98
waitstaff, 106
dinners, business
 about, 174
 declining drinks, 176
 drinking politely, 175
 pouring shots, 175
 serving superiors, 175
directions
 about, 203
 actions with, 210
 asking, 203–210
 conversation, 76
 distance, 209–210
 giving, 210–212
 making directions flow, 211–212
 pointing, 204
 street locations, 210
 where, 204–206
 which direction, 207–209
disliking with adjectives, 100–101
distance, directions, 209–210
districts, shopping, 112
DMZ, 142
doctors
 body parts, 270–271
 describing ailments, 269–271
 diagnosis, 272
 finding, 267–269
 getting medical help, 267–274
 hospitals, 263
 medical history, 272
 medical terminology, 273
 prescriptions, 273–274
dog, year of, 255
dragon, year of, 255
drama for improvement, 281
drinking
 about, 107–108
 declining drinks, 176
 drinking politely, 175
 homes, 181–183
 pouring shots, 175
 serving superiors, 175
dying, expression, 296–297

• E •

eating
 about, 93, 174
 acceptable behavior, 284
 chopsticks, 288
 cuisine, 98–101
 declining drinks, 176
 dining out, 101–107
 disliking with adjectives, 100–101
 drinking politely, 175
 homes, 181–183
 hunger, 95
 liking with adjectives, 100–101
 meal time, 94
 menus, 101–102
 ordering at restaurants, 102–103
 ordering at roadside shops, 103–104
 paying for meal, 106–107
 popular dishes, 99–100
 pouring shots, 175
 restrooms, 106
 rice bowls, 287–288
 serving superiors, 175
 setting time for meal, 100
 sitting down to eat, 95–97
 spoons, 287–288
 table manners, 98
 waitstaff, 106
elders
 acceptable behavior, 284
 body language, 21
 introducing, 58–60
electronics shopping in Korea, 122
emergencies
 about, 263
 body parts, 270–271
 calling police, 264–265
 describing ailments, 269–271
 diagnosis, 272
 finding doctors, 267–269
 getting medical help, 267–274
 lost and found, 266
 medical history, 272
 medical terminology, 273

emergencies *(continued)*
  prescriptions, 273–274
  reporting accidents, 264–265
  shouting for help, 263–264
English verbs and adjectives, 34–35
essential words, conversation, 71–73
ethnicity, conversation, 77–79
exactly, expression, 290–291
expressions, common
  about, 293
  awesome, 297
  dying, 296–297
  it's annoying, 295
  keep up good work, 299
  a little, 295
  queasy, 297–298
  refreshing, 298–299
  resignation, 294
  by the way, 294–295
  what a pity, 293–294
expressions, favorite
  about, 289
  exactly, 290–291
  fast, 289
  good, 291
  hurry, 289
  I don't know, 291
  like that, 292
  oh dear, 292
  okay, 289
  one moment please, 291
  really, 290
  that's enough, 292
  turned out well, 292
  what are you doing, 291

fast, 289
good, 291
hurry, 289
I don't know, 291
like that, 292
oh dear, 292
okay, 289
one moment please, 291
really, 290
that's enough, 292
turned out well, 292
what are you doing, 291
faxes, sending, 161
fees, check, 201
films, 130–131
finding
  accommodations, 218–220
  doctors, 267–269
  office items, 166–169
  people in office, 170
  phones, 152
first names, 285
fishing, 142
floor heating, Korea, 285–286
fluency
  basic phrases, 18–20
  pronunciation, 17–20
  puzzling words, 18
  speaking rhythm, 18
  stressed syllables, 17
  syllable pronounciation, 17
flying time, transporation, 238
food
  about, 93, 174
  acceptable behavior, Korea, 284
  chopsticks, 288
  cuisine, 98–101
  declining drinks, 176
  dining out, 101–107
  drinking politely, 175
  homes, 181–183
  hunger, 95
  Korean cuisine, 98–101
  liking and disliking with adjectives,
    100–101
  meal time, 94
  menus, 101–102

• F •

face, losing, 284
fall season, 145, 248
farmer's market, 122
Fashion Street, 117
Fashion Valley, 117
fast expression, 289
favorite expressions
  about, 289
  exactly, 290–291

ordering at restaurant, 102–103
ordering at roadside shop, 103–104
paying for meal, 106–107
popular dishes, 99–100
pouring shots, 175
restrooms, 106
rice bowls, 287–288
serving superiors, 175
setting time for meal, 100
sitting down to eat, 95–97
spoons, 287–288
table manners, 98
waitstaff, 106
forests, 142
formal
  introductions, 51–55
  Korean, 25–27
  polite speech, 25–26
  usages, conversation, 71–73
friends
  house invitations, 136
  introductions, 57–58
  office, 172
fun places
  about, 129–135
  bars, 134–135
  clubs, 134–135
  concerts, 130
  films, 130–131
  galleries, 130
  karaoke room, 132–133
  museums, 130
  performances, 130
  theatres, 130
future tense verbs, 33–34

• G •

galleries, 130
gaming, 148–149
getting medical help, 267–274
giving
  directions, 210–212
  invitations, 135–137
  thanks, 64–65
goat, year of, 255
good expression, 291

goodbye, saying, 65–67
Goodwill Guide Services, Korea Tourist
    Organization, 260
grammar
  about, 5
  speech parts, 28
green, 119
greetings
  about, 49
  introductions, 50–51
Gregorian calendar, 252
grey, 119
grocery shopping, 122
grooming, homes, 184

• H •

hand shaking, introductions, 51
handshakes, body language, 22
Hangeul, 10
hanging out in homes, 179–181
health hazards, gaming, 148–149
help, shouting for, 263–264
hobbies, 139–142
holidays
  Buddha's Birthday, 253
  Children's Day, 253
  Christmas Day, 254
  Chuseok, 254
  Constitution Day, 253
  Independence Movement Day, 253
  Korean Thanksgiving Day, 254
  Liberation Day, 254
  Lunar New Year's Day, 253
  Memorial Day, 253
  National Foundation Day, 254
  travel to Korea, 252–254
home community conversation, 74–76
homes
  about, 176–177
  accidents, 185
  cleaning up, 186–187
  drinking, 181–183
  eating, 181–183
  grooming, 184
  hanging out, 179–181
  hygiene, 184

homes *(continued)*
  smallest room, 177–178
  staying over, 184–186
  touring, 178–179
  trash, 176–177
  visiting, 178–187
horse, year of, 255
hospitals, 263
hostels, 217
hotels
  about, 215, 238, 239
  accommodations, 216
  bed and breakfast, 215, 217
  beds, 216
  broken machinery, 226–227
  check out rooms, 224–225
  checking out, 228–230
  cleanliness, 228
  complaints, 226–228
  details, 223–224
  finding, 218–220
  hostels, 217
  motels, 216–217
  noisy neighbors, 227
  public baths, 217–218
  reservations, 220–222
  saunas, 217–218
  temperature problems, 228
houses
  about, 176–177
  accidents, 185
  cleaning up, 186–187
  drinking, 181–183
  eating, 181–183
  grooming, 184
  hanging out, 179–181
  hygiene, 184
  smallest room, 177–178
  staying over, 184–186
  touring, 178–179
  trash, 176–177
  visiting, 178–187
hunger, 95
hurry expression, 289
hygiene, homes, 184

• *I* •

I don't know expression, 291
Il Mare, 131
immigration, going through, 238
improvement tips
  CDs, 280
  Korean dictionaries, 281
  Korean drama, 281
  Korean movies, 280–281
  Korean restaurants and bars, 280
  Korean songs, 280
  Korean television, 281
  Korean word and phrase lists, 282
  Koreans, 279
  language tapes, 280
  multimedia resources, 280
  travel to Korea, 282
Independence Movement Day, 253
informal introductions, 51–55
informal polite form, verbs, 32
informal polite speech, 25–26
installment paying, 200
Internet
  about, 161–163
  cyber cafes, 148–149
interrogative pronouns, 29
intimate polite speech, 25–26
introductions
  about, 49
  asking names, 61–64
  bowing, 51
  describing people, 62
  formal, 51–55
  greetings, 50–51
  informal, 51–55
  introducing friend or peer, 57–58
  introducing seniors, 58–60
  introducing yourself, 55–56
  making, 49–60
  office, 173
  parents, 58–60
  salutations, 50–51
  shaking hands, 51

invitations
about, 135–137
friends to house, 136
giving, 135–137
islands, 142
Itaewon, 112
it's annoying expression, 295

• J •

jobs, 83–87

• K •

keep up good work expression, 299
Korea House Handicraft Shop, 122
Korea Tourist Organization, 260
Korean-English dictionary, 307–329
Korean script, 10
Korean Thanksgiving Day, 254
Korean wave, 130
Korean Web sites, 281

• L •

landscape, nature, 144–145
language tapes, 280
last names, acceptable behavior, 285
leaving
airports, 238
messages, 157–159
messages at businesses, 157
messages at someone's home, 157–158
recorded messages, 158–159
legal help, 263, 274
legs, crossing while sitting, 286
Liberation Day, 254
like that expression, 292
liking with adjectives, 100–101
listening, 5
locations in conversation, 76
losing face, 284
lost and found, 266
Lunar New Year's Day, 253

• M •

mail, 160–161
making
calls, 152–155
directions flow, 211–212
introductions, 49–60
markets, shopping, 112–114
meals
paying for, 106–107
setting time for, 100
time, 94
medical help
about, 267
describing ailments, 269–271
diagnosis, 272
finding doctors, 267–269
medical history, 272
medical terminology, 273
prescriptions, 273–274
meetings
office, 173–174
speaking up, 173–174
members of family conversation, 87–90
Memorial Day, 253
menus, eating out, 101–102
messages
at businesses, 157
leaving, 157–159
recorded, 158–159
at someone's home, 157–158
money
about, 191
ATMs, 196–197
banks, 192–193
cash, 197–199
changing, 192–195
check fees, 201
checks, 201
conversions, 191–192
credit cards, 199–201
debit cards, 199–201
paying in installments, 200
personal checks, 201
purchases, 197–201
types, 191–192

monkey, year of, 255
monsoon rains, 145, 248
months
    about, 125–126
    conversation, 82
    travel to Korea, 248–251
motels
    about, 215
    accommodations, 216–217
    bed and breakfast, 215, 217
    beds, 216
    broken machinery, 226–227
    check out rooms, 224–225
    checking out, 228–230
    cleanliness, 228
    complaints, 226–228
    details, 223–224
    finding, 218–220
    hostels, 217
    hotels, 216
    motels, 216–217
    noisy neighbors, 227
    public baths, 217–218
    reservations, 220–222
    saunas, 217–218
    temperature problems, 228
mountains, 142
multimedia resources for improvement, 280
museums, 130
Myeongdong, 111

• N •

names
    acceptable behavior, 285
    country, 74
National Foundation Day, 254
native Korean numbers, 42–43
nature
    forests, 142
    landscape, 144–145
    mountains, 142
    recreation, 142–147
    seasons, 145–147
    train rides, 144–145

    waterfalls, 142
    wildlife, 142
New Year's Day, 253
no thank you, acceptable behavior, 287
nodding, body language, 22
noisy neighbors, accommodations, 227
nouns, speech parts, 28
numbers
    about, 41
    counters, 44–46, 45
    native Korean, 42–43
    Sino-Korean, 41, 43–44, 193

• O •

occupations in conversation, 83–87
office
    about, 165
    asking directions, 170–172
    commenting about other people, 174
    computers, 169–170
    finding items, 166–169
    finding people, 170
    introductions, 173
    meetings, 173–174
    peers and superiors, 172
    speaking up, 173–174
oh dear expression, 292
okay expression, 289
Old Boy, 131
one moment please expression, 291
orange, 119
ordering
    at restaurant, 102–103
    at roadside shop, 103–104
ox, year of, 255

• P •

packing for travel, 259
parents, introductions, 58–60
particles
    about, 38
    common, 40
    dropping understood words, 39

sentence, 39
speech parts, 38–40
parts of speech
about, 27–28
adjectives, 36–37
adverbs, 37–38
grammar, 28
nouns, 28
particles, 38–40
pronouns, 29–31
questions, 40–41
suffixes, 37
verbs, 31–35
past tense verbs, 33–34
paying
in installments, 200
for meals, 106–107
peers
introductions, 57–58
office, 172
people in office, finding, 170
performances, 130
personal checks, 201
personal pronouns, 29–31
phones
communications, 151–159
finding, 152
phonetics, 9–10
pig, year of, 255
places, travel, 258
plain polite speech, 25–26
pointing
directions, 204
out best item, shopping, 117
police
about, 263
calling in emergencies, 264–265
polite speech
about, 25–26
formal polite, 25–26
informal polite, 25–26
intimate, 25–26
plain, 25–26
popular dishes, eating, 99–100
possessive pronouns, 31

pouring shots, business dinners, 175
prescriptions, medical, 273–274
present tense verbs, 33–34
pricing, shopping, 123
pronouns
demonstrative, 29
interrogative, 29
personal, 29–31
possessive, 31
pronunciation
about, 10
consonants, 13–17
fluency, 17–20
vowels, 10–12
public baths, 217–218
public displays of affection, acceptable
behavior, 287
public transporation, 233
purchases
currency, 197–201
shopping, 123
purple, 119
puzzling words, 18

• *Q* •

queasy expression, 297–298
questions
conversation, 71–73
speech parts, 40–41

• *R* •

rabbit, year of, 255
rains, monsoon, 145, 248
rat, year of, 255
really expression, 290
receiving invitations, 135–137
recorded messages, leaving, 158–159
recreation
about, 139
hobbies, 139–142
nature, 142–147
red, 119
refreshing expression, 298–299

refunds, shopping, 123
remote areas, 203
reporting accidents, 264–265
reservations, accommodations, 220–222
resignation expression, 294
respect, body language, 21
restaurants
 ordering, 102–103
 tips for improvement, 280
restrooms, 106
rhythm, speaking, 18
rice bowls, acceptable behavior, 287–288
Rodeo street, 117
Romanization of Korean, 10
rooms, hotel, 224–225
rooster, year of, 255

• S •

salutations, introductions, 50–51
saunas, 217–218
saying
 goodbye, 65–67
 sorry, 64–65
schools, cram, 87
script, Korean, 10
seasons
 about, 128
 conversation, 80–82
 nature, 145–147
 travel, 247–248
Sejong, King, 10
self-deprecation, 283–284
sending faxes, 161
seniors
 acceptable behavior, Korea, 284
 body language, 21
 introductions, 58–60
sentence particles, 39
Seoul, 111
serving superiors, 175
setting time for meal, 100
shaking hands, introductions, 51
shoes in house, acceptable behavior,
 285–286

shopping
 about, 111, 256
 antiques, 122
 asking for help, 115–116
 bargaining, 123
 browsing, 114–115
 buying, 123
 checking for sizes, 118–119
 clothes, 117–121
 colors, 119
 comparing merchandise, 116–117
 comparing several items, 117
 department stores, 112–114
 districts, 112
 electronics, 122
 groceries, 122
 markets, 112–114
 pointing out best item, 117
 pricing, 123
 purchasing, 123
 refunding, 123
 shopping for specific items, 121–122
 small shops, 112–114
 souvenirs, 122
 stores, 111–116
 trying on clothes, 120–121
shouting for help, 263–264
Sino-Korean
 counters, 45–46
 numbers, 41, 43–44, 193
sites, travel, 257
sitting
 acceptable behavior, Korea, 284
 down to eat, 95–97
small shops, shopping, 112–114
smallest room, homes, 177–178
snake, year of, 255
soccer, 148
songs for improvement, 280
sorry, saying, 64–65
sounds, basic, 10
souvenirs shopping, 122
speaking
 about, 5
 rhythm, 18
 up in meetings, 173–174

speech parts
  about, 27–28
  adjectives, 36–37
  adverbs, 37–38
  grammar, 28
  nouns, 28
  particles, 38–40
  pronouns, 29–31
  questions, 40–41
  suffixes, 37
  verbs, 31–35
speech styles, 25–27
spoons, acceptable behavior, 287–288
sports
  about, 148–149
  baseball, 148
  boating, 142
  fishing, 142
  gaming, 148–149
  soccer, 148
  wrestling, 148
_Spring, Summer, Fall, Winter...and
    Spring,_ 131
spring season, 145, 248
staying over in homes, 184–186
stores
  department store shopping, 112–114
  shopping in Korea, 111–116
street locations, directions, 210
stressed syllables, 17
study areas, conversation, 85
subways
  about, 238
  transportation, 240–242
suffixes, 37
summer season, 145, 248
superiors
  introductions, 57–58
  office, 172
  serving, 175
syllables
  consonants at end, 16–17
  pronounciation, 17
  stressed, 17
system requirements, CD, 340

• _T_ •

table manners, 98
taxis
  about, 238
  transportation, 239–240
technical support, CD, 340
Techno Mart, 122
television for improvement, 281
temperature problems, accommodations,
    228
temples, Buddhist, 238
tense, verbs, 33–34
thank you, no, 287
thanks, giving, 64–65
that's enough expression, 292
theatres, 130
tiger, year of, 255
time
  about, 125, 126–129
  travel, 247–256
tips for improvement
  CDs, 280
  Korean dictionaries, 281
  Korean drama, 281
  Korean movies, 280–281
  Korean restaurants and bars, 280
  Korean songs, 280
  Korean television, 281
  Korean word and phrase lists, 282
  Koreans, 279
  language tapes, 280
  multimedia resources, 280
  travel to Korea, 282
titles, acceptable behavior, 285
touring homes, 178–179
tourists
  Goodwill Guide Services, 260
  Korea Tourist Organization, 260
trains
  about, 238, 256
  nature, 144–145
  transportation, 244
transportation
  about, 233
  airport, 233–238

transportation *(continued)*
  airport check-in, 234–235
  Buddhist temples, 238
  buses, 238, 240
  flying time, 238
  hotels, 238
  immigration and customs, 238
  leaving airport, 238
  subways, 238, 240–242
  taxis, 238, 239–240
  trains, 238, 244
trash, home, 176–177
travel
  about, 247
  agencies, 259–260
  around town, 239–244
  buses, 240
  business, 256
  dates and times, 255–256
  days, 248–251
  destinations, 256–259
  holidays, 252–254
  months, 248–251
  packing, 259
  places, 258
  seasons, 247–248
  shopping in Korea, 256
  sites and activities, 257
  subways, 240–242
  taxis, 239–240
  timing, 247–256
  tips for improvement, 282
  trains, 244
  travel agencies, 259–260
  vacation, 256
  years, 254–255
trying on clothes, shopping, 120–121
turned out well expression, 292
tutoring conversation, 87

• V •

vacation travel, 256
verbs
  about, 31, 303–305
  adjectives like, 36–37
  conjugating, 32–33
  dictionary form, 32
  with English verbs and adjectives,
    about, 34-35
  forms, 32
  future tense, 33–34
  informal polite form, 32
  past tense, 33–34
  present tense, 33–34
  speech parts, 31–35
  stem, 32
  tense, 33–34
  verb stem, 32
visiting homes, 178–187
vowels
  differences, 12
  pronunciation, 10–12
  sound, 10–11

• W •

waitstaff, eating, 106
waterfalls, 142
weather conversation, 80–82
Web sites
  Goodwill Guide Services, 260
  Korean, 281
  Korean dictionaries, 281
  Korean movies, 280–281
  Korean songs, 280
  Korean television, 281
  Korean tourist information, 259
  Wiley technical support, 340
weeks, 125–126
what a pity expression, 293–294
what are you doing expression, 291
where
  are you from conversation, 73–79
  directions, 204–206
  someone lives conversation, 76–77
which direction, 207–209
white, 119
wildlife, 142
winter season, 145, 248
word and phrase lists for improvement, 282
wrestling, 148

• Y •

year of dog, 255
year of dragon, 255
year of goat, 255
year of horse, 255
year of monkey, 255
year of ox, 255
year of pig, 255
year of rabbit, 255
year of rat, 255
year of rooster, 255
year of snake, 255
year of tiger, 255
years, travel, 254–255
yellow, 119
yourself, introductions, 55–56

• Z •

zodiac
  animals, 255
  Chinese, 254–255
  dog, year of, 255
  dragon, year of, 255
  goat, year of, 255
  horse, year of, 255
  monkey, year of, 255
  ox, year of, 255
  pig, year of, 255
  rabbit, year of, 255
  rat, year of, 255
  rooster, year of, 255
  snake, year of, 255
  tiger, year of, 255

Notes

Notes

Notes

Notes

Notes

Wiley Publishing, Inc.
End-User License Agreement

READ THIS. You should carefully read these terms and conditions before opening the software packet(s) included with this book "Book". This is a license agreement "Agreement" between you and Wiley Publishing, Inc. "WPI". By opening the accompanying software packet(s), you acknowledge that you have read and accept the following terms and conditions. If you do not agree and do not want to be bound by such terms and conditions, promptly return the Book and the unopened software packet(s) to the place you obtained them for a full refund.

1. **License Grant.** WPI grants to you (either an individual or entity) a nonexclusive license to use one copy of the enclosed software program(s) (collectively, the "Software") solely for your own personal or business purposes on a single computer (whether a standard computer or a workstation component of a multi-user network). The Software is in use on a computer when it is loaded into temporary memory (RAM) or installed into permanent memory (hard disk, CD-ROM, or other storage device). WPI reserves all rights not expressly granted herein.

2. **Ownership.** WPI is the owner of all right, title, and interest, including copyright, in and to the compilation of the Software recorded on the physical packet included with this Book "Software Media". Copyright to the individual programs recorded on the Software Media is owned by the author or other authorized copyright owner of each program. Ownership of the Software and all proprietary rights relating thereto remain with WPI and its licensers.

3. **Restrictions on Use and Transfer.**

   (a) You may only (i) make one copy of the Software for backup or archival purposes, or (ii) transfer the Software to a single hard disk, provided that you keep the original for backup or archival purposes. You may not (i) rent or lease the Software, (ii) copy or reproduce the Software through a LAN or other network system or through any computer subscriber system or bulletin-board system, or (iii) modify, adapt, or create derivative works based on the Software.

   (b) You may not reverse engineer, decompile, or disassemble the Software. You may transfer the Software and user documentation on a permanent basis, provided that the transferee agrees to accept the terms and conditions of this Agreement and you retain no copies. If the Software is an update or has been updated, any transfer must include the most recent update and all prior versions.

4. **Restrictions on Use of Individual Programs.** You must follow the individual requirements and restrictions detailed for each individual program in the "On the CD" appendix of this Book or on the Software Media. These limitations are also contained in the individual license agreements recorded on the Software Media. These limitations may include a requirement that after using the program for a specified period of time, the user must pay a registration fee or discontinue use. By opening the Software packet(s), you agree to abide by the licenses and restrictions for these individual programs that are detailed in the "On the CD" appendix and/or on the Software Media. None of the material on this Software Media or listed in this Book may ever be redistributed, in original or modified form, for commercial purposes.

5. Limited Warranty.

(a) WPI warrants that the Software and Software Media are free from defects in materials and workmanship under normal use for a period of sixty (60) days from the date of purchase of this Book. If WPI receives notification within the warranty period of defects in materials or workmanship, WPI will replace the defective Software Media.

(b) WPI AND THE AUTHOR(S) OF THE BOOK DISCLAIM ALL OTHER WARRANTIES, EXPRESS OR IMPLIED, INCLUDING WITHOUT LIMITATION IMPLIED WARRANTIES OF MERCHANTABILITY AND FITNESS FOR A PARTICULAR PURPOSE, WITH RESPECT TO THE SOFTWARE, THE PROGRAMS, THE SOURCE CODE CONTAINED THEREIN, AND/OR THE TECHNIQUES DESCRIBED IN THIS BOOK. WPI DOES NOT WARRANT THAT THE FUNCTIONS CONTAINED IN THE SOFTWARE WILL MEET YOUR REQUIREMENTS OR THAT THE OPERATION OF THE SOFTWARE WILL BE ERROR FREE.

(c) This limited warranty gives you specific legal rights, and you may have other rights that vary from jurisdiction to jurisdiction.

6. Remedies.

(a) WPI's entire liability and your exclusive remedy for defects in materials and workmanship shall be limited to replacement of the Software Media, which may be returned to WPI with a copy of your receipt at the following address: Software Media Fulfillment Department, Attn.: *Korean For Dummies,* Wiley Publishing, Inc., 10475 Crosspoint Blvd., Indianapolis, IN 46256, or call 1-800-762-2974. Please allow four to six weeks for delivery. This Limited Warranty is void if failure of the Software Media has resulted from accident, abuse, or misapplication. Any replacement Software Media will be warranted for the remainder of the original warranty period or thirty (30) days, whichever is longer.

(b) In no event shall WPI or the author be liable for any damages whatsoever (including without limitation damages for loss of business profits, business interruption, loss of business information, or any other pecuniary loss) arising from the use of or inability to use the Book or the Software, even if WPI has been advised of the possibility of such damages.

(c) Because some jurisdictions do not allow the exclusion or limitation of liability for consequential or incidental damages, the above limitation or exclusion may not apply to you.

7. U.S. Government Restricted Rights.
Use, duplication, or disclosure of the Software for or on behalf of the United States of America, its agencies and/or instrumentalities "U.S. Government" is subject to restrictions as stated in paragraph (c)(1)(ii) of the Rights in Technical Data and Computer Software clause of DFARS 252.227-7013, or subparagraphs (c) (1) and (2) of the Commercial Computer Software - Restricted Rights clause at FAR 52.227-19, and in similar clauses in the NASA FAR supplement, as applicable.

8. General.
This Agreement constitutes the entire understanding of the parties and revokes and supersedes all prior agreements, oral or written, between them and may not be modified or amended except in a writing signed by both parties hereto that specifically refers to this Agreement. This Agreement shall take precedence over any other documents that may be in conflict herewith. If any one or more provisions contained in this Agreement are held by any court or tribunal to be invalid, illegal, or otherwise unenforceable, each and every other provision shall remain in full force and effect.

NESS, CAREERS & PERSONAL FINANCE

0-7645-9847-3

0-7645-2431-3

Also available:
- Business Plans Kit For Dummies
  0-7645-9794-9
- Economics For Dummies
  0-7645-5726-2
- Grant Writing For Dummies
  0-7645-8416-2
- Home Buying For Dummies
  0-7645-5331-3
- Managing For Dummies
  0-7645-1771-6
- Marketing For Dummies
  0-7645-5600-2
- Personal Finance For Dummies
  0-7645-2590-5*
- Resumes For Dummies
  0-7645-5471-9
- Selling For Dummies
  0-7645-5363-1
- Six Sigma For Dummies
  0-7645-6798-5
- Small Business Kit For Dummies
  0-7645-5984-2
- Starting an eBay Business For Dummies
  0-7645-6924-4
- Your Dream Career For Dummies
  0-7645-9795-7

ME & BUSINESS COMPUTER BASICS

0-470-05432-8

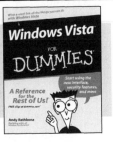

0-471-75421-8

Also available:
- Cleaning Windows Vista For Dummies
  0-471-78293-9
- Excel 2007 For Dummies
  0-470-03737-7
- Mac OS X Tiger For Dummies
  0-7645-7675-5
- MacBook For Dummies
  0-470-04859-X
- Macs For Dummies
  0-470-04849-2
- Office 2007 For Dummies
  0-470-00923-3
- Outlook 2007 For Dummies
  0-470-03830-6
- PCs For Dummies
  0-7645-8958-X
- Salesforce.com For Dummies
  0-470-04893-X
- Upgrading & Fixing Laptops For Dummies
  0-7645-8959-8
- Word 2007 For Dummies
  0-470-03658-3
- Quicken 2007 For Dummies
  0-470-04600-7

OD, HOME, GARDEN, HOBBIES, MUSIC & PETS

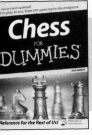

0-7645-8404-9

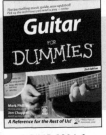

0-7645-9904-6

Also available:
- Candy Making For Dummies
  0-7645-9734-5
- Card Games For Dummies
  0-7645-9910-0
- Crocheting For Dummies
  0-7645-4151-X
- Dog Training For Dummies
  0-7645-8418-9
- Healthy Carb Cookbook For Dummies
  0-7645-8476-6
- Home Maintenance For Dummies
  0-7645-5215-5
- Horses For Dummies
  0-7645-9797-3
- Jewelry Making & Beading For Dummies
  0-7645-2571-9
- Orchids For Dummies
  0-7645-6759-4
- Puppies For Dummies
  0-7645-5255-4
- Rock Guitar For Dummies
  0-7645-5356-9
- Sewing For Dummies
  0-7645-6847-7
- Singing For Dummies
  0-7645-2475-5

TERNET & DIGITAL MEDIA

0-470-04529-9

0-470-04894-8

Also available:
- Blogging For Dummies
  0-471-77084-1
- Digital Photography For Dummies
  0-7645-9802-3
- Digital Photography All-in-One Desk Reference For Dummies
  0-470-03743-1
- Digital SLR Cameras and Photography For Dummies
  0-7645-9803-1
- eBay Business All-in-One Desk Reference For Dummies
  0-7645-8438-3
- HDTV For Dummies
  0-470-09673-X
- Home Entertainment PCs For Dummies
  0-470-05523-5
- MySpace For Dummies
  0-470-09529-6
- Search Engine Optimization For Dummies
  0-471-97998-8
- Skype For Dummies
  0-470-04891-3
- The Internet For Dummies
  0-7645-8996-2
- Wiring Your Digital Home For Dummies
  0-471-91830-X

parate Canadian edition also available
parate U.K. edition also available

able wherever books are sold. For more information or to order direct: U.S. customers visit www.dummies.com or call 1-877-762-2974.
customers visit www.wileyeurope.com or call 0800 243407. Canadian customers visit www.wiley.ca or call 1-800-567-4797.

WILEY

SPORTS, FITNESS, PARENTING, RELIGION & SPIRITUALITY

0-471-76871-5

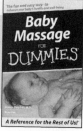

0-7645-7841-3

Also available:
- Catholicism For Dummies
  0-7645-5391-7
- Exercise Balls For Dummies
  0-7645-5623-1
- Fitness For Dummies
  0-7645-7851-0
- Football For Dummies
  0-7645-3936-1
- Judaism For Dummies
  0-7645-5299-6
- Potty Training For Dummies
  0-7645-5417-4
- Buddhism For Dummies
  0-7645-5359-3

- Pregnancy For Dummies
  0-7645-4483-7 †
- Ten Minute Tone-Ups For Dummie
  0-7645-7207-5
- NASCAR For Dummies
  0-7645-7681-X
- Religion For Dummies
  0-7645-5264-3
- Soccer For Dummies
  0-7645-5229-5
- Women in the Bible For Dummies
  0-7645-8475-8

TRAVEL

0-7645-7749-2

0-7645-6945-7

Also available:
- Alaska For Dummies
  0-7645-7746-8
- Cruise Vacations For Dummies
  0-7645-6941-4
- England For Dummies
  0-7645-4276-1
- Europe For Dummies
  0-7645-7529-5
- Germany For Dummies
  0-7645-7823-5
- Hawaii For Dummies
  0-7645-7402-7

- Italy For Dummies
  0-7645-7386-1
- Las Vegas For Dummies
  0-7645-7382-9
- London For Dummies
  0-7645-4277-X
- Paris For Dummies
  0-7645-7630-5
- RV Vacations For Dummies
  0-7645-4442-X
- Walt Disney World & Orlando
  For Dummies
  0-7645-9660-8

GRAPHICS, DESIGN & WEB DEVELOPMENT

0-7645-8815-X

0-7645-9571-7

Also available:
- 3D Game Animation For Dummies
  0-7645-8789-7
- AutoCAD 2006 For Dummies
  0-7645-8925-3
- Building a Web Site For Dummies
  0-7645-7144-3
- Creating Web Pages For Dummies
  0-470-08030-2
- Creating Web Pages All-in-One Desk
  Reference For Dummies
  0-7645-4345-8
- Dreamweaver 8 For Dummies
  0-7645-9649-7

- InDesign CS2 For Dummies
  0-7645-9572-5
- Macromedia Flash 8 For Dummies
  0-7645-9691-8
- Photoshop CS2 and Digital
  Photography For Dummies
  0-7645-9580-6
- Photoshop Elements 4 For Dummie
  0-471-77483-9
- Syndicating Web Sites with RSS Feed
  For Dummies
  0-7645-8848-6
- Yahoo! SiteBuilder For Dummies
  0-7645-9800-7

NETWORKING, SECURITY, PROGRAMMING & DATABASES

0-7645-7728-X

0-471-74940-0

Also available:
- Access 2007 For Dummies
  0-470-04612-0
- ASP.NET 2 For Dummies
  0-7645-7907-X
- C# 2005 For Dummies
  0-7645-9704-3
- Hacking For Dummies
  0-470-05235-X
- Hacking Wireless Networks
  For Dummies
  0-7645-9730-2
- Java For Dummies
  0-470-08716-1

- Microsoft SQL Server 2005 For Dummi
  0-7645-7755-7
- Networking All-in-One Desk Referen
  For Dummies
  0-7645-9939-9
- Preventing Identity Theft For Dummies
  0-7645-7336-5
- Telecom For Dummies
  0-471-77085-X
- Visual Studio 2005 All-in-One Desk
  Reference For Dummies
  0-7645-9775-2
- XML For Dummies
  0-7645-8845-1